T0294964

WHERE TEXAS MEETS *the* SEA

Number Twenty-One
Clifton and Shirley Caldwell Texas Heritage Series

WHERE TEXAS MEETS

the ★ SEA

CORPUS CHRISTI
& ITS HISTORY

ALAN LESSOFF

University of Texas Press
· AUSTIN ·

Publication of this work was made possible in part by support from
Clifton and Shirley Caldwell and a challenge grant from the
National Endowment for the Humanities.

Copyright © 2015 by the University of Texas Press
All rights reserved
Printed in the United States of America
First edition, 2015
First paperback printing, 2018

Requests for permission to reproduce material
from this work should be sent to:
Permissions
University of Texas Press
P.O. Box 7819
Austin, TX 78713-7819
http://utpress.utexas.edu/index.php/rp-form

The paper used in this book meets the minimum requirements of
ANSI/NISO Z39.48-1992 (R1997) (Permanence of Paper). ∞

Library of Congress Cataloging-in-Publication Data

Lessoff, Alan, author.
Where Texas meets the sea : Corpus Christi and its history / Alan Lessoff.
— First edition.
pages   cm — (Clifton and Shirley Caldwell Texas Heritage Series ; number 21)
Includes bibliographical references and index.
ISBN 978-1-4773-1224-7 (pbk. : alk. paper)
1. Sociology, Urban—Texas—Corpus Christi. 2. Corpus Christi (Tex.)—
History. I. Title. II. Series: Clifton and Shirley Caldwell Texas heritage series ;
no. 21.
F394.C78L47 2015
976.4'113—dc23
2014031552

doi:10.7560/768239

For Tom Kreneck, historian and archivist, mentor and friend

∾

The men and women I saw were all near to me.
Others the same—others who look back on me because
I look'd forward to them.

Walt Whitman,
"Crossing Brooklyn Ferry"

CONTENTS

~

INTRODUCTION

∽

T his book has two agendas. First, it uses Corpus Christi, Texas—a
midsized city along the Gulf of Mexico about halfway between
Houston and Brownsville, significant especially for its port, petrochemicals industry, tourist sector, and military installations—as a
gateway to understanding the system of cities that took shape in Texas
during the twentieth century. The emergence of a dynamic network
of cities between Houston and Los Angeles transformed the United
States and North America in myriad ways: in politics, economics, culture, environment, and much else besides. Corpus Christi illustrates
many forces that generated urban Texas and the urban Southwest.

Normally, writers on cities and city systems start with large metropolises, which in Texas means Dallas–Fort Worth, Houston, San
Antonio, and Austin. They take for granted that the large cities' economic and political dynamics, their mindsets and living patterns,
apply as well to satellite or secondary places. This book looks at urban
Texas from its self-conscious periphery rather than its confident core.
A midsized city may reveal qualities that pervade a region more readily than the largest cities, with their webs of commerce, finance, and
information that extend across continents.[1]

The agenda just sketched will make the book useful to readers and scholars of urban history and related fields, particularly in Texas and the U.S. Southwest and West, but in other regions as well. The theme of an urban region as seen from the perspective of a secondary city will recur throughout this book. By perspective, I mean both my analytical point of view as a professor of urban history and the point of view of residents, whose ruminations, conversations, and debates have reflected an acute—perhaps too acute—awareness of second-tier status in a region whose major cities are bounding ahead.

To make a place relevant to experts on cities no matter where they are, professional historians usually move from the particular to the general. Corpus Christi thereby becomes a case study of themes in the overall urbanization of Texas and the Southwest. But I also intend this book to move from the general to the particular, to show how large patterns visible in cities across the Southwest or the United States have been at work in Corpus Christi and help to explain it. This leads to the book's second agenda, which arises from the author's connection to Corpus Christi and his ambition to write a book useful to people there and across South Texas and to readers in other Texas cities.

People in secondary cities—even port cities, with their far-flung commerce and contacts—are apt to consider their place merely regional, in the sense of provincial. Significant or exciting events happen elsewhere. In the late twentieth and early twenty-first centuries, Corpus Christi often struggled economically and socially, falling further into the shadow of the great Texas metropolises, places renowned for energy and growth. In the years when I worked in the city and later as I visited and researched there, I came to see the resultant notion—that Corpus Christi stood out in large measure because it had failed to grasp opportunities that its regional neighbors had seized—as a cloud hanging over discussion and assessment of the city's situation and options. I could—I came to believe—do my part to counter the perception of Corpus Christi as a place whose shortcomings set it apart by stressing that its structure, layout, economy, life, and problems arose from and illustrated large patterns among southwestern, U.S., and modern cities. The book then weaves together and balances the perspective of the urban historian—who may have an allegiance to a city but whose methods for researching cities and whose models of urbanization and urban life are not tied to the place under study—with the mindset of the local and public historian, whose goals and approach flow from personal dedication to and professional involvement with a place.

My own engagement with Corpus Christi came by accident; I had never been within 140 miles of the place before 1992, when I interviewed for an assistant professor's position at the institution soon to be renamed Texas A&M University–Corpus Christi. At the time, Texas had embarked upon a loosely organized policy of upgrading public education in the southern part of the state. My new employer, hitherto a limited commuter school on the site of a defunct Baptist college, was expanding into a full university according to the urban-public model common in U.S. cities. This change meant, among other things, that education and research would emphasize matters relevant to the metropolitan area. Appropriately, the university, situated in the largest Texas city south of San Antonio, included a focus on urban affairs, one aspect of which was urban and public history. While background and training gave me the potential to add value, I knew almost nothing about Corpus Christi and its history before I went there. To the extent that my experiences inform this book, it describes on-the-job training as an urban and public historian.

Until I moved to Corpus Christi in August 1992, my thinking about cities—their growth, their economy and politics, their layout and appearance, their atmosphere and problems—was based on northeastern U.S. or European models. Having traveled in Texas and the Southwest, I was aware that their cities had their own history, structure, and atmosphere. But I had few tools for understanding the place on its own terms, and only loose preconceptions about it. Fortunately, my years in South Texas came in the aftermath of a period of burgeoning research on cities throughout the American West. That phase of scholarship on southwestern and western cities was to some degree a byproduct of the so-called Sunbelt debate of the 1970s–1980s. This research's strength stemmed from its recognition that southwestern (and, to a lesser degree, southern) urbanization probably amounted to a significant new phase in American geography, politics, and life. Urban affairs experts and social scientists, including historians, sought to understand how and how much these newly dynamic cities and this newly influential urban region differed from the so-called Rustbelt, which stretched from Boston and Baltimore to Milwaukee and St. Louis. Since the 1980s, the varied trajectories and experiences of cities across the United States have revealed the contrast between Sunbelt and Rustbelt to be too sweeping and straightforward. Whatever its shortcomings, that period of writing on the urban Southwest and West provided me with concepts and issues, a starting point for analyzing Corpus Christi and fitting it into the sweep of U.S. urban history.

When it came to learning about my new home in particular, my mentor was Thomas Kreneck, now-retired director of the special collections department at A&M–Corpus Christi, a remarkable expert on the documentation of Texas urban history and of the history of South Texas. Tom and his assistants over the years, the late Norm Zimmerman and then Grace Charles, Jan Weaver, and Ceil Venable, helped me compile packets of documents that would introduce students—as well as me—to phases and issues in the city's history and to sources and techniques for researching the place and its peoples. Key sections of this book start from documents that we organized during the 1990s into assignments for students. Our pedagogical agenda was to demonstrate how anyone might use sources readily available in Corpus Christi— and similar sources available in most U.S. cities—to research common themes in urban and local history. Careful readers will note that the research is built outward from two large repositories of documents that have equivalents in almost every U.S. city: the A&M–Corpus Christi archives and the local history collection at the Corpus Christi Public Library. Ideas and references encountered in those two places led me to most other sources consulted—or in the case of interviews and photos, sources that I created.

The special collections library at A&M–Corpus Christi, an archetype of a university-based, urban and regional history archive, thus provided the frame around which I constructed my knowledge and eventually this book. At the core of this wide-ranging center for South Texas research stand two huge sets of primary sources compiled by characters in this book: the papers of the civil rights leader Hector P. García and the books, pamphlets, and other printed materials collected by the South Texas historian and bibliophile Dan E. Kilgore.

In my first months at the university, Tom made a stack for me of every significant published historical account of the city to that time. I could then absorb what themes writers on Corpus Christi perceived in its history and what issues they stressed. What I found in reading this stack of books and articles puzzled and fascinated me. I right away hit upon a mindset and outlook—a tension in most writing about Corpus Christi—that became one of this book's overarching themes and key analytical points.

While Corpus Christi had produced its share of regional historical writing, almost none of it qualified as urban history, not simply by professional or academic standards, but even by good local or amateur standards. That is, little of what had been written about Corpus Christi's history took as its central task the explanation of how the physical city, its institutions, and its life came to be what they were by the late twentieth century. Events and developments since the 1870s–1890s, and above all since the 1910s–1930s, formed the contemporary city. But into the 1990s, writing about the place was preoccupied with people and events before 1880, when Corpus Christi was still a marginal coastal town of around 3,250 people, a far cry from the port and regional metropolis of 300,000 that I came to. This disjuncture arose from the basic way that Corpus Christians have discussed, reflected upon, and taken lessons from the South Texas past.

Corpus Christi's portion of the coast of the Gulf of Mexico, the so-called Coastal Bend, which straddles the mouth of the Nueces River, played a significant role in two grand, competing stories of the founding of Texas. The area figures in the south-to-north Tejano saga of explorers and conquistadores, missionaries and *empresarios*, vaqueros and carters, invasion, expropriation, and borderland violence. The area also looms large in the east-to-west Anglo-Texan epic of frontier settlements, ranchers, vigilantes, and rangers, the Texas Revolution, the Mexican War, the Civil War, Reconstruction, and railroads. These two stories help a great deal in understanding the origins of the region, its role in the formation of Texas, and its basic ethnic loyalties, preoccupations, and conflicts. Neither story in its customary form devotes much attention to the modern, urban environment in which people live.

Texas's founding stories offer drama, grandeur, heroism, and tragedy. They impart—in the manner of most epics—unforgettable lessons about group identity, personal character, and standards of behavior.

The enduring power and pervasiveness of the Texas frontier epics, then, should not surprise a newcomer. What caught my attention was the tepidness of the follow-up into the era of urbanization and of influential cities. It was clear to me that the urban transformation of the twentieth century amounted to a new Texas epic as large as the story of the revolution, ranchers, and rangers. Corpus Christians, however, showed little sustained interest in the forces and events that directly shaped their contemporary environment. This changed in a tentative way only around the turn of the twenty-first century, with the retrospection and reflection that moment prompted. In South Texas, newcomers from every direction absorbed the practice of deliberating over regional history and character by drawing upon frontier and wilderness lore, even though the relevant phases of regional history were long past by the time most migrants, drawn by twentieth-century developments, arrived.

The juxtaposition that I found between the modern city, where people lived, and the frontier place they dwelled upon in writing and art seemed at first unnerving and frustrating. From other writers, especially the urban historian Carl Abbott, I came to understand that I was observing one city's version of a ubiquitous theme in the southwestern and western portions of the United States. As would make sense in an arid region—where people concentrate according to the natural or engineered availability of freshwater—the human geography of the American West consists of strings or zones of fairly dense settlement. The spaces between concentrations of population, however, and the sparse settlements in those spaces affect the consciousness even of those living in such all-encompassing metropolises as Dallas–Fort Worth or Denver. The everyday life of the West takes place in the city, but its imaginative life fills the spaces between.

For the most part, historians are in the business of events and trends that can be documented, not heritage or myth. And South Texas's myths have often obscured or diverted attention from the region's geographic, environmental, and economic circumstances and its political and ethnic conflicts. Still, I have not made it a priority to overturn or pick apart the myths and lore of Corpus Christi. For one thing, explorers and *empresarios*, ranchers and rangers, did create the preconditions and foundations for the modern city. In the case of South Texas's famed ranching families—the Kings, Klebergs, Kenedys, Driscolls, and so on—the relationship was direct: they deliberately sought to build up Corpus Christi as a service town and port for the hinterland that they largely owned. On top of that, the lore and myths of South Texas are themselves documentable historical forces. Heritage stories are not as powerful as the Gulf of Mexico or the Texas coastal plain, and they did not create as much wealth or as many jobs as the oil industry or the Port of Corpus Christi. Still, they underpinned people's discussions and arguments about the city and their competition to shape the city in image and actuality. Myth and lore even employ people to the extent that the region's allure for tourists hinges on its distinctive intertwining of the frontier and the Gulf Coast.

The person who most effectively demonstrated to me the benefits of treating with respect South Texans' sense of the grand and dramatic was Joe B. Frantz, former director of the Texas State Historical Association and first holder of the Walter Prescott Webb Chair of History and Ideas at the University of Texas. Semiretired in Corpus Christi, Frantz befriended me in 1992–1993, near the end of his life. He retained enough health to explain the city as he understood it and to introduce me to a number of people in this book, especially Oscar Flores and the Westside Business Association. As his biographer and former student David McComb explains, Joe had a facility for discerning what might catch someone's attention and for drawing that person into what he cared about most, Texas's history and culture. He sensed that he could spark a durable interest in Corpus Christi and other Texas cities if he could demonstrate to me what intricate, intellectually challenging cities these were.[2] Joe prized South Texas's heritage and lore for what they revealed about the mindsets and concerns of different groups of people he worked with. Later in this book, I recount episodes when Joe went too far in accommodating people's penchant for lore at the expense of history, with costly consequences, literally and figuratively.

Epic or heroic versions of the past make historians wary in part because they often amount to winners' history; they validate triumph and power. To its critics, the Anglo lore of Texas counts as a conspicuous example of this pattern. Into the 1990s, triumphalist versions of Anglo South Texas lore were certainly manifest in Corpus Christi, though usually expressed in a less brazen manner than in the early and mid-twentieth century. Anyone familiar with South Texas anticipates that ethnic tensions will play out in competing versions of history and heritage. Beyond that, I became curious about ways that people measured the heroic past against the mediocre present. As I encountered it in Corpus Christi, part of the attraction of the epic past related to a sense, expressed to me continually and in many different ways, that the present did not measure up.

In 1992, on one of my first days in my Corpus Christi job, a colleague in the middle of an admirable career remarked ruefully, "Now you've reached the end of the road. You can't get any farther away from things than here." Anyone who has been around professors knows that they are inclined to this species of gloom, except at Harvard or Oxford, and sometimes there. But I learned that many people shared the sentiment that Corpus Christi had become an end of the line. I also learned that there was a historical and geographic basis for this frame of mind, even if the mood went beyond what a fresh observer might concede was justified.

From my urban-history perspective, Corpus Christi did not seem peripheral. The urbanization of Texas and the Southwest reshaped the country and continent in the second half of the twentieth century, so (it followed) places such as Corpus Christi had profound historical significance. Much of this significance came from the city's being the Gulf port at the northeastern gateway into Tejano South Texas and, beyond that, into the vast Mexico-U.S. borderlands. Corpus Christi stood near the edge of the United States, but it was near the core of a new version of North America. Much of this book explores the tension between Corpus Christi as an edge place within the United States of the industrial era and as a potentially pivotal place within a system of cities and commerce oriented more toward Latin America, the Caribbean, and the Pacific.

For a century, the United States, not the borderlands or the Gulf of Mexico, did the most to form Corpus Christians' geographic as well as historical frame of reference. The city grew at a remarkable rate between 1920 to 1960 on account of its position within the Texas urban network and its commercial and industrial links to the U.S. urban system beyond. In the city's most dynamic era, little of its economy—other than, of course, labor—hinged on ties with Mexico. Moreover, local accounts stressed the city's role as a Texas seaport, but only occasionally expressed a common identity or interest with other Gulf ports. In a political-economic and political-cultural sense, Corpus Christi thrived as an outpost and manifestation of Anglo America, channeled through Texas. For decades, being the city where Texas meets the sea—as a booster slogan from the years after the 1926 opening of the deepwater ship channel put it—seemed to present only opportunities. As recently as the mid-1950s, it seemed reasonable for Corpus Christi to aim to emerge as one of Texas's metropolitan centers. By the 1970s, such a prospect had bypassed the place. The city ranked among the continent's leading ports and functioned as an indispensable processing center for the petrochemical industry. Yet within Texas, Corpus Christi had settled into a second-tier or satellite status. Houston and San Antonio above all, but also Dallas–Fort Worth and Austin, not only overshadowed Corpus Christi but also delimited it.

Corpus Christians fretted that their city had failed to take advantage of the Sunbelt era of urban growth of the 1960s–1980s, when Texas's system of cities asserted a national and international presence. That was the background of the disappointment that people expressed to me in the 1990s. In the 1930s–1950s, entrepreneurs and professionals from across Texas and around the United States sought opportunities in the "fastest growing city on the coast," as one author observed in 1955, "by far the most versatile, the most progressive, and the most promising" of the Texas Gulf Coast cities outside Houston.[3] By the 1970s, civic and business leaders were worrying about statistics indicating a steady outmigration of ambitious young people to other Texas metropolises. By the 1990s, the city's oil-and-gas sector relied on Houston, Dallas–Fort Worth, and San Antonio, or Wichita and Oklahoma City farther afield, for finance, corporate management, and technical and professional expertise.

The city's niche within tourism in an odd way reinforced its self-image as second tier and dependent. Corpus Christi carved out a position as an accessible, relatively inexpensive waterfront resort town for middle-class Texans from the state's inland cities. People from Dallas, Austin, and San Antonio viewed Corpus Christi as a relaxed place to hang around on the beach, go fishing or sailing, watch birds, maybe surf. Corpus Christians expressed appreciation for this recreation-oriented, Gulf Coast way of life. But a waterfront vacation atmosphere has drawbacks if a city's goal is to attract people who thrive there during workdays, the creative-class types driven to challenge themselves amid a large concentration of innovators and entrepreneurs. An unkind epithet that I heard applied to Corpus Christi expressed this particular frustration: "mecca for underachievers." Few would have said that about Houston or Dallas in the 1990s or about Corpus Christi in the 1940s–1950s.

It was in this context that the frontier epics of South Texas seemed a judgment upon Corpus Christi's present. Frontier myths and borderland lore were unfamiliar to me, but I knew a lot about medium-size

NOVEMBER - IN CORPUS CHRISTI

Of course our friends from less fortunate climates won't believe us when they see our "typical November" shot, but WE know it's true. In fact, we can prove it any time we want to don bathing suits and head out to Padre or South Beach, just a few minutes away from our bustling downtown business district. The fact is, our average temperature during November will be a comfortable 64.9 degrees — and that's merely the average. There'll be many an 85.9 degree day while the rest of the nation is getting out the snow plows.

We're not trying to rub it in. We just feel every community has the right to put their best foot forward. So come on down and join us — for your vacation, for your convention, or — just for fun.

YOU . . . NOVEMBER, 1964

Figures 0.1 and 0.2. The Gulf Coast city marketed to migrants in the 1940s as the Port of Play and Profit in a chamber of commerce brochure and as a "just for fun" escape "while the rest of the nation is getting out the snow plows" in a tourist magazine in the 1960s. Courtesy of the Dan Kilgore Collection, Special Collections and Archives, Bell Library, Texas A&M University–Corpus Christi.

cities fearful of stagnation and decrepitude. Sympathy for Corpus Christi's sense of disappointment and provincialism gave an impetus to my teaching and writing that I hope comes through in this book. Still, I confess that much of the book was researched and nearly all of it written after I, too, left the place in 2000 for professional opportunities elsewhere.

This book's content and organization, therefore, arises from its mix of agendas and audiences. I have not recounted Corpus Christi's history step-by-step. I have instead examined juxtapositions and interactions between Corpus Christi's historical sensibilities, which have their roots in the nineteenth century, and the city's development, geography, appearance, and social, cultural, and political dynamics, products mostly of the twentieth century. The book is less a history of Corpus Christi than a consideration of different ways that the city reveals and relates to its history. It dwells upon regional and historical crosscurrents that shaped the city, along with varied, often conflicting local understandings of the city's history, character, possibilities, place, and role in South Texas and along the Gulf of Mexico.

Among urban historians, there has long existed a division of opinion—mostly friendly, with opposed sides not always clear-cut—over the extent to which regional history and culture matter in understanding cities such as Corpus Christi. In what substantive ways might cities in Texas, the Southwest, and the West differ from cities in other regions, and to what extent did the regions themselves generate these differences? These differences have proved difficult to measure, so supporters of the regionalist position—the view that a region's cities have distinctive qualities—often resort, as I have in this book, to impressionistic observations about the legacy of history; about practices, quarrels, and sensibilities inherited from the past; and about atmosphere and the power of the environment. The antiregionalist side of the case has the advantage of being easier to support with specific evidence. Most traceable differences between southwestern cities and those elsewhere, this argument roughly goes, result from the timing of the region's urbanization. Southwestern and western cities might be better understood as twentieth-century cities; their institutions, politics, economies, geographies, and living patterns illustrate a distilled form of twentieth-century urbanism, with fewer holdovers or survivals from previous eras to distract attention. Call to mind familiar images of Chicago versus Dallas–Fort Worth, or Philadelphia versus Houston, to grasp the point being made. I remain attached, more or less, to the distinctiveness position. But this book will underscore the rationale for also considering Corpus Christi a product of twentieth-century urbanization and urbanism.

Corpus Christi's status as a significant yet secondary Texas city makes it an appropriate place from which to contemplate cities and urban systems in the state and the Southwest. While indispensable to Texas, Houston and Dallas–Fort Worth transcend it. Such highly networked cities absorb and thrive on a multitude of cultural influences; their forte is exchange and interchange. Meanwhile, the smallest cities, those that function merely as local markets and service centers, tend to reflect a narrow range of influences; for the most part, they absorb and embody the culture of their hinterland. Corpus Christi is a medium-size city that manages to be both cosmopolitan and provincial, networked and local. It is an indispensable provider of urban services to its region and at the same time a port of international significance. Its industry and military bases—and increasingly, its coastal research institutes—give it a range of connections throughout North America. Yet the city has evinced a keen self-consciousness concerning its perceived small-town atmosphere and its lack of power relative to Texas's four main metropolises. Such a place illustrates tensions between regional and cosmopolitan influences shaping southwestern cities more clearly and distinctly than larger or smaller places.

While a book examining an urban region from the perspective of a medium-size city will have value to scholars of cities everywhere, I have also worked to create a tool for people in the Corpus Christi area and its portion of South Texas. An emphasis on how Corpus Christi illustrates patterns evident in many other places and shares difficulties with those other cities can help counter the city's sense of distinctiveness and provincialism. Corpus Christians often talk about their city as though it is alone at the end of the road. They express the worry that their city might have special defects of circumstance or character, that in addition to being midsized, the place might be destined for mediocrity, permanently unattractive to people with large goals. Books cannot solve problems, but they can make misconceptions untenable. History and geography have infused the place with distinctive features. Even so, the city is a product and illustration of large trends. The problems that have made Corpus Christians anxious about its viability are partly local but not only so. To some degree, they reflect limitations attributable to its place and role within the urban system of Texas. Yet in part, the city has confronted issues typical of midsized cities across the United States and indeed around the world.

The first half of the book revolves around the tension that I perceived in a twentieth-century city with a nineteenth-century regional, historical sensibility. Chapter 1 sketches the city as an analytically inclined newcomer—such as I was initially—might describe it. I offer an outline of the city's geography and spatial structure and then divide the city's history into a plausible set of phases. Chapters 2 and 3 turn the perspective of chapter 1 on its head. They elaborate on competing bodies of regional lore that molded the city's outlook and self-presentation: the east-to-west epic of Anglo South Texas and the south-to-north saga of Mexican South Texas. Southern Texas's experience as disputed territory—a place where frontiers came together violently—has meant that ethnic, nationalistic disputes often take the form of conflicts embedded in frontier heritage and lore. The Mexican heritage of South Texas hinges on an alternate or stolen frontier process. Pioneer ancestors—from south of the area, not east of it—were steadily building a Hispanic region when Anglo intruders arrived, suppressed and blighted what Mexicans were creating, and imposed a new frontier.

Chapter 4 examines how competing outlooks on the city and its place in South Texas appeared in local quarrels over sculptures and monuments. As in many cities, diverse groups have used public art— sculptures, monuments, murals, and such— to put their stamp upon the city and shape its identity. Of the crosscurrents that made Corpus Christi's public art raucous, ethnicity caused division and suspicion to be sure, but it was not the most persistent source of argument. The bitterest, most enduring disputes revolved around differences in education, social class, and outlook: cosmopolitan versus regional orientation, elite versus popular taste, professional versus amateur influence. In this, Corpus Christi again illustrates the divergent reference points and aspirations that one might expect in a city with a strong regional sensibility but also with manifold connections to national and international networks.

Chapter 5 concerns downtown Corpus Christi and decades of schemes to embellish, redevelop, or preserve it. An unforgettable physical setting, with its prolonged, crescent-shaped bayfront and forty-foot bluff, downtown defined the city's image for residents and visitors and embodied its sense of history and civic identity. As in most U.S. cities, the central city had come to seem a problem by the mid-1960s, when the consequences of outlying shopping centers and office strips became clear. For the next half century, plans for the central business district were surrounded by tensions over the motives of pro-revitalization interests, the sincerity of their assurances that even as they plotted to attract tourists and conventioneers, they intended to protect downtown and the bayfront for local people to use and take pride in.

Historic preservation efforts, meanwhile, concentrated on the central city, and not just because of its visibility and prestige. Until World War II, Corpus Christi had not spread beyond the limits of this diffuse area, so nearly every structure that residents considered worth preserving was located there. Buildings cherished by historical activists in the 1970s–2000s were intended when new—whether early in the century or after World War II—to convey the impression that Corpus Christi was no longer a crude outpost but a component of modern, urban America. Except for a few instances that, I argue, prove the rule, Corpus Christi's record in using history to reinvigorate the central city was meager. In keeping with the city's self-consciousness, preservationists were apt to blame their disappointments on special defects in Corpus Christi's historical or civic sensibilities, but, I further argue, the real culprits were geographic and practical obstacles and, at times, bad luck. The illustrative case was the 1914 Nueces County Courthouse, subject of a decades-long preservation battle that, rightly or wrongly, disheartened preservationists while discrediting preservationism with local government and the public and adding to the city's sense of its own incapacity in comparison with Galveston or San Antonio.

The final chapter dwells upon ways that Corpus Christi's place within Texas and the Southwest infused the city's political economy and shaped its responses to the stagnation evident by the mid-1960s. In the 1940s–1960s, apex of the city's aspirations, the port, petrochemicals, and related industries attracted a cohort of ambitious, talented entrepreneurs, engineers, and professionals. Self-confident and close-knit, this generation of Anglo commercial and civic leaders organized a political alliance that stressed business-government cooperation as the key to maintaining the city's dynamism and its reputation (at the time) for progressive planning and policy. Urban affairs experts label such alliances "progrowth" or "commercial-civic" coalitions. Common in U.S. cities, these alliances took on an especially organized form in the mid-twentieth-century Southwest, where they worked through quasi political parties such as Corpus Christi's Better Government League and where self-perpetuating civic groups such as Corpus Christi's Area Development Committee oversaw planning and set priorities for public works and services.

The results seemed to justify this oligarchic approach until economic stagnation undermined deference to the elite, as well as its own self-confidence and capacity to perpetuate itself. Hispanic and black activists demanded an open, responsive political system, even as middle-class Anglo neighborhoods expressed more and more resistance to the commercial-civic leadership's emphasis on big-ticket, civil-engineering and public-building projects. This atmosphere generated fractiousness, recrimination, and self-defeating policies. But as in much of Texas, the city's political and civic leaders—increasingly Hispanic as well as Anglo—adapted to this more pluralistic, contentious environment well enough to avoid paralysis most of the time.

Most political and civic activists conceded that the city was better off with a more open style of politics. Still, they hankered for the mid-century elite's self-assurance, coherence, and sense of direction. The city's politics retained its progrowth orientation, though of necessity in a less coherent way. After the 1970s, it was hard to discern what direction the city should take, let alone how one might rally support for and pursue a particular vision coherently. The circumstances within Texas and along the Gulf of Mexico that caused Corpus Christi to prosper between the 1920s and the 1950s now seemed to limit and hamper the city. In effect, by the 2000s, Corpus Christi sought ways partially to secede from a Texas urban system in which it was stuck in the second tier, an instrument of other cities' endeavors. It sought autonomous political, economic, and cultural ties, ones that did not go so often through Dallas, Houston, or Austin. Yet in its regional identity and historical sensibility, the city remained, to be sure, firmly and proudly Texan, the place where Texas meets the sea.

I drafted this introduction in the summer of 2011. I redrafted it in mid-June nearly a year later. The weather was clear and pleasant for the first draft, gray and chilly the second time around. I was not in Corpus Christi, but in a city of comparable size and status nearly seven thousand miles away. Bielefeld, Germany, where I finished the first draft of this book while a guest scholar during 2010–2011, also had a population of a little over 300,000, though its hinterland, as one would expect for fertile Westphalia as opposed to arid South Texas, consisted of a dense network of towns and a large aggregate population. Both cities showed signs of emerging from periods of drift, their recoveries sparked by the resurgence of sectors that had seemed stagnant or even in decline: energy production and processing in Corpus Christi's case, specialized manufacturing in the Bielefeld region.

This contrast suggested that renewed prosperity might present the two cities with differing prospects for autonomy and self-generated growth over a period of years. The shale oil boom that took hold in South Texas during the 2010s signified multinational enterprise; capital came from around the world, and a large share of the profit would flow whence investment came. It would be decades before the vast Eagle Ford field to the northwest of Corpus Christi petered out, but when that happened, how much shale oil wealth would the city retain for its own use? In seeking to explain the resilience of German manufacturing after the 2008 recession, the *Economist* in April 2012 told the story of a family-owned Bielefeld firm that paid high wages to skilled workers who manufacture complex lighting control systems. Revenues from contracts for Italian opera houses and Las Vegas casinos flowed into the city and stayed there. Like many of Germany's midsized metropolitan regions, the Bielefeld area featured a web of such firms that supported one another, the magazine explained.[4]

Just as Corpus Christians look toward San Antonio and Austin, Bielefelders look westward to the Ruhr region, the cluster of cities surrounding Düsseldorf, Dortmund, and Essen. Corpus Christi, with its sweeping bay along the Gulf of Mexico and its high bluff set back from the shore, has a dramatic setting. Bielefeld defines nondescript; it does not even have a river, which Germans assume is essential to a proper city location. An elaborate joke known throughout Germany as the "Bielefeld Conspiracy" asserts that the city is so nondescript that it must be an illusion concocted for some untoward purpose. The plausible grounds for the conspiracy start with pointed questions, "Do *you* know anyone from Bielefeld? Have *you* ever been there?" The place sits in a pass in the Teutoburg Forest, which, like the Nueces Valley, has profound, even disturbing associations with national history and nationalistic lore.

So far as I know, other Texans have never suggested that Corpus Christi does not exist. Texans often express affection for and ties to Corpus Christi, something one rarely hears from residents of the huge German state of Nordrhein-Westfalen regarding Bielefeld. Art and photographs depicting Corpus Christi are spread throughout the state; it figures regularly in Texan and Tejano popular songs. Texans worry in summer and fall when hurricanes threaten it. It is easier to amuse oneself by alleging the disappearance of a city with no river than one along the Gulf of Mexico. What ties the two cities together is the reality of the urban life that takes place in them. In Dallas or Dortmund, in Essen or Austin, big-city dwellers would profit from understanding these midsized cities not as lesser versions of themselves, but as their own types of places and as places with which their fates are intertwined.

Chapter 1

A CITY OVER SPACE
& ACROSS TIME

∽

C *orpus Christi* is located along the southern coast of Texas at the mouth of the Nueces River, about halfway between Houston and the Rio Grande. With a metropolitan population of over 428,000 (in 2010) and a municipal population in excess of 305,000, the city has a Gulf of Mexico–style, waterfront-and-petrochemical economy centered on the Port of Corpus Christi. Since World War II, the area has also hosted a string of military bases. A seaside city with a sparsely populated hinterland and year-round clear weather, Corpus Christi offers a practical location for naval air training, and the army maintains a large helicopter maintenance facility there. A popular destination for beach vacations and water sports, especially among Texans, the city provides governmental, professional, medical, and retail services to the Coastal Bend region, which extends in an arc from roughly Victoria in the north to small towns such as Falfurrias toward the south.

Even with these assets and relationships, Corpus Christi does not count among Texas's dominant cities. The incorporated city is eighth largest, while the metropolitan statistical area (MSA) ranks seventh.[1] Economically, politically, and culturally, Corpus Christi has evolved into a satellite of Houston and San Antonio; Dallas–Fort Worth and Austin loom powerfully as well.

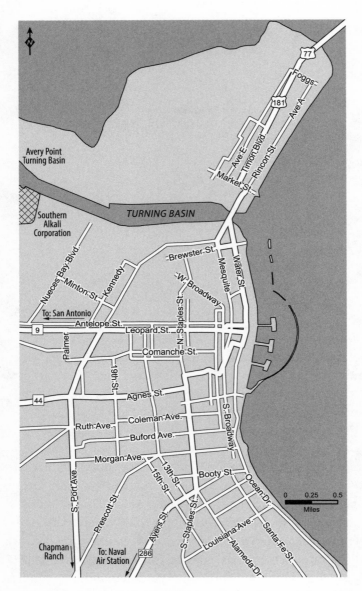

Figure 1.1. Corpus Christi in 1941, the year that the naval air station opened on Flour Bluff (off the map to the south). The Anglo middle-class city had begun its expansion along Southside thoroughfares—Staples, Alameda, and Santa Fe. The Port of Corpus Christi, which opened in 1926, is visible at the upper center; the ship channel extension during the 1930s to the Southern Alkali plant at Avery Point is on the upper left. By Crystal K. Williams, GEOMAP, Illinois State University, based on a map at the front of the city's WPA guide, *Corpus Christi: A History and Guide* (Corpus Christi, 1942).

This chapter sketches the city's geographic situation and physical site, the city's layout and appearance, and the stages of its history. The two chapters that follow consider the city's history, culture, and political economy and its place in South Texas, Texas, and the Southwest from the perspectives of different residents. Comprehending a social or historical phenomenon such as a city often entails recognizing and maintaining a tension between analyzing from without and depicting from within. This chapter sets up the analytical side of that dual perspective. It is built around another type of tension, between the city's spatial logic—where the city fits in its immediate and extended region and how its areas relate to one another—and its temporal logic—how the city, its parts, and their relationships have developed over time.

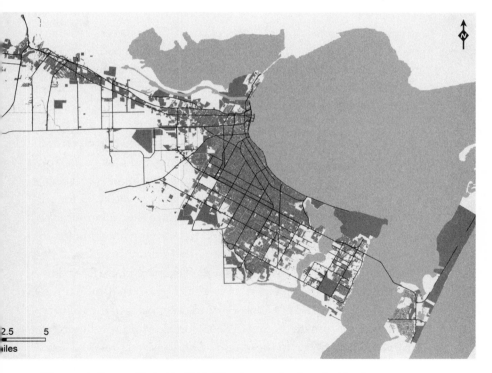

Figure 1.2. Corpus Christi in 2000. The city remained marked by the crescent bay even as municipal limits extended thirty miles from the Nueces River at Calallen in the northwest to annexed portions of Padre and Mustang Islands across Laguna Madre in the southeast. By Crystal K. Williams, GEOMAP, Illinois State University, based on a Planning Department land-use map, City of Corpus Christi.

A Satellite City in the Texas System

In 1900, Texas was a straggling mix of the post–Civil War South, mired in stagnation and dependency, and the Gilded Age West, thriving with a boom-and-bust, resource-extraction economy. Its population was about 80 percent rural. In the half century after the opening of the Spindletop oil field in 1901 and the Houston Ship Channel in 1914, Texas went through a stunning transformation, developing a system of cities capable of exerting far-flung influence. Approximately 45 percent of Texans were living in cities and towns by World War II, and 80 percent by the 1980s.[2] In the 2010 census, Dallas–Fort Worth ranked fourth and Houston sixth among the country's ten largest MSAs, and Houston, Dallas, and San Antonio counted among the ten largest incorporated cities.[3]

Through the decades of rapid urbanization, Texas's economy remained resource based, built on oil and gas, but also on cotton, grain, and cattle. The key variable in the story is the degree to which entrepreneurs and financiers in Houston and Dallas–Fort Worth—and in cities like Corpus Christi—managed to retain capital extracted from the land and its resources. The state's new, urban-based commercial and civic leadership, a mix of native Texans and migrants, invested profits from the oil bonanza in durable forms of wealth: banking and finance; petrochemical manufacture and other industries; engineering, exploration, construction, geological expertise, and similar support activities for oil and gas production worldwide; aeronautics, electronics, communications, biomedical research, and computers. Research- and technology-based enterprises eventually caused Austin, theretofore a modest state capital and university town, to thrive as well. Texas avoided a fate common in peripheral regions injected with wealth generated by natural resources. Texas's cities did not allow cities in other parts of the country or the world to subordinate them in a neocolonial fashion and thereby reap most of the benefits from the state's oil and gas reserves.

By the Sunbelt period of the 1960s–1980s, Texas's old straggle and dependency were long gone. Texas-style rhetorical bravado at times masked a lingering sense of cultural provincialism, but the basis even of that was diminishing. Geographers and historians began to posit a Texas-dominated zone of financial and commercial activity that extended in an oblong pattern through Colorado and into Wyoming. This Greater Texas, or even Imperial Texas in some formulations, roughly recalled those maps that circulated between the Texas Revolution of 1835–1836 and the Compromise of 1850 to illustrate the maximum claims of Anglo-Texans against Mexico. Economically, even if not politically, reality had caught up with the dreams of the Texas Republic.[4]

Within the boundaries of Texas itself, a multicentered system of cities took shape, what geographers label a "megaregion." Trace on a map a large isosceles triangle roughly 260 miles long on the tall sides and 200 miles at the base, with Dallas–Fort Worth at the apex and Houston and San Antonio at the base vertices.[5] By the early 2000s, the area included in this Texas Triangle accounted for well over half the population of Texas, perhaps 6 percent of the United States population, and perhaps 7 percent of total U.S. gross domestic product. The ability of the state to weather the worst of the recession of 2008–2009 seemed to reinforce the Texas Triangle's position even before the shale oil boom of the 2010s generated a new round of petrochemical wealth.

The triangle is hardly self-contained. Roots or shoots like those of an aggressive tree or plant or—for a less provocative metaphor—like the radiating arms of a star stretch hundreds of miles in many directions. On the shoots and the arms outside the triangle, one finds outposts or gateways that link the core of Texas to its zone of influence and beyond: Beaumont and Port Arthur to the east; Abilene and Midland-Odessa to the west; Lubbock and Amarillo to the northwest; Corpus Christi along the South Texas coast; Laredo and the Brownsville-Harlingen-McAllen region in the Rio Grande Valley. In its settlement patterns and economic activity, Texas does amount to a sort of empire. It has a core territory, outposts and ports on its frontier, and an expansive sphere of influence.[6]

Concepts such as the Texas Triangle and Greater Texas contradict notions of geography evoked by Texas's familiar outline map. More than the map of any other state or indeed the maps of most countries, the map of Texas has become a symbol with a life of its own. This serendipitous product of migration, politics, and war seems like a natural unit, so much so that people overlook the environmental, geographic, economic, and cultural divisions into which Texas is segmented.[7]

When one takes into account the territory encompassed by the outline map, Texas consists of vast spaces, of dusty, creaky, Dairy Queen towns dispersed through arid plains. Outside the triangle, one moves through sparse landscapes. But when one diverts attention from the wilderness to where most people live, one understands how Texas went from being about 80 percent rural in 1910 to about 80 percent urban by the 1980s. The core of Texas is densely settled and evenly developed, with a regular pattern of towns. It is hot in the summer, to be sure, but hardly barren and uninviting. Except in drought years, most places in the urbanized core even have sufficient water, though the limitations of water supply clash with the methods and goals of Texas urbanization, a situation that global warming is likely to magnify.[8]

Of the Texas Triangle's satellite or peripheral cities, Corpus Christi is the only one that was seriously envisioned as having metropolitan potential before it settled into secondary status during the Sunbelt years, when other Texas cities accumulated people, wealth, and power. If Corpus Christi's midcentury promoters had succeeded, the triangle would have been a trapezoid. Defining the South Texas port as a satellite of Texas's core metropolises, while generally true, is not the complete truth. The city functions as a metropolis in relation to its own hinterland. Through the port, the military bases, and other activities, the city maintains myriad connections throughout the hemisphere and beyond.

Nevertheless, few would dispute the characterization of Corpus Christi as secondary or satellite within Texas. What does it mean for a city to have a secondary position in a system of cities? Geographers and historians use two large models to describe the relationship of cities to one another and their hinterlands. Of these, the "central place" model, identified with the German geographer Walter Christaller, seems the less appropriate one for Corpus Christi. In this model, cities at the top of the hierarchy perform overall or coordinating functions, and lower-ranking cities perform subsidiary, localized, or everyday activities. Corpus Christi illustrates this pattern as a location for branch operations of corporations, banks, and law firms headquartered in San Antonio, Houston, or Dallas; as a vacation destination for Texans; and as a provider of commercial, professional, governmental, and medical services to South Texans. By the late twentieth century, nearly all significant petrochemical and other industrial operations surrounding the port had come under out-of-town ownership. Yet even when owned by out-of-towners, such activities sparked ongoing interactions between the city and hemispheric, and indeed transnational, markets; they might be subsidiary, but they are not localized. The port, the petrochemical industry, the military, and the Mexico-U.S. borderlands infuse Corpus Christi with influences from across the United States, Mexico, the Caribbean, and many other places.

An alternative model treats cities as nodes having variable presences in networks of commerce, finance, and communications. In this model, secondary or satellite cities depend—often uncomfortably—on metropolitan cities to define the goals and direction of the regional economy, to channel investment capital, and to find markets for products. The situation of the Port of Corpus Christi illustrates the concept. This feat of civil engineering bears no resemblance to a provincial port. Thirty-four nautical miles (around forty statute miles) of channel dredged to forty-five feet, with five turning basins, the port begins in the Gulf of Mexico and stretches through Aransas Pass, over the Intracoastal Canal, across Corpus Christi Bay, and about eight more miles inland parallel to the Nueces River. Ringed by perhaps five thousand acres of dock, warehouse, bulk storage, and industrial sites, and lined with service roads and twenty-six miles of port-owned railroad track feeding three long-distance freight lines, the port handled an estimated 85 million tons of cargo annually in the early 2000s, consistently ranking as the sixth- or seventh-busiest port in the country in tonnage handled. For all this, the Port of Corpus Christi operates in the shadow of the Port of Houston, which handles perhaps 225 million tons a year, the largest port in the country in foreign tonnage and the second in overall tonnage, the continental hub for petrochemical operations.[9]

Texas oil and gas, along with cotton and grain from the South Texas hinterland, caused the Port of Corpus Christi to thrive after its opening in 1926. But petrochemicals, which by the 1980s were accounting for over 80 percent of cargo tonnage, left Corpus Christi vulnerable to decisions made in Houston and other cities where petrochemical enterprises had their headquarters. The decline of onshore production in South Texas, punctuated by the oil bust of the 1980s, drove home the hazards of such dependence, at least for a time. Espousing autonomy and diversification, port officials invested in a range of activities, including cold storage and cruise ship terminals, and sought independent commercial connections to Mexico, Latin America, and Asia. The results of these efforts were mixed even before the South Texas shale oil boom of the 2010s refocused attention on the port's traditional core activity.

Carl Abbott, the historian of cities in the western United States, recasts the terminology of central places and networks in a way that makes sense for urban Texas. Abbott distinguishes between "networked cities" such as Houston, which act "as gateways and links between national and world regions," and "regional cities" such as Corpus Christi. To some degree, these regional cities conform to Christaller's image of provincial places that "develop in step with their adjacent hinterlands, serving as economic and cultural centers for relatively limited contiguous regions."[10] But Abbott accounts for the reality that all cities of any consequence are bound up in webs of trade, capital, and information. His question is where, on balance, those networks are organized and managed. In his model, networked cities make decisions regarding jobs and investment, whereas regional or satellite cities have such decisions made for them. Corpus Christi is on the receiving end of many more political, professional, and business decisions than it makes for other cities.

Second-tier status is not the same as decay or a poor living environment. In comparison with midsized cities from Fresno, California, to Rockford, Illinois, Corpus Christi retained a diverse, durable economy with many strengths and attractions. Residents often expressed the view that a manageable city with an easygoing, waterfront life was preferable to a clogged, overwhelming metropolis. One could appreciate such moderate-growth sentiments, given the dreary round of commutes, subdivisions, and strip malls that people live with in much of the metropolitan United States. But these sentiments made business, civic, and professional leaders anxious because of the historical memory of unfulfilled potential and because of concern that secondary status might mean a withering of opportunities for investment and employment. A city in "station keeping" mode, remarked a Corpus Christi Regional Economic Development Corporation report in 2006, might be preferable to the "rapidly declining economies" of some American cities. Still, such a city faced a cycle of declining services, decaying neighborhoods, poverty, and out-migration. The public services, amenities, and way of life that people appreciated depended "on *primary* industries that pay wages higher than the area's average and on companies that need our area's assets."[11] In an inadvertent illustration of Abbott's model, such development reports were often frustratingly vague when it came to listing the city's assets worth investing in. Someone someplace else would make that call.

The drift of control of Corpus Christi enterprise toward Texas's dominant cities was punctuated by embarrassing defections of high-profile personalities and firms in retail and services as well as

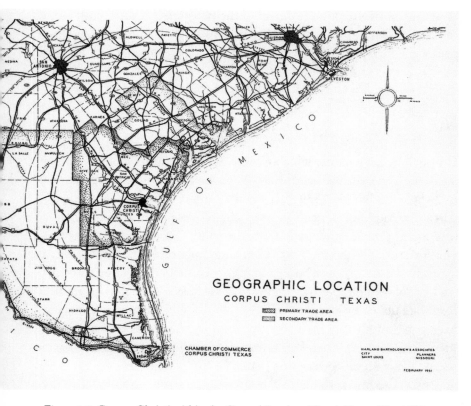

Figure 1.3. Corpus Christi within the Coastal Bend and South Texas. The 1953 comprehensive plan defined the city's immediate hinterland, its "primary trading area," as the eight counties from Refugio on the north to Kleberg on the south and then west to Live Oak, midway to San Antonio. From *Comprehensive Plan for the Corpus Christi Area* (St. Louis: Harland Bartholomew and Associates, 1953), plate 1.

petrochemicals. The H-E-B supermarket chain (a familiar grocery presence in Central and South Texas) moved to San Antonio in 1985. In 1996, the developer Robert Rowling, whose family had made over $500 million in South Texas oil and gas, held out the possibility of the city becoming a corporate headquarters location when he bought the Omni Hotel chain and planned to base operations in one of his two high-rise hotels along the Corpus Christi Bayfront. A year later, Rowling moved himself and Omni to Dallas, though he retained substantial real estate holdings in his hometown. In 2005, Whataburger, a hamburger chain known across the Southwest, signaled its local roots by buying naming rights for a downtown stadium, home field for a Texas League team sponsored by Nolan Ryan. In 2009, Whataburger's departure for San Antonio contributed to the defeat of the two-term mayor Henry Garrett, a well-liked former chief of police. In local accounts, Joe Adame won the race not so much because he would become the first elected Hispanic mayor as because his record as a developer might send "a clear message that Corpus Christi is open for business."[12]

Where Texas Meets the Sea

Corpus Christi's name, which evokes Spanish Catholic customs and attitudes, can deceive the unwary about the city's provenance. Settled by Anglo traders in 1839, the town resulted from the east-to-west spread of Anglo-American society, which overwhelmed the Hispanic settlement process underway from the south. At the time of the Anglo-American influx, the Texas Gulf Coast was on Mexico's frontier, a sparsely settled region whose land grants contained vagaries and contradictions exploitable by Anglo lawyers. Mexican society in its full form had not come closer to the area than Laredo or San Antonio, and even San Antonio retained an outpost atmosphere. Mexicans officials identified Corpus Christi Bay as a site for a future port, but they had no reason to act on this perception before 1836.[13]

Both Hispanic and Anglo-Americans saw towns as integral to the spread of their culture, so the siting and structure of towns reveal these peoples' goals for places they settled and their methods for achieving those goals. The Spanish and the Mexicans tended—at least in theory—to locate and lay out towns according to a formula. The New

Laws of the Indies of 1542 outlined rules and procedures that Hispanic surveyors followed even after the laws ceased to have force.[14] Anglo-Americans imposed no equivalent guidelines, but their surveyors did bring customs and practices concerning what made a town look respectable and inviting to settlers. The much-misunderstood grid pattern embodied their ideals.[15] The clearest signal of who founded and built Corpus Christi is that the early city took the shape of a slightly irregular grid of streets to and from the original harbor along the current Water Street. Far from being oriented around plazas, this grid made no provision even for a town square. For Anglo-Americans, this was a place to come ashore and move inland.

After establishing a trading post there in 1839, Henry Lawrence Kinney, a Pennsylvania-born merchant and land dealer, named the town after the crescent-shaped bay, itself named by Spanish colonizers of the surrounding coastal plain in the mid-1700s. Anglo town promoters habitually engaged in wishful thinking concerning a town site's geographic advantages, but Kinney had made a shrewd choice. His site, twenty miles inland from Padre and Mustang Islands, barrier islands along the Gulf of Mexico, promised protection from hurricanes. This relatively safe position compensated for the shallowness of the passes and the bay, whose sandbars were usually within five or six feet of the surface and periodically less than that. For a town builder, another inviting feature is the forty-foot Corpus Christi Bluff several hundred yards west of the natural shoreline, reputed to be the highest point on the flood-prone Texas coast. (High Island near Galveston also makes this claim.) The dramatic bluff behind the gorgeous, sweeping bay encouraged nineteenth-century boosters to label the place "Naples of the Gulf." Although this might seem excessive to jaded travelers of the twenty-first century, early settlers described their first glimpse of the town after arduous journeys over land or sea as a "vision of heaven."[16]

Kinney was also drawn to the first harbor south of the Nueces River for less forthright reasons. In Mexican eyes, the river was the southern boundary of Texas during the uneasy peace that followed the Texas Revolution of 1835–1836. The Texans, one recalls, claimed everything to the Rio Grande. Kinney thus set up shop in disputed territory, the best location for smuggling and similar operations. Kinney never gave up dubious dealings in Mexico, even after the Mexican War ended with the border 160 miles south at the Rio Grande. Ultimately, Kinney died from his Mexican adventures, shot in 1862 on a street in Matamoros, reportedly caught in a gunfight while on his way to a tryst. Between 1848 and the Civil War, Kinney did engage in conventional town promotion. He brought the Lone Star Fair, Texas's first state fair, to Corpus Christi in 1852, the year that the rickety town of around 700 people became an incorporated municipality. Kinney hoped to illustrate that his prospective port, 150 miles southeast of San Antonio, was not a remote, dangerous place but one of interest to all "Friends of the South West."[17] The choice of words reveals where Kinney saw his town to be located or at least where commerce and settlers could go from it.

Ever since, promoters and civic leaders have deployed various geographic terms to describe Corpus Christi in relation to Texas, the United States, Mexico, and the Gulf. When not Naples of the Gulf, Corpus Christi might be the Chicago of the Southwest or the Long Branch of the South, labels that sum up an enduring tension between the city as a hub of commerce and as a resort for people getting away from business. During the so-called Ropes Boom in the years before the Panic of 1893 (named for Elihu Ropes, an investor from New Jersey), a railroad promotion magazine urged "Capital" to "Take Notice" of the town at the gateway of the "extreme southwest" of Texas. With proper railroad connections and port facilities, the place could be "the conduit of commerce" for the "trans-Mississippi country," a "Chicago No. 2," with direct connections for Texas beef to New York and even Great Britain. Another pamphlet from the Ropes Boom proclaimed Corpus Christi "the future deep-water harbor for a larger extent of territory and a larger population than are now tributary to any one seaport in the world," a natural outlet for Denver, Kansas City, St. Louis, and Omaha.[18]

In these boosterish geography lessons of the late 1800s, *Southwest* and *the Gulf* evoked not just commerce, ports, and hinterlands. For Anglo-Americans, the South Texas coast also implied warm weather and a less hemmed-in life. Boosters declared winters to be milder than those in soon-to-be-obsolete Chicago (indisputably true) and summers to be comparable (true if one compares an average South Texas summer to the worst heat experienced in Illinois). "Swept by the salty sea-breezes fresh from the Gulf of Mexico," the city might develop into a year-round retreat for inland Texans. "The cooling sea breezes," the 1890s boosters stressed, meant that "the thermometer *never touch[es] ninety-two degrees.*"[19] (Maybe their thermometer was broken.)

The South Texas coast also signified a long growing season—along with cheap, mainly Mexican labor—to potential farming migrants from the upper Mississippi Valley, who had become a target of recruiting efforts by the early twentieth century. "Sea—Sunshine—Soil," proclaimed the subtitle of a Commercial Club booklet in the 1910s, "an ideal city for your vacation—summer or winter, for your business, for your farm to be near." By then a "modern, progressive city," in aspiration at least, Corpus Christi was "in the very heart of the largest, richest, most rapidly developing section of the 'Great Southwest.'"[20] Backers of the deepwater port in the 1920s published maps showing the city's "strategic location" at the center of American and world trade. "This is the Gateway to the United States from South American waters," insisted a Commercial Club briefing to the Army Corps of Engineers. States as far away as Montana were "actively tributary," and the "immediately contiguous" hinterland contained "some of the largest live stock ranches in the world," along with rapidly developing agricultural lands.[21]

With the opening of the port in 1926, the chamber of commerce hit upon a catchphrase that recurred over the next decades: "Where Texas Meets the Sea." This slogan "aptly," the chamber proclaimed, summed up the city's commercial position. It also, this book argues, expressed how residents generally understood the place.[22] An apt slogan did not stop publicists from concocting others as the occasion suggested. With the advent of large-scale industry in the 1930s and the opening of the naval air station in 1941, population leapt from 10,522 in 1920 to 57,301 in 1940 and nearly doubled again to 108,287 in 1950. Corpus Christi's transformation into a "Port of Play and Profit" and the "Wonder City of the South" epitomizes circumstances that made the World War II decade decisive in the American West's emergence as a powerful urban region.[23]

By the 1970s, terms that described Corpus Christi in promotional publications had narrowed in vision as the city settled into the second tier. "Escape City" offered "low-cost, unskilled, trainable" labor in "a right-to-work state," explained the chamber of commerce in the

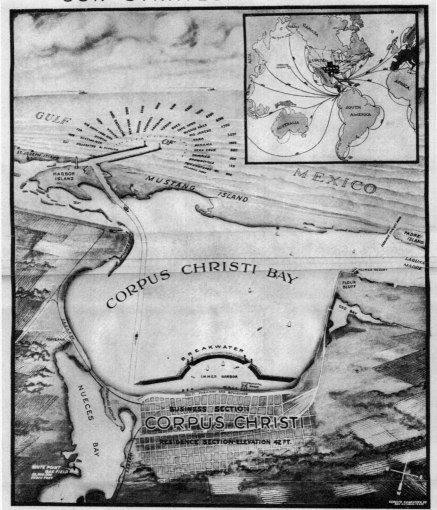

OUR STRATEGIC LOCATION—Perspective view of the Corpus Christi Bay Section with key map inset. No more forcible illustration of our commanding position in the development of extensive trade relations with South America and Mexican ports could be presented than the above map, showing at a glance the commanding position of our Port. It shows strikingly that this is the Gateway to the United States from South American waters and that our outlet to the Sea is nearer the Panama Canal than any other developed Port on the Gulf Coast. **STUDY THE MAP AND OUR STRATEGIC POSITION.**

Figure 1.4. "Our Strategic Location." Promoters of the deepwater port created this as "a forcible illustration of our commanding position" as "Gateway to the United States from South American waters." The half circle at the upper left lists distances to ports as far-flung as Hamburg, Cape Town, and Buenos Aires. From "Brief of the City of Corpus Christi, Texas, and the Corpus Christi Commercial Association, submitted to the Board of Engineers," September 20, 1920. Courtesy of the Dan Kilgore Collection 6205, Special Collections and Archives, Bell Library, Texas A&M University–Corpus Christi.

mid-1970s, which treated inhabitants' limited skills and alternatives as a selling point. The geographic situation of the "Sparkling City by the Sea" still offered attractions to professionals and managers, even if not to the mass of people. "We're Texas's favorite wave-washed resort city," trumpeted an Industrial Commission ad in *Business Week*, "a culture bent" city with industrial "sites next to interstates, labor, fishing, hunting and sailing all so plentiful and low-cost."[24] This shift in tone underscores the relevance of Abbott's dichotomy between networked and regional cities. In the early twentieth century, boosters imagined reconfiguring a continent from the vantage point of Corpus Christi Bay. Later in the century, marketers invited others to find uses for it.

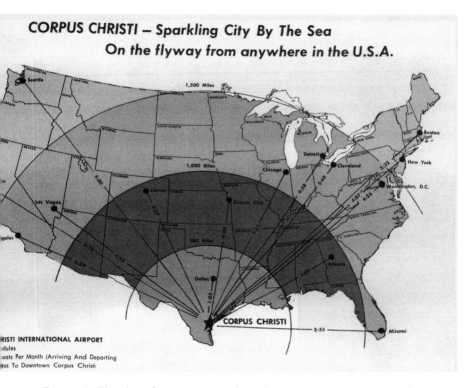

Figure 1.5. Chamber of commerce map from the 1960s proposing Corpus Christi as an accessible location for conventions. From "Corpus Christi Convention Climate." Courtesy of the Dan Kilgore Collection 4961, Special Collections and Archives, Bell Library, Texas A&M University–Corpus Christi.

Of the regional terms offered by promoters to locate Corpus Christi, "Texas" seems to have meant the most to local people. My own searches during 2010 of online yellow-pages listings—a rough way to measure where people locate their city—suggest that businesses and institutions used "Texas" or "South Texas" in their names two to four times more often than "Coastal" or "Coastal Bend" and five to seven times more often than "Gulf" or "Gulf Coast." "Southwest" and "South" also fall far behind "Texas." The iconography of Texas—the Lone Star flag, the outline map, armadillos, cowboy hats and boots—is ubiquitous on signs, in print, and on the Internet. Residents consider Corpus Christi to belong to South Texas and Texas, to a lesser extent to the Gulf of Mexico, the Southwest, and the South, and finally, though often reluctantly, to the U.S.-Mexico borderlands.

In the phrase "where Texas meets the sea," the accent is upon Texas. Commercial and financial networks extended into the city through the Texas metropolises, which also served throughout the twentieth century as Corpus Christi's main political and cultural reference points. By contrast, one finds surprisingly little discussion in Corpus Christi of other Gulf Coast cities east of the Sabine River as having comparable character or similar economic, planning, or environmental problems. During the 1920s–1950s, Corpus Christi took an active part in the movement for the Intracoastal Canal. But even that endeavor illustrated the city's linkages to Texas more than to the Gulf of Mexico. In New Deal–era Washington, the head lobbyist for the Gulf Intracoastal Canal Association was the former Corpus Christi mayor and *Corpus Christi Caller* editor Roy Miller, a protégé of South Texas political figures such as Vice President John Nance Garner and Congressman Richard M. Kleberg of the King Ranch family. The impetus for the Intracoastal Canal came largely from Texans, who at times expressed suspicion of their Louisiana collaborators. Oriented around the Mississippi and concerned about competition from Houston, Louisianans did "not share [Texas's] degree of enthusiasm," as an Army Corps history put it.[25]

A Southwestern City, More or Less

Corpus Christi might be where Texas meets the sea, but which Texas? Texas encompasses nearly 270,000 square miles, larger than France, as the boast goes. And like France, Texas is not a coherent entity geologically, environmentally, geographically, or ethnographically. The Coastal Bend amounts to one segment of the Texas coastal plain, a terrain that varies from flat and scrubby lowland to rolling brush or grassland as it stretches from the Edwards Plateau beyond San Antonio to the Piney Woods north of Houston. This is one of at least four major environmental regions (depending on how they are defined) into which Texas is divided. Likewise, Texas evinces social and cultural crosscurrents from the South, the Southwest, the Great Plains, and Mexico. So do sections within the state, including the Coastal Bend.

Much of the Anglo-American population of Texas originated in migrations from the South. Since the Civil War, Corpus Christians have debated the degree to which the city might be characterized as southern. I classify Corpus Christi as an eastern gateway into the Southwest rather than as an outlier of the South. The city's history, politics, economy, culture, and appearance entwine it with San Antonio, Laredo, and other places to the west. The landscape and environment of the area likewise suggest the Southwest rather than the South. Once one moves southwest of the Houston metropolitan area through the Texas coastal plain, especially beyond Victoria, space stretches out, with no visual boundary into the brush country of southwest Texas and northern Mexico.

At 97°24'7"W longitude, Corpus Christi is almost directly south of Austin, Fort Worth, Oklahoma City, Wichita, Lincoln, and Sioux Falls. This line of cities has had special significance for scholars of the West since the 1930s, when Walter Prescott Webb identified the ninety-eighth meridian as the start of the massive zone of semiaridity that, he argued, set the West apart from other American regions.[26] The relevance of Webb's idea becomes evident when one passes from Victoria toward Corpus Christi; it is also evident when traveling southeast from San Antonio toward the Gulf Coast.

The environment of the Southwest concentrates settlement because of people's need for access to limited freshwater supplies. Corpus Christi fits this pattern well. Approached from any direction except from the north along the coast, a sparsely settled landscape gives way to a large city with a dense, evenly built fabric. In this arid-zone pattern, hinterland towns are much smaller than the regional city. The largest towns in Corpus Christi's orbit include Kingsville, in Kleberg County, with over 26,000 people in 2010, and Alice, in Jim Wells County, with around 20,000 people. Every other hinterland town outside Corpus Christi's metropolitan statistical area has at most 5,000–6,000 people. Five towns within the MSA contain approximately 8,000–10,000 people, which is to say that Corpus Christi has no large incorporated suburbs, a product of Texas municipal law as well as the arid environment.[27] This pattern of a large city surrounded by sparse countryside reinforces the association of the Southwest with space and not cities. The connection of this pattern to freshwater has led numerous observers to follow Webb in applying to the Southwest the archaeological term "oasis civilization."[28]

Corpus Christi shares with the urban Southwest the endless search for a "larger and more adequate" water supply. One downtown landmark, Artesian Park, testifies to this challenge. While camping along the bay in 1845–1846, General Zachary Taylor's troops sank a well that yielded sulfurous water. Always attentive to promotional opportunities, Henry Kinney deeded the land to the town, with the idea that the well might have medicinal qualities. Freshwater being the more immediate problem, Kinney and his successors reserved what they could from nearby arroyos, sank wells where they could, and relied on cisterns. These efforts afforded the town a barely tolerable supply until the last years of the nineteenth century, when a private company began pumping water from a dam on the Nueces River near the current neighborhood of Calallen, about fifteen miles west of the central city.[29]

The city took this system over as the basis for a municipal system. In the fall of 1929, the city dedicated La Fruita Dam at Mathis, about thirty-five miles up the Nueces River. Lake Lovenskiold reservoir, named for P. G. Lovenskiold, the mayor who pushed the water-supply expansion, was supposed to be sufficient for four times the population that then lived in the city. Cost cutting on construction contributed to

the dam's failure during heavy rains in November 1930. The prospect of
attracting the port's first large manufacturer—Southern Alkali, a joint
venture of Pittsburgh Plate Glass and American Cyanamid—spurred
the dam's rebuilding with funds from the Depression-era Reconstruction Finance Corporation. Like industries drawn to the port over the
next decades, Southern Alkali required considerable freshwater, which
set up an ongoing tension between residential and industrial demand.
By the late 1950s, industry accounted for nearly 40 percent of Nueces
County's water demand, even though firms were increasingly making
use of seawater in cooling.[30] Meanwhile, Corpus Christi's population
had quadrupled, pushing the Mathis reservoir, now renamed Lake
Corpus Christi, to its limits. The coalition of business and civic interests that at the time dominated public-works policy resisted pressure

Figure 1.6. The Wesley Seale Dam, finished in 1958, and Lake Corpus Christi along
the Nueces River at Mathis, Texas. The University of Texas report that included
this picture in 1961 recognized the reservoir's eventual limitations: "Even with this
firm supply of fresh water, Corpus Christi is looking beyond the immediate future,
planning long-range area water resource management." From *Corpus Christi: Area
Resources for Industry* (Austin: Bureau of Business Research, 1961), 133.

from the federal Bureau of Reclamation to establish a comprehensive water system for eight South Texas counties and instead supported the construction of an enlarged Mathis dam, the Wesley Seale Dam, finished in 1958.[31]

Backers recognized that the new Mathis dam was a temporary solution, especially as outlying towns outgrew their groundwater supplies and began tapping into Lake Corpus Christi. In 1965, the Area Development Committee (ADC), the self-perpetuating elite organization that oversaw planning and public works, set off a bitter controversy when it shifted direction and came out in support of the Bureau of Reclamation's regional water plan. The plan's central feature was a dam on the Frio River, a branch of the Nueces, at Choke Canyon near Three Rivers, seventy-five miles northwest of Corpus Christi. The Choke Canyon reservoir would yield about 28 percent less water than an alternate site five miles north of the city boundary along the Nueces River. The closer site, known as R&M, after the Reagan and McCaughan engineering firm that outlined it, was estimated to cost at least twice as much as Choke Canyon, mainly on account of higher land prices. R&M would put more water under municipal control, but the city would likely have to fund the project itself, while the Bureau of Reclamation would underwrite Choke Canyon. Amid the many-sided quarrels, upstream communities generally favored Choke Canyon, while city residents and businesses favored R&M. Conservationists raised additional issues, above all potential damage to fish and shrimp breeding grounds through alteration of the nutrient and saline content of estuaries.[32]

The controversy pushed Corpus Christi's government and civic leadership into formal cooperation with surrounding counties. The new Coastal Bend Regional Planning Commission hired the St. Louis planning firm Harland Bartholomew and Associates, with whom the ADC and the city had a lengthy relationship, to develop regional plans on a variety of matters, the "most important" of which was water.[33] The consultants' report stressed the obvious: "Municipal, industrial, agricultural, and tourist growth" were "critically tied to the provision of water." The consultants called for consolidating twenty-eight area water districts and control agencies into a Coastal Bend Water Authority. Corpus Christi politicians sensed that the city was being tied into engineering systems and administrative arrangements that would be regretted later. In 1967–1968, Corpus Christi's state representatives fought legislation authorizing a consolidated water authority, on the grounds that it would be a "vehicle for Choke Canyon." Despite a 1970 referendum favoring the R&M site, the city yielded to state and federal pressure. The Choke Canyon Dam ended up being a joint project of the city and the Nueces River Authority, a reclamation agency dating to the New Deal period.[34]

Bitterness lingered long after the dam went into operation in 1982. As conservationists had anticipated, damming the Nueces watershed exacerbated problems that cycles of drought placed upon shrimp and fish breeding grounds along the coast. In the early 1990s, the city and the Nueces River Authority agreed to a regime of freshwater releases into the estuaries. Underscoring the disappointing results of Choke Canyon, Corpus Christi in 1995 began a $230 million project to pipe in water from Lake Texana, northeast of Victoria, 100 miles away. By the 2000s, Corpus Christi was dependent on Lake Texana for around half its drinking water.[35]

By the 2010s, prolonged drought, aging mains, and intensifying petrochemical industry demand due to the South Texas shale oil boom made water's limits on regional development inescapable. "The economic value of water supplies and the nature of industrial use," the *Corpus Christi Caller-Times* remarked in January 2013, left the city few alternatives to restrictions on residential use. At the time, industry still accounted for 40 percent of annual use. Since inflow into the reservoirs was in "drastic decline," as the executive director of the Nueces River Authority put it, the city, regional agencies, and petrochemical executives mulled everything from desalination to handing out rain barrels, which no one any longer called cisterns. The "clear gold" of water was essential to the pursuit of the "black gold" behind the region's renewed prosperity. The shale oil boom—much of which centered on Three Rivers in the vicinity of Choke Canyon—threatened a watershed already under pressure from deepening cycles of "drought and dry climates."[36]

The limitations imposed by water supplies, along with the arid landscape, explain the appearance and layout of southwestern cities, especially when one further takes into account the timing of their most rapid development. The urban Southwest grew mainly in the age of the internal combustion engine, and its cities show only small or weak vestiges of the urban forms fostered by docks, railroads, and tramways. At first glance, cities like Corpus Christi seem to epitomize "sprawl," a pejorative term that urban affairs experts often resist, whether they approve of spread-out, auto-oriented cities or deplore them. Sprawl implies formlessness, whereas observation reveals a logical structure.[37]

"What actually bothers the critics is not that southwestern cities are formless, but that they are unfamiliar," notes Carl Abbott. When taken on their own terms, southwestern cities amount to the *most* comprehensible cities." Places such as Corpus Christi are multicentered and linear rather than concentrated around hubs of transportation and commerce. They are horizontal rather than vertical. Their vistas are open and seemingly boundless. In southwestern cities (and indeed in outlying, post–World War II portions of many northeastern and midwestern cities), one orients oneself by driving along highways and thoroughfares and absorbing the sensation of crystalline growth. These cities "cluster straightforwardly around their highways." Central business districts (CBDs) feature aggregations of high rises, but they end with surprising abruptness, giving way to a fabric of "low-slung, horizontal" buildings, subdivision upon subdivision of ranch houses and bungalows, interrupted by apartment courts and commercial strips. In the Southwest, the built area is continuous; the cities "spread *evenly* rather than thinly across their sites," as Abbott explains.[38]

This describes how one moves through Corpus Christi and what one sees, except along the bays—a big exception. Corpus Christi is unusual in being a southwestern city along the Atlantic basin. In any western direction from the city, one enters the Southwest. Along the coastal road from Corpus Christi to Galveston, most of which consists of the two-lane Texas State Highway 35, one passes through marshes, estuaries, and fishing or resort towns, similar to what one finds anywhere along the U.S. coastline from South Texas to Cape Cod.

The Port, Petropolis, the Northside, and the Westside

With these descriptors in mind—low, even, linear, open, and multicentered—the layout of a city like Corpus Christi becomes easy to grasp. Using Texas's generous annexation laws, the city expanded over the decades to a length of more than thirty miles from the Nueces River at Calallen to the Gulf of Mexico on Padre Island. Through this expansion, the city retained the oblong or crescent shape that it initially took from the bay.

By automobile, one usually approaches from the northwest. Interstate 37 from San Antonio and U.S. Highway 77 from Houston meet north of the river in San Patricio County, home of the Irish Catholic colony San Patricio de Hibernia, whose settlement Mexico encouraged in its search for a buffer against Anglo Protestants from the United States. The San Patricio colony laid the foundation for a Catholic presence that came to include Czechs as well as Irish and Mexicans. The highway bridge over the Nueces River calls no attention to the momentous territorial dispute once focused on the site. Mexico's insistence that Texas ended at the river provided James K. Polk's administration the opportunity to prod Mexico into the disastrous war of 1846–1848, which ended with Mexico ceding the Rio Grande border and much else under the duress of foreign occupation.[39]

Driving east, about ten miles still from Corpus Christi's contiguous street grid, one passes Calallen, named for Calvin J. Allen, the rancher who began developing it before World War I. The municipality annexed Calallen and the neighboring Tuloso-Midway section starting in the 1960s. These residential suburbs, detached from the bulk of the city, have a meaningful form of governmental independence: they maintain two of the five independent school districts within municipal boundaries. Commuters also come to Corpus Christi from Robstown to the west and from Portland or Aransas Pass across Nueces Bay. But a large majority of metropolitan Corpus Christians live in the contiguous urban fabric; myriad subdivisions of detached houses and garden apartments stretch into the plain in the crystalline fashion of the Southwest. Texas municipal law encouraged Corpus Christi to absorb urbanizing land on its border before suburbs could gain legal autonomy. In the early 2000s, the municipality accounted for nearly 70 percent of the population in its metropolitan statistical area, a level of central-city control of the MSA greater than that existing in San Antonio or Houston.

By far the most important autonomous jurisdiction along the South Texas coast appears to the left as one drives east from Calallen: the Port of Corpus Christi Authority. The port has almost no residents, but its

Figure 1.7. William H. Parker, a Corpus Christi photographer, captured the spectacle of a refinery at night in this undated image from the 1950s. Courtesy of the William H. Parker Collection 126-8bw, Special Collections and Archives, Bell Library, Texas A&M University–Corpus Christi.

intricate mesh of industrial architecture, pipelines, railroads, towers, and tanks is an unforgettable urban landscape, spectacular by night. At the end of the twentieth century, the Port of Corpus Christi Authority controlled over 21,000 acres, 16,000 of which were submerged, stretching from the west end of Nueces Bay to Harbor Island in the Gulf of Mexico. Of the seven port commissioners who governed this domain, three were appointed by the city, three by Nueces County, and one by San Patricio County, an arrangement implemented in 2004 to settle disputes over Nueces County's long-standing control of the port authority majority. San Patricio County's involvement recognizes the port's expansion across Nueces Bay into the La Quinta area—planned site of container facilities—and Ingleside, where regional governments hoped that investment related to the Eagle Ford shale oil field would replace 3,000 jobs lost with the 2005 decision to close Naval Station Ingleside.[40]

The port authority operates, among other facilities, around a dozen liquid docks for petrochemicals, along with dry docks, wharves, warehouses, cold storage, and a convention center. Numerous enterprises lease port authority land: refineries, petrochemical plants, and private petrochemical docks and storage facilities. The roster of industrial firms lining the Corpus Christi Ship Channel underscores the centrality of petrochemicals and high-energy manufacturing along the Texas coast. Over the last decades of the twentieth century, local plants matured and corporate control became more concentrated, but the mix of industries persisted. In the early 1960s, five major refineries lined the port, four of which—Delhi-Taylor, Pontiac, Southwestern, and Suntide—were run by regionally owned independents, who seemed, as a 1961 study put it, to "have adapted themselves well" to oil-industry consolidation and vertical integration. At that time, Sinclair was the only integrated oil company with a large refinery in Corpus Christi. Well-known corporations had plants in other industries: Celanese and Pittsburgh Plate Glass in industrial chemicals, Reynolds and American

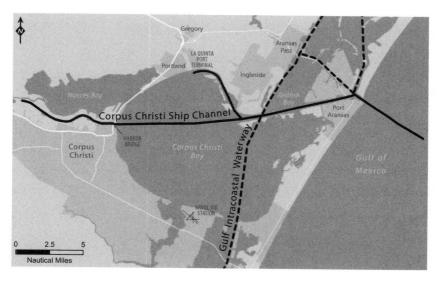

Figure 1.8. By the early 2000s, the massive Corpus Christi Ship Channel, dredged to forty-five feet, stretched over thirty-four nautical miles from the Gulf of Mexico to the Viola Turning Basin near the Nueces River on the left. The La Quinta Port Terminal, projected for container facilities, and the former Naval Station Ingleside, site of Eagle Ford–related development by the 2010s, appear north of Corpus Christi Bay in San Patricio County. By Crystal K. Williams, GEOMAP, Illinois State University.

Smelting and Refining in metals, Corn Products in food processing, and Halliburton in cement manufacturing.[41]

At the end of the century, after decades of consolidation and re-shuffling, Reynolds still employed 900 workers producing aluminum hydrate, but the major chemical plants were owned by DuPont, Oxy-chem, and Elementis Chromium. Industry consolidation was also evident among refiners. Valero and Ultramar Diamond Shamrock (which merged in 2001) had headquarters in San Antonio. Citgo had its home in Houston, Koch in Wichita, and Trifinery (which processed petroleum into asphalt) in Omaha. Out-of-town control did not mean second-rate facilities. The Koch refinery could produce 300,000 barrels a day, half of that company's capacity, and Valero's refinery could handle up to 125,000 barrels. Overall, Corpus Christi's refining operations had a capacity of 673,000 barrels a day in 2001, accounting for 4 percent of the country's refining capacity and contributing $161 million a year to the local payroll.[42]

Three railroads had converged on Corpus Christi by 1914, and the ship channel eventually meshed with them. The port and its industries, therefore, reinforced an overall pattern of functional and residential segmentation in the city. Corpus Christi's north and west sides acquired a reputation as belonging to commerce, transportation, and industry and to people who could not live elsewhere. Desirable residential sections, especially for the Anglo middle class, took shape toward the southeast and south. A few exceptions, such as Hillcrest, northwest of the central business district, remained Anglo-American into the 1960s, by which time those who could afford it were leaving.

While technologically impressive and visually spectacular, refineries and industrial chemical plants at the Port of Corpus Christi use processes and generate by-products that pose undeniable dangers to workers and the public. Given the city's elongated geography, most Corpus Christians can put their version of "petropolis"—a term coined by the environmental scholar Christopher Sellers—out of their minds most of the time. Into the 2000s, no major oil spills had occurred in Laguna Madre, though a 1979 spill in the Bay of Campeche reached beaches well up the Texas coast. Of more immediate danger to bird nesting grounds and marine-life breeding grounds in the estuaries were fertilizer and other types of agricultural runoff.[43]

Concerns over air and ground contamination were most pronounced in neighborhoods nearest the ship channel. No refinery or chemical plant accidents have matched the April 1981 grain dust explosion at the port's public grain elevator, which killed nine workers and did $30 million in damage. Yet accidents and fires were recorded regularly. Rumors abounded that chemical releases occurred more frequently than reported. Plant safety engineers conceded that hazards were ever present, even when thorough regulations and procedures were followed. Many studies sought to measure toxin levels in surrounding neighborhoods. Bad publicity, threats of legal action, and enhanced federal limitations on emissions persuaded refiners to buy and demolish hundreds of nearby houses in order to create a buffer zone and to improve emergency reporting and outreach.[44]

In Corpus Christi as elsewhere, the assumption that cities should be segmented into functional territories, thereby allowing incompatible economic activities to take place in different parts of a city, guided planning, zoning, and real estate development. People with less power and fewer resources ended up living closest to the least desirable activities. Mexican Americans had been concentrated by the 1920s in the so-called Hill area west of the central business district atop the Corpus Christi Bluff. The new Nueces County Courthouse, built in the 1970s, and Corpus Christi City Hall, built in the 1980s, came to occupy this rough area. African Americans, generally around 5 percent of the city's people, settled north of the Hill. This portion of the Northside area became known as the "Cut," perhaps because it was cut from the bluff during railroad construction. Segregation of blacks was stringent in a city where Jim Crow laws and practices took hold. Into the late 1960s, an estimated 97 percent of blacks lived in segregated neighborhoods, half of them in two Northside census tracts.[45] Both the Hill and the Cut were accessible to the waterfront and the rail yards, but were removed from the tree-lined streets of Anglo-owned bungalows that by the 1920s and 1930s had spread southward from the bluff.

In zoning ordinances in 1937 and 1948, the city reserved the north and west for industry, business, and multifamily residences, a sensible decision given the location of the port, but one that ratified the city's racial and ethnic divisions.[46] Interstate 37, constructed in the 1960s, divided and isolated the Northside, another logical decision from a

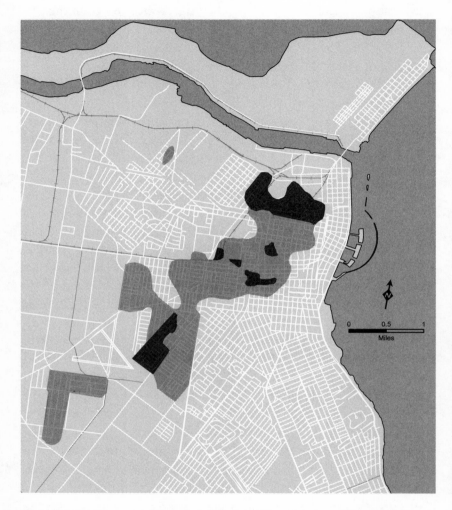

Figure 1.9. Racial patterns in housing during the Westside's formative years. The darker shades represent African American areas—the Northside and a newer area east of old municipal airport. Tejanos were meanwhile moving from the old Hill barrio immediately south of the Northside as far as the Molina district to the west of the airport. By Crystal K. Williams, GEOMAP, Illinois State University, based on *A Preliminary Report upon Housing, Corpus Christi, Texas* (St. Louis: Harland Bartholomew and Associates, 1951), plate 3.

planning perspective, but one with racial implications. African Americans then spread north into Hillcrest, accelerating white flight from that region. Smaller black sections gradually emerged several miles southward in the Westside, which was predominantly Hispanic.

As the Hispanic population expanded from around one-third at midcentury to over half by the 1990s, Hispanics spread throughout the Westside and eventually across the city. The Westside, a wedge of land that fans southeast from Interstate 37 roughly to the Crosstown Expressway or perhaps Ayers Street, was by the 1960s a famous center for Mexican American politics, business, and culture. It was the home of Dr. Hector P. García and his American GI Forum and of the region's Labor Council for Latin American Advancement, which pursued the decisive *Cisneros* case against educational discrimination. Radio and television personalities such as Domingo Peña broadcast from there. The Galván Ballroom was there, along with Estrada Motors, La Malinche Tortillas, and much else besides.

Like the Northside, the area suffered from decrepit housing, poverty, and social ills. But it also featured subdivisions of wooden and brick-sided ranch houses not visibly distinguishable from Anglo neighborhoods to the south. As Corpus Christi Tejanos gained a larger, more secure position within the city's economy, they bought housing throughout the Westside. Families with barely enough resources sought neighborhoods such as Molina, outside the city limits until the mid-1950s and thus not subject to codes regarding plumbing and utilities that might have priced the unfinished houses beyond reach. Hector García became a national figure through his campaigns across South Texas for equal treatment and educational opportunities for Mexican Americans, but much of his local stature came from persistent battles to ensure that water, sewer, and electrical services were delivered to such neighborhoods, along with assistance for building improvements. By the 1990s, Molina had developed into a settled and tight-knit, even if still often poor, neighborhood. This was the childhood home of the slain Tejano music star Selena, as well as of political figures such as Carlos Valdez, who in 1992 won election as the county's first Hispanic district attorney, and the educator and activist Danny Noyola, valedictorian of the area's West Oso High School who eventually became superintendent of the West Oso Independent School

District.[47] By century's end, outright housing discrimination no longer blocked Hispanics from living anywhere in the city. Still, the struggle for affordable housing prompted the emergence of unserviced, flood-prone *colonias* on unincorporated land throughout Nueces County. One survey in the early 2000s counted eighty-eight such settlements, where immigrants lived alongside Texas-born Hispanics and some members of other ethnic groups.[48]

Downtown, Seawall, and Bluff

At Mesquite Street, where Interstate 37 ceases to be a freeway, Corpus Christi Bay is already visible, but the drama of its crescent is not yet apparent. This is because the Corpus Christi seawall grades upward to a crest of fifteen feet above sea level, over three and a half feet above the storm surge of September 14, 1919, the most significant date in the city's history. Constructed in 1939–1941, the seawall extends outward over 600 feet from the original shoreline at Water Street and then runs 12,000 feet south from the ship channel, fortifying the straggling central business district against the Gulf.[49]

As one enters the CBD, to the right on the slope of the bluff are the offices of the *Corpus Christi Caller-Times*, the city's major newspaper for over a century. Artesian Park, site of the army's futile quest for freshwater, is visible down the bluff from the Caller-Times building. Immediately to the left one sees an eclectic Greek Revival building, abandoned and crumbling despite miscellaneous efforts at preservation and protection. Upon its opening in 1914, the Nueces County Courthouse, like county courthouses across Texas, was cherished as a symbol of the town's urban potential and urbane ambitions. It was "dignified and magnificent in architectural lines and complete in every detail," a pamphlet pronounced shortly after it opened. The building, however, grew stuffy and cramped as county business expanded. By 1977, when the county left downtown for its bland new structure beyond the bluff, county workers and lawyers alike had come to despise the old courthouse. Disagreements over its aesthetic and economic value set the stage for a decades-long stalemate over whether to salvage Corpus Christi's first National Register building and to what end.[50]

Advocates on both sides of the argument cited the courthouse's location at the city's so-called Gateway. Whether by railroad or automobile, travelers have entered Corpus Christi roughly at the same area toward the northern end of the CBD. Starting in the mid-1990s, architectural, planning, and citizen groups debated proposals to "create a more attractive entryway to the city."[51] After several times rejecting renovation of the old courthouse as too expensive and impractical, the U.S. government opened a new federal courthouse at I-37 and Shoreline Boulevard, on the crest of the seawall. The federal courthouse now shares the Gateway with sculptor Robert Perless's *Orion's Belt*, three fifty-five-foot-long weathervanes atop twenty-foot piers, installed in 2002 after a quarrel over whether a constructivist sculpture by a Connecticut artist made an appropriate symbol for the city.[52]

Dominating the scene to the north is a structure that took its place as a "symbol of a city" upon its opening in 1959: the Harbor Bridge over the ship channel. During the 1950s, the powerful Area Development Committee gave priority to fixing an egregious flaw in the port's 1920s design: a bascule drawbridge that formed a bottleneck for both ships and cars at the ship channel's entrance. The Harbor Bridge became the ADC's most lauded accomplishment. A mile long and shaped somewhat like Napoleon's hat, with a 138-foot clearance for ships, the steel bridge was nearly as striking an engineering feat as the seawall and the port. By the late 1980s, port and city officials gingerly called attention to the reality that it was reaching the end of its projected lifespan. High and grand as the bridge was, ships were becoming ever taller. To accommodate cruise ships and other contemporary vessels, Corpus Christi might require an even higher bridge, or a bridge with a more mundane location up the ship channel, or perhaps a tunnel, an idea first sketched in the 1950s. By 2013, replacing the bridge, estimated at $1 billion, had moved beyond discussion into financing. With construction planned to begin in 2017, Corpus Christians were resigned to losing a cherished landmark. "There is no more dramatic sight in this part of Texas than coming off the Harbor Bridge at night, with the city lights rising before you," the columnist Murphy Givens wistfully remarked in 2006, "although, presumably, a new bridge would provide a similar experience."[53]

Figure 1.10. Postcard of the Harbor Bridge at the entrance to the ship channel, 1962. This landmark, with its "Napoleon's hat" shape, is scheduled for replacement starting in 2017. Courtesy of the Dan Kilgore Collection, Special Collections and Archives, Bell Library, Texas A&M University–Corpus Christi.

When one continues to the seawall and then south on Shoreline Boulevard to the T-head piers extending into the bay, the basic layout of central Corpus Christi becomes apparent. Waterfront activities had gravitated toward the north even before the ship channel's opening in 1926. Retail, services, and government occupied the lower portion of the CBD, beneath the bluff. In Uptown, atop the bluff, a separate financial and business center took shape, especially after the 1927 opening of the Nixon Building, later the Wilson Building, the city's first large office building. Resort activities clustered in segments along the shore. Hotels arose along the waterfront starting across the ship channel on North Beach (later known as Corpus Christi Beach) and then continuing south past two high-rise hotels that during the 1980s came to define Shoreline Boulevard's skyline, along with the twin skyscrapers of One Shoreline Plaza, completed in 1988. Hotels continued beyond the south end of the seawall.

As in most American cities, retail and services had begun to disperse from the CBD by the 1960s. Meanwhile, Padre and Mustang Islands emerged as attractive competitors to the Corpus Christi Bayfront as locations for hotels and condominiums. When Nueces County built its new courthouse and Corpus Christi its new city hall west beyond Uptown during the 1970s–1980s, even government partly abandoned the central city. In fits and starts, a strategy emerged that kept portions of the central city vital despite the CBD occupying too stretched-out an area even for the functions it had contained at its height. Beginning in the 1960s with designation of the Bayfront Arts and Science Park at the point where the ship channel meets the bay, and the construction there of the Corpus Christi Museum of Science and History and the Art Museum of South Texas, Corpus Christi, like many American and European cities worried about their downtowns, used museums and other cultural attractions, entertainment, and convention facilities as anchors around which restaurants, shops, and residence might grow. Across the Harbor Bridge, the Texas State Aquarium, opened in 1990 and dedicated to Gulf of Mexico marine life, and the World War II aircraft carrier *Lexington*, docked on Corpus Christi Beach since 1992, helped attract hotels and condominiums north of the ship channel, despite competition from the barrier islands.

This anchor strategy depends upon a cluster of activities in proximity. Corpus Christi concentrated on the northern CBD and Shoreline Boulevard, a reasonable emphasis, but one that meant that other areas received only sporadic attention. By the 2000s, swaths of downtown had no prospect of being reused by the public or private sector. The south bayfront especially featured stretches of vacant land and abandoned car dealerships. Misgivings over the southern half of downtown animated a prolonged controversy over Memorial Coliseum, opened in 1954 but abandoned in 2005 in favor of the new American Bank Center at the north bayfront. Opinions could differ over the aesthetic appeal and practicality of the coliseum, a low-slung structure that military veterans compared to a Quonset hut, but it was the city's most visible surviving building by Richard Colley (1910–1983), the first local architect to achieve a national reputation. In 2010, the city council ended the dispute and short-circuited preservationists' push for landmark designation by ordering the coliseum demolished. The city pinned its hopes for the southern CBD on Destination Bayfront, an alliance of civic activists and downtown property interests similar to the group that had organized the Bayfront Arts and Science Park in the northern CBD four decades earlier. That earlier endeavor, however, began at the high point of business-civic authority in the city's politics, an antediluvian era from the perspective of the 2010s. In November 2013, voters rejected bonds for Destination Bayfront by a crushing 2–1 margin.

As landscaped after World War II, Shoreline Boulevard consisted of a broad sidewalk on the bayfront side of the seawall and then six lanes of traffic divided by a median strip. This "windshield view" drive along the bay became so essential to the city's Gulf Coast experience that residents long resisted proposals for rerouting traffic to create a waterfront park. In 1997, William "Dusty" Durrill, a businessman and philanthropist devoted to downtown improvement, persuaded the city council to vote to shift the roadway away from the shoreline. An outcry forced the council to reverse itself, but Durrill placed the notion on the agenda. In 2004, voters approved the rerouting of portions of the boulevard.[54] The city began the laborious transformation by constructing a small water park on North Shoreline across from the arena and the convention center. The city then undertook the rerouting of South Shoreline where Destination Bayfront would have gone.

Corpus Christi Bay so captivates people that they might overlook the city's other defining feature, to the east: the Corpus Christi Bluff. In the late 1800s, powerful South Texas ranching families made evident their stake in the city by building townhouses on Upper Broadway, atop the bluff. The heiress Clara Driscoll, whose family held over 125,000 acres in the Corpus Christi vicinity, outdid everyone by occupying the penthouse of her twenty-story Driscoll Hotel. Even before her hotel came to dominate the skyline in 1941, residences were making way for offices, though the ranchers' presence on Upper Broadway endures indirectly. The Catholic Kenedy family, associates of the Kings and Klebergs of the King Ranch, donated their lot for Corpus Christi Cathedral, built in 1940. Already in 1901, the Kings had donated land for the First Presbyterian Church, which later moved a few blocks to the south along Upper Broadway. The First Methodist Church became rooted in the area, as did the Episcopal Church of the Good Shepherd and its private school. The Kings, who were Presbyterians, donated land for the Catholic Spohn Hospital, whose building on North Beach was swept away during the 1919 hurricane, along with patients and the nuns who tried to protect them.[55] The bluff was so central to Corpus Christi's geographic and visual logic that the coastal town signaled its urban ambitions by sponsoring City Beautiful–style landscaping there in 1914, the same year as the construction of the Greek Revival courthouse. Placed on the National Register of Historic Places in 1989, the Bluff Balustrade also suffered stretches of neglect, but the municipality and civic groups periodically intervened to protect the landscaping and restore its allegorical fountain, *Queen of the Sea*.[56]

Figure 1.11. Claimed as the highest point on the Gulf Coast, the Corpus Christi Bluff provides a strong rationale, along with Corpus Christi Bay, for the city's location. On Upper Broadway behind the City Beautiful landscaping from the 1910s are, *left to right*, Corpus Christi Cathedral, the Wilson (formerly Nixon) Building, the 600 Building (designed in part by the well-known local architect Richard Colley), and the former Driscoll Hotel, remade into a bank building. Photo by Kenny Braun, 2014.

Southside and the Islands

At the southern end of the seawall, Shoreline Boulevard feeds into Ocean Drive, which extends eight miles southeast to Oso Bay, boundary of the contiguous city. Laid out in the 1940s, Ocean Drive fulfills the vision of a seaside parkway articulated by the promoter Elihu Ropes in the 1880s–1890s. Off and on, planners tried to outdo Ropes. In 1967, the Harland Bartholomew planning firm proposed a Florida Keys–style offshore highway across man-made islands in Corpus Christi Bay, all the way from the CBD to Oso Bay.[57] The city eventually preserved Oso Bay as the Hans and Pat Suter Wildlife Refuge, named for a Swiss immigrant chemist devoted to wetlands preservation and his wife, a chemistry teacher and well-known environmentalist. Along Ocean Drive, access to the bay becomes piecemeal. Private houses and apartment buildings occupy sites with majestic views. Some sections along the drive were retained for the public, including Ropes Park, near the site of Ropes's Alta Vista Hotel, completed in 1891 but still unopened when the Panic of 1893 bankrupted the promoter.[58]

Ocean Drive, with its eclectic, at times extravagant houses, is the main place where Corpus Christi conspicuously displays oil-derived wealth.[59] Behind Ocean Drive run parallel thoroughfares: Santa Fe Street, Alameda Street, Staples Street. These are connected by perpendicular boulevards: Louisiana Avenue, Texan Trail, Brawner Parkway, Doddridge Street. Around these streets, the Southside area took shape before spreading farther south to Oso Creek and beyond. Driving along these interior thoroughfares, one grasps what scholars of the urban Southwest mean when they talk about the region's cities taking on a crystalline, linear, low, and even pattern.

South of the CBD, pleasant bungalows in the Furman Avenue and Blucher Park areas embody the Anglo middle-class city of the 1920s and 1930s. Starting with the Del Mar area, one passes through street after street of rambling, wood-frame houses—generally one-story, though sometimes two—on pier-and-beam foundations, half hidden by vegetation. This is the Anglo city of the 1940s–1950s, Corpus Christi's great phase of growth. Farther south, one enters the 1960s–1970s: brick-sided ranch houses, flexible despite their standard outward appearance, but with slab foundations that crack in the clay soil, setting homeowners at loggerheads with their insurance companies. Approaching Oso Bay along Alameda or moving beyond South Padre Island Drive down Staples, the 1980s and 1990s arrive: houses more varied and lavish, with high ceilings, picture windows, and expansive garages dominating the facades.

After the mid-1950s, Alameda and Staples usurped the CBD's commercial role. They became Corpus Christi's first linear-city, retail-and-service zones, a succession of shopping centers, small and large office strips, supermarkets, and miscellaneous stand-alone businesses, punctuated by churches, hospitals, and schools. Six Points, where Staples meets Alameda, was home to the first satellite business district. It gave way to Parkdale Plaza at Staples and Gollihar, opened in 1957, the first suburban-style shopping center. Both had fallen on hard times by the 1980s, when Sunrise Mall and Padre Staples Mall and then Moore Plaza (at Staples and South Padre Island Drive) emerged as automobile-age downtowns. Every evening and Saturday, intersections along "SPID" (pronounced "S-P-I-D") generated perilous traffic snarls as drivers barreled off the elevated highway onto the Texas-style frontage roads. As residential subdivisions moved steadily across a new set of parallel thoroughfares on the far Southside beyond SPID—Holly, Saratoga, Yorktown—the miscellany of commercial structures came, too. The shift of commerce southward along all these arteries turned the city's first enclosed mall into a shell, Cullen Mall (at Alameda and Airline), constructed in 1963 and torn down in the late 1990s. The malls along SPID struggled as well through store closures and ownership changes in the 1990s and 2000s, victims of relentlessly evolving retail practices. In August 2008, in the depths of a South Texas summer, the electric utility briefly cut off Sunrise Mall for unpaid bills.[60]

Ocean Drive continues beyond the southeastern edge of Corpus Christi's mainland over a causeway onto Ward Island, which separates Corpus Christi Bay from Oso Bay, and then onto Flour Bluff, its name derived from a clash between Texas militia and Mexican smugglers in the vicinity during the Texas Republic.[61] The area was an unimpressive fishing and beach village until 1940, when the U.S. Navy took possession of 2,050 acres for one of its two largest air training stations. Handed a $25 million project that would right away employ five thousand construction workers and upon completion would account for at least as many active-duty and support personnel, Corpus Christi expeditiously built a water line two dozen miles from its treatment plant at Calallen and extended Lexington Boulevard (the future SPID) to Flour Bluff. During World War II, the Corpus Christi Naval Air Station trained 35,000 aviators, most famously President George H. W. Bush.[62]

By 1949, the navy's overhaul-and-repair center was employing four thousand civilians, more direct employees than any single industrial operation in South Texas, including those at the port. In 1959, the navy closed the repair facility, throwing thousands out of work until 1961, when the U.S. Army opened the helicopter repair operation eventually known as the Corpus Christi Army Depot. With addition of a naval hospital and smaller naval air stations at Kingsville and Beeville, regional officials found themselves in the fortunate but awkward position of having a military presence so comprehensive that some portion of it was always threatened by cutbacks. Naval Air Station Chase Field, in Beeville, fell victim to the Base Realignment and Closure Commission (BRAC) process in 1991. Almost from its construction in the late 1980s, the mine warfare station at Ingleside lived under threat from BRAC until the definitive closure vote in 2005.[63]

Back in 1947, meanwhile, the navy turned over its training center on Ward Island to a group of Texas Baptists who planned to establish a private University of Corpus Christi. Led by the oilman and developer Guy Warren and the supermarket operator H. E. Butt, the Baptist businessmen undertook a $1 million fund drive that attracted much non-Baptist support on the grounds that a "progressive metropolis" needed a "great university."[64] In 1935, the city had founded a municipal junior college, Del Mar College. Centrally located at Ayers and Baldwin, Del Mar had the potential to grow into an urban public university along the lines of the University of Houston, also begun as a junior college. Into the 1970s, the notion of expanding Del Mar College into a university continued to appear. But the Gulf of Mexico's violence, oddly, diverted regional efforts toward exposed Ward Island. The University of Corpus Christi was already struggling when Hurricane Celia in 1970 caused damage beyond its capability to recover. In 1973, the state opened an upper-level branch of Kingsville's Texas A&I University on the site. This evolved into Corpus Christi State University and then Texas A&M University–Corpus Christi (TAMU-CC) in 1993.

TAMU-CC swelled from four thousand students, mostly part-time, in 1992 to around ten thousand students two decades later, including a residential undergraduate body. The university estimated that it was injecting nearly $329 million a year into the local economy by the early 2000s. The university further claimed that it retained thousands of students who would have gone to Austin, Houston, or Dallas and enrolled thousands more who might not have gone to college at all. The expansion of professional schools and cultural and arts programs promised to turn Corpus Christi into an importer of skilled labor for the first time since the 1960s. Graduate programs and research institutes concerned with environmental and coastal matters and marine science had the potential to provide Corpus Christi with an intellectual identity, entrepreneurial opportunities, and national and international connections distinctive within Texas and not run through Houston, San Antonio, or Austin.[65]

South around Oso Bay from Ocean Drive runs Ennis Joslin Boulevard, named for a utilities executive whose "lucky" investments—in his words—gave him ownership of lucrative sites along South Padre Island Drive.[66] With the Hans and Pat Suter Wildlife Refuge—an urban sanctuary for shorebirds—on the left along Oso Bay, one passes the city's main sewage treatment plant as well as houses and apartments facing the water. This point marks the end of the crystalline urban fabric and the beginning of the seaside city, alternately ramshackle, pleasant, and garish. A causeway on SPID over Oso Bay connects to Flour Bluff, the residential neighborhoods of which are generally Anglo and lower middle class, with a few fancier subdivisions along Oso Bay and Laguna Madre. Annexed in the 1960s, Flour Bluff off and on has expressed a sense that the city treats it as a stepchild.

Across Flour Bluff to the east, one arrives at the four-mile causeway over Laguna Madre to Padre Island. Except for 1927–1933, when a grooved wooden causeway conveyed cars whose drivers dared it, the barrier islands, twenty miles from the central city, remained inaccessible until 1950. That year, a $2 million causeway (later renamed for John F. Kennedy) opened. Promoters began touting the "Isle of Adventure . . . where shining sea and sand and sky meet for 110 miles of beaches and dunes," an exotic resort filled with the lore of pirates, shipwrecks, and treasure.[67] By 1958, around 315,000 cars were crossing to the island each year; the traffic catalyzed the movement to designate the Padre Island National Seashore, established 1962. By comparison with construction on South Padre Island near Brownsville, development on North Padre Island remained slow. In the mid-1960s, tourists complained that North Padre beaches were litter-strewn disgraces, unsuitable for family vacations. In 1969, the *Caller-Times* reprinted a letter from an army sergeant to a newspaper in San Antonio, a city essential to Corpus Christi tourism: "I have never seen a beach as cluttered with glass, beer cans, plastic bags, and rusted metal as is Padre Island!"[68]

During the 1970s, and especially after Hurricane Allen in 1980, the county and the state upgraded the Gulf beaches. Meanwhile, the city annexed segments of Padre Island north of the national seashore, as well as portions of Mustang Island beyond Packery Channel, the almost imperceptible border between the barrier islands, silted over more or less continuously since the dredging of Aransas Pass for the ship channel in the 1920s. Investors had begun putting capital into condominium and single-family housing projects by the mid-1960s, but the island's population grew from only 31 residents in 1960 to 667 by 1980. Development on the barrier islands was contentious from the start, especially against the backdrop of the new environmental consciousness. By the 1970s, coastal scientists and engineers traded arguments back and forth over whether Laguna Madre could accommodate thousands of residences with direct access for recreational boats. Did it make any sense to encourage people to build on a barrier island in a hurricane zone?[69]

The Texas oil bust of the 1980s promised opponents a reprieve, but by the mid-1980s, development "quietly" revived. By 2000, the island's population had reached 6,444, a figure projected to double over the next decade, largely on account of a $30 million project to dredge Packery Channel, enabling the circulation of water, marine life, and boats between Laguna Madre and the Gulf of Mexico.[70] Supporters of the dredging pointed to promises by an Austin investor to construct over $1 billion in resorts and housing along the channel's bank. As real estate grew troubled later in the 2000s, the developer raised the ire of locals by demanding additional concessions, including limitations on the hallowed Texas practice of driving on the beach. Almost no large-scale construction took place between the channel's opening in 2006 and the international real estate collapse amid the Panic of 2008. Once again, North Padre fell short of other Gulf Coast and Atlantic resorts in population and activity.

Disputes over barrier island development illustrated contradictions inherent in Corpus Christi's identity as a city of "sand, waves, and wind." Along with the port, industry, the military, and regional services, tourism counted among Corpus Christi's fundamental businesses. By 2009, the city was ranked as the sixth-biggest tourist destination in Texas, but at times it came in second or third, behind San Antonio and sometimes Galveston. The South Texas city regularly ranked first for in-state travel, another way in which it acted as a satellite of San Antonio or Dallas–Fort Worth.[71] Urban business and civic interests are attracted to tourism, despite its reputation as a low-skill, low-wage sector, because it is labor intensive and entrepreneurial; to some degree, cities can control it themselves. Corpus Christi's attractiveness for in-state travelers partially protected its tourism from national trends in commerce, industry, and politics. Municipal officials stressed that up to half of local sales-tax revenues came from nonresidents. Furthermore, the city relied on hotel taxes to underwrite culture and amenities.[72]

Yet the city also marketed "fun 'n sun" to its own residents. The Gulf of Mexico was a way of life. Corpus Christi never developed a large urban public park; the municipality instead treated the bay and the Gulf as its public space. "This beautiful city," proclaimed a brochure from the 1910s, offered "a veritable paradise" to visitors from the "hot, stifling atmosphere of the towns and cities of the interior of the State." The city's "gifts[,] which the God of Nature and human enterprise have prepared," beckoned also to migrants. A Corpus Christi Industrial Commission pamphlet from the 1970s promised tired executives a "'get away' factor" in a laid-back atmosphere: "This is not a bottled-up community of frustrated people[;] every citizen, rich or poor, is but a few minutes away from the opportunity to 'rest and look' or actively use the geographic beauties of the city."[73]

For a city that must compete with Austin and Houston for ambitious young people—"men of large hearts and keen vision" (as the 1910s pamphlet put it)—a reputation as the site of "permanent vacation" (in the words of a 1999 retrospective) is an ambiguous asset.[74] Go-getters might spend a weekend as if escaping their cares in a Jimmy Buffett song, but would they want to stay there to live and work? Of popular songs set in Corpus Christi, the best known, "Corpus Christi Bay" by the Austin songwriter Robert Earl Keen, captures the misgiving that someone might absorb the atmosphere too much. The song's narrator lets himself drift and dissipate so badly that, as Keen poignantly sings, even the chance to live his life over would not matter. The narrator's brother pulls himself together and moves to Houston.

Nineteenth-Century Town, Twentieth-Century City

In 1934, Coleman McCampbell, a professional writer from a well-known Corpus Christi family, began a perceptive book on his home-town by considering how geography explained the "shifting kaleido-scope of phases" in the city's history. Like any "Southwest" city of consequence, Corpus Christi was "the focus and trading nucleus of a spacious region," with "its history, its development, its resources aris[ing] out of and [existing as] part of the fabric of that region." A few years later, the city's Works Progress Administration guide elaborated along the same lines, noting that the city's "almost overnight" rise since the 1920s had been "based largely upon surrounding natural wealth— chiefly that of agriculture and petroleum—and upon the shipping of its exports through a deep-water port." With an obligatory dose of frontier romance in the prose, the guide summarized Corpus Christi's "authentic story" as the transformation of a "small village of smugglers and lawless men" into "an important commercial and industrial center, a great cotton and oil port, the home of the country's largest Naval Air Station, and an all-year playground for thousands of vacationists."[75]

Even though the city was still taking shape as they wrote, McCampbell and the Texas Writers' Project articulated how Corpus Christi's evolving relation to the Texas urban network and how its site along the South Texas coast explained history as well as appearance. Corpus Christi's story hinged on developments in the Coastal Bend, the Nueces River Valley, the U.S.-Mexico borderlands, and Texas and the Southwest overall. Just as one can explain basic geography and layout, one can identify a succession of historical periods, each marked by its own combination of political, economic, and social dynamics.

At the risk of excessive neatness, one can identify four periods, each revolving around the city's changing relations to its hinterland, Texas, and the Southwest. From the 1830s to the 1870s, Corpus Christi was an outpost town, a spearhead of Anglo-American expansion into a contested region.[76] From the 1870s to the 1910s, it was a coastal town, the gateway and service center for a region that Anglo-Americans controlled and were colonizing. From the 1910s to the 1960s, it was a crystallizing city; in this period, the pillars of Corpus Christi's modern political economy were built. From the 1960s into the 2000s, Corpus Christi was a developed city, a "mature" place, as economists use the term.[77] Thriving enough to upgrade its appearance and amenities and to attempt to tackle ethnic tensions, environmental damage, and other long-standing problems, the city nonetheless faced concerns that it was trapped within networks and relations that once benefited it immensely but might soon no longer do so.

OUTPOST TOWN (1830s–1870s)

Henry Lawrence Kinney and his partner the Alabaman W. P. Aubrey established their first South Texas trading post in 1838 at Live Oak Point near the current town of Fulton in Aransas County. With a record of scandal and failure in his home state of Pennsylvania and in Illinois, Kinney was "conspicuous," as a nineteenth-century historian remarked, "among the many marked and original characters who have figured in Texas history." A year later, the "Hustler of the Wilderness," in the words of another Texas writer, moved his operation south to Corpus Christi Bay, at least in part to place his contraband dealings beyond effective reach of Texan or Mexican authorities. For decades, Mexican settlers had pushed into the coastal plains and established ox-cart routes across the region, but Kinney's outpost represented the first known effort to build a town along this section of the coast. By 1840, the trader acquired title to the land from Enrique Villarreal, the Mexican officer who held the grant. In these negotiations, Kinney seemed to acknowledge Mexico's jurisdiction in the disputed area in exchange for Mexican forbearance. This infuriated some Texas republicans, who later brought treason charges against Kinney for his alleged role in the Mexican capture of a Texas revolutionary leader who happened to be a business rival. Acquitted for lack of evidence, Kinney returned to his outpost. The Mexicans for their part jailed him briefly as a spy.[78]

When Zachary Taylor's army arrived in 1845, Corpus Christi consisted of "some half dozen American stores," a British visitor noted, "and a grog shop or two." Population suddenly burgeoned to two thousand civilians and three thousand soldiers. After the war, Kinney, capitalizing on the attention, advertised for settlers in Ireland, Great Britain, and Germany. The booster publicized ideas for trade routes from Corpus Christi across the Southwest and into Mexico, and spent a fortune on the 1852 Lone Star Fair, which backfired by demonstrating that Corpus Christi was too distant for most Texans to reach easily through countryside racked by banditry, interethnic violence, and spillover from Mexico's internal strife. Desperately in debt, Kinney mortgaged his remaining Corpus Christi holdings and embarked, without success, on an 1854 filibustering expedition to Nicaragua. His frantic property dealings entangled the town in convoluted lawsuits that persisted after he was murdered in Matamoros in 1862.[79]

The town endured, growing in population from 689 in 1850 to 2,140 in 1870. A series of setbacks underscored the place's uncertain prospects. Frustrated by the difficulties of navigating the shallow bay during the Mexican War, the army in 1849 chose Port Lavaca, east of Victoria, for its depot. The federal government recognized Corpus Christi as a port in 1852, the year of the fair and the city's incorporation. But shipping to Corpus Christi involved the cumbersome transfer of cargo from steamships to lightering barges or skiffs that could clear the sandbars. During the 1850s, the city authorized bonds for dredging, but with little result until 1874, when an eight-foot channel permitted the first regular steamship service. By 1886, silting had again forced steamships to stop at Rockport.[80] In effect, Corpus Christi's value remained too prospective to warrant federal and state support for harbor construction.

Yellow fever ravaged the town in 1854 and 1867. The Texans had suppressed most Native American resistance in the area by the late 1850s. Yet events such as the occupation of Brownsville in 1859 by the paramilitary nationalist Juan Cortina dramatized ongoing Mexican-American hostility along the Rio Grande border, which few Mexicans accepted as legitimate anyway. Not that Anglos practiced peace among themselves. During the Civil War, Union efforts to hamper Confederate cotton exports brought fighting to the southern Gulf Coast. A

Union blockade force failed to occupy the town during the so-called Battle of Corpus Christi in 1862, but the Civil War plagued the area with divided loyalties, raids and guerrilla attacks, disrupted trade, and grinding shortages. After the war, the place remained an insecure outpost on the edge of a disputed border region.[81]

COASTAL TOWN (1870s–1910s)

Nearly one-third of Corpus Christi's population died in the 1867 yellow fever epidemic. A hero of this catastrophe, a former state judge named Edmund J. Davis, tended the sick in his house on the bluff. An antisecessionist who incurred Texans' wrath for his wartime exploits in the Union army, Davis returned to work with the Texas Republican Party. As an attorney, he defended freedmen's rights and pursued claims by Texas Unionists whose property the Confederates had confiscated. His term as the state's Reconstruction Republican governor, 1870–1874, made him anathema even in his hometown, which, despite its minimal stake in slavery, became pervaded by Lost Cause and Redeemer sentiment. Even in Corpus Christi, to which he had moved in 1849 and where he had married into a pioneer family, Davis, a Florida native, was denounced as a carpetbagger governor.[82]

Corpus Christi did have a substantive grievance against its hometown governor. The war set off a new wave of violence in the Nueces and Rio Grande areas, but Reconstruction-related political and racial violence in other parts of the state diverted attention and resources from beleaguered South Texas. Along the border, the Civil War mingled with Mexico's war to oust the French-installed Emperor Maximilian. Juan Cortina and other northern Mexican nationalists assisted the Union side during the Civil War. Afterward, the nationalists supported bandit and guerrilla groups operating north of the Rio Grande. These bandit groups were often of mixed ethnicity and could include a mixture of former Confederates, southern guerrillas, and demobilized or deserted Unionists. They raided settlements and ranches, stealing cattle and horses from Mexican-owned ranchers as well as from Anglo operations such as the King Ranch.

This turmoil culminated in March 1875, when at least thirty-five Mexican raiders—reportedly allied with Cortina—marched toward Corpus Christi, seizing hostages along the way. Upon learning of a shootout at a general store in Nuecestown, near the current Calallen, Corpus Christians sent posses that drove the Mexicans southward. The band killed an uncertain number of Texans before retreating across the border. After a wounded captive was tried and hanged at Corpus Christi, vigilantes spread across the countryside, murdering hundreds of Tejanos and Mexicans, most uninvolved in the raiding. Atrocities in the Nueces region continued for several years "on the ranches, roads, and wherever they were found," an Anglo businessman later told a congressional investigation. The Redeemer government of Texas, meanwhile, used the Texas Rangers as a border police force. In cooperation with the authoritarian Mexican president Porfirio Díaz, who took power in 1877, the Rangers shut down most of the raids and killings. Even the Rangers, not known for their Mexican sympathies, labeled Anglo vigilante reprisals "horrible."[83]

This pacification proved to be a turning point because it left Anglo landowners with the upper hand throughout the Coastal Bend. During the 1870s–1880s, the region's great ranching operations—the Kings and Klebergs of the King Ranch, their allies the Kenedys, the Coleman-Fulton Pasture Company, the Driscolls, and others—extended their holdings in an enormous arc around Corpus Christi. The ranchers reorganized their businesses into diversified land, cattle, and transport operations. By the 1880s, the ranchers were constructing mansions on the bluff, "visible manifestation of the stockmen's fortunes," in the words of the local historian Dan Kilgore. They allied with town merchants to underwrite banks and other institutions, including the *Corpus Christi Caller*, founded in 1883.[84]

The Army Corps of Engineers and the State of Texas remained wary of schemes for a ship channel across Corpus Christi Bay. Except when locals managed to open a channel that soon silted back up, shipping still depended on lighters or barges. During the post–Civil War years, cattle were so cheap and transport was so dear that cattlemen found it cost-effective to strip animals of their hide, tallow, and horns in hide-and-tallow plants along the shore, where carcasses would be left to rot or tossed into the bay. Until rising land prices and changing tariffs made sheep herding unprofitable, Corpus Christi briefly flourished as a wool market, shipping 1.5 million pounds of wool by the 1890s. Even with the shallow bay, Corpus Christi had surpassed Brownsville by the early 1880s to become southern Texas's busiest port.

With support from the ranching families, the railroad promoter Uriah Lott managed to bring three lines to the city between 1875 and 1904. These connected the town first to Laredo and Mexico and then to Brownsville, San Antonio, Houston, and beyond. The network of railroads encouraged the subdivision of ranchlands for farms. In the early 1900s, land companies and railroads published magazines such as the *Gulf Messenger* and the *Gulf Coast Line*, which lured midwestern farmers with promises of long growing seasons, cheap labor, and healthful conditions. Satellite towns such as Alice (founded in 1888 and named for Richard King's daughter who married Robert J. Kleberg Sr., cementing the famous family alliance), Kingsville (1904), and Robstown (1906, named for Robert Driscoll) were intended as railroad service centers for these new farmers. The booster Elihu Ropes's schemes briefly doubled the population to over eight thousand before the boom's collapse in 1893. By 1910, Ropes seemed prescient. South Texas seemed developed and diversified enough to support a city as opposed to a town.[85]

CRYSTALLIZING CITY (1910s–1960s)

Between 1910 and 1960, Corpus Christi vaulted from a coastal town of 8,222 to a city of 167,690. Such growth can seem like the inevitable result of natural advantages of geography and resources. That view was held by the region's most powerful, knowledgeable economic interests—the landholding families and their allies—in the early twentieth century. To them, Corpus Christi was a good bet, and they devoted considerable time and money to it. Still, the daunting costs of a ship channel inclined the Army Corps of Engineers to look seriously at sites along the coast from Rockport to Harbor Island near Aransas Pass.[86] The corps imagined an alternate future for South Texas, which might have featured not a regional metropolis but a string of medium-sized cities from Rockport to Corpus Christi. This alternate form of urbanization came to exist in the Rio Grande Valley and the Midland-Odessa region in West Texas.[87]

Efforts at Harbor Island had not progressed much when the hurricane of 1916 destroyed the railroad line there. Then the hurricane of 1919 devastated the coast even more than Corpus Christi, where estimates of deaths ranged as high as 600. Corpus Christi and its allies turned their disaster into an argument for state and federal backing for the ship channel. "The storm of September 14, 1919, with few exceptions, destroyed everything at Port Aransas and on Mustang, Harbor, and St. Joseph's Islands," city officials reiterated to the Corps of Engineers and Congress in 1920. "Practically the entire loss sustained by the City of Corpus Christi," the brief claimed, came from debris from the barrier islands thrown ashore by the storm surge.[88]

This way of understanding the sequence of events—that the storm of 1919 persuaded relevant interests of the superiority of a lengthy ship channel to Corpus Christi—echoes Texans' understanding of the relation between the 1900 Galveston hurricane and the emergence of the Port of Houston. For decades before the 1900 storm, Houstonians had made similar arguments on behalf of dredging Buffalo Bayou into the Houston Ship Channel, which was indeed done from 1902 to 1914. But this cause-and-effect sequence overlooks the speed with which Galveston recovered after the catastrophic storm. With new wharves, a massive seawall, and a raised grade level in the central city, Galveston again became the country's leading cotton port by 1912. Likewise, the Army Corps of Engineers could have returned to Harbor Island or Aransas Pass rather than settling on Corpus Christi Bay.

Storm protection was part of the reason for Houston's ascendency, and Corpus Christi's too. Beyond that, economic and technological changes were making such ship channels into reasonable investments. Traditional seaports such as Galveston, one historian notes, "had been founded on the [saltwater] principle that a region's major city ought to be located at the site of its best harbor."[89] This principle became outmoded after 1900. Houston, like Corpus Christi, offered an excellent site for railroads. The two cities offered space for industry and for storage tanks and pipelines for oil and gas. The vast quantities of freshwater used by modern industry would need to have been pumped to Galveston or Aransas Pass. Spindletop in 1901 probably explains more of Houston's ascendency than the great storm. Proponents at first envisioned Corpus Christi as devoted to the shipping of cotton and other agricultural products, more like Galveston than Houston. Still, in the era of railroads, petrochemicals, and heavy industry, bringing ships to railroads and factories made economic, technological, and even environmental sense. Already in 1920, Corpus Christi revealed an understanding of these considerations when making its case for an inland port:

The four railways now serving Corpus Christi have convenient access to this proposed location, and there is ample room for the construction of all necessary piers, docks and slips, and railway switches and terminals, and ample room for all necessary extensions of these facilities for years. . . . The Nueces River . . . is capable of supplying an unlimited quantity of fresh water, which is absolutely essential. . . . It is well known that there is not water supply at Port Aransas that is adequate nor is an adequate water supply ever possible. This alone makes Aransas Pass forever unsuited for an adequate port service.[90]

In the Corpus Christi area, questions of economic and infrastructure development became intertwined with cultural and ethnic tensions and political rivalries. While debates over port location were taking place, the Coastal Bend experienced conflict—common in Texas and the Southwest—roughly between probusiness, modernizing reformers, and entrenched powerbrokers such as the Parrs of Duval County. For example, Nueces County saw angry battles leading up to an election on a 1916 local-option ordinance (that is, a referendum to impose prohibition on the county). This was adopted by 218 votes; prohibition was a bellwether issue between reformist drys and traditionalist wets. Anglo migrants to South Texas, along with the land companies that encouraged them, were determined to create a respectable, modern atmosphere. This intention—along with racist and ethnocentric attitudes—explains the support that the region's most economically innovative interests gave to the early twentieth-century movement to disenfranchise most South Texas Tejanos and drive nearly all of them from politics. Old-line political operatives such as the Parrs based part of their power on extending patronage to Mexican South Texans and manipulating their votes.[91]

For their part, Tejanos in the Corpus Christi area were divided over the fallout from the Mexican Revolution of the 1910s. Mexico's upheaval set off the first large-scale migration northward since the Treaty of Guadalupe Hidalgo, but also led to renewed fighting in the Rio Grande Valley, much of it sparked by the scheme for a nationalistic uprising known as the Plan de San Diego. Taken together, mass migration into Texas of rural and urban Mexican workers and the decision of most South Texas Hispanics to distance themselves from nationalistic aspirations for reunion with Mexico marked the founding episode of modern Tejano South Texas and of the Mexican American rights movement.[92]

Amid all this, Robert Kleberg Sr. of the King Ranch and other progress-minded business leaders backed a Progressive Era–style civic improvement movement, led by the youthful editor of the *Corpus Christi Caller*, the Kansas native Roy Miller. As mayor starting in 1913, Miller pushed street, water, and sewerage improvements, a new city hall, a municipal fire department, and other innovations that gave the coastal town the appearance and functions of a modern city. Miller's landscaping of Corpus Christi Bluff—lauded by one writer as "easily the most striking example of municipal beautification to be found south of San Antonio"—was intended, like the 1914 Nueces County Courthouse, to proclaim that Corpus Christi had arrived.[93] Defeated by a coalition of Parr allies and other rivals, Miller returned to being editor of the *Caller*. After the 1919 hurricane, rival factions united to form the Storm Stricken Area Committee, similar to the group that took charge after the 1900 Galveston hurricane. And as in Galveston, the relief committee—renamed the Deep Water Harbor Association, with Kleberg as chair and Miller as secretary-treasurer—expanded its agenda. Miller perceived the huge benefit to the town of the ship channel, which was authorized in 1922 and dedicated on September 14, 1926, the seventh anniversary of the storm. Corpus Christi would henceforth be a "real city, a great metropolis."[94]

In keeping with the wildcat aura surrounding the early years of the Texas oil boom, local lore marks the advent of the oil-and-gas industry with blowouts that reveal success in a spectacular way. On January 2, 1916, "the roar of escaping gas," audible "easily for seven miles," announced "the biggest strike of gas in the world" at White Point, north of Nueces Bay.[95] By 1930, the port had gained the capacity to handle oil, and by 1935 oil had passed cotton, with five million barrels shipped. Corpus Christi "is showing consistent progress toward becoming one of the outstanding refining sections of the Gulf Coast," proclaimed a chamber of commerce magazine in 1937, when eight refineries were processing 45,000 barrels of crude daily.[96]

The port and petrochemicals partly cushioned Corpus Christi from the Great Depression. In addition to petrochemical operations, the city attracted producers of inorganic chemicals and metals, drawn by accessible, cheap natural gas for their high-energy production process-es. In 1934, the $7 million Southern Alkali plant "put Corpus Christi on the nation's industrial map."[97] So eager were Corpus Christi leaders to secure this multinational enterprise that they extended and deep-ened the ship channel in addition to rebuilding the Mathis dam. The naval air station also resulted from shrewd promotion of resources and geography, cheap land along the coast, and good flying weather.

"The keystones in the city's growth," the Dallas Federal Reserve explained in 1951, "have been the oil and gas industry, manufactur-ing, the naval air training station, agriculture, and the tourist trade." "Phenomenal growth" resulted in a city of "youthfulness," remarked the Federal Reserve article, both in the age of its entrepreneurs and its industrial plants, about three-fifths of which had been built in the pre-vious ten years. Despite the Latin name, the report observed, Corpus Christi was "essentially an 'American' city"; its 35 percent Hispanic population marked the place as part of South Texas, while its 5 per-cent black population was "considerably smaller than in most of the Gulf Coast cities." Since its civic leadership had the "will and energy to promote further development," the city "has a very bright future."

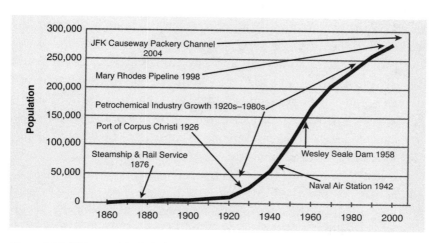

Figure 1.12. This municipal chart straightforwardly illustrates the link between the city's burst of growth after 1920 and the advent in quick succession of the deepwater port, petrochemicals and related industries, and the naval air station. It also ties the city's growth to water-supply projects such as the Wesley Seale Dam (1958) and the Mary Rhodes Pipeline to Lake Texana (late 1990s). Based on a chart prepared by the Department of Development Services, City of Corpus Christi.

In 1951, its problems, like those in "other rapidly growing cities of the Southwest," seemed, apart from the "fundamental" challenge of water, to be "growing pains" in schools, public facilities, and zoning.[98]

DEVELOPED CITY (1960s–2000s)

Within fifteen years, the optimism of the 1950s had faded, and confidence in and the cohesion of the city's commercial-civic leadership had frayed. Over the last decades of the twentieth century, Corpus Christi grew steadily enough in population, housing, and infrastructure. The government and civic groups impressively upgraded the city's appearance, its cultural and educational institutions, and its amenities. But by the 1970s, the notion that the city would join the ranks of Texas's metropolises had dissipated. Austin's surge past Corpus Christi was especially discomforting, since Austin founded its growth on new activities—computers and information technology—that were intertwined with the University of Texas and linked to dynamic sectors with international implications.

By comparison to northeastern or midwestern industrial cities such as Rochester, New York, or Youngstown, Ohio, Corpus Christi's foundation remained broad, unthreatened with dissolution. Yet the city still relied on the set of activities around which it had crystallized in the middle of the century: the port, petrochemicals, the military, tourism, and professional, commercial, and governmental services for South Texas. When the oil-and-gas sector went on one of its periodic upswings, some of the optimism of midcentury returned. By 2011, Eagle Ford shale oil had again made managing growth a practical challenge. Millions of barrels of oil and billions of cubic feet of gas could generate "jobs and growth with no end near." But caution ran through even enthusiastic accounts. "Texas has had its hopes raised and dashed by oil and gas" before, the *Caller-Times* remarked. The 1980s Texas oil bust imprinted on the next two generations a wariness of the "gold-mining mentality," even when rising world prices "flooded the energy industry with money."[99] Sectors that expanded steadily between the 1980s bust and Eagle Ford—tourism, education, health care, and other regional services—cushioned the city from precipitous declines but reinforced its regional status within Texas. Corpus Christi deepened its ties to South Texas, while Austin networked with the world.

Anxiety over dependence on slow-growing activities and on those directed from more dynamic cities obscured the level of drama and change the city experienced after the 1960s. Manifestly, the most important change was the ascension—amid tension and against resistance—of Hispanic Corpus Christi to a greater level of political, economic, and cultural influence. Especially after 1983, when a court ruling pushed the city from an at-large city council to a system that mixed at-large and single-member districts, Hispanic political influence grew, though in fits and starts. The city elected its first Hispanic-majority city council in 1997, at which time the area's congressman, its state senator, its three state representatives, the city manager, the chief of police, the superintendent of the Corpus Christi Independent School District, the county judge (the Texas term for county executive), the county sheriff, and the district attorney were all Mexican Americans.[100] After Joe Adame's two terms, voters in 2012 chose Nelda Martinez, a city councilwoman, as the second elected Hispanic mayor, though Hispanics were still usually a slight minority on both the city council and the county board.

Accompanying this growing presence in politics and government was an increased Hispanic—and to a lesser degree black—presence in business and the professions, as well as in civic institutions. Outright discrimination was rarer than in the past, though habits of condescension endured. Since the 1970s, the Anglo political, business, and civic establishment had made it increasingly clear that it understood that the region's ethnic changes would transform politics and civic and business life. Still, the city struggled at moments when this abstract principle turned into a real shift in authority. Turning points such as election in the 2000s of Yolanda Olivarez (a banker) and then Ruben Bonilla Jr. (a lawyer and businessman) as chair of the Port Authority Board of Commissioners signaled an erosion of the Anglo establishment's determination to keep the most strategic matters in its own hands. Into the 2010s, city and county politics were so racked by factionalism that it frustrated efforts to confront the area's acknowledged problems. But political arguments now often cut across ethnic lines rather than breaking down along them. This change was itself a sign that Corpus Christi might be entering a new stage. In this new era, the greatest challenge would be to translate shifts in politics, the professions, and business into enhanced access and opportunities for residents in a city fragmented by class and neighborhood as well as ethnicity.

Henry Lawrence Kinney began the town as an Anglo-American outpost and a launching point into the Mexican Southwest. A trader and smuggler, Kinney adapted to Corpus Christi's situation at the edge of a disputed borderland beset by ethno-national conflict. As town promoter, he envisioned an Anglo-Texan city with Tejanos in a secondary role, the direction that Corpus Christi took after his death, in 1862. Between Reconstruction and World War II, the city coalesced and thrived as an extension and component of the Anglo-Texan urban system. By the late twentieth century, the geographic and economic orientation that had caused Corpus Christi to flourish constrained it. A secondary city within Texas, Corpus Christi by the early twenty-first century had the motive and the potential to remake itself in the alternate geographies of the Gulf of Mexico and the U.S.-Mexico borderlands. The analysis of the city over time—the division of its history into stages—brings one back to the analysis of it in space—Corpus Christi as the product of its location on Corpus Christi Bay, to the south of the Nueces River. Each new historical era raised in new ways the questions of what it meant to be a city of the South Texas coast—the place where Texas met the sea—and of what limitations and possibilities that entailed.

Chapter 2

A TEXAS SEAPORT
IN TEXAS LORE

                        ∽

T *he last chapter* sketched Corpus Christi's geography and periodized its history from the author's perspective. This chapter and the next emphasize local accounts. For convenience of presentation, I group these into Anglo accounts, with their east-to-west perspective, and Hispanic accounts, which view the region south to north. Members of both major ethnic groups have differed among themselves over what to highlight and how to interpret it. Moreover, Anglo and Hispanic understandings have interacted with and addressed each other; the two sets of stories are inseparable. On top of that, Euro-American ethnic and religious groups have their own variations on the frontier and pioneer story derived from Anglo-Texan heritage and lore. African American perspectives stand as an alternative, often overshadowed counterpart to Anglo and Hispanic narratives.

Most of the events and eras described in chapter 1 appear in local accounts of Corpus Christi history, its picture books and guidebooks, newspapers, heritage publications, and so on. But local discussions—from virtually every angle, ethnic, political, or whatever—dwell on the city's story differently from how I have just done. Corpus Christi's story is an episode in the urbanization of Texas, but its residents are inclined to emphasize "Texas" rather than "urbanization." The urban career of Corpus Christi has taken place mainly since 1900; it is a story of civil engineering and city planning, the ship channel, agribusiness, petrochemicals, finance, the military, tourist promotion, cultural institutions, subdivisions, and ethnic neighborhoods and movements. As traditionally understood, Texas history occurs mainly before 1900; it is a story of explorers, missionaries, *empresarios*, pioneers, rangers, ranchers, cowboys, and farmworkers, with town promoters and townspeople as supporting characters.

Much about the way that Anglo and Tejano Corpus Christians handle their past supports the contention, commonly made by urban scholars, that Texas's nineteenth-century heritage is an obstacle to understanding the state's urban realities.[1] Even so, people's inclination to keep Corpus Christi's history tied to South Texas's regional lore—even as they gradually incorporate new themes prompted by the urban experience—reflects more than a hankering for romance amid the mundaneness of modern life. Even with its hyperbole and misdirection, the region's frontier and rural heritage have shaped the way people live in and perceive their city. This lore draws attention to ways that landscape, environment, and regional history and culture have infused and molded the city. Casting this lore aside would distort understanding as much as an excessive preoccupation with the frontier past has done. It would remove a shaping force from the city's story and experience.

The Eighth Wonder Misconstrued

The Port of Corpus Christi is an impressive example of the kind of vast reengineering of the environment on which modern cities are founded. Only in places, however, is the port accessible for people to contemplate. For example, boat tours of the Corpus Christi Ship Channel have never taken hold as they have in Houston, Hamburg, or other great ports.

The Corpus Christi seawall, more than two miles long, offers the most familiar experience of Corpus Christi as an engineered environment. Starting eighteen inches below the water line and filled with gravel supported by timber and steel, the seawall rises in twelve-inch-by-twenty-one-inch concrete steps to fourteen feet above sea level.

The hurricane defense system then slopes upward even more to a crest fifteen feet above sea level along Shoreline Boulevard, itself the high point of a landfill project that expands the central city 600–850 feet outward from Water Street, which before construction of the seawall had merited the name. Two concrete T-head piers, each with heads 1,000 feet by 300 feet, lying 750 feet beyond the shore punctuate the seawall, along with a smaller L-head pier to the south. Completed in 1941, the seawall needed minimal maintenance until it showed signs of cracking and erosion in the 1980s, near the end of the life expectancy predicted by its engineers. A $43 million repair program during the 2000s put the structure into trustworthy shape. Designed by the Dallas engineering firm Myers and Noyes, the seawall in 1988 was designated a Texas Historic Civil Engineering Landmark. When it was built, enough people still remembered the 1919 storm, despite all the newcomers who had arrived during the 1920s–1930s, that as the local columnist and historian Murphy Givens recounts, it right away became "a showpiece": "People would drive by and marvel. It was, and is, a sight that never grows stale." For visual effect, the seawall competes with Galveston's, though the latter is five times longer. To Givens, the seawall stands as the city's candidate for "eighth wonder of the world."[2]

Most residents are not so effusive as Givens, but they appreciate the seawall. Every sunny day—most of the year—people walk or run along the seawall or fish from its steps or drive along Shoreline Boulevard and look at the bay. The seawall's visual power depends on its simplicity and functionality. It consists of two miles of concrete steps that break the waves, backed by a landfill. The designers used no self-conscious artistry to call attention to their achievement. The only effort on the seawall to explain it consists of a plaque near the Lawrence Street T-Head, sponsored by the Texas branch of the American Society of Civil Engineers. Right behind this modest memorial and overshadowing it is a flamboyant symbol of the Gulf of Mexico, a twenty-three-foot bronze sculpture of two sailfish, *Wind in the Sails*, by Kent Ullberg. One has to think for a minute to realize that the object on which one is standing—a manifestation of the human drive to reshape the world for human purposes—is in its way as grand as the gulf to which Ullberg's sculpture alludes.

By refraining from articulating their own messages, the seawall's designers created an elongated pedestal for others to fill. In 1991, the philanthropist William "Dusty" Durrill paid $1 million to construct atop the seawall eight Spanish-style gazebos called miradors. A beer distributor and real estate investor—a personality admired across ethnic lines for his cut-the-red-tape manner—Durrill became a civic activist in midlife through a determination to turn private misery to public benefit. In 1978, his daughter, Devary, died after her Ford Mustang burst into flames in a crash. With $12 million won in a lawsuit against the car company, he and his wife, Shirley, established a foundation dedicated to, among other causes, the history, preservation, and beautification of Corpus Christi. Each mirador contains a plaque recounting a familiar moment in South Texas lore and history. But none of the plaques discusses the seawall itself, the port, or indeed any local event since the founding of King Ranch in 1853. The miradors depict Corpus Christi during a time of wilderness, exploration, the frontier, and pioneers. In 1997, Durrill underwrote the Mirador de la Flor at the People's Street T-Head, a vibrant memorial to an unmistakably contemporary Corpus Christi personality, the Tejano singer Selena, who was murdered by a former employee at a local motel in 1995.[3]

From the seawall's original planning stages, Corpus Christians have been inclined to use it to commemorate nature, the frontier, and Texas lore—anything but the city and its technology. In 1927, the chamber of commerce invited Gutzon Borglum, later the sculptor of Mount Rushmore, to design a monumental seawall in collaboration with the city's municipal engineer and a Texas A&M University architecture professor. Ousted as the sculptor of Stone Mountain, Georgia, the artist had opened a San Antonio studio to work on another of his troubled projects, the Trail Drivers Monument.[4] The "colossal" treatment Borglum proposed in March 1928 went beyond the "simple and dignified beauty" stated as the project's goal.[5] Borglum intended his seawall to symbolize the ongoing Anglo-American saga of man against wilderness. It was to be the north end of a "grand avenue" to the Rio Grande, a roadway lined by 10,000 palm trees and flowering plants. Among the plantings would be statues depicting "soldier and adventurer, conquistadore and farmer; covered wagons and armies, bandits and heroes." At the boulevard's south end, on the Mexican border, Borglum

Figure 2.1. A view north along the simple, concrete steps of the Corpus Christi Seawall, with one of the Spanish Revival miradors added in the 1990s. The Selena memorial, Mirador de la Flor, is in the background to the left. Photo by Kenny Braun, 2014.

envisioned "a heroic bronze statue of Edwin Cameron, the first Texas cowboy," an unselfconscious gesture of defiance to Tejanos and Mexicans, who insist that their ancestors brought ranching techniques to Texas. For the head of the seawall, in the middle of Corpus Christi Bay, Borglum promised to donate a thirty-two-foot-tall statue of Christ stilling the waters, another forceful symbol, given the city's name and the fact that the project would defend the city from storm surges on the scale of the one that occurred in September 1919.[6]

The plan's mix of boosterism, exuberance, and storm protection won support, especially for the portions in Corpus Christi itself. Borglum's seawall would transform "the nightmare of debris and filth" along the waterfront into "a thing of beauty and a joy to behold," asserted the *Corpus Christi Caller*.[7] Bad luck, murky local politics, and Borglum's penchant for alienating supporters combined to scuttle the program. An October 1930 bond election fell 179 votes short of the needed two-thirds majority, from 2,806 votes cast. The washout a month later of La Fruita Dam (see chapter 1) delayed a new vote on the seawall. Protestant fundamentalists, meanwhile, denounced the Christ colossus in the bay as a Papist graven image, an attitude that dovetailed with that of South Texas's Ku Klux Klan. In the 1930s, Borglum lobbied for Public Works Administration funding, but the cautious PWA declined to support Corpus Christi, in whose convoluted feuds the sculptor had managed to involve himself. Borglum gave up on "a town where the crooks and the 'respectable people' are so like scrambled eggs." When the city finally secured voter support in 1938, it did so by insisting that the revised seawall was "an entirely different type of structure" from what Borglum had proposed.[8]

Political discretion, therefore, may have contributed to the seawall's stark majesty, which left a symbolic blank space that others perceived as needing filling. People who use the bayfront appreciate Durrill's miradors as lookouts and resting places. But the structures adhere to the Spanish Revival style common in the Southwest and have little to do with the seawall's austere functionality. Spanish colonial romance and the epic of pioneers and ranchers conspire to distract from the seawall as a manifestation of the engineered city.

Cities, Texas, and Corpus Christi

Modern Corpus Christi, with its ship channel and seawall, its street upon street of shingled cottages and brick-sided ranch houses, and its refineries and petrochemical plants, adds up to an urban epic as romantic in its way as the wilderness and the frontier. Residents, though, experience these places, and visitors perceive them, as mere present-day city life. Since its greatest growth occurred between 1910 and 1960, Corpus Christi never had many structures or places that appeared worth drawing attention to on historic grounds. San Antonio, with the Alamo and other missions and much else, offers an obvious contrast to Corpus Christi for its ability to tie the city to Texas heritage and lore. Like Corpus Christi, Galveston features a splendid physical site along the Gulf of Mexico, but it can boast of pirates, a role in the Texas Republic and the Civil War, and above all a sumptuous Gilded Age heyday. Because Galveston declined as a port after World War I, its central-city real estate faced little development pressure. Bypassed by commerce, Galveston held on to outmoded Victorian buildings that came to seem invaluable assets as the historic preservation movement gathered momentum in the 1960s–1970s.[9]

Preconceptions of what counts as historic and Texan can stand in the way of an appreciation of modern Corpus Christi and the ways that it reshaped South Texas after World War I. This chapter nonetheless argues that to understand Corpus Christi as a city, one needs to appreciate South Texas heritage and lore and the outlooks and sensibilities associated with them. Often, Texas-based experts on cities and urban history treat attempts to reconcile "Texas" and "cities" as not worth the effort. They hesitate to talk about Texas as a distinct urban region or system. Even if one accepts the validity of concepts such as the Texas Triangle, discussed in chapter 1, the seemingly Texan aspects of Texas's cities might merely be matters of style, image, or promotion. Given Texas's shifting links to the South, Midwest, Southwest, borderlands, and northern Mexico, historians and geographers wonder what, if any, economic, political, or cultural patterns or technological and design practices might distinguish Texas's cities from cities in all those regions. Robert Fairbanks, a historian of Dallas, "takes exception to scholars who argue that regions like the South"—or, by extension, the Southwest or Texas—"leave such an indelible mark on their cities that they create a unique typology of urban form." "Dallas's so-called uniqueness," he argues, resulted more from American urban patterns and styles during the decades when Dallas began rapidly to develop than from any heritage or personality or situation imparted to Dallas by Texas. Dallas, in this view, illustrates city-building ideas and practices and political and economic conditions that prevailed during the early twentieth century more than any regionally based characteristics.[10]

Indeed, scholars of Texas cities have never bothered to construct a model or typology of an archetypal Texas city; they have found it more effective to borrow social-science and historical models created to study cities in other places and then apply them to this or that city in Texas. Even the notion of a Sunbelt, which became popular among journalists and urban-affairs experts during the 1970s–1980, suggests that metropolitan Texas stands at the center of urban trends from the Carolinas to Los Angeles; in this model, Texas cities shared their most important characteristics and dynamics with the urban South, Southwest, and West.[11] Environmental perspectives, which gained popularity starting in the 1980s, directed attention to local and regional factors shaping cities and stressed the interplay of Texas's cities with the state's varied landscape, ecology, resources, and climate. Such environmental and geographic factors have the advantage of offering a more tangible source of regional distinctiveness than culture, heritage, or identity.[12]

Perceptions and sensibilities matter, though they defy systematic verification. Corpus Christians of various backgrounds and perspectives repeatedly and in innumerable ways have expressed the notion that their city belongs to Texas and takes its character from the South Texas coast. The familiar saga of Texas history—set in the 1700s and 1800s, with explorers, missionaries, and *empresarios*, pioneers, rangers, and ranchers as protagonists—has remained relevant to urbanized Texas, a huge portion of whose residents descended from post-1920 migrants, people drawn by cities and their opportunities. In museum exhibits and at historical sites, as well as in books and classes, when Texans did pay attention to urban and commercial-industrial Texas, they often recast that modern story to conform to old themes and to convey familiar lessons about frontier individualism and the Texas spirit.[13] All Texas's cities, and all cities in the western United States, share with Corpus Christi significant connections to landscapes and hinterlands. Despite the scale of the post-1920 migrations, segments of these cities' populations retained personal ties and family memories that extended to nearby towns and farms. Yet a preoccupation with the Texas saga went beyond what direct or family connections warranted. The Texas saga, in both its Anglo and its Hispanic versions, became a prism through which people comprehended regional history and culture.

Professional scholars often start from the "debilitating" assumption, as the literary scholar Harvey Graff remarks with regard to Dallas, that their agenda involves "'disprov[ing] myth' with the 'facts.'" Dallas's "origin myth," as Graff explains, amounts to a version of the Anglo-Texan lore of frontier fortitude and self-reliance applied to city building: "great men creating a great city out of nothing but sheer willfulness." Such imagery needs to be taken seriously, since it often has political as well as cultural consequences. In Dallas—and in other Texas cities, including Corpus Christi—the image of the urban promoter as a type of Texas pioneer for decades ratified a local politics dominated by a self-perpetuating, commercial-civic elite that equated the well-being of business with progress and the public good. "An overly narrow and misconceived search for fact," Graff emphasizes, "excludes the enormous power of myth in making history."[14]

Lore and myth, in this view, become tools that people use to shape their city's identity and to put forth competing agendas for it. Myths and lore can mold a city in concrete ways—as, for example, the miradors atop the Corpus Christi Seawall try to do—but also through their effects on attitudes, goals, and activities. Historians do need to set the record straight, "to establish the limits of myths, propose alternate narratives, and offer causal explanations," to quote Graff again.[15] But heritage and lore are an aspect of what happened. Conventional Texas images and themes in Corpus Christi's historical narrative appear indispensable not simply because residents insist upon them. They draw attention to the city's place in the physical, historical, and cultural environment of South Texas and of Texas overall. The rest of this chapter illustrates this point through an examination of the Texas-style motifs found in business, civic, tourist, and religious publications as well as in local historical writing.

"Possibly True"

In the 1910s, Corpus Christi and Galveston both launched promotional spring festivals called Splash Day. Galveston's continued until 1965, although gay groups later reinvented the festival with a pride theme.[16] In 1938, Corpus Christi transformed its festival into Buccaneer Days, with Jean Laffite as patron saint. Galveston had a documentable claim to the pirate, who had used Galveston Island as a base for forays against Gulf of Mexico shipping. Nevertheless, as a Corpus Christi tourist magazine claimed, Laffite was also "thought to have used numerous inlets and lagoons along this section of the coast as a hide-away after his cut-throat depredations." The marketing value of this formulation is that it mattered not at all who thought Laffite had frequented the Coastal Bend area, nor on what sources they based this idea. For the record, pirates did station themselves on Padre Island, and some of them probably had associations with Laffite. As the city geared up for the 1939 edition of the celebration, the *Caller-Times* observed that the pirate-themed festival created the right atmosphere for "pleasure-seeking Corpus Christi" to "plunge into the summer season." Buccaneer Days evolved into the city's most elaborate promotional event, complete with floats, parades, and costume balls. The highlight grew to be the annual ritual of bathing-beauty queens in pirate costumes capturing the mayor, who was then made to walk the plank into the bay.[17]

After the 1950 opening of the Padre Island Causeway, promoters extended this buccaneer romance to the "Isle of Adventure," where "many came by intent to bury loot." Well into the twentieth century, artifact hunters were finding doubloons, pieces of eight, mysterious rotted chests, "and all the other trappings of the legendary treasure tale," a guidebook from 1950 remarked. Padre Island enticed people eager to relive a "wide-eyed childhood where a filched bedsheet, nailed to a rickety mast, constituted a pirate ship plying in backyard seas." "Anything is feasible," the guidebook stressed, "on the very spot where the fabulous Jean Laffite is said to have cached his ill-gotten gold." The Antiquities Code of Texas, a state legislative response in 1969 to the private salvage of a 1554 Spanish wreck along Padre Island, ended treasure hunting as an advertised tourist activity on public land, though the hunting and trading of artifacts continued, half hidden.[18]

Figure 2.2. Pirates on a float during the Buccaneer Days parade, June 1939, as photographed by John "Doc" McGregor. Reprinted by permission of the Corpus Christi Public Libraries.

According to boosters, Jean Laffite ought to belong to Corpus Christi, and he suited its image, so phrases such as "is thought to have" and "is said to have" filled gaps in the evidence. Other Gulf Coast characters from the age of exploration, however, could be placed near Corpus Christi with less conjecture. Most local accounts of course begin with the area's indigenous people, the Karankawas. Through disease, encroachment, and harassment, the Karankawas had dwindled to perhaps a hundred people by the 1840s–1850s, when the group's vestiges were caught fatally between Mexicans and Anglo-Americans battling for the area. Native American history and lore haunts Corpus Christi in the shadow of the clash between Anglo and Hispanic cultures. The paucity of archaeological and documentary evidence of the Karankawas leaves people free to confront the Native American past in their imaginations. The South Texas–born writer Bret Anthony Johnston captures the tenor when, in one of his stories, he has a lonely man "carry on," rambling to friends and acquaintances about a miscellany of archaeological information and legends, a preoccupation shared by his son, who had died of a fever caught at Camp Karankawa. These people, the boy and his father had learned, "stood over six feet tall, wore no clothes and were known cannibals; they slept on dry palms, tattooed themselves from head to foot."[19]

Spain enters next. Extrapolating the Spanish presence backward as close to Columbus as possible heightens the romance of it. This explains the prominence in South Texas lore of two enduring "is thought to have"-style stories: conjectured visits by the Spanish explorer Alonso Álvarez de Pineda in 1519 and by the castaway Álvar Núñez Cabeza de Vaca in the 1530s. Both came near the bay, though no primary documents support the supposition that either actually saw it. The 1519 expedition took on special significance when, after World War I, the "possibly true" tale (as the city's WPA guide put it) that Álvarez de Pineda named the bay because he discovered it on Corpus Christi Day, June 24, 1519, became a fixture in promotional and heritage writing and in local celebrations and rituals.[20] Álvarez de Pineda died before he could report on his discoveries, and no account by a crewmember has surfaced. The primary record consists mainly of other Spaniards referring to the voyage. A contemporary map—probably drawn by participants in the expedition—shows that Álvarez de Pineda and his comrades fairly accurately charted the Gulf of Mexico. In 1974, an archaeological dig near Harlingen, Texas, uncovered a carved stone tablet purportedly left by the 1519 expedition, although this is almost certainly a later fabrication. The tablet commemorates the Spanish captain's alleged exploration of the Rio Grande, another doubtful claim that became rooted in Texas history textbooks, this time through an error made by the great historian Carlos E. Castañeda.[21]

The provenance of the story that Álvarez de Pineda named Corpus Christi Bay is itself uncertain. During the opening celebration for the Port of Corpus Christi in 1926, a historical pageant began with "a fiesta in Spain celebrating the feast of Corpus Christi," because on that feast day "in 1519 Alverez de Pineda [sic] . . . discovered a body of water and named it Corpus Christi." This close association between the city and a Spanish explorer did not emerge from consideration of Corpus Christi's Mexican residents, though Tejanos later became the legend's guardians. Rather, the story conformed to the early twentieth-century preference among southwestern Anglos for Spanish colonial lore and Mission Revival style and may even have been concocted by Anglo boosters.[22]

Careful writers, aware that Texan, Mexican, and Spanish historians all doubted the story's veracity, handled it warily. After claiming that "the history of the city's name dates back to 1519," Coleman Mc-Campbell added that the story is "tradition": Álvarez de Pineda is *"believed* to have been the first white man to view the site" (emphasis added). Civic and business elites were not as circumspect. From the start, Álvarez de Pineda—known locally as Pineda—figured prominently in pageantry and paraphernalia surrounding Buccaneer Days. In 1954, the Anglo social group that ran the Buccaneer Days pageant began naming its ceremonial king "Alonso," after "the discoverer of Corpus Christi Bay."[23]

Before the 1920s, romantic stories about the city's origins tended to home in on the expedition of René-Robert Cavelier, sieur de La Salle, who supposedly reached and named the bay on another Corpus Christi Day, June 14, 1685. An account reprinted in a 1910s tourist brochure elaborated on the possibly true details: "The sky was cloudless, the atmosphere balmy, and the beautiful shell beach, backed by a verdure-covered bluff, seemed very alluring to the adventurous Frenchman after his long and tempestuous voyage . . . [La Salle] named the peaceful harbor Corpus Christi, in honor of the day."[24] La Salle's colony met its dreary end near present-day Port Lavaca, over eighty miles northeast of Corpus Christi. Whether La Salle visited the bay or not, the episode does have relevance for the region's documentable history because it prompted expeditions from Mexico to counter French encroachment on the Spaniards' frontier. This included Alonso de León's 1689 expedition, which named the Nueces River.[25] Threats from the French and later the English eventually prompted the Spanish to target southern Texas for colonization. Neither Pineda nor La Salle has relevance to Corpus Christi as a city, any more than the conjectured visits of Jean Laffite. Even so, local writers dwell upon them because they make Corpus Christi a participant in Texas's age of exploration. A chamber of commerce typescript history from 1969 illustrates how this mishmash of legends could set the stage for the city:

> Long before the settlement of Corpus Christi, sea-faring Spanish "conquistadores" plied the waters of the Gulf of Mexico, and it was one of these, Alonso Alverez [*sic*] de Pineda, who discovered the blue waters of Corpus Christi Bay in the year 1519. The event took place on the Festival Day of Corpus Christi. . . . The Bay was

named to fit the circumstance. . . . The Spanish, the Portuguese, the English and the French alternated in making port in Corpus Christi Bay and in visiting the coastal islands . . . The galleons of Hernando Cortez appeared here as did the vessels of Jean Lafitte's freebooting band. At one time, the buccaneers held such sway in the area that Padre and Mustang Islands are said to have become mines of buried treasure. . . . Reminiscent of the days of the roving raiders is the annual Buccaneer Days celebration, usually held in late April or early May, when citizen buccaneers control Corpus Christi once again and even force the mayor to walk the plank.[26]

Dan E. Kilgore, the city's most important bibliophile and document collector, felt obliged to use source-based history to combat such free-booting of the truth. "It is entirely possible that Pineda was the first white man to see Corpus Christi Bay," Kilgore insisted. "But known facts hold no evidence on which it can even be supported as a tradition." As for La Salle, "unfortunately the records of his explorations of the area were lost." The oldest "recorded instance of the bay being called Corpus Christi came in 1766." In that year, a Spanish officer named Diego Ortiz Parilla used it when making a map. If Parilla did not name the bay himself, he was almost certainly using the name given it by someone associated with the recently established Falcón colony at Petronila, the first durable Spanish settlement in the current Nueces County.[27] Enveloped in social ritual and bearing class and ethnic connotations, the Pineda legend managed to outlast Kilgore, who died in 1995. A point of pride and eventually of intergroup competition, the story remained impervious to repeated recountings of the evidence against it. In 2011, Herb Canales, director of the Corpus Christi Public Library system, closed a step-by-step review of the matter with the prose equivalent of a sigh: "The known facts do not support Álvarez de Pineda, though this has not deterred Corpus Christi groups from using the legend as if it were fact."[28]

"The Most Original and Fearless of Texans"

For most Anglo-Texans, pre-Columbian and Spanish Texas are background to the main story, which begins with the Austin colony in the 1820s and ends around the 1880s with the fencing of the range. Throughout the twentieth century, the pivotal episode in the creation of Anglo Texas remained the Texas Revolution of 1835–1836, a first-rate story that happens to be true, full of bravado, stubbornness, miscommunication, ruthlessness, brutality, and luck. Like any good epic, it has a hero with outsized flaws, Sam Houston, and a villain, Santa Anna, with admirable tenacity and a plausible grievance against the protagonists. Until the late twentieth century, Anglo-Texan versions of the Texas Revolution rarely acknowledged moral ambiguities explicitly, though they were at times present as a subtext. Popular accounts distorted the independence war into an Anglo uprising against Mexican treachery and tyranny, a foundation story for a national community based upon race and ethnicity. In school history classes, South Texas Anglos absorbed the notion of Tejanos as potential enemies, outsiders in their own country. Numerous Mexican Texans could recall painful childhood experiences of Anglo schoolchildren holding them somehow responsible for the Alamo and Goliad.

Anglo-Texans have wanted their towns to figure in Texas's national epic. Local historians of Corpus Christi dwell upon it, even though the closest significant revolutionary episode happened at Fort Lipantitlan near San Patricio, twenty-five miles away. Henry Lawrence Kinney founded his trading post on the bay in the fall of 1839.[29] By the late twentieth century, groups such as the Nueces County Historical Society only occasionally devoted programs to details of the independence war in South Texas. But the subject continued to inspire interest and stir emotions.

To cite a well-known example of the intensity of these preoccupations, Dan Kilgore devoted thirty-five years and a small fortune to amassing over 10,000 books, pamphlets, ephemera, and documents; this archive has been the starting point for serious research into Corpus Christi history since the collection's acquisition in 1984 by the local state university. Yet in Kilgore's lifetime, this achievement was overshadowed by controversy surrounding his 1977 presidential address to the Texas State Historical Association. Kilgore explained that according to a newly translated Mexican eyewitness account, Davy Crockett did not die in the fight for the Alamo, but was bayoneted and shot after being captured. "The die-hard Swingin' Davy crowd"—in the words of the Texas essayist Stephen Harrigan—lambasted Kilgore, having already inflicted "hate mail and outraged phone calls" on the translator. That the Mexican account praised Crockett's "nobility" and deplored his murder weighed little. Why would a rational person consider this a libel upon Crockett's memory? The quarrel made sense to those caught up in what Harrigan, author of his own Alamo novel, terms the "weird, primal fascination" that surrounds Crockett's death.[30]

In setting, characters, ethics, and violence, the Texas Revolution counts as a frontier story; it seems to suit Texas naturally. But it represents a way of looking at the region that reduces Corpus Christi and its influence to afterthoughts. As a historical matter, towns were indispensable components of Anglo-American westward expansion—and of Hispanic American northward expansion. Town builders saw themselves as constructing and anchoring the civilization that would displace the wilderness. The association of the West with disorder and violence held no romance for town promoters or dwellers until the frontier phase was safely in the past. The imperative of order and respectability was so strong that historians doubt that western cities ever had much of a Wild West atmosphere, with the exception of the early years of mining and cattle towns, which featured famously high ratios of unattached young men. In the same decades, eastern and midwestern cities, with their class and religious strife, individual and gang violence, and police brutality, could make the West seem tranquil. Philadelphia—cited by western town builders in the mid-1800s as a model of respectability and public spirit—experienced at least five race or ethnic riots in the 1830s–1840s. Chicago—reference point for western town builders by the late 1800s—appeared capable of generating an American version of the Paris Commune in the years marked by the 1877 railroad strike, the 1886 Haymarket affair, and the 1894 Pullman strike.[31]

Western cities did not display any special inclination toward lawlessness, but local conditions within the West did create violent subcultures. Central Texas from the 1860s to the 1890s qualified as one of the worst. There, amid the disruption and rancor of the Civil War and Reconstruction, one expert explains, "white-Indian warfare, vigilantism, cattle-range conflict, outlaw activity, community feuds, ethnic and racial tension, agrarian discontent, and political tumult" occurred simultaneously.[32] Likewise, the Civil War intensified strife in the trans-Nueces region and along the Mexican border, setting off a tumultuous period in Corpus Christi's hinterland. Perched at the gateway to the contested zone between the Nueces and the Rio Grande, Corpus Christi could claim Texas-style banditry and bushwhacking as a "significant attribute" of its history, as Dan Kilgore insisted.[33] Disorder, brutality, and vigilantism ran through Corpus Christi's story not because it was a frontier or western town, but because it was located in a volatile, disputed territory.

Some notorious incidents in Corpus Christi reveal twentieth-century conflicts more than Old West ones. After 1900, commercial agriculture drew Anglo Protestant settlers from the Midwest, who made the region receptive to moralistic reformism. In 1916, prohibitionists imposed their stance on Nueces County with a slim victory in a local-option referendum. The newcomers also energized South Texas movements for poll taxes and white primaries, on the grounds that political bosses "herd[ed] illiterate Mexicans like so many sheep" to the polls and thereby perpetuated the region's retrograde civic culture.[34] The Corpus Christi area became receptive to the 1920s version of the Ku Klux Klan, with its ethno-religious vigilantism. Catholics—an ethnically diverse constituency in the Coastal Bend area, consisting of Mexicans, the Irish, Czechs, and others—defended themselves against the Klan with armed patrols around churches, schools, and parish houses. In October 1922, the Nueces County sheriff, Frank Robinson, an ally of Judge Walter Timon, a political boss whom the moralists despised, shot the Klan leader Fred Roberts outside a Corpus Christi grocery whose owner was linked with the Klan. In July 1925, constables allied with the Klan were involved in a shootout outside a Corpus Christi brothel that killed four people. Local writers have seen a frontier aspect in this fighting. "The old west hadn't died in Corpus Christi," remarked Kilgore in explaining that in the 1920s perhaps "over half the men here still wore guns."[35] Yet these clashes were not so much relics of the Old West as they were products of the 1920s, with its headlong urbanization and development and angry cultural conflicts.

There was nothing particularly frontier about western cities in the 1800s, and nothing particularly western about urban strife. Townspeople put a stop to the Wild West as soon as they could. Having accomplished that, they embraced the gunfighter legend. Writers on Texas cities such as Corpus Christi invoke an atmosphere of struggle and violence as a way to fill their subject with Texan personality and to fit the city into Texas lore.

The city's WPA guide noted that Corpus Christi was "rich in the lore of Texas." "Sturdy pioneers" filled the town's "turbulent" early history, enduring "siege and plundering, raids of bandits, alternate land booms and depressions, droughts, floods, fires, and storms."[36] Such portrayals of the city as enacting prototypical Texas dramas enhance a preoccupation with the decades before 1880, directing attention away from Corpus Christi's post–World War I emergence as a significant regional city.

The town's founder, Henry Lawrence Kinney, among "the most original and fearless of Texans" despite his Pennsylvania origins, wove Corpus Christi into the drama of Anglo Texas from the moment he settled the place. "A restless adventurer, a romantic dreamer, yet a man of action," a true Texas archetype, Kinney, whose "colonel" was unearned, came to Texas in the late 1830s, a refugee from business and personal failure in the North. With few scruples about contraband trade and about meddling in Mexican factional politics, Kinney gained repute as "a loyal Texan, within the limits of his own code." As noted earlier, Texas republicans accused him of acknowledging Mexican claims to the trans-Nueces region and of aiding the 1841 Mexican capture of the Texas Revolution hero (and Kinney business rival) Philip Dimmitt, who committed suicide while in custody. Kinney survived a Republic of Texas treason prosecution in part through intervention of Texas president Mirabeau B. Lamar, who valued Kinney as an informant regarding border affairs. Kinney rehabilitated himself enough to serve four terms in the state senate after Texas's annexation in 1845, even as he strove to take advantage of publicity surrounding General Zachary Taylor's encampment at Corpus Christi that year. The 1852 Lone Star Fair and other failures threw Kinney into debt, which his foray into Central American filibustering deepened. Kinney, whose Unionism helped prompt his departure from Civil War Corpus

Christi, schemed to recover his fortunes up to the day he was killed in Matamoros in March 1862.[37]

Founder of the first Anglo-American settlement south of the Nueces, member of the 1845 constitutional convention, host of the army that brought the United States flag to the Texas mainland, Kinney makes Corpus Christi matter in the creation of Anglo Texas. With warts larger than life and maybe larger than his virtues, he represents a local allegory for the ambivalent image that Anglo-Texans have of themselves. "Smuggler, politician, merchant, gunhand, developer, dreamer, horseman, swindler," runs a typical summation. Historians whose perspective is Mexican Texas likewise see Kinney as a contradictory symbol for the Anglo settlers: at times a defender of Tejano rights, but a manipulator who accumulated land titles through bullying and trickery and whose acknowledgment of Mexican claims to the trans-Nueces region meant nothing when the crisis came.[38]

Kinney's Corpus Christi exhibited the provisional nature of Anglo Texas in the republican and early statehood years. Upon his death, his town consisted mostly of ramshackle residences scattered along a few dusty, unpaved blocks near the waterfront. The Union blockade of the southern Gulf Coast—which included an August 1862 bombardment and attempted landing that the press grandly labeled the Battle of Corpus Christi—left the town drained and dreary by 1867, when a yellow fever epidemic reduced the population to as few as 700 people, a figure that had rebounded to over 2,100 by 1870.[39] In the 1850s–1860s, Indianola, on Matagorda Bay, was the region's main port and entry point for immigrants headed for Central Texas; that town received a railroad connection in 1871, a decade before the completion of Corpus Christi's first railroad, the Texas-Mexico line to Laredo. Indianola had 5,000 people in 1875, when the first of two severe hurricanes hit. The place was a ghost town by 1887.

This town rivalry played out against the banditry and vigilantism that marked the decades after the Anglo influx across the Nueces, from which Indianola enjoyed some distance. The "Cart War" of 1857, when Anglo teamsters attacked Mexican carters operating from the coast to San Antonio, and the 1859 fighting in the Rio Grande Valley between Juan Cortina's militia and the Texas Rangers, caught the attention of officials in Mexico City and Washington. Corpus Christi was stymied, a local paper complained in 1858, by an atmosphere in which Americans treated "the shooting of Mexicans" as "doubtless a harmless amusement."[40] The Civil War exacerbated this turmoil, leading to the 1875 Nuecestown raid and the ensuing reprisals against area Tejanos. While the area's small black presence and peripheral relation to the cotton South removed Corpus Christi from the main sources of tension during Reconstruction, the state's post–Civil War disarray became a major episode in local experience in the context of the unsettled border zone. Hostility toward the Radical Republicans, including E. J. Davis, the Corpus Christi Unionist who became the state's Reconstruction governor, simmers in local writing. Such attitudes endure in part because many Corpus Christians accept the notion of Reconstruction as a "desperate" time that saw Texans "oppressed by military occupation and groaning" under mismanagement by corrupt carpetbaggers. More relevantly for Corpus Christi, the state's political turmoil slowed response to the "virtual reign of terror in outlawry and brigandage" between the Nueces and the Rio Grande. In local accounts—Anglo ones at least—the Redeemers become heroes for reestablishing the Texas Rangers in 1874 and directing them to bring the borderlands under control, which they did by using means often indistinguishable from those of the vigilantes and posses.[41]

The border violence enshrined in Texas lore ended with the tightening of the Anglo hold on the town's hinterland, making it possible for commerce and agriculture to thrive there. Retaliations for the Nuecestown raid were "indiscriminate," explains the city's 1952 centennial history, an expanded version of the WPA guide, in which vigilantes slaughtered "not only the outlaws, but also innocent Mexican settlers, ranchmen, and traders." However deplorable, the episode put an end to "insecurity," which meant that "the people of the bayside town could turn at last toward a more constructive era." When the "Tex-Mex" rail line reached Laredo in 1881, the narrow-gauge railroad symbolized Corpus Christi as a force for Anglo-American progress in southern Texas. "Like the bison, the antelope, the cattle drive," remarked the historian Coleman McCampbell, "wagon trails and ox-carts [were] doomed."[42]

"A Cowboy, Just like Anybody Else"

Historians who would emphasize South Texas's urban element might disdain to dwell upon ranching, the most stereotyped, conventional part of Texas lore. In fact, the ranch economy and ranch life provide the most direct link between the familiar Texas drama and Corpus Christi's meaning as a city. In South Texas, towns did not represent the aftermath or antithesis of the ranchers' lonely battle with wilderness. South Texas's ranch families valued towns as tools in the conquest of the land. Their ambitions depended on connecting themselves to continental trading networks via railroads and a port. Likewise, they needed a service and distribution center for farm families whom they enticed to their subdivided holdings and for merchants in the satellite towns they named for family members, along the railroads that they underwrote. Corpus Christi began to take shape as a consequential town after the 1870s largely because landowning families and syndicates perceived it as the place to concentrate transportation and regional services. In urban studies parlance, the landowning families identified Corpus Christi as their gateway to the urban network and as the central place on the South Texas coast.

The South Texas epic of the King and Driscoll ranches, spread around the world via Edna Ferber's 1952 novel *Giant* and George Stevens's movie version, makes no sense without Corpus Christi, and vice versa. The landholding families treated Corpus Christi as integral to their operations and set themselves up as "boosters of the small but growing coastal town."[43] In addition to mansions and hotels, ranch interests underwrote transportation, finance, and industry as well as the town's religious, cultural and social institutions. Spohn Hospital, Driscoll Hospital, the *Corpus Christi Caller*, and the Corpus Christi National Bank all manifested King and Driscoll money. Denizens of the ranches embraced a self-depreciating, rustic image. Long after they became managers of far-flung modern businesses, they had themselves photographed wearing cowboy hats and riding horses. An executive of Corpus Christi National Bank from 1929 to 1970 and chair of the port commission from 1929 to 1952, Richard King, grandson of the founder of the King Ranch, shared with Robert Driscoll Jr. credit for guiding the port's formative decades. King, however, insisted that ranching was in his "blood" and that banking was not his strong suit: "Sometimes I think I don't understand all I know about figures and finance." While Robert Kleberg Jr. was transforming the King Ranch into a multinational oil-and-gas and agricultural enterprise, his brother, Congressman Richard M. Kleberg, served on the House Agriculture Committee. When Congressman Kleberg helped bring the naval air station to Flour Bluff, Clara Driscoll, longtime Democratic national committeewoman, contributed toward the purchase of the site.[44]

Clara Driscoll appears in local accounts as an especially formidable personality—"something, even by Texas standards," remarks a Driscoll Foundation official history—who brought the unyielding ethos of the ranches into the whirl of modernizing, urbanizing Texas. Known throughout Texas as a catalyst for the Alamo's preservation, a cosmopolite, and a Democratic powerbroker, she wielded a "fiery-eyed" assertiveness in behalf of her family, causes, and town, which fed a "Driscoll legend" befitting a socialite two generations removed from Ireland and less than one from a South Texas ranch. An oft-repeated Corpus Christi legend claims that Driscoll built the Robert Driscoll Hotel on Upper Broadway four stories higher than the neighboring White Plaza Hotel, the city's second tall building, because, having lost control of the White Plaza in a lawsuit, she wanted to "stand at a window and vent her displeasure on it." Versions of the story (which her biographer, alas, demonstrates to be improbable) render the verb "to vent" with more specificity.[45]

At the end of the western tale, the cowboy rides away, leaving the townspeople to their settled lives. At the end of Corpus Christi's Texas drama, the city integrates itself into modern networks of commerce and finance, but at the cost of a spirit derived from the land. In 1998, directors pushed out Stephen J. "Tio" Kleberg as operating manager of the King Ranch. Great-great-grandson of the original Richard King, Tio Kleberg represented the fourth generation of Klebergs to oversee what was by then not merely a ranch bigger than Rhode Island, but also an intricate, professionally managed corporation. While recognizing this reality, the *Caller-Times* nevertheless lamented "a corporate end to a cowboy era." Although both a "businessman in the modern sense" and the "last of the great South Texas patrons," Kleberg could not "sidestep trouble inside a climate-controlled corporate high-rise as readily as he did an advancing steer." "He is a cowboy, just like any-body else," remarked one of the Tejano ranch hands known as *Kineños*. King Ranch and its workers were "part of his life," added the ranch's onetime official historian. "I don't think any corporate suit in Houston has a clue as to what that means."[46]

"Yankee Colonel Promoters"

The town promoter, the booster, is a fixture in the story of Corpus Christi and other Texas cities, counterpoint to the brave pioneer and the dogged rancher but also a town-based manifestation of pioneer tasks and values. The booster lore of nineteenth-century Corpus Christi surrounds three "Yankee colonel promoters": Henry Lawrence Kinney, both a frontier figure and a town booster; the railroad builder Uriah Lott, from Albany, New York; and the New Jersey–born sales-man Elihu H. Ropes, who actually had been a Union colonel.[47] His-tories of Corpus Christi recount their adventures with melodramatic flourishes typical of western boom-and-bust stories. At times suspi-ciously urbane in manner and image, the town promoter can inject a deceptive sophistication and alien values into the supposedly down-to-earth West. Ropes, whose investments and promotion started the four-year boom dashed in the Panic of 1893, appears as "fluent of tongue," with "impressive" credentials and "a portfolio of exciting ideas." This "magnetic personality" turned "staid and conservative citizens" into "giddy" speculators. The Yankee promoters all saw their hopes dashed, and each died in reduced circumstances. Two died amid the fallout from their failures: Kinney at age forty-eight, murdered in 1862; Ropes in 1898 at age fifty-three, driven from town by "irate" citizens, his health broken, his Alta Vista hotel "a glamorous and va-cant hulk," and his wrecked dredge abandoned in the barrier island sand. Lott lived into his seventies but ended dependent on his backers, the Klebergs of the King Ranch.[48]

Even while recounting these boosters' delusions, deceptions, and disappointments, Corpus Christi writers refrain from dismissing them altogether. "Rascal or prince? Promoter or swindler?" summa-rizes Bill Walraven, a *Caller-Times* columnist and a popular local his-torian. "Whatever Kinney was, he did lay out the townsite, encourage

European settlers, promote Corpus Christi all over the world."[49] Alone of the three, Lott raises few moral questions, standing instead as a cautionary tale for entrepreneurs long on vision but short on capital. Organizer between the 1870s and 1900s of three railroad lines that connected the nascent port with Houston, San Antonio, and the Rio Grande Valley, Lott won praise upon his death for "waste places settled and civilization advanced," as the *Caller* put it, his achievement marred by "no great fortune in tainted millions."[50] Even Ropes, a Union veteran who took down local former Confederates with him, appears not as a rogue but "a man ahead of his time." "His ideas were all right," conceded Mary Sutherland, whose *Story of Corpus Christi* (1916) reflected the perspective of its publisher, the Daughters of the Confederacy, "but he came on about twenty years too soon, and did not fully understand the subject."[51]

"A hustler and promoter like Kinney," Walraven remarks, "was exactly what the town needed to survive." "A man like [Lott] could never be considered poor," he continues, since he "made the country rich by opening it to immigration and the development of farms and towns" while enhancing the case for a deepwater port.[52] Whatever the boosters' excesses, accounts stress their stories as significant episodes for Corpus Christi and as illustrations of the challenges facing city builders in South Texas. From the 1840s to the 1900s, Corpus Christi's three Yankee colonels all sought to attract visitors, settlers, and capital to the town, dredge a ship channel, and construct other transportation and commercial facilities. Without doubt, Corpus Christi needed such improvements if it were to grow from an outpost into a significant port and city.

Paeans to boosterism in Texas and the Southwest are so ubiquitous and self-serving that skeptics are inclined to discount them too readily. Harvey Graff, for example, assails a notion that runs through Dallas's booster lore: the North Texas city had "no reason to exist" and would have remained an insignificant place but for the business elite's enterprise and governance. The like-minded Patricia Evridge Hill deplores "the myth of Dallas as the product of local businessmen's ability to 'sell' others on an indistinguishable piece of prairie." Hill and Graff emphasize geographic factors conducive to Dallas's growth, "a natural river crossing" amid "a large, fertile hinterland," along with transportation and trade routes running east-to-west and north-to-south.⁵³ Such arguments have value for undermining facile self-justifications. Even so, it is not so easy to write off the boosters just because one is suspicious of the political consequences of exaggerated praise of them. Cities do not grow on their own, even when the geographic situation is favorable. Powerful, well-connected people exert disproportionate influence over which places develop and in what ways. Apart from unusual cases such as Washington, D.C.—or the Texas example, Austin, until its economy diversified in the late twentieth century—American cities have overwhelmingly been commercial, transportation, and industrial centers. Inevitably, they have taken their tone and direction from entrepreneurs and capitalists. Booster lore has had unsavory political uses, but booster activity was essential to the transformation of potential town sites into cities.

Cities resulted from the interplay between circumstances conducive to urban growth and the shrewdness, persistence, and luck of town promoters, not from just one or the other. On a general level, cities emerge inexorably as centers for developing hinterlands or as nodes in networks of extraction, production, and exchange. But specific cities depend upon the "determination of many citizens," as a Corpus Christi economist put it, to take advantage of resources and geography. A region might urbanize for impersonal reasons; individual cities manifest successful town promotion. Not counting Fort Worth for the moment, how many promising town sites existed within a 150-mile radius of Dallas? Between 1880 and 1990, Dallas's municipal population rose from around 10,000 people to over 1,000,000. Between 1940 and 1990, the Dallas–Fort Worth metropolitan region expanded from around 600,000 people to nearly 3,900,000. Without its long history of aggressive commercial-civic activism, highlighted by the famously self-perpetuating, probusiness governing alliance that ruled for decades during the twentieth century, would Dallas be nearly as large today?⁵⁴ Maybe the development of more open, democratic cities would have been worth a slower rate of growth, but that is a different argument.

To direct the point to the South Texas coast, a port city would probably have arisen in the vicinity, even though every plausible site required expensive reengineering to make it safe and accessible. Corpus Christi emerged on Corpus Christi Bay partly for contingent reasons. The Anglo-American influx across the Nueces River created a situation conducive to seaport development. Still, for any of several possible cities to benefit, promoters had to identify one site as preferable and then overcome its shortcomings. Through engineering and organizational feats such as Lott's railroad lines and later the Port of Corpus Christi and the Corpus Christi seawall, Corpus Christi's promoters made a plausible but flawed site into a good place for Texas to meet the sea.

Kinney understood the tasks involved in town promotion by his arrival in the Corpus Christi region in 1838. The Panic of 1837 ended his youthful career as a canal contractor and land dealer in Peru, Illinois, another potential transportation center, where the Illinois and Michigan Canal met the Illinois River. Kinney's smuggling, filibustering, and double-dealing made his South Texas life a frontier romance, but his town promotion followed formulas. The arrival of Taylor's army in July 1845 represented a public relations windfall. After serving with Texas troops at the Battle of Monterrey, Kinney promoted his "Naples of the Gulf" in the "Italy of America" on both sides of the Atlantic. He and his partners bought up the land of hard-pressed Mexican grantees on larcenous terms and then subdivided the properties into farms, offered for cheap prices, and town lots, offered dear. Kinney reportedly spent $45,000 in borrowed money to promote his 1852 fair, which attracted a mere 2,000 of the 20,000–30,000 anticipated visitors. Recognizing that a port that could handle only shallow-draft packet boats hardly merited the title, Kinney invested in a steam dredge and persuaded the municipality to invest more, though little was accomplished before the Union troops burned the dredge during the Civil War. Kinney's diverse activities illustrated mainly that the town—prone to yellow fever and closer to the turmoil of the Mexican borderlands than to any prospering region of Texas—remained a premature enterprise.[55]

When Uriah Lott relocated to South Texas in the late 1860s, he also brought relevant town-promoting experience, having worked in his twenties on the Chicago and Alton Railroad in Illinois. Though he never made much money for himself, his ventures corresponded better than Kinney's to the region's level of development. By 1881, when his Corpus Christi, San Diego and Rio Grande Railroad, or Texas Mexican Railroad, reached Laredo, Corpus Christi Bay had been dredged to eight feet, deep enough for shallow-draft steamships engaged in the wool and hide trades. The railroad connection diverted Mexican trade to Corpus Christi. Laredo tripled in population from 3,521 in 1880 to 11,319 in 1890. The Kings, Klebergs, Kenedys, and Driscolls put capital into Lott's San Antonio and Aransas Pass Railroad, which had connected the port town to Houston, Central Texas, and the Hill Country by the time it fell under the control of the Southern Pacific Railroad in the 1890s. Lott's final venture, the St. Louis, Brownsville and Mexico Railway, which reached Brownsville in 1904, had the explicit purpose of encouraging midwesterners to migrate to ranches subdivided into farms connected to markets by strings of railroad towns. Lott had "the entire map of South Texas indelibly impressed in his mind," remarked a Brownsville paper. Upon the railroad builder's death in 1915 in the King Ranch's Casa Ricardo Hotel, Corpus Christi mayor Roy Miller proclaimed Lott's enterprises to have been "probably more resultful for the people of Corpus Christi than [the work of] any other one man."[56]

Whatever their failures and shortcomings, Kinney and Lott understood boosterism and knew that it was arduous and time-consuming. By comparison, the so-called Ropes Boom seems overeager and amateurish. In 1889, Ropes, who, among other occupations, had managed advertising for the Singer Sewing Machine Company, stopped in Corpus Christi on his way to California, where he was traveling for his health. The high bluff gave him a vision of a Gulf Coast resort comparable to what Henry M. Flagler was promoting in South Florida. With dredging, Corpus Christi might become the best-protected harbor along the hurricane-prone Texas coast. Casting aside California, Ropes went home and lined up investors—including, apparently, members of the Roosevelt family—for his project to combine a "Chicago of the Southwest" with a "Southern Newport and a Long Branch."[57]

Ropes returned to Corpus Christi with enough funds to purchase and subdivide thousands of acres and to construct a streetcar to a hotel overlooking the bay. He brought a dredge and plans for Port Ropes on Mustang Island near Packery Channel. A proposed Deep Water Terminal Railroad would run across Laguna Madre near the site of the modern Kennedy Causeway, linking to Corpus Christi's rail terminals and thence throughout the Americas. "The problem of deep water on the Texas Coast, without government aid," asserted a *Houston Post* article reprinted as a flyer, "seems to be near solution." Port Ropes would have been Texas's first port for ocean traffic, since sandbars hampered access to Galveston Bay until 1896 and the Houston Ship Channel was a quarter century in the future. As a resort, "Corpus Christi is the most beautifully located city by the sea in America," with its bluff "commanding the most magnificent water view" ever seen. With the cost of living and taxes "ridiculously low," vacationers could "spend the summer months right here at the seaside *as cheaply as they can live at home.*"

Under the influence of this "medium of unlimited capital," some property prices became inflated from $8 to $1,000 an acre. "Local people were not inclined to stay out of what appeared to be a 'sure thing,'" the city's WPA guide observed. Even before the 1893 depression, signs abounded that Ropes had overextended himself and the town with him. He threw a ball to celebrate the 1891 completion of his hotel, but the resort never opened; photos of vacationers there have been retouched. After a stint as a girl's school, it stood abandoned until a 1927 fire completed demolition begun by the 1919 hurricane. Even before the panic, northeastern newspapers questioned Ropes and his plans, prompting him to file a $100,000 lawsuit against one Boston paper. As the depression began, Ropes abandoned his broken-down dredge and returned, brokenhearted, to New York. The crash returned Corpus Christi's population to 4,700, nearly its preboom level.[58]

At the height of the Ropes Boom, "speculators, horse racers," and drifters "traded in everything and anything, provided it could be bought on time," recalled Mary Sutherland. "This class was the first to go, they brought nothing with them and carried nothing away." Yet the Daughters of the Confederacy historian expressed little rancor against the Yankee huckster who had bankrupted "good people" among her acquaintances. By the mid-1910s, "the schemes planned by Colonel Ropes [had] become realities," the city had grown in the direction he predicted, "and fortunate [were] the men who bought real estate and kept it."[59] His story, commemorated a century later by a historical marker at the bayside Ropes Park, near the site where his hotel had been, amounts to a booster parable. Ropes pursued in a rush enterprises that gradually did become mainstays of the town. His activities and publicity illustrated where the city's opportunities resided and what tasks Corpus Christi needed done.

"Epitome of the Anglo Establishment"

Despite her conspicuous devotion to the Lost Cause, Sutherland sin-
gled out a native Kansan, "honest, upright" Roy Miller, Corpus Christi's thirty-two-year-old progressive mayor, as "not the least" of "the
many blessings enjoyed by our city on the coast." From Sutherland's
perspective, it helped that Miller had attended school in Houston and
married into a Corpus Christi family.[60] In style and substance, Miller
embodied the town's transition to a city. Born in 1884, valedictorian
of his Houston high school and a scholarship student at the University of Chicago, Miller operated less like a nineteenth-century booster
than a twentieth-century public relations professional. After a stint as
a railroad journalist and publicist in Houston, Miller was recruited by
Robert Kleberg Sr. in 1904 as public relations agent for Uriah Lott's St.
Louis, Brownsville and Mexico Railway. By age twenty-four, Miller
was editor of the *Corpus Christi Caller*. He remained a protégé and
friend of the Klebergs, whose city-building and modernizing agenda
he praised and pursued. Miller also identified with John Nance Garner, the area's congressman starting in 1903. Miller's rivalry with Walter E. Pope, an attorney, property investor, and state legislator allied
with Duval County's Archie Parr, became a local episode in the battle
of land developers and modernizers against ranchers and traditionalists, which played out across southern Texas and which had parallels
among political and business leaders across the Southwest.[61]

In 1913, Miller replaced one of Pope's allies as mayor. Over three
terms, Miller's administration provided Corpus Christi the accouter-
ments of a respectable city: streets, sewers, a water supply, a city hall,
and a wharf. The City Beautiful–style landscaping that he oversaw
for Corpus Christi Bluff signaled the town's urban aspirations. At the
same time, Walter Timon, longtime Nueces County judge, oversaw the
1914 courthouse, which expressed the same aspirations. An old-style
politician with a dubious reputation, Timon cooperated with Miller's
city-building progressives; they had common enemies, especially Pope
and the Parrs. Defeated for a fourth term by Pope's law partner, Miller returned to the *Corpus Christi Caller* in time to devise the strategy
of using the dreadful 1919 hurricane and tidal wave as an argument
for a deepwater port. The Miller-Kleberg and Pope factions set aside

rivalries during poststorm recovery and the port campaign. This despite the fact that Miller, whose own house had been destroyed in the storm, had made well-founded charges that Pope's waterfront properties posed a significant obstacle to bayfront and port improvement.

Ever the publicist, Miller organized a celebration to open the port on the storm's seventh anniversary, September 14, 1926. Twenty-five thousand people came by special train and excursion boat from as far away as Beaumont. The chair of the celebration, Robert Driscoll Jr., provided—along with the Klebergs—much funding toward the lobbying effort for the port. Driscoll chaired the Port of Corpus Christi commission until he died, in 1929, and was succeeded by banker Richard King. Miller and his allies had turned Corpus Christi's bleakest date into a festival to introduce the city where Texas met the sea. Acknowledging political divisions that had often stymied the port campaign in the decades preceding the catastrophe, the program dedicated the event to civic leaders "big enough to rise above provincial strife, always using honorable means to reach a worthy end." These experiences gave Miller an expansive perspective on Gulf Coast navigation, leading to his second career, as director of the Intracoastal Canal Association.[62]

When turning their attention from the nineteenth to the twentieth century, Corpus Christi's Anglo-American historians tend to identify turning points with commercial-civic leaders in the mold of Miller, a sophisticated professional allied to scions of long-established but modern-minded families like the Klebergs. Twentieth-century town promotion in this way balances an outward-looking perspective with a localized consciousness. Twentieth-century promoters, even those with Yankee provenance, seemed to "fully understand the subject" in a way that Mary Sutherland complained that interloper Ropes did not.

Corpus Christi histories identify the next major turning point, the advent of petrochemicals and industry, with personalities such as Maston Nixon, a World War I artillery officer and former cotton farmer who in the 1920s developed the first two skyscrapers atop the bluff, the twelve-story Nixon Building (with funding from Robert Driscoll) and the fourteen-story White Plaza Hotel (in partnership with Clara Driscoll). As head of the chamber of commerce's industrial committee in the mid-1930s, Nixon lured Southern Alkali, the port's first major factory. To ensure a regular supply of the natural gas, on which the plant's investors insisted, Nixon organized a supply and pipeline company known as Southern Minerals, or SOMICO. Deals such as these became the foundation for the port's industrial zone, with its strengths in petrochemicals, inorganic chemicals, and metals. Nixon's group marketed Corpus Christi to industry not just for its ship channel and labor costs, but also for the "industrialist's dream" of "gas wells in sight of ship masts . . . low priced fuel at tidewater!"[63]

By the 1950s, Nixon had built SOMICO into a pipeline, production, and supply company worth $100 million. This was a key example of the midsized petrochemical operations that made Corpus Christi seem headed for metropolitan status until the Coastal Bend petrochemical industry fell under out-of-town control after the 1960s. For years, Nixon operated Southern Minerals from the city's oldest surviving building, Centennial House on Upper Broadway, in the shadow of his 1920s skyscrapers. Local accounts portray Nixon not as a free-wheeling Texas tycoon, but as a gruff, frugal skeptic. Bill Walraven relates that the farmer turned oilman woke each day at 4:15 a.m., became agitated over the newspaper, drank a scotch to go back to sleep, and then started the workday at 8. Nixon made a point of recounting how, during World War I, he had let slip an opportunity to acquire a large share of Humble Oil, ultimately a component of Exxon.[64]

Into the 1970s, initiative in Corpus Christi's developmental politics and civic affairs came from Anglo business and professional figures who, like Nixon, occupied the intersection between petrochemicals, the port, urban real estate, and South Texas ranches and farmlands. Two founders of the Area Development Committee, the panel of business and political leaders that controlled the city's planning and public works during the 1950s–1960s, were Guy I. Warren, a Kansas-born engineer who made a fortune in South Texas oil during the 1930s and 1940s, much of which he invested in Corpus Christi real estate, and Lon Hill Jr., president of Central Power and Light, the regional electrical utility, and son of Lon C. Hill, a Brownsville lawyer and merchant who had worked with Lott on railroad and town development in the Rio Grande Valley.[65]

Of the younger personalities whom Warren and Hill drew into civic activism, the most important proved to be Hayden Head, a corporate attorney from a family of business lawyers in Sherman, Texas. After graduating from the University of Texas Law School in 1937, Head set up practice in Corpus Christi, having perceived opportunities in oil and gas analogous to the North Texas banks and railroads represented by his family. The attorney impressed founding figures in South Texas petrochemicals, including Maston Nixon and the landowner Rand Morgan, his eventual father-in-law. These mentors helped him gather a roster of industrial clients from among the plants lining the Port of Corpus Christi: DuPont, Celanese, and Pittsburgh Plate Glass, along with major petrochemical operations. A fighter pilot in World War II, Head endured a stint as a German prisoner of war after being shot down near the Baltic coast. Upon Head's return to Corpus Christi, Nixon engaged the lawyer to lobby in Washington in behalf of natural gas deregulation, an episode that enhanced Head's political experience and connections. On his own account and through marriage, Head accumulated considerable investments in oil and land.

Head became a factor in Corpus Christi politics soon after his homecoming in 1945. As in much of the Southwest, modern-minded business leaders sought to switch from the commission municipal format, which had become a disappointment since its widespread adoption following the 1900 Galveston hurricane, to the council-manager system, with its reputation for professionalism and business-mindedness. A Corpus Christi commission allegedly allied with Duval County's George Parr tried to co-opt this movement by hiring a city manager without redefining its own powers. During a city commission meeting, Head took the floor, denounced the commissioners as schemers, and presented a lengthy recall petition. A board member chastised him for wasting their time. The commissioners, the returned fighter pilot and POW admonished, were "badly mistaken" in underestimating him and his allies.[66] Head put together a Better Government League, which soon forced the old-line commissioners to resign rather than face recall. Modeled on progrowth, "good government" movements then taking shape across Texas and the Southwest, the Better Government League fielded a slate that won by a landslide in a special election in March 1946 on a council-manager platform.[67] This coalition's hold remained shaky until 1955, when an election victory, along with a favorable charter revision, led to a run of dominance that lasted until good-government coalitions broke apart across the Southwest in the 1970s.

As Hill, Warren, and other midcentury, commercial-civic activists aged, Head emerged as their heir, a South Texas powerbroker on the level of Houston's Jesse Jones or Dallas's Robert Thornton. Beyond force of personality, Head's influence came from his corporate and political connections, which gradually shifted from conservative Democrats such as Governors Allan Shivers and John Connally to probusiness, promilitary Republicans such as Senator John Tower. Like many powerbrokers, Head avoided elected office, preferring to work through organizations such as the Area Development Committee or appointed positions such as chair of the Coastal Bend Council of Governments, which was essential to regional water planning. Head's determined support for the Choke Canyon project fueled suspicions that port industries mattered more than the city's people when it came to water supply. Despite his efforts to stay behind the scenes, his clients and alliances made him a lightning rod, as did his reputation for—in the *Corpus Christi Caller*'s words—"rigidity, arrogance, and ruthlessness." In 1978, *Texas Monthly* labeled Head the "kingpin behind the Anglo establishment." He stood at the center, the magazine charged, of a "snug coterie of downtown bankers, corporate lawyers, oilmen, and big landowners," complacent amid the city's stagnation. To this, Head wryly responded that he was not so much kingpin as the "epitome of the Anglo establishment."[68]

Having started as a protégé of Corpus Christi's first generation of oilmen and industrialists, Head became the veteran leader of a self-styled "Group" that kept a semblance of Texas-style, commercial-civic rule alive in Corpus Christi after such downtown establishments had frayed elsewhere. His support for business cooperation with local government, especially in regard to planning, public works, and transportation, was typical of the period's progrowth coalitions across the Southwest. On the surface, his inclination toward an active public sector at the local level contradicted the staunch free-market conservatism that he advocated for state and national politics. Head's outlook shared an affinity with that of Arizona Republican Barry Goldwater, who entered politics in the late 1940s as a probusiness municipal reformer dedicated to the physical and economic development of Phoenix. When, in 1964, Head backed Goldwater for U.S. president over fellow Texan Lyndon Johnson, this apostasy did not hurt him in his hometown. His local alliances extended into both parties and major ethnic groups.

The most important career Head helped launch was that of Democrat Solomon Ortiz, the county's first Hispanic sheriff and U.S. congressman. In a twist that illustrates the personal and family webs in South Texas politics, Ortiz continued for fourteen terms in Congress until defeated by 799 votes in the 2010 Republican sweep by Blake Farenthold, grandson of Head's second wife, Annie Morgan Farenthold.

Within Corpus Christi, Head seemed to have few implacable critics, despite his methods and conservatism. Environmentalists at times derided him as "lawyer for the polluters." Typical for Texas during this period, the harshest criticism came from elsewhere on the political right, from antiestablishment Anglos such as Jason Luby, a onetime South Texas organizer for George Wallace who won three terms as Corpus Christi mayor during the 1970s. Luby labeled Head "my number one enemy," which Head in 1982 proved by backing Ortiz's successful campaign for Congress against Luby. Others who clashed with the powerbroker appreciated his civic sense and his dedication to "work[ing] without much fanfare and publicity," as the civil rights leader Hector García commented after Head's death in a private plane crash in 1987. He "put together a power structure by persuasion and not by force," recalled one former mayor. "It meant the world to me that he thought I would be a good candidate," remembered another. Ruben and Tony Bonilla, local lawyers who both became national presidents of the League of United Latin American Citizens, criticized Head for his patronizing, "right kind of Mexican" attitude. Tony Bonilla nonetheless remembered Head as "class gentleman" whose "word was solid." If "Head called you to his office, you went," the *Corpus Christi Caller* columnist Nick Jimenez recalled. The reporter added that like García, Head had a reputation for "integrity" and was upfront about his agenda and sympathies. Jimenez disclaimed any "yearning for a return to the day of decisions made behind closed doors." Still, the city had benefited when the Anglo and Hispanic figures with the most leverage were "absolutely trusted by their followers, but they could also bank on a measure of respect by opponents."[69]

"I had a lot of admiration for Hayden Head," local NAACP chair Lena Coleman explained in a 1997 *Caller-Times* series on civic leadership. "But I would like to see young people take a chance to explore new horizons." By 2000, Corpus Christi's conversation over civic leadership had expanded beyond nineteenth-century boosters in the mold of Kinney, Lott, or Ropes and twentieth-century commercial-civic activists in the mold of Miller, Nixon, and Head. Accounts included women as well as men, educators, environmentalists, philanthropists, and social reformers as well as businesspeople, public officials, and professionals. Black and Hispanic Corpus Christians appeared alongside the Anglo elite.[70]

Some of this broader sensibility reflected a more open-ended notion of who made up the city and what caused it to thrive. But some also reflected the city's uncertain economic and geographic situation at the end of the twentieth century. The boosters, modernizers, and powerbrokers were products of and spokesmen for particular phases and specific projects: water and rail transportation, commerce and finance, petrochemicals, industry, the military, and tourism. By the 1990s, Corpus Christians lamented that their city had grown too diffuse and factionalized, that it lacked the coherent leadership provided, warts and all, by Head. But Head's outlook and methods had been formed in the oil and petrochemical boom of the mid-twentieth century and were suited to that era. In the early twenty-first century, the city's leadership may have seemed less capable of making and pursuing coherent policies in his manner because the city's circumstances and prospects were themselves ambiguous.

At the start of the twentieth-first century, South Texas's frontier and rural heritage still pervaded historical accounts of Corpus Christi. People's sense of regional history, however, seemed more often to encompass the city itself. The oil and petrochemical industries had begun to receive attention proportionate to their influence. The port generated official, popular, and scholarly histories. The port's promoters—Roy Miller, Robert Driscoll Jr., and others—took their place alongside the flamboyant boosters of the nineteenth century as founding figures of the modern Corpus Christi economy.

In his long-running history column in the *Caller-Times,* Murphy Givens sought a balance by dwelling on frontier, Texas Republic, and Civil War topics while also offering accounts of twentieth-century politics, infrastructure, religious institutions, and other matters.[71] In the 1990s and 2000s, Givens and his predecessor as the paper's history columnist, Bill Walraven, produced picture books emphasizing the centrality of the 1919 storm, the port, and the seawall in creating modern

Corpus Christi. In 1997, the Nueces County Historical Society revised Walraven's 1982 illustrated history of the city, adding a chapter by another reporter on the contemporary city and reworking illustrations to shift the balance forward in time. In 2005, Walraven published a lengthy history of the South Texas oil industry, a commission from the Corpus Christi Geological Society. And throughout 1999, the *Caller-Times* published well-researched retrospective supplements emphasizing education, architecture, transportation, business, and other modern themes.[72]

The Anglo-Texan lore of wilderness and frontier, ranchers and rangers, diverted Corpus Christians from observing and appreciating urban influences that surrounded them. But no account of South Texas urbanism would be truthful if it slighted geography and environment, if it considered the city without also stressing the land. South Texas's geography, environment, rural history, and even its myths gave character and life to Corpus Christi. Between a fierce plain and a ferocious sea, Corpus Christi occupies a powerful landscape that grips the imagination and makes tough demands on those who would thrive there. Corpus Christians might profit from more sustained attention to the city. Still, they exhibit a healthy instinct when they leave land and sea in their story, hurricanes and prickly pears as well as explorers, ranchers, rangers, Mexican migrants, and midwestern farmers.

From Kinney through Lott and Ropes and across the twentieth century, promoters realized that the city and the region had to sell each other. Civil engineering projects such as the port and the seawall overcame the shortcomings of the site to realize the potential of the region. The South Texas environment continued to govern Corpus Christi's appearance, political economy, and living patterns as much as the city shapes South Texas. As the next chapter explains, people from multiple ethnic groups—not just Anglo South Texans—retained connections and mindsets formed in the small towns, ranches, and farms of the Nueces region.

Chapter 3

CITY ON A FRONTIER
OF PEOPLES

∽

N ick Jimenez, a longtime *Caller-Times* columnist and editor, recalls
being intrigued by the "semi-rural, semi-urban" atmosphere he
encountered when he arrived in Corpus Christi from San Antonio in
the late 1960s. People's mindsets seemed still "tied in with the land."
Numerous acquaintances had lives intertwined with relatives in surrounding small towns. Corpus Christi Tejanos had little nostalgia for
the grinding conditions of South Texas agricultural labor, which they
or their parents had left behind. But people measured the good life in
small-town terms, telling the young reporter of their aspirations for "a
little ranch out in Duval County," Jimenez recalled. "As a San Antonio
kid, I never heard anyone say, 'Let's buy a ranch.' What the hell would
you want to buy a ranch for?"[1]

Hispanic as well as Anglo-Americans came to the Nueces region
with a cultural predisposition toward rural heritage and frontier lore.
Circumstances and experiences in South Texas heightened this inclination, which meant that sensibilities shaped on ranches and farms
and in small towns infused Corpus Christi. The consequences jumped
out at Jimenez, who came, after all, from the Texas city long regarded
as the intellectual, artistic, and commercial capital of the Hispanic
Southwest. One can critique as marketable hodgepodge the pervasive

Spanish and Mexican motifs in San Antonio's architecture, tourist sites, celebrations, and image making. The River Walk and La Villita are far removed from Spanish and Mexican town-building practices. Still, such places reinforce the city's strongly felt Hispanic "symbolic identity," as the geographer Daniel Arreola puts it.[2]

By contrast, Corpus Christi remains marked by its origins as an Anglo-American foundation, a tool in the extension of U.S. power, society, and economy into South Texas and beyond. Even so, geographers and ethnographers identify Corpus Christi as a component of a major subregion within both Texas and the Mexico-U.S. borderlands: the Tejano "homeland" that Arreola and others discern by observing vernacular architecture and landscaping, arts and crafts, and everyday culture such as the preparation of common foods. The city's location at the northeastern gateway to the vast borderlands—stretching 1,500 miles to the Pacific—meant that Corpus Christi would absorb and reflect borderland influences in myriad ways.[3]

Corpus Christi's Anglo origins complicate its place in Tejano South Texas. Despite the troubled ethnic history of all South Texas towns in the century and a half after the Texas Revolution, Tejanos can claim San Antonio, Laredo, and other Spanish- or Mexican-era towns as their regional heritage. In the Coastal Bend, the hinterland shaped Hispanic identity and outlook more than the city itself. The trans-Nueces region has a deep, powerful, and long-standing association with Hispanic heritage and Tejano history. Since the 1920s, Corpus Christi has been a force in Tejano politics and culture. But for Mexican Texans as for Anglo-Texans, rural South Texas, more than the city, evokes experiences that seem fundamental and themes worth arguing over. When explaining their outlook and agenda, for example, Corpus Christi–based movements such as the American GI Forum referred far more often to South Texas's rural story and the struggles and sensibilities of small-town Tejanos than they did to equivalent experiences in their city. As Jimenez observed, this sense of connection to the region's farming and ranching towns was personal in many Mexican South Texan families. Hispanic Corpus Christi remained intertwined with and defined by the ranching and farming towns of South Texas until late in the twentieth century.

Tejano Corpus Christians, like most Hispanic Texans, come mainly from families who moved north of the Rio Grande during the enormous migration that began around 1910 with the outbreak of the Mexican Revolution. Thousands of Mexicans, to be sure, remained in southern Texas after the Treaty of Guadalupe Hidalgo, and thousands more migrated temporarily or permanently from south of the Rio Grande between 1848 and 1910. Still, in the six decades after annexation, South Texas's recurrent ethno-national conflict, its dispossession of preannexation inhabitants despite treaty guarantees, and its endemic racial oppression did not create an inviting atmosphere for people from south of the river. In 1915, a new wave of vigilantism and reprisals in reaction to the irredentist Plan de San Diego—which came in the context of Mexico's civil war and the cross-border raids and paramilitary movements associated with it—sent a new stream of refugees southward across the Rio Grande. Yet neither this turmoil nor accelerated Anglo efforts to disfranchise and segregate South Texas Hispanics reversed the south-to-north trend.

Between 1910 and 1930, the number of Mexican-born people living in Texas doubled from 125,000 to 266,000, and the state's Spanish-surnamed population nearly tripled, from 233,000 to 684,000. During the 1930s, the political situation in Mexico stabilized, but the Great Depression exacerbated tensions in Texas. These factors slowed and in some cases reversed Mexican migration, at times through voluntary repatriation encouraged by the Mexican government but also through coerced deportation by U.S. and Texas authorities. All these events had the seemingly contradictory but, in reality, logical effect of enhancing the sense among Tejanos, old families and recent migrants, that South Texas was not a temporary home but a permanent one, a homeland, as Arreola terms it. Tejanos increasingly insisted on organizing to affirm their status and protect their rights within Texas and the United States.

During World War II and the decades after the war, Tejanos in the Corpus Christi area grew even more South Texan in demography and identity. The wartime and postwar Bracero program, which sought to limit Mexican agricultural workers to temporary residence—mostly unsuccessfully, despite deportation programs such as Operation

Wetback during the 1950s—in any case accounted for only a small portion of documented and undocumented migration from Mexico into postwar Texas. Through natural increase and migration, the number of Mexican Texans had surpassed 1 million by 1950 and had approached 4 million by 1990, around one-fourth of the state's people. The combined Tejano and Mexican-born population of South Texas went from 135,000 people in 1910 (37 percent of the region's people) to around 670,000 in 1960 (49 percent) to over 1.7 million by 1990 (71 percent). By 1970, around 79 percent of Mexican Texans had been born in Texas. (The term "Mexican Texans" refers to U.S.-born citizens, naturalized immigrants, and resident aliens of Mexican extraction. The term "Mexican Corpus Christians" is used analogously.) This is compared to around 71 percent of the state's overall population, a figure that reflects the Lone Star State's welcoming reception of millions of Anglo migrants during the Sunbelt era.

This trend toward a relatively U.S.-born Hispanic population was evident in the Coastal Bend, despite the area's proximity to the borderlands and myriad personal connections across the Rio Grande. In 1970, the U.S. Census Bureau recorded around 40 percent of Corpus Christi's municipal population of 204,552 as Spanish-language speakers or as having a Spanish surname. Around 94 percent of the city's Hispanics were listed as born in the United States. Of Corpus Christi Hispanics, 87 percent were natives of Texas, a figure greater than the state's overall proportion of native-born Hispanics. Of the city's total population—Anglo, Hispanic, and black—97 percent were born in the United States, but only 73 percent of the city's total U.S.-born residents were Texas natives, a subset that of course includes migrants from all over the immense state. Around 8.4 percent of the city's population came from the southern states, and around 5.9 percent from the north-central region, with smaller proportions from the Northeast and the West. The large majority of these internal U.S. migrants were non-Hispanic whites. Only 2,142 people, around 1.5 percent, were immigrants from somewhere other than Mexico.[4]

Such figures, rough as they are, reinforce the common view that modern Tejano identity in the Corpus Christi area took shape in the half-century after 1910, when the subdivision of ranchland for commercial agriculture combined with the Mexican Revolution to catalyze rapid expansion of the area's Mexican-derived population. Many Corpus Christi Hispanics, to be sure, can trace branches of their families to ranchers, merchants, and others already in the area before the Anglo grip on the region tightened in the 1870s. But because twentieth-century migrants mainly found work on ranches and farms, huge numbers of people have personal or family memories of the rural dimensions of South Texas development from the 1910s to the 1960s. By 1950, around one-third of employment in South Texas was agricultural labor. That figure represents thousands upon thousands of Tejanos and Mexicans on Anglo-operated cotton farms, frequently as part of the migrant cycle known as the Big Swing. The memory over generations of this experience and of the struggle to improve or escape it pervades the region's historical sensibilities.[5] This background goes far toward explaining the rural references that stamped the outlook of many Mexican American Corpus Christians.

These ties across South Texas and the way people talk about them raise analytical issues related to how people can orient themselves differently in the same city. The concept of a "spatial narrative" describes how people "'mark' or 'inscribe' the space within the impersonal-built environment of the city with meaning," as the historian Timothy Mahoney puts it.[6] In the West and Southwest, a landscape and wilderness consciousness inclines city people in any case to include hinterlands and wilderness in their narratives over space. With regard to Hispanic Corpus Christi, these ties and perceptions seem personal and direct, reinforcing a sense of history that encompasses the South Texas region. In story after story, Mexican Corpus Christians connect their own lives and accomplishments to the harsh working and living conditions and constrained educational opportunities faced by earlier generations in Benavides, Alice, or Three Rivers. As Jimenez observed to this author, this sensibility seemed to fade toward the end of the twentieth century. Still, this region-wide sense of space created a "different outlook" from that common to those living in places like San Antonio, where Mexican American residents were conscious of a "long urban history," the *Caller-Times* columnist and editor concluded.[7]

Personal and family memories of the Nueces region may have exerted a longer, deeper hold upon Hispanic than upon Anglo Corpus Christi. This despite a web of relationships to the South Texas countryside to which Anglo ethnic and religious groups could point. These broad ethnic and religious ties between city and region reinforced the appeal of Texas frontier lore among South Texas Anglos. In other parts of the United States, Irish and Jews counted among the most urban-oriented European immigrant groups. In Corpus Christi, descendents of the Irish Catholic settlers of San Patricio, who remained visible in civic affairs throughout the twentieth century, drew attention to their broad, regional identity. Among Jews, families such as the Weils, Alsatian immigrants who began ranching near Bishop, Texas, in the 1880s, remained influential into the 1970s.[8] German influence was not as pronounced as elsewhere in Texas, but Czech migrants took up farming in areas such as Karnes County, between San Antonio and Corpus Christi. Among British American South Texans, descendents of the pre-1880 pioneer and ranch families exerted an obvious presence in heritage and cultural matters. Midwestern and southern migrants who by the early twentieth century farmed the subdivided ranchlands around Corpus Christi were generally Protestant and Anglo-American in culture, a background that also nurtured durable family connections and regional and small-town identities. The region's bewildering political alliances become more comprehensible when one realizes that small towns around Corpus Christi became centers of evangelical and Pentecostal Protestant movements, Hispanic as well as Anglo.

The Lure of Spanish Heritage

Agricultural development and migration into and around rural South Texas placed an enduring mark upon Corpus Christi's Tejano life and culture. Yet as was the case among Anglo Corpus Christians, until late in the twentieth century the city's Tejanos—at least those active in historical and heritage matters—seemed not drawn to that powerful story as the subject matter for history in an organized sense. People tended to recount these matters as family experiences, although often articulating the implications of such experiences for South Texas ethnic politics. Like Anglos, Corpus Christi Tejanos for a long time seemed preoccupied with events, people, and lore from the nineteenth century and earlier. Why would a generation molded by migrations from Mexico and the struggles of Mexicans and Mexican Americans in South Texas during the twentieth century reach beyond that undeniably significant story to the lore of the Spanish Empire? Like South Texas Anglos, the region's Hispanics enjoyed the romance and adventure associated with exploration and the frontier. But more basic to the answer is the intricate, tense dialogue that evolved between Hispanic and Anglo lore.

Anglo-Texan lore depicts civilization advancing from the east into a receding wilderness in the west. Tejano lore—long an undercurrent, but forcefully asserted in the second half of the twentieth century—envisions a settlement process moving from south to north before being overwhelmed by Anglo aggression and conquest. These two epics compete for the region rather than the city, both because Corpus Christi was an Anglo foundation and long an Anglo stronghold and also because wilderness and frontier imagery pervade historical sensibility throughout southern Texas.

The highlighting of the Spanish and Mexican frontier eras draws attention to the dual geographic location of South Texas among Tejanos. Rooted in Texas and dedicated to their status as Mexican Americans, Tejanos by implication accepted the South Texas that resulted from Anglo colonization, with its U.S.-oriented urban and commercial networks and Rio Grande border. Yet Spanish frontier lore also dissolves the border, situating the Tejano homeland within the Mexico-U.S. borderlands and Spanish America beyond it. That alternate geography predated Anglo South Texas and endured through the harshest periods of subordination.

Sustained Spanish presence near the site of Corpus Christi extends for a century before the arrival of the town's founder, Henry Lawrence Kinney, in the 1830s. Continuous settlement dates from the 1760s. Yet local Hispanics have stretched their heritage as far back as conceivable, to Alonso Álvarez de Pineda. As recounted in the previous chapter, the legend of the Álvarez de Pineda expedition having discovered and named the bay on Corpus Christi Day in June 1519 was given currency by Anglo boosters during the 1920s. The Anglo social elite built rituals around this story—for example, King Alonso, who reigned over the Buccaneer Parade and Ball, or the Order of Pineda, a young women's social group. But by the 1970s, Hispanic Corpus Christians began to assume custodianship of the Pineda story to the point of defending it from doubting historians from both ethnic groups.

Some prominent Corpus Christi Hispanics, such as Oscar Flores, cofounder and longtime president of the Westside Business Association (WBA), which in the 1980s sponsored Pineda Plaza in Westside Corpus Christi, expressed a belief that the explorer was "responsible for our name." In contrast to Anglo tourist and promotional publications, however, Hispanic groups usually refrained from asserting in print that the 1519 naming of the bay was more than a "legend." The WBA used that word in the inscription on the statue of Álvarez de Pineda it erected in Pineda Plaza in 1984, in order to mollify the historian Dan E. Kilgore, who also fought Anglo-promoted manifestations of the story. Though she seems to have been less circumspect in conversation, Clotilde García, sister of the civil rights leader Hector García and an enthusiastic proponent of Spanish heritage, in print labeled the story a "tradition" that is "believed by some historians."[9]

Hispanics who adopted Álvarez de Pineda received encouragement from the most renowned Texas historian living in Corpus Christi. In a 1989 testimonial on behalf of Oscar Flores, Joe B. Frantz, former director of the Texas State Historical Association and holder of the Walter Prescott Webb Chair of History at the University of Texas who had semiretired to the Coastal Bend, affirmed that the explorer "was the first European to see the region, and he gave it the name Corpus Christi, a unique appellation." Frantz knew that the Pineda story was both implausible and irrelevant to Mexican South Texas, whose history for practical purposes began in the mid-1700s, when the bay's name also appears in Spanish records.[10] In his varied work, Frantz displayed an ambivalent attraction to the customary Anglo-Texan epic, and he undermined aspects of the Anglo-Texan story that denigrated Tejanos as less than full Texans. To serve his goal of broadening ownership of Texas history, Frantz was inclined to validate the epic of Hispanic Texas, even at questionable points.

Anglo-American narratives of the Corpus Christi area had long cast Mexicans and Tejanos as supporting characters in the Anglo-Texan saga of settlement and progress. The region's Hispanics appeared as noble rancheros, "wily" banditos, and "childlike" farm or ranch hands stubbornly holding to folklore, traditions, and heedless mores.[11] The city's WPA guide acknowledged tensions documented in the 1930s by the sociologist Paul Schuster Taylor. The Federal Writers' Project nonetheless cheerfully depicted migrant Mexican workers as a "color-ful" aspect of South Texas life, calling the cotton picker "the successor of the Mexican vaquero of yesterday." On Saturdays during harvests, cotton workers, dressed in Stetsons and silk shirts, filled downtown Corpus Christi, spending "lavishly," with "a gay disregard for tomor-row, and a present desire for red coconut candy, strawberry soda, and canned tomatoes." While "upon their labor rests much of the prosper-ity of the region," Mexicans provided the city with an air of romance, since in their music, folklore, foodways, and festivals, "everyone is merry."[12]

Like counterparts from the Gulf Coast to Los Angeles, Mexican Corpus Christians loathed portrayals of themselves as "happy poor people," "quaint but oblivious," to quote one historian of California.[13] Such depictions rankled even when Tejanos perceived moneymaking opportunities in Anglo visitors or residents who came to restaurants, vendors, or shops for supposedly authentic folk-culture experiences. Treatment of Mexicans as local color began to fade from tourist and promotional writing amid the civil rights activism of the 1950s and 1960s. Still, enough lingered that in 1969, Paul Montemayor, a highly regarded Corpus Christi labor organizer, insisted that Tejanos would no longer abide Anglo versions of Texas history in which "the Mexi-cano is pictured as a thing with no culture, no history, no beginning."[14]

The quest for Spanish roots and lore thus amounts to a search—sometimes awkward—for a countermythology, a history extending back beyond Anglo Texas. Among Mexican Americans, efforts to identify with a Spanish past have long stirred argument. Themes of Spanish romance and heritage play into disputes over which aspects of Mexican identity and history in the United States should be em-phasized. Critical writers assert that this search for Spanish heritage amounts to a romance that is unthreatening and marketable to Anglo-Americans; explorers, missionaries, and colonizers appear as precur-sors to and equivalents of Anglo pioneers and ranchers. Spanish heri-tage emphasizes the Spanish dimension of Mexican ethnicity at the expense of indigenous roots. It allegedly diverts attention from the harsh reality of displaced landowners after annexation, of exploitation and violence, of struggling Mexican migrants, farmworkers, urban la-borers, and labor and civil rights activists.[15]

Scholars more sympathetic to Spanish-heritage activity counter that the critics overlook the intellectual atmosphere in which Mexican American consciousness developed in the 1920s–1950s. The grand, even mystical nationalism of the Mexican Revolution animated efforts to assert Mexican ethnic pride across the Southwest. Texas-based groups such as the League of United Latin American Citizens (LULAC), founded in Corpus Christi in 1929, maintained ties with Mexican revolutionary figures such as José Vasconcelos, who in 1928 visited activists in Corpus Christi. In 1925, Vasconcelos had published *La raza cósmica*, which claimed that the mestizo peoples of Latin America were destined to succeed Anglo-Americans as the continent's leading civilization. "We belong to tomorrow," Vasconcelos wrote, while "the Anglo-Saxons are gradually becoming more a part of yesterday." Within this atmosphere, Hispanics who depicted South Texas as an episode in the "Spanish cavalcade" asserted the region's place within Latin American "culture and civilization," as an early LULAC activist noted. The Southwest's relation to Latin civilization had been overshadowed but not negated by the Anglo-American conquest.[16]

Many scholars have noted that the Mexican American generation of the mid-twentieth century shared a civil rights mindset with ethnic and racial minorities across the United States. By this, one means that ethnic Mexicans sought incorporation into U.S. society and recognition as equal citizens. From the start, LULAC insisted that Tejanos embrace U.S. citizenship and act as patriotic Americans, a position that might imply repudiation of their Mexican cultural heritage. But the Mexican American rights movement took shape at a time when pro-immigrant intellectuals and activists were arguing for ethnic heritage as a desirable feature of American identity. In this view, which acquired the label "pluralism," Americanness meant having come from somewhere. By this reasoning, Mexican Americans should be celebrated as another sort of American, like Irish Americans or Italian Americans. Mexican Texans did sometimes hesitate to identify with African, Native, and Asian Americans, groups that seemed to most U.S. whites not to contribute positively to a European-dominated cultural mosaic. Was Spanish heritage, then, a device for signaling that one was another sort of European white? Or did it express rejection of Anglo-American notions of whiteness and an embrace of ethnic and racial intermixture, as Vasconcelos and his followers intended? Given that Anglo-Texan accounts of the state's history confounded Texanness with Anglo-American ethnicity, the insistence that Spanish and Mexican heritage made a person Texan, too, had powerful albeit ambiguous cultural and political implications.[17]

Corpus Christi Hispanics who promoted Spanish-heritage themes did not intend to emphasize the assimilationist and accommodationist implications that later critics deplored. They meant for Spanish heritage to convey precedence and pride. These themes were an example of the "foundation" stories that many ethnic groups deployed in the face of what one historian calls "the Anglo-American myth of foundation," the "notion that the United States was an English country" in culture and politics as well as language. Proponents saw Spanish heritage, the historian Cynthia Orozco explains, as legitimizing the "hybrid identity" that Mexican Americans sought, the possibility of being "both Mexican and American and not purely Mexican or American."[18]

After the 1920s, Corpus Christi figured large in Mexican Texans' politics, business, and culture. Still, the city did not symbolize Tejano historical sensibilities; the region did. Elsewhere in the Southwest, cities did embody the heritage of New Spain and Mexico, though often in confusing ways. Attracted to the romance of the Southwest and also seeing promotional possibilities in a Hispanic regional identity, Anglo-Americans incorporated Spanish and Mexican motifs—sometimes carefully done but often ersatz—in buildings, furnishings, and much else. Hispanics appropriated these motifs for their own agendas.[19] Moreover, in San Antonio, Laredo, Tucson, and other southwestern cities whose founding predates Anglo entry, tangible evidence survived in layouts and buildings of a Spanish and Mexican past. Mexican Americans in those cities could rally around their urban heritage and use urban history to assert legitimacy. Houston is even more manifestly an Anglo-Texan city than Corpus Christi, but the sheer size of its Mexican American population (fourth largest in the country) and the intensity and cosmopolitan character of its cultural and educational institutions invigorated interest in the Mexican American experience there.[20]

By comparison, Corpus Christi did not offer an inviting subject. In appearance, structure, and dynamics, the city embodied the expansion of Anglo-American commerce and power into southern Texas. It was an agent in the displacement of preannexation Mexican society and in the transformation of Mexicans who remained and Mexican migrants who came afterward into a constrained laboring class. Until the 1970s, the city retained an Anglo-American majority in a predominantly Hispanic region.

All this shaped historical activity among Corpus Christi's Mexican American business and professional class. Clotilde García was a leader in the Spanish American Genealogical Association (SAGA), which in the main helped Corpus Christi Hispanics trace their family backgrounds, generally to northern Mexico. But Clotilde García also devoted time and money to publishing documents related to Blas María de la Garza Falcón (1712–1767), who led the Spanish expedition that settled the region in the 1760s. She published a booklet on Enrique Villarreal (1788–1846), from whom Kinney acquired the site. Even though Villarreal founded no town, García labeled him "the first settler, colonizer, and rancher of Corpus Christi." By celebrating the Falcón colony, by placing Corpus Christi Bay in the province of Nuevo Santander (not in Spanish or Mexican Texas), and by noting that Kinney built his town on Villarreal's land, García and her colleagues in effect asserted that the Anglo city rested on Hispanic land, a formidable argument for the legitimacy of the Tejano presence.[21]

This mindset also gave energy to an alternate history of South Texas ranching that underscored the Mexican roots of cowboys, cowboy culture, and ranching methods. The quintessence of western Americana proves to be a Hispanic creation. This is a forceful example of the impulse to reveal the Hispanic foundations of Anglo South Texas, especially because, during these same years, research accumulated on the drawn-out, often unsavory process by which Anglo settlers gained control of Hispanic land grants. The Anglos who put together the King Ranch and the region's other legendary ranching operations adapted a form of business established by Mexicans. To teach them and to do the practical work on their ranches, King and Kleberg relied upon the *Kineños*, whose counterparts continued to work the ranches surrounding Corpus Christi even as cotton workers surpassed ranch hands in number, becoming the stereotyped Mexican labor in the region.[22]

Pineda Plaza represents a distant, even imagined Spanish past, but sponsors located it at a symbolic and strategic point in modern Tejano South Texas. The intersection of Agnes and Laredo Streets is the gateway into Westside Corpus Christi along Texas State Highway 44, which runs westward to Robstown, a stronghold of Hispanic politics and life in the Coastal Bend. In this way, Pineda, or at least his image and legend, became a starting point for a spatial narrative of Hispanic Corpus Christi.

The Westside Business Association, which sponsored the plaza, was formed in 1980 amid a successful fight against a state plan that would have diverted traffic along Highway 44 onto South Padre Island Drive. This plan would have hindered the flow of traffic from Robstown, Alice, and other Hispanic-majority towns into the commercial heart of Mexican Corpus Christi. For decades, Westside business owners had expressed exasperation over the accessibility advantages of Anglo-owned shopping centers on the Southside. The Agnes-Laredo corridor was one of several commercial strips that formed as the Tejano city spread westward from the old Hill enclave in Uptown Corpus Christi. The corridor was the first place encountered by rural and small-town Tejanos driving into the city. As Jimenez remarks, it was "the 'hometown' for many of the city's families," where modern Hispanic Corpus Christi "got started."[23] Pineda Plaza, for example, is adjacent to the site of the former Estrada Motors, for decades the area's leading auto dealership catering to a mainly Hispanic clientele. The owner, E. G. Estrada, invested his profits in banking and media. His dealership served as a venue for early shows of Domingo Peña, for years South Texas's most familiar Tejano radio and television personality.

Pineda Plaza was one of a number of efforts to rejuvenate the area, which had deteriorated by the 1980s. Several blocks to the east along Agnes Street, the WBA worked to develop the Center for Hispanic Arts. This building, opened in 1993, was meant as a community and education center as well as exhibition space. After struggling financially from the start, the center evolved into an arts education facility run by Texas A&M University–Corpus Christi.[24]

Figure 3.1. Pineda Plaza, where Highway 44 splits into Agnes and Laredo Streets, late 1990s. Estrada Motors, in the background, has since given way to an auto body shop. Photo by Mineke Reinders.

The WBA leader Oscar Flores managed King Furniture, four blocks farther east at Agnes and 14th Street. This store, with its cartoon-king logo, shared a building with the Galván Music Store and Ballroom, a landmark of Hispanic South Texas. The furniture store's founders, Angela and Salvador Varela, were associates of the building's developer, Rafael Galván Sr., an entrepreneur who became the city's first Hispanic policeman as well as a political powerbroker. The Galván's son Bobby and the Varelas's daughter, Alicia, who married in 1965, eventually broke down the wall between the businesses they operated jointly.[25]

In the 1990s, the international success and then dreary murder of the singer Selena Quintanilla-Pérez drew attention to Corpus Christi's role in the Tejano recording business. Selena was identified locally with the Molina section, which originated as a *colonia* on the Westside's edge. By the century's last decade, clubs and recording studios for Tejano and other genres of Mexican-Texas music were scattered across the city, reflecting the partial diffusion of Mexican American life from the Westside. Before Hispanic cultural venues began to spread through Corpus Christi, the Galván Ballroom anchored the neighborhood and boasted of being the largest jazz venue in South Texas. Rafael Galván Sr. and his four musician sons were the city's main connection to national popular music. Their jazz band was the ballroom's featured act, but their hall also hosted touring stars such as Tommy Dorsey, who played the opening concert in 1950. Duke Ellington gave a Valentine's Day concert in 1952. The Galván family recalled having trouble finding lodging for Ellington and his band in the segregated city. Ellington played to an Anglo and Hispanic crowd; a second concert for a black audience never materialized. Normally, the ballroom was one of the few places outside the Northside where African Americans could hold social functions. The Galváns played with black musicians, although mainly in Northside clubs such as the Down Beat and the Cotton Club. Jazz, a form of music that embodies the country's convoluted racial interactions, illustrated the complexities of a triracial city that usually imagined itself biracial.

Figure 3.2. The Galván Ballroom, c. 1953, with King Furniture in the background to the right. Courtesy of the Rafael Sr. and Virginia Galván Family Papers, Special Collections and Archives, Bell Library, Texas A&M University–Corpus Christi.

In 1960, the Galváns helped create the Texas Jazz Festival. Later, the brothers branched out into other careers; Eddie Galván gained recognition as a music educator in the public schools and the local state university. Memoirs of Corpus Christi's Mexican American generation regularly allude to the ballroom as a social center. "The Galvan ballroom always had the best of bands," one woman stressed in her memoirs, and the Galván brothers' orchestras were "as professional as any in New York City."[26]

The Galváns' story illustrates the geographic fluidity of Hispanic Corpus Christi. Mexican Corpus Christi became centered on the Westside but was never confined there. In 1982, the municipal government bought the Galván family house, which was not in the Westside but several blocks south of the old Hill barrio. The city moved the Galván house to the north bayfront, where it became a fixture in the preservation site known as Heritage Park. Built in 1908 for an Anglo lawyer's family but purchased by Galván in the early 1940s, the rambling house hosted Senator Lyndon Johnson and Mexican president Lazaro Cardenas during the 1940s–1950s. The house came to reflect the powerbroker status exerted by Galván and his circle of business and civic leaders, which included the Corpus Christi–based organizers of LULAC in 1929.[27]

LULAC, likewise, predated the shift to the Westside. From the start, the group operated on a scale and with a scope larger than any neighborhood. Its founding president, Ben Garza Sr., a Corpus Christi restaurateur and property investor, had roots in the *mutualista* and fraternal society movements that thrived from San Antonio and Corpus Christi to the Rio Grande Valley. In all these places there appeared chapters of the Order of the Sons of America, a rights-oriented fraternal society that became a component of LULAC. LULAC came to embody the integrationist and civil rights agenda identified with the Mexican American middle class, which prompted critics off and on to accuse it of excessive respectability and weak connections to barrio life. In Corpus Christi, however, the group retained strong ties to neighborhood politics and to family and patronage networks.

Through the 1960s–1980s, when the Corpus Christi brothers William, Tony, and Ruben Bonilla all served as national presidents, LULAC's national image as a moderate voice for the civil rights agenda and ethnic pride obscured the rough-and-tumble role these activists played in Corpus Christi and South Texas. In 1983, a reporter noted that the Bonillas, attorneys with diverse business interests, "make no apologies" for ambitiousness, outspokenness, and success, even when success threatened their ties to the Westside. The reporter quoted Tony Bonilla: "Hell, we didn't work our butts off getting through college and law school to live in a shack or drive a team of mules." Tony, LULAC's then president added, "Nobody objects when they see a successful Anglo lawyer living on Ocean Drive." By then, all three owned houses in affluent sections of the Southside. Still, into the 2000s, when Ruben Bonilla exercised considerable power as chair of the Port of Corpus Christi Commission, he and Tony Bonilla ran their law firm at the Bonilla Plaza office and shopping center, at another strategic Westside intersection, Morgan and Port Avenues.[28]

Figure 3.3. The documentary photographer Russell Lee, then living in Austin, accompanied Dr. Hector García around Westside Corpus Christi in April 1949. Among a wide variety of scenes, Lee recorded pit privies in Molina, then a *colonia* outside the city limits. García's credibility within Corpus Christi came partly from his campaigns to improve services and health conditions in such areas. Reprinted by permission, Russell W. Lee Photograph Collection, e_rl_139iief_0007, Dolph Briscoe Center for American History, University of Texas at Austin.

One block west of Bonilla Plaza, at Bright Street and Morgan Avenue, is a nondescript building that embodies the Westside's web of relationships throughout South Texas and across the Southwest. Largely vacant since 1996 and ever-more rundown, the cluttered doctor's office of Hector P. García mirrored García's unadorned, often gruff style. Corpus Christians associated him with this building, though from 1946 to 1966, the years that made his reputation, his office was two blocks west on Morgan. In either place, the medical practice was crowded daily with patients who paid what they could afford, even as García made the office a coordinating point for the Hispanic rights movement. "Amid the squalling infants and the humble elderly," the *Caller-Times* noted in 2004, activists strategized and politicians solicited support, a scene etched in local historical discussions of modern Corpus Christi. "I've never been there when his office wasn't packed," recalled Mayor Mary Rhodes when García retired in March 1996, four months before his death. Responding to the newspaper's call for comments upon the release of a 2002 documentary, a local woman recalled visiting with her father and "hearing conversations of leadership and being frustrated because of the Hispanic community not being equal." García "was a very, very strong person" who inspired her to be a "strong woman in the community."[29]

Funding problems and internal disputes hampered plans by the García family and the American GI Forum—the Hispanic veterans and rights group that García founded in 1948—to remake the office into a museum and education center. The building's "decidedly modest" character was central to García's image as the community's conscience, a figure who earned respect and exerted authority through "the evident selflessness of his conduct, of his life," as Nick Jimenez stressed. Numerous accounts portray him as fiercely dedicated, neglectful of self and family, helpful in countless ways, but given to overwork and bursts of temper. As he was gaining fame in the early 1950s, the novelist Edna Ferber caught this intense idealism in her fictional Dr. Guerra in the best-selling *Giant*. Though he never sought personal wealth, "he died rich because of everything he did for everybody," remarked Josh Hinojosa, a young Corpus Christi businessman who in the 1990s helped organize the García statue and plaza front of the Texas A&M University–Corpus Christi library, which houses the GI

Forum leader's enormous manuscript collection. Hinojosa added that typical patients included "two of my uncles, one with a broken arm and one with a leg, and [García] never charged them anything."[30]

By 2004, García's office was "boarded and covered with graffiti," one admirer lamented, the area "surrounded by junk and high weeds." García himself remained a presence in the city, despite family worries that "nobody knows who Papa is," as his daughter, Cecilia, recalled when the state authorized Hector P. García Day in September 2009. His image appeared on everything from the telephone book to concert announcements. The city's main post office was named for him, as were a park and, fittingly, an indigent clinic at the hospital where he once practiced on a segregated ward.[31]

Such a strong personality casts a large shadow over his contemporaries. García inspired but also depended on the generation of professionals and businesspeople, organizers and activists, who between the 1920s and 1980s constructed the institutional, economic, and political foundations of Mexican American Corpus Christi. Stances, decisions, and actions move the world, but alliances and institution building make stances and actions possible. Likewise, local expressions of pride in García often emphasize honors and renown at the expense of what he did and what made it possible for him to do it. Statements praising him can depict him as a heroic figure headquartered in Corpus Christi more than as an integral figure within it. "We had a Presidential Medal of Freedom winner in our city, in our lifetime, for work transforming the South Texas region," remarked Juan M. García, a lawyer and politician unrelated to the doctor, alluding to Hector García's 1984 award. As an "American civic rights pioneer," Dr. García deserved "a place in the pantheon of such greats as Martin Luther King and Cesar Chavez," the *Caller-Times* editorialized in 2005.[32] As he grew older, García inadvertently fed such tendencies. Like many successful people from humble backgrounds—his father, a schoolteacher in a town in Tamaulipas, came north during the Mexican Revolution and ran a dry-goods store in the Rio Grande Valley—Hector García took much pride in the recognition he eventually received. His biographical files contain curricula vitae from later years that list in detail awards and appointments to national commissions and advisory councils, starting in 1961, when he served on a diplomatic delegation for the John F.

Kennedy administration. The CVs offer a line or two of summary but no explanation of actions during the 1940s and 1950s that led to the appointments and honors in the first place.[33] A biographer might wish that the aging García had been more analytical about how he and Corpus Christi remade each other, but anyone who has framed an award certificate for the living-room wall understands the impulse.

This tendency to emphasize García as a historical figure who lived in Corpus Christi rather than as a manifestation of the place also stems from the approach he adopted to the region's and the city's politics and issues. García was not from this section of South Texas, and he established his practice there after World War II partly by happenstance. Yet he grasped local people's sense of space and regional heritage, the practical and symbolic importance of rural South Texas for Corpus Christi. Though he was an urbane professional with experiences in different parts of the United States and in wartime Europe, he never exhibited impatience with or condescension toward the provincial influences with which South Texas infused Corpus Christi. He did not look down upon the small towns of the Nueces region, nor did he regard them as distinct from the city.

The dramatic actions for which García is most remembered concerned glaring cases of bigotry, abuse, or neglect in small Texas towns. The Felix Longoria incident—the refusal of an Anglo funeral home in 1949 to hold a wake for an army private killed in the last months of World War II, an outrage that García used to draw international attention to the circumstances of Mexican Texans—occurred in Three Rivers, seventy miles to the northwest. He organized the American GI Forum to combat discrimination in Corpus Christi in veterans' health care, benefits, and education, as well as to ameliorate the wretched sanitary conditions and rampant tuberculosis he found in barrios such as Molina. Nevertheless, early fact-finding missions took him to Mathis and Orange Grove, where he documented decrepit labor camps and "unbearable" schools, "not even a poor excuse for institutions of learning." Soon, García and his allies were pressing the U.S. Justice Department to investigate abuses by small-town police forces in Sinton and Skidmore. The Pete Hernández case, which ended in a 1954 U.S. Supreme Court ruling concerning anti-Hispanic discrimination, revolved around a murder among agricultural workers in Jackson County, near

Figure 3.4. This commemorative telephone book, produced not long after Hector García's death in July 1996, stresses the civil rights leader as a statesman recognized by Presidents Lyndon Johnson, John Kennedy, and Ronald Reagan (all on the right). The collage also shows García as a younger man, but no image evokes the relentless activism in the 1940s–1950s on which his reputation was based. Courtesy of the Special Collections and Archives, Bell Library, Texas A&M University–Corpus Christi.

Victoria.[34] García and his GI Forum colleagues thus devised strategies between 1945 and 1960 to fit the regional mindset of South Texas Hispanics. The city was intertwined with the countryside and was a launching point for action in it.

By the 1960s, García's story had melted into the southwestern and national story of Hispanic civil rights. In scholarly studies and popular accounts, the GI Forum and García's initiatives can seem less and less tied to anywhere specific.[35] Yet García remained a character of Corpus Christi and of the Westside. Within his city, García usually preferred negotiation. But when needed, he resorted to confrontation, starting with the treatment of Hispanic veterans but extending to sanitation and services in barrios and *colonias*, segregation, educational opportunity, and representation in politics and the judicial system. Insisting that with political mobilization, local "discrimination and segregation and inequalities will finish," García and the GI Forum organized poll tax drives. Such efforts, along with his own prestige and force of personality, gave him the credibility to press issues with what the biographer Ignacio García called "orderly militancy," a "passionate and demonstrative" but civil style that dramatized the Mexican American goal of inclusion and respect. He "chose his battles very carefully," Jimenez explained, and always gave "the guy on the other side of the table a way to get out." His typical triumph, the journalist added, enabled a hitherto-resistant Anglo authority figure to proclaim, "All we needed was Dr. Hector to bring this to our attention."[36]

When asked, García would lend his voice to Anglo-establishment lobbying efforts, for example, concerning local military bases. The result of such an approach—along with myriad practical favors he arranged for people on the Westside—was a kind of political machine based not on the influence peddling of the stereotyped boss, but on his own credibility and reputation. A generation of Hispanic politicians first ran for office based on his encouragement, and Anglo politicians who sought Hispanic votes visited his clinic before announcing their candidacies. Upon his death in 1996, a former mayor recalled him as an "expert" negotiator, "very aggressive" but not alienating: "He worked very hard to make sure that people he trusted were appointed to our boards and committees." García's presence and persistence made him, as one scholar told the *Caller-Times* in 2000, "unquestionably the [area's] single most important figure, as an agent of change for Hispanics."[37] This was true even though nearly every dramatic event emphasized to date in his biographies happened somewhere *other than* Westside Corpus Christi.

"Education Is Our Freedom"

The American GI Forum's slogan, "Education Is Our Freedom," expressed the link made by the Mexican American movement between civil rights, equality, opportunity, and education. García's documentation of wretched conditions in segregated schools in small South Texas towns was crucial in building Hispanic support for his movement. In Corpus Christi, he put his prestige and political connections behind legal actions and protests related to education. These efforts included a 1971 incident in which he was arrested along with seventeen young Hispanics during a sit-in at the Corpus Christi Independent School District (CCISD) headquarters.[38]

The context of García's arrest was Anglo resistance to a 1970 federal court ruling in the *Cisneros* case, the best-known Corpus Christi–originated episode in the national Hispanic rights movement. (That is, as opposed to Corpus Christi-based groups using incidents in small Texas towns to call attention to conditions across the region—the pattern outlined above.) The case, which led to federal court oversight of CCISD schools that lasted into the 1990s and that produced numerous judicial precedents, illustrates the broad appeal of the rights-and-opportunity agenda in Corpus Christi. Observers have sometimes identified this agenda with the Mexican American middle class, but in Corpus Christi it drew together a variety of groups across different areas of the city.

In 1968, relying on legal help from the Mexican American Legal Defense Fund (MALDEF), Jose Cisneros, appalled by his children's stories of "broken windows and dirty bathrooms" at their school, put his name first among twenty-five Mexican and African American plaintiffs. The plaintiffs were mostly members of the United Steelworkers union connected to the Port of Corpus Christi's Reynolds Aluminum plant.[39] The USW workers acted with encouragement from the local union leader Manuel Narvaez and from Paul Montemayor. A onetime

Corpus Christi taxi driver, Montemayor became an organizer for the national USW and national director of the Labor Council for Latin American Advancement (LCLAA). For a time, he was the highest-ranking Mexican American in the AFL-CIO.

Montemayor, who died in 1978 at age sixty, embodied the role of the port and its industrial working class in the transformation of Hispanic Corpus Christi. Unions such as the USW fought for opportunities at the port, whose firms had blatantly confined Hispanics to low-level or dangerous occupations. Under the leadership of Montemayor, Narvaez, and their colleague Mike Zepeda, the USW also pushed civil rights and equal education in a way that dovetailed with the agenda of Hector García and his colleagues and with commercial-civic groups such as the WBA, which included LCLAA officials among its leaders. Alliances and friendships between labor leaders and civic, business, and professional figures were common in civil-rights-oriented ethnic campaigns around the country.

Montemayor had the ability to persuade people to "stand out," as Nick Jimenez recalled, "a hard thing to do for Hispanics of that age." For Montemayor, class, ethnic, and neighborhood solidarity were interdependent. He once publicly chastised William Bonilla, a former LULAC national president, for moving to Ocean Drive: "You are a Mexican making money and living in an Anglo neighborhood." Shortly before his death, Montemayor worried to a reporter that success itself challenged the working-class neighborhood politics he felt essential: "Most of our members [now] make 20 to 40,000 a year, and they move over to the Anglo neighborhoods." Indeed, by the 1980s, five of the eight Hispanics still listed—along with two African Americans—as plaintiffs in the *Cisneros* case lived outside the customary boundaries of the Westside.[40]

In keeping with the centrality of education to their agenda, Mexican Corpus Christians pushed strenuously for schools to be named after local Hispanic figures. Such proposals targeted schools throughout the city, not just on the Westside. CCISD did name an elementary school after the Texas Revolution hero Lorenzo de Zavala, alongside the district's David Crockett and Sam Houston schools. Mexican American Corpus Christians sought this honor for more recent characters too. As early as 1951, Corpus Christi named a Westside school after

Vicente Lozano, a merchant and patriarch of a prominent commercial-civic family. In 1967, a year before the filing of the *Cisneros* case, the district named a Westside school for Dr. José Antonio García, whose practice in Corpus Christi preceded that of his famed younger brother and who in 1940 became the first Hispanic elected to the school board. When, in 1990, a group of Corpus Christians persuaded CCISD to name a Southside school after the civic leader and ballroom operator Rafael Galván, they presented a long list of relatives who had studied or taught in the district. The family's success, the dedication ceremony program noted, proved "that pride can be found in knowing that you have served your country well, that the best gift each parent can give a child is a good education."[41]

In 1999, a public campaign persuaded CCISD to name a new school on the Southside after Corpus Christi's most significant twentieth-century Hispanic educators, the linguist E. E. Mireles and his wife, the folklorist Jovita González Mireles. In 1941, E. E. Mireles, a Chihuahua native who, like Hector García's family, came to Texas during the Mexican Revolution, organized a successful effort to repeal state restrictions dating to World War I on teaching foreign languages in public schools. Mireles then mounted an attack on South Texas's suppression of Spanish. He devised Spanish and bilingual programs for preschool and elementary children and for adults, precedents that contributed to the national bilingual movement. The national press took notice in 1944, when *Time* magazine profiled Mireles, who symbolically kept Shakespeare and Cervantes together on this desk and who believed "that in time his bilingual children will lead their adults a long way toward inter-American understanding."[42]

Jovita, from a preannexation Tejano family, was a Spanish teacher as well as a writer of fiction and poetry and a scholar of Tejano folklore, a protégé of the University of Texas folklorist J. Frank Dobie. Jovita became widely known in Corpus Christi through educational efforts concerning Mexican cuisine, customs, and folklore.[43] Together, the Mireleses wrote textbooks based on their experiments in grade-school Spanish instruction. In arguing that a school should be named for the Mireleses over other worthy residents, the columnist Nick Jimenez emphasized their dedication to multilingualism as a "liberating act" and "a bridge to international understanding." Like Lozano, J. A.

García, and Galván, the Mireleses called attention to the modern city and the ways that Hispanics have shaped it. Naming public places after people like the Mireleses, Jimenez remarked, "has nothing to do with fairness"; instead, such commemoration "can give us fuller understanding of the history behind us all."[44]

The Mexican American, rights-and-pride tendency represented by LULAC, the GI Forum, the *Cisneros* case, and LCLAA exerts such a powerful presence in Corpus Christi that it can obscure competing lines of thought and activity. The ethnic nationalism identified with the Chicano movement, for example, also had deep roots in the region. Starting in the 1960s, activists with a Chicano perspective engaged in a dialogue, sometimes tense and competitive, with civil-rights-minded groups. As elsewhere, Mexican American–style leaders bristled at the Chicano charge that they were assimilationist and self-serving. Even so, groups such as LULAC under the Bonillas absorbed some of the concerns and style of the Chicanos. After the mid-1970s, moreover, Chicano activists combined their original, confrontational style of protest with nuts-and-bolts political mobilization and community organization. In elected and appointed offices, the beneficiaries were usually Hispanic professionals and businesspeople with moderate reputations, San Antonio mayor Henry Cisneros being the archetype.[45] In Corpus Christi by the 1980s, the Chicano emphasis on inclusion and cultural autonomy had taken its place among the streams feeding Hispanic politics alongside the older rights-and-pride activism.

In the Corpus Christi region, *Chicanismo* evokes a small-town-oriented spatial understanding that parallels the overall regional understanding among Mexican Americans. *Chicanismo*'s intellectual roots appear in places like the former Texas A&I University, renamed Texas A&M University–Kingsville, as well as in San Antonio. Chicano activism thrived in satellite cities such as Robstown. The Chicano movement's political expression, La Raza Unida Party, developed from political campaigns in Crystal City, Cotulla, and Carrizo Springs.

Raza Unida's public face was a Corpus Christian. The charismatic young attorney Ramsey Muñiz, a onetime football star at CCISD's Miller High School, was working as an antipoverty activist in Waco in the early 1970s when he emerged as the central figure in the Chicano attempt to build a statewide grassroots party. Having overcome a difficult background, Muñiz expressed the struggles and hopes of Tejanos, especially the young, with clarity and force. When he gained 214,000 votes in the 1972 gubernatorial election on a third-party ticket, his potential seemed enormous. As Raza Unida faded as a separate party in the mid-1970s, colleagues worried about Muñiz's self-discipline, concerns that proved justified in 1976 when he skipped bail to Mexico after a drug-trafficking arrest, the start of a spiral that ended in 1994 with a prison term of life for multiple drug convictions. In Corpus Christi, Muñiz's descent became an allegory for the Chicano years: expansive ideals followed by crushing and at times tawdry disappointments.[46]

"Much More Urbanized than the Mexicans"

The United Steelworkers emphasized the *Cisneros* plaintiffs as an interracial coalition of parents who would no longer tolerate schools that "shortchang[ed] their children" and who were determined to fight a school district bent on "keep[ing] Mexican-American [*sic*] and Blacks in their own place."[47] The labor union repeatedly called attention to its alliance building between Hispanics and blacks. Such episodes of cooperation—along with episodes of interethnic tension—figure prominently in the politics and social history of southwestern and Texas cities that residents understood as comprising three or more major racial groups: Los Angeles, Phoenix, Dallas–Fort Worth, and Houston. In Corpus Christi, however, relations between Tejanos and African Americans come to the fore only sporadically. This was in part because the epic of Anglo-Hispanic conflict has overwhelmed other stories. Also, blacks' typical experiences did not fit readily into South Texas's frontier, ranch, and small town heritage.

During the twentieth century, the black percentage of Corpus Christi's population hovered around 5 percent, slightly less if one includes the metropolitan area, since around 90 percent of black residents of the Coastal Bend live in the city. This added up to about 10,500 people by 1970, rising to around 13,000 people by 2000, a town's worth of people within a medium-sized metropolis. In San Antonio, the black population remained around 7 or 8 percent during the second half of the twentieth century. But because San Antonio has over four times the population of Corpus Christi, a fairly small percentage still means a substantial number of people. San Antonio's African American East Side has thus exerted a large presence in the city's history, politics, and heritage. That and the fact that ethnic divisions among Euro-Americans had a more manifest role in San Antonio's politics and life has meant that the South Texas binary of Anglo and Hispanic dominates San Antonio history less than it does Corpus Christi's.

By contrast, the Coastal Bend's remoteness before the 1870s and its ranching orientation meant that slavery did not become rooted there; the 1860 census counted 216 slaves and 1 free black in Nueces County, about 7.5 percent of the population. Around the turn of the century, cotton farmers on subdivided ranchland attempted to recruit black as well as Mexican agricultural labor, but with mixed success. In the 1930s, the sociologist Paul Schuster Taylor noted that blacks in Nueces County were "much more urbanized than the Mexicans, both as to residence and as to occupation." Taylor correctly guessed that growth of the port would reinforce this trend. In outlying towns, black workers tended to be found at the cotton gins, cottonseed oil mills, and grain elevators of large operations such as the Coleman-Fulton Pasture Company. Taylor reported that while blacks might account for as much as 20 percent of migrant farm labor, resident agricultural labor was more on the level of 97 percent Mexican and 3 percent black. Some blacks acquired small farms or worked as ranch hands, as they did throughout the Southwest. But in the Corpus Christi area, blacks were generally town workers: "stevedores, carpenters, cooks, or domestic workers," as Taylor summarized.[48]

The black experience thus stood as a town-oriented counterpoint to the ranch-and-farm perspective of every other group. As a percentage, black population peaked before World War I: 9.8 percent in 1900, 460 people out of 4,700 total. Like blacks in other small cities in that period, men made their livings as draymen and laborers, both skilled and unskilled; women worked as domestic servants, cooks, and seamstresses.[49]

In accounts of African American Corpus Christi, the person who usually appears as the founder was a remarkable character whose education, professionalism, and urbanity make him a marked contrast to frontier figures such as Henry Lawrence Kinney. Born a slave in Virginia in 1844, Solomon Coles learned to read as a teenager and took advantage of postemancipation educational opportunities, becoming in 1872 the first black student admitted to Yale Divinity School. Graduating in 1875, Coles accepted an offer in 1877 from the American Missionary Association to minister to a small black Congregational church in distant Corpus Christi. Coles threw himself into educational matters, resigning his ministry in 1880 to become principal of the city's first school for African Americans. Even after Coles moved to a similar position in San Antonio in 1894, he remained a paragon for black Corpus Christians. Local accounts recall him as determined and encouraging, but a disciplinarian of whom misbehaving students were "mortally afraid." In 1925, a year after Coles's death, the school district named the new black high school on the Northside after him. Even after school desegregation in the 1960s, Northside residents identified with the Coles building, which was converted into a neighborhood elementary school in 1973. In a physically isolated neighborhood, the Coles School served as anchor, community center, and symbol. In 2005, residents sued to block its closure as part of a consolidation plan, eventually settling with CCISD for the school's conversion into an alternative high school and training and community center.[50]

As befit a population that was urban in experience and aspirations, symbolic personalities of twentieth-century black Corpus Christi continued Coles's model of the educated professional devoted to civic improvement. Among the best-known organizers of desegregation campaigns in the 1950s and 1960s were Drs. W. Boyd Hall, a dentist and president of the local NAACP, and H. J. Williams, a physician. In 1971, their colleague Harold Branch, pastor of St. John Baptist Church, became the first African American elected to the city council in the twentieth century. In 1994, CCISD named a Southside middle school after another local civil rights activist, Elliot Grant, pastor of St. Matthew Baptist Church, which, like the Coles School, served as an institutional anchor of the old Northside. In 1984, Grant became CCISD's first black school board president. These four men organized efforts to enable blacks to disperse beyond the Northside, first into Hillcrest, the formerly white middle-class enclave south of the port, and then into subdivisions on the Southside, some specifically developed for blacks. In the 1950s, Hall built a house on Ocean Drive, the first black homeowner on the city's most exclusive street.

The breakdown of strict residential segregation had dramatic effects on the Northside, whose black population fell from 4,305 in 1960 to 2,610 in 1990. This downward trend probably would have appeared even if Interstate 37 and the approaches to the Harbor Bridge had not isolated the area further during the 1950s–1960s. About one-fifth of Corpus Christi's African Americans still lived there in the late twentieth century, and they had an average family income below the federal poverty rate. The Reverend Branch pushed hard for housing opportunities for African Americans, and his own congregation moved in the 1960s from the Northside to a specially developed African American subdivision on the Southside. Branch continued to live in the Northside, despite the plummeting value of his house and the realization, as he put it, that "those who can get out economically are doing so." The Northside was especially vulnerable to odors and potential contamination from the port's chemical plants. As new investment was stymied by litigation over industrial pollution and by the area's reputation, Branch lamented in 1998 that there was "nothing to do but sit and wait for [the community's] slow death."[51] The Northside's institutional cohesiveness and community identity meant that its dissolution evoked regret, despite the neighborhood having been established largely as the result of restriction, oppression, and poverty.

Founded in 1874, St. Matthew Baptist Church remained on the Northside at the end of the twentieth century, along with two other venerable African American congregations: St. Paul United Methodist and Holy Cross Catholic. All struggled with membership: St. Matthew dwindled to 500 congregants from a high point of 1,500, while St. John Baptist, which had moved to the Southside, was gaining members. The small size of the city's black population and the Northside's confined area, ministers recalled, encouraged interdenominational cooperation, enhancing the churches' reputations as focal points of the city's black life. Even as established churches sought to adapt to the neighborhood's economic decline, area residents were drawn to small evangelical or missionary churches, such as God's Street Ministry, which held services in an old liquor store. The congregation's minister,

Frances Houston, told the *Caller-Times* in 1998, "The other churches wouldn't touch the people we deal with here."[52]

In a neighborhood isolated from the start by transportation routes—first railroads and then Interstate 37—residents expressed dismay over planning for the new Harbor Bridge. The two most discussed approach routes would isolate the Northside further, with one cutting a corner from the property of St. Paul Church. One member, resigned to the church falling victim to the bridge, remarked, "But Jonah was released from the whale's mouth, too."[53]

Ethnic Commemoration and the Visual City

When Corpus Christi sought to commemorate its ethnic heritage, it tended to do so in the central city rather than in the scattered and, in the case of the Northside, threatened neighborhoods where ethnic life had taken place. Starting in the 1980s, as chapter 5 details, the city did this in a blunt way by moving historic houses associated with different ethnicities to Heritage Park in the cultural zone toward the north end of the Corpus Christi Bayfront.

By the 1980s and 1990s, public institutions, civic and commercial organizations, and residents assumed that buildings, sites, and exhibits ought to highlight the city's Hispanic heritage and ties to Mexico. The city, to be sure, featured massive evidence of its place within Tejano South Texas and the Mexico-U.S. borderlands. Storefronts, signs, the painting and decoration of houses, gardens, murals, and innumerable other everyday elements—especially on the Westside, but in different ways throughout the city—marked Corpus Christi as vibrantly Tejano.[54] But vernacular architecture and popular decoration do not fulfill conventional notions of style. The Westside was an unmitigated manifestation of the gritty, resourceful Tejano present. The apparent ordinariness and practicality of most of the Westside inhibited people from appreciating it as a historical area worth documenting and protecting.

The central city required retrofitting if it were to project the Mexican presence in something resembling due proportion. Since the city's founding, Tejanos had lived, worked, and run businesses throughout the central city, but few sites survived to dramatize that. The Hill barrio was in Uptown near Leopard and Waco. As Hispanics moved westward beyond Staples Street after World War II, the Hill area decayed, so much so that by the 1970s–1980s it offered swaths of cheap land for a new courthouse and city hall surrounded by parking lots. In the early 1980s, a preservation survey commissioned by Nueces County found only three significant structures remaining in the old barrio. One of these, the Grande-Grossman House, was moved to Heritage Park in 1982, the same year as the Galván's home, whose original location, as discussed earlier, was slightly outside the old barrio. The Grande-Grossman House, built in 1904 and identified with a family that ran a popular cantina in the late 1800s, evoked Hispanic life before the digging of the deepwater port. In Heritage Park, it served initially as local headquarters for LULAC. The so-called French-Galván House, renovated into a multicultural center and exhibition space, symbolized the mid-twentieth-century Mexican American movement and the growth of Hispanic influence in politics, culture, education, and the professions.

That these two houses needed to be moved if they were to be reused illustrated the difficulty of remaking central Corpus Christi so that it would appear and feel Hispanic as well as Anglo. The 1982 preservation study lamented that the Uptown "Spanish Colony" had been "lost" to "road and highway improvements" and in general to the CBD's "gradual redevelopment and rebuilding." Without such a neighborhood, the central city's visual and historical associations remained overwhelmingly Anglo-American. The study reported that few downtown buildings revealed the early twentieth-century fashion for Mission or Spanish Revival architecture.[55] Architects and builders had used such regionalist styles for residences on the Southside. But in the central city over most of the twentieth century, Anglo Corpus Christians reached for European or standard American styles for civic and commercial buildings in order to project urbanity and sophistication.

When Corpus Christians began to seek a more Hispanic image for their city, they approached this task as other southwestern cities did. Sometimes they reached for styles and motifs that looked stereotypically Mexican, sometimes they carefully adapted Mexican or Latin American design practices to the project at hand, and sometimes they mixed stereotype and study. This held for both Tejanos and Anglos.

Hispanic developers and civic groups, whether operating on the West-side or elsewhere in the city, sometimes systematically incorporated Mexican forms, materials, colors, and so on. Other times they appropriated elements of Spanish Colonial or Mission Revival styles, not visually different from what Anglos did when they had the same goal. In any case, starting especially in the 1970s, efforts to use Spanish, Mexican, and Latin American elements to balance the prevailing Anglo-American atmosphere became evident in central Corpus Christi as well as in residential neighborhoods and shopping and office centers. More and more structures featured round arches, light-colored stucco walls, red tile roofs, and colorful tile work.

Some such projects—for example, the miradors that the philanthropist Dusty Durrill sponsored atop the Corpus Christi seawall in the 1990s—created juxtapositions between Spanish romance and modernist civil engineering. A few Anglo-Mexican juxtapositions

Figure 3.5. Museum officials planned the 2006 Legorreta + Legorreta addition (*left*) to Philip Johnson's acclaimed 1972 Art Museum of South Texas (*right*) as a sophisticated example of a meeting between Mexican and Anglo-American forms. The landscape architect Robert Zion's water garden is in the foreground. Author photo, 2011.

were planned with exquisite care, above all the addition completed in 2006 by the Mexican architectural firm Legorreta + Legorreta to Corpus Christi's most noteworthy building in an architectural sense, Philip Johnson's 1972 Art Museum of South Texas. Other late twentieth-century public buildings in southwestern or Latin American styles included La Retama Public Library in Uptown, opened in 1986, and the new federal courthouse along Shoreline Boulevard, completed in 2001. In 1988, when the city leased a former city hall annex on Shoreline Boulevard for use as the Art Center of Corpus Christi, the community group involved renovated the building in a Spanish Colonial style, with a pale yellow facade, a courtyard, and a tile roof. The center maintained this theme during an expansion in the 2000s, which was largely underwritten by the Durrill Foundation.[56]

Ambiguities and tensions permeated these efforts to retrofit downtown to account for Hispanics' role in the city's history and life. The fundamental tension arose over the audience and constituency for such a reshaped image. Was the goal mainly local, to provide symbolic support for a more inclusive city? Or was the goal to foster a marketable, regionalist ambiance? Although a latecomer to the Spanish-heritage enterprise, Corpus Christi's experience paralleled San Antonio's and Santa Fe's. In those cities and many other places, Anglo establishments had long used Spanish motifs in architecture, design, and culture to infuse their environment with a dash of romance and exoticism and to promote the tourist and convention trade. And as in Corpus Christi, groups of Hispanics in other southwestern cities identified with imperial Spanish imagery as a form of regional lore that they could use to assert ethnic pride, even as critics deplored Spanish heritage as an accommodation to Anglo-American preconceptions of intrepid Spaniards and mundane Mexicans. Questions of trust exacerbated this confusion of purpose. To the end of the twentieth century, Mexican Corpus Christians regularly expressed the suspicion that the Anglo establishment still assumed its own greater competence, even in projects whose purpose was recognition of the Hispanic presence. Hispanic civic leaders worried that their Anglo counterparts would find ways to assert control, impose their preconceptions on such projects, and create a muddle through incomprehension.

This gnarled cultural politics was bound up with straightforward questions of money. Even in cities less economically troubled than Corpus Christi, political, civic, and business leaders find it hard to make a consistent case that historical sites and cultural amenities should be fiscal priorities. Municipal officials cast about for public-private partnerships, foundations, investors, and other ways to make culture and history pay more of their own bills. Local governments push the cost of heritage and culture onto tourists through hotel and sales taxes and entrance fees. This in turn rechannels the priorities of city managers and planners, historical commissions, and site and museum administrators in ways they would not have welcomed had the revised priorities been anticipated from the start.

"The Citizenry's Pride in Its Hispanic Past"

The most agonizing episode in this convoluted politics of ethnic commemoration involved a set of borrowed reconstructions of long-destroyed artifacts lacking any concrete connection with Corpus Christi and South Texas. This was fitting, since Corpus Christi had no pre–Texas Revolution structures or places—no missions, presidios, courtyards, or plazas—with a direct, powerful association with the Spanish or Mexican past. For two decades starting in the 1990s, Spanish-built replicas of Christopher Columbus's 1492 fleet, the most generic representation imaginable of the Spanish presence in the Americas, carried the burden of dramatizing the Hispanic role in Corpus Christi.

The quincentenary in 1992 of Columbus's first voyage revealed the extent to which historical consciousness had transformed in many countries over the past decades. Attentiveness to the disease, destruction, and conquest that Columbus set in motion made it no longer possible to celebrate the explorer unabashedly. The Spanish government, on the other hand, used the event to attract positive attention. Among its activities, the Spanish commissioned reconstructions of the *Niña*, *Pinta*, and *Santa Maria*, meticulously researched and magnificently crafted at a cost of over $6.5 million. After visits to European ports, the Spanish sent *las carabelas* under sail across the Atlantic, where they toured North American ports in conjunction with an estimated 1,500 quincentenary events held throughout the United States. In March 1992, during a ten-day stay in Corpus Christi, Texas's official quincentenary city, the fleet drew an estimated 106,000 people, its largest U.S. crowds. This reception, along with enthusiastic lobbying, convinced Spanish authorities that "the citizenry's pride in its Hispanic past" qualified Corpus Christi as a long-term home for the replicas. The Washington-based Spain '92 Foundation spurned more lucrative offers and accepted $1.6 million to lend the fleet to Corpus Christi.[57]

The Columbus Fleet Association, a Corpus Christi group, promised to pay the Spanish and maintain the ships. Early plans called for the ships to be moored along Corpus Christi Beach between the aircraft carrier USS *Lexington* and the Texas State Aquarium. Partly for fear of storms, the association moored them instead at Cargo Dock One in the ship channel beyond the Harbor Bridge, outside normal tourist routes. There, in April 1994, an ocean barge plowed into the *Pinta*, which rammed the *Santa Maria*. The two ships suffered over $1.5 million in damage. Before the collision, conflicts between the Corpus Christi group and Spain's representatives had already led the head of the Spain '92 Foundation to threaten to repossess the ships. The Spanish perceived the fleet association as being in disarray. The association in turn demanded the replacement of a Spanish liaison who publicly expressed "doubts that [the ships] would ever be properly managed under our auspices." The Washington-based Spanish lawyer responsible for the ships communicated worries over inadequate maintenance, unclear authority, and a failure fully to incorporate the fleet "into the overall tourism industry of Corpus Christi." Even before the barge collision, attendance had fallen tens of thousands of people, and revenue hundreds of thousands of dollars, below projections.[58]

All the while, Hispanic groups expressed consternation that a "power struggle" within the fleet association had diverted *las carabelas* from their "future" as "a historical, cultural and economic joint venture with tremendous potential among Spain and the United States," in the words of Fernando Iglesias, a Spanish-born Corpus Christi businessman prominent in the campaign to secure the ships. The enthusiastic involvement of LULAC, SAGA, and the WBA in South Texas's quincentenary celebration was a major reason that the Spanish assumed that the replicas would succeed in Corpus Christi. Of eighteen members of the 1992 Quincentenary Commission, eleven, including Iglesias, were Hispanic. But of twenty-five members of the initial board of directors of the Columbus Fleet Association formed in 1993, seven had Hispanic surnames. Including Iglesias and Janet Rice, chair of the Quincentenary Commission, only four members of the 1992 commission continued as directors of the Columbus Fleet Association. At the time of the 1994 barge collision, ten of thirty-two board members were Hispanic.

This discontinuity arose largely from the need—once the goal became to make the ships a permanent exhibit—to involve the Greater Corpus Christi Business Alliance and the city government, represented by Rick Stryker, director of the city-run Corpus Christi Museum of Science and History. Still, a sense that downtown establishment figures had displaced the project's initiators lay behind some of the divisiveness that disconcerted Spain's representatives. In April 1993, as negotiations for the ships verged on success, unease over "the great danger of ill-feeling when some are given more credit than others" prompted Rice to prepare memoranda for the fleet association chair, William H. Crook, director of the VISTA (Volunteers in Service to America) program and later an ambassador during Lyndon Johnson's administration, that detailed events and participating groups back to 1987, when state senator Carlos Truan had arranged the invitation for *las carabelas*. Rice wanted Crook to be "fully informed of the effort and the participation that went into that great event which so united our city and strengthened our ties to Spain." Rice eventually left the fleet association board, persuaded that it had undermined the goodwill established between the Quincentenary Commission and the Spanish.[59]

Fearful of "municipal embarrassment" should the Spanish make good on their repossession threat, city officials and the business alliance devised a bailout package that included $2.9 million for a dry dock connected to the Corpus Christi Museum of Science and History, where people could tour the damaged *Pinta* and *Santa Maria*; the *Niña* would remain in the bay. The shipwrights' repair work, it was hoped, would both attract visitors and offer a history lesson. At the city's acquisition of the ships in 1993, Mayor Mary Rhodes lauded them as having symbolic value that went "way beyond any kind of monetary tag." A year later, the city wavered on guaranteeing its own bailout.

The city council instead assigned the bonds for the bailout package to the city's hotel-motel tax, meaning they would have the potential to drain as much as 12 percent of the Convention and Visitors Bureau budget, should attendance continue to fall short of projections. The city could not allow the Columbus fleet to "be a big failure," Mayor Rhodes explained, "because the next time we go out and bid, it will be thrown in our face."[60]

Meanwhile, starting in 1990, when it opened an exhibition of artifacts from the famed 1554 Spanish shipwreck off Padre Island, the Corpus Christi Museum of Science and History had shifted its emphasis toward Spanish-colonial exhibits with tourist potential. A product of the junior museum movement of the mid-twentieth century, the museum was built in the 1960s as a locally oriented municipal agency with close ties to the public schools, and for decades, it charged no admission fees. Around the time when the city lobbied the Spanish for the Columbus ships, the museum acquired *Seeds of Change*, a Smithsonian exhibition on the environmental and agricultural dimensions of the Columbian Encounter. Despite qualms over such a shift away from its educational and local-service mission, the museum wove the three exhibitions—the shipwreck, the ships, and the *Seeds of Change*—into a "World of Discovery" display that opened in May 1995. "In one visit," the curator Don Zuris told the *Caller-Times*, "a visitor can see the whole effect of 500 years of European contact."[61]

The city tried to keep the Columbus fleet and its debts separate from the museum and its finances. The museum raised its admission from a nominal $3, implemented in 1990, to $7 and then to $8 for adults, a prohibitive amount for many Corpus Christi families. The bulk of these added fees went to the fleet association, which operated as a sort of subcontractor or lessee within the museum. The arrangement had turned "a potentially catastrophic situation" into "a world-class attraction," the association's new director remarked hopefully in May 1995. Attendance at the museum jumped by 13 percent but soon stagnated. This drop happened despite determined promotion, including a ten-week truck tour by the *Niña* around Texas, a trip deplored by Spanish officials as potentially damaging to the only one of the three ships still seaworthy. The Spanish further complained that the fleet association had diverted the insurance settlement from the barge accident to operating expenses and debts. On top of all that, the Spanish insisted, the *Santa Maria* and the *Pinta* could have been repaired in the water. This implied that the $2.9 million dry dock had been a waste from the start. Worse, it had subjected the ships to dry rot and termites. When, in July 1997, an arbitrator ruled that the fleet was entitled only to $1.7 million in insurance compensation for the accident, not the $2.2 million–$2.3 million it had sought, the spiral into bankruptcy became uncontrollable. Right after Columbus Day in 1999, the museum closed access to the ships and rolled its entry fee back to $5.[62]

The *Caller-Times* expected Spain to "send the repo man to reclaim the *barcos*."[63] In January 2000, Dusty Durrill intervened by filing a lien that in effect seized the ships as collateral for a $1 million loan that he had guaranteed seven years earlier as part of the arrangement to acquire the fleet. Durrill now found himself in a thankless position, a target of criticism for his involvement in decisions in the mid-1990s that contributed to the impasse at decade's end. In addition to his loan guarantee, Durrill had advanced hundreds of thousands from his foundation to bring the ships and keep them running. As fleet association chair in the aftermath of the April 1994 barge accident, Durrill had helped arrange the bailout that included the dry dock. Durrill responded to Spanish and local criticism by recalling the fleet association's struggle to find a contractor willing to repair the ships in the manner that the Spanish advised: "We sent out 102 bids and got back three—nobody wanted to work on wooden ships." To a *New Yorker* reporter, Durrill insisted that he and others saw the fleet at the time as "a major visible flag-flyer for our tourism industry." "The Columbus ships were a perfect way to tell" the story of Spain and the Americas, he added. "And why not in Corpus Christi?"[64]

The *New Yorker* cited an unnamed "Hispanic leader" who labeled Durrill's approach a "well-meaning" throwback to the days of the Anglo "*patron*."[65] Ethnic politics played a huge role in the decision to pursue the Columbus fleet, in dubious measures taken to retain them, and in bickering over their management. Still, the *New Yorker* erred in depicting Durrill as representative of old patterns of condescension. In the risks he took to bring the ships to the city and keep them there, he acted in line with his long-standing cooperation with Hispanic civic groups on heritage projects. The fundamental miscalculation was the notion that the ships would provide Corpus Christi "a particularly dramatic link to its own heritage," a notion shared across ethnic lines.[66] Corpus Christi's ties to imperial Spain are too abstract to ensure that Mexican American identity would rally around replicas of Columbus's ships, no matter how exquisitely crafted.

Spanish Embassy attorneys sued to have the liens removed, but Durrill staved off repossession long enough for the city government to work out a new bailout package. The Columbus exhibition reopened in May 2001. The city would draw on the hotel-motel tax for the bonds for the exhibition plaza and dry dock in a manner that was supposed to free up more money for the ships. A $3 supplement tacked back onto the museum's admission price would cover insurance and maintenance, which the city would henceforth oversee. This deepened a relationship with which the museum's staff had never been comfortable. Stryker, a professional curator with experience in Michigan and Delaware before coming to Corpus Christi in 1985, had expressed concern from the start that his role as the city's voice in the fleet association would conflict with his responsibilities to the museum. Indeed, the ships' supporters accused Stryker of looking out for the museum, to their detriment. "I've been in the museum business for 25 years," Stryker remarked in 2000, "and I've never had people hate my guts so" as they did over the dry dock fiasco.[67]

The conjuncture of the Columbus fleet, Seeds of Change, the 1554 shipwreck exhibit, and other artifacts had the potential to elevate the Corpus Christi Museum into a regional center for Spanish-era archaeology and history, an impressive purpose, though quite removed from the original rationale in the 1960s for a municipal museum. After recovering briefly once the ships reopened in 2001, museum attendance resumed its decline; over 108,000 people visited in 1998 but fewer than 60,000 in 2004.[68] The museum continued to collect and display artifacts related to modern Corpus Christi, but the Age of Exploration overshadowed the city. Unlike city museums elsewhere in the United States that were integral to public-history initiatives, the museum played a negligible role in coordinating and advising movements for downtown preservation, historic districts, and projects related to neighborhood, ethnic, business, labor, and transportation history.

At the time las carabelas reopened in May 2001, the museum also

Figure 3.6. The *Pinta (left)* and the *Santa Maria* deteriorate in dry dock at the Corpus Christi Museum of Science and History, 2011. Author photo.

opened a Gallery of Cultural Encounters, featuring a thirty-two-foot domed wooden ceiling built in Castile in the 1530s and acquired from the Philadelphia Museum of Art in 1995. As with the Columbus ships, the ceiling was a beautiful work of craftsmanship with no links to Corpus Christi. The former *Caller-Times* publisher Ed Harte and his wife donated $1 million for the display hall, whose initial exhibit featured artifacts from the ill-fated La Salle expedition to Matagorda Bay in the 1680s. According to Stryker, the museum planned ultimately to use the hall to display material on the regional influence of the Karankawas, the French, and the Spanish.[69]

The museum struggled until 2005, when an advisory group drafted a revised mission statement conceding that the municipal museum would concentrate in a general way on South Texas as "the cultural crossroads of the New World." Portions of the advisory group's proposal for a "Hispanic Heritage Center" addressed the modern and urban experience of the region's Mexican-descended majority, but the document emphasized exploration and settlement. Of the nineteen collections the proposal listed as supporting regional Hispanic study, four focused on Corpus Christi after the 1926 opening of the port.[70] From $8 for adults when the Columbus fleet reopened in 2001, the museum's entry fee had risen to $11.50 by 2010, $9 for senior citizens, and $6 for children over five.

Upon director Stryker's retirement in 2012, the city contracted with a company run by Dusty Durrill's son, Bill, who ran a number of entertainment ventures, to manage the museum. The younger Durrill promised to hold the line on ticket prices, remodel the building, maintain accreditation and professional staff, and implement "kid-friendly" interactive exhibitions on regional history and ecology. Relieved to be rid of a financial, administrative, and political burden, the city agreed to a profit-sharing arrangement that included a municipal subsidy during the transition period. The deal caught the attention of curators and directors around the country, who noted how unusual it was to contract the operation of a public museum to a private company. Standard American practice would have suggested a public partnership with a foundation or a nonprofit organization, the arrangement in place for over forty years at the museum's neighbor, the Art Museum of South Texas.[71] Exhausted after years of struggle and apprehensive about the new management, the bulk of the staff resigned or asked for transfers to other municipal agencies. The museum's role as a low-key educational and civic institution for the community had long fallen by the wayside.

"The problem isn't that the Columbus ships closed," Stryker observed in October 2000, during the impasse caused by the Spanish repossession threat and Dusty Durrill's lien. "It's that they didn't go away."[72] The ships' condition remained heartbreaking; any visitor could perceive the *Pinta* and *Santa Maria* decaying in dry dock in the early 2010s. They had become a monument not to interethnic pride, but to the perils of community building through generalized symbolism. In 2013, Bill Durrill conceded the failure of his father's vision: the dry-docked ships "have been an albatross around the museum's neck for a long time." If the city cannot give them away, the younger Durrill remarked, it should consider demolishing them.[73] Indeed, the city unceremoniously destroyed the *Pinta* and the *Santa María* over two days in August 2014.

As with Anglo frontier lore, Spanish colonial heritage formed an indelible and understandable—though at times distracting and distorting—aspect of Corpus Christians' perspective on their city's history, geography, and culture. Corpus Christi's situation as a gateway into Tejano South Texas and the Mexico-U.S. borderlands fostered a sense of regional geography in which city wove into country and past wove into present. Probably the most effective symbols of the city's ties to Hispanic America were not those that fixed people's identity at some point in the past—like the Columbus ships or self-conscious, mission-style motifs in local architecture and urban design. The buildings, storefronts, signs, and gardens of the Westside summed up Tejano South Texas and the larger borderlands precisely because these tended toward the miscellaneous, jerry-rigged, and nondescript. Every form on the Westside had equivalents in the towns spread across South Texas, across the Rio Grande, and into northern Mexico. Corpus Christi acts as an entryway into a section of Texas and North America that has no hard or clear borders between city and region, United States and Mexico, or Anglo and Tejano.

Religion offered an example of the intricate networks—sometimes formal and sometimes improvised—that tied Corpus Christi to South Texas and beyond. Religion anchored distinct racial and ethnic communities, yet it also created arenas for mediation across groups. Like the ethnic groups with whom their stories intertwine, historians of Corpus Christi churches have customarily begun their accounts by highlighting frontier episodes and "pioneer missionaries." As throughout the West, congregations that resulted from spiritual pioneering organized and sustained town life. Clerical hierarchies and denominational conventions tied the area culturally to the wider urban world in the same way that railroads and merchants built links to urban commercial networks. In addition, churches embodied the city's divisions; Catholic, Baptist, and Presbyterian histories all note that congregations were segregated as soon as numbers and resources permitted. Yet from the start, Protestant sects endeavored to win Mexican converts, to the point of sponsoring Hispanic pastors and underwriting church buildings. The Catholic Church countered this perceived threat in part by positioning itself as a protector of Mexican residents against egregious discrimination and deprivation.[74]

From this competition emerged webs of relationships not readily apparent to observers who concentrate on the secular aspects of political, economic, or social life. Catholicism brought Irish, Czech, and German settlers together with Mexicans and with an increasingly Hispanic clergy. Meanwhile, evangelical Protestantism shaped influential Hispanic figures, including Congressman Solomon Ortiz and his ally Richard Borchard, the first Hispanic Nueces County judge. Both came from evangelical families in nearby Robstown. Borchard's father, from a South Texas German family, integrated himself into his Hispanic wife's farm-laborer world and its fundamentalist Protestantism. Such experiences helped these politicians build connections throughout the region and across its cultures.

While Nick Jimenez was at first surprised by the small-town perspective of Corpus Christi Hispanics, he grasped this religious geography; he came from a Hispanic Protestant family in San Antonio. Immersion "at least one day out of the week in this sort of Anglo culture," the journalist explained, gave Borchard and Ortiz a sense of "something you can talk about." The late twentieth-century spread of charismatic Protestantism and Pentecostalism across southern Texas and Mexico reshuffled relationships yet again. This trend created new divisions within families, even as it gave new form to Hispanic folklore and customs, such as faith healing. It brought working-class Hispanics into class-based denominations with long-standing appeal to working-class whites and blacks. As in every American metropolitan region, congregations appeared everywhere, in expected places and grand buildings as well as in odd corners and strip malls.[75] This maze of institutions and shifting communities, large and small, illustrates how some identities and divisions within Corpus Christi and South Texas were enduring and definable, while others were provisional and shifting. The border region itself shared this ambiguity: a zone of division between peoples with opposed heritages and clashing points of view and yet a place where people revise identities and relationships that can be fixed neither in doctrine nor in stone.

Chapter 4

PUBLIC SCULPTURE & CIVIC IDENTITY

∾

C orpus Christi's most vividly remembered life of the late twenti-eth century ended in a nondescript place. On March 31, 1995, Yolanda Saldívar fatally shot Selena Quintanilla-Pérez at a Days Inn near Interstate 37 on the far Northside. The singer, a few weeks shy of her twenty-fourth birthday, had gone to retrieve financial records from her former fan club president and business partner, who had been fired for embezzlement. Barely known to most Anglos, even in her home-town, Selena, from a family of musicians, had been a star for a decade. Acclaimed as queen of the regional genre known as Tejano, Selena was especially beloved in northern Mexico and South Texas. In perfor-mance and elsewhere, she emphasized her working-class background and demeanor and her Mexicana appearance. Young Hispanic women absorbed this as a validating message: they could be themselves and still be admired and glamorous.[1]

An estimated 15,000–20,000 mourners came to a vigil at the Bay-front Convention Center. Indignation joined grief when, on the day of Selena's funeral, the radio vulgarian Howard Stern broadcast a de-grading parody. The emotion surrounding Selena's murder took the U.S. media by surprise; the outpouring of response dramatized the vigor, scope, and complexity of Latino popular culture within the United States. Many Hispanic professionals and businesspeople also underestimated Selena's popularity and significance. Attentive reporters noted that the affair shed light on social divisions among Mexican Americans, illustrating the hazards of generalizations about Hispanic culture in the Southwest.

Corpus Christi's civic and political leaders scrambled to keep up with calls for appropriate recognition. As with Hector García's medical office, places associated with Selena revealed a great deal about the geography and daily life of the Hispanic city, but these sites were scattered and unprepossessing. The Quintanillas did eventually open a museum in their Westside recording studio, not far from their home in the Molina neighborhood. Selena also ran a boutique, but this was in an unremarkable building on the Southside near South Padre Island Drive. Responding to sentiment for a conspicuous memorial, the city in April 1996 renamed the 2,500-seat Bayfront Auditorium for Selena.

A variety of proposals for a central-city monument came together in the Mirador de la Flor, or "Outlook of the Flower," a reference to her hit song "Como la Flor." Underwritten by the philanthropist Dusty Durrill, this "Spanish-style, open-air pavilion" overlooking the bay was a rectangular cousin of the eight miradors that Durrill had sponsored atop the Corpus Christi seawall a few years earlier. The monument was decorated with mosaics, an elaborate tile mural (partly painted by schoolchildren), and other features intended to add a Hispanic atmosphere to central Corpus Christi. Highlight of the mirador was the sculptor Buddy Tatum's life-size bronze statue of Selena as she appeared in concert.[2]

In subject matter, style, and iconography, the Mirador de la Flor appeared special to contemporary South Texas. Yet the project adopted a standard form for twentieth-century North American monuments to a person. Rather than the venerable sculpture on a pedestal, designers began regularly to place a portrait within an architectural setting that illustrated the commemorated person's character and life; famous examples include Washington's U. S. Grant, Franklin D. Roosevelt, and Martin Luther King memorials. Originally, the monument included wooden slats attached to the concrete column against which Selena seemed to lean. Fans were allowed to write messages on the slats until city workers—tired of cleaning graffiti that overflowed onto the column and even the statue—removed them. When that did not stop the graffiti, the city in 2000 constructed a four-foot-tall steel barrier to keep

Figure 4.1. Selena depicted in concert, surrounded by the antigraffiti barrier at the Mirador de la Flor, 2014. Photo by Kenny Braun.

visitors away from the statue and column. "People want to leave messages," remarked Abraham Quintanilla, Selena's father, but defacing his daughter's memorial "is not the right way to do it." Despite signs pleading with fans no longer to leave markings, the barrier displaced the graffiti onto the walls around the mirador. The slats had been a well-intentioned "mistake," noted the *Caller-Times* columnist Nick Jimenez. As with many sites of pilgrimage, the messages had begun as "acts of devotion," but they crossed the line into "disrespect" for other fans and for the city itself.[3]

Inviting graffiti was imprudent in part because for millennia people have used graffiti as much to assert their presence as to express themselves, which makes it inherently an ill-disciplined activity. The Selena monument itself raised questions of "ownership," as Jimenez observed soon after the monument's dedication in 1997. "We say who we are with the bayfront," the columnist elaborated. "The Selena statue now says we are unmistakably an Hispanic community." Bickering that surrounded the monument's placement and design was "about turf," added Javier Villarreal, a scholar of Tejano culture at Texas A&M University–Corpus Christi.[4] Jimenez and Villarreal made clear that Hispanic versus Anglo was only the most manifest source of division revealed by the Selena memorial. In addition to ethnicity, the monument proclaimed Selena's working-class identity and popular-culture sensibility. The Selena portrayed in the statue—tight pants, bra halter, jacket, jewelry, and microphone—was a pop music star in the global youth culture. Even her cowboy boots were a pop symbol, no longer regional in content. Although she began in a South Texas genre, she developed into a pan–Latin American star by appropriating mass-culture influences. The monument captured this spirit. It made little pretense of refinement or uplift, seeking instead an emotional connection with fans. Like Lubbock's statue of Buddy Holly and Port Arthur's commemorations of Janis Joplin, the Selena monument celebrated the role of mass culture in modern Texas as much as it acknowledged the Mexican American contribution to Corpus Christi. Civic leaders in all three cities recognized that a memorial to a popular music figure who died prematurely would draw tourists, but in ways that countered the reputation for sophistication and professionalism that they also sought for their towns.[5]

The involvement of Durrill underscored the complexity of the monument's cultural politics. Outsiders might find it remarkable that local Hispanics embraced a monument whose sponsor, architect, tile makers, and sculptor were all Anglo. But this configuration made sense, given local understandings of who belonged to the establishment and who were the upstarts. The self-made businessman's anti-establishment style gave him credibility among Hispanic civic groups, whose heritage projects he consistently supported. Arts advocates complained bitterly over the way that Durrill had taken the Mirador de la Flor proposal to the city council after the Municipal Arts Commission (MAC), the body responsible for vetting public art projects, had signaled that it might resist the design. Durrill "has determined to have his own way" on the bayfront, MAC's chair wrote Mayor Mary Rhodes in February 1997, "the principle [sic] crown jewel in the city's inventory of assets."[6] Detractors, for their part, considered the arts commission a bastion of socially connected elitists who would, if left in charge, line the bayfront with obscurities that would make them feel cosmopolitan but would alienate everyone else.

Of the artists involved in the project, only the tile makers, a local firm associated with the area's best-known ceramicists, expressed consternation at having been recruited into "doing a community art project on city property without MAC approval."[7] The sculptor, Tatum, had had earlier difficulties with MAC and appreciated Durrill's ability to maneuver around the commission. This despite the fact that sidestepping MAC meant that the artist had no approved design to insist upon when Selena's family asked for changes.[8] Tatum was trained in foundry techniques, but he earned his living as an accountant. He counted as a local artist in a city that had seen decades of tension over efforts by arts professionals associated with the Art Museum of South Texas and with area universities to assert authority over aesthetic standards in exhibitions and public art. Feelings ran so deep that local artists such as Tatum preferred to put up with the importunities of patrons rather than struggle to satisfy the art professors, curators, and educated laypeople on MAC's art review panels. In contrast with the Arthur Ashe statue controversy in Richmond—a famous 1990s clash between urban cultural politics and art review procedures—the quarrel over the Selena memorial among Durrill, MAC, and the city council was for the most part kept out of the press. Still, the strategy that Durrill used to gain city council sanction for a monument opposed by the city's arts commission revealed as much about the politics of public art in Corpus Christi as it did about the monument's content.[9]

Beyond reflecting complex issues of ethnicity, class, and culture, the Selena monument reveals ambivalence over the state of urban life in Corpus Christi as well as over the ability of public art to embody civic ideals in an age when the spatial diffusion of cities mirrors their social divisions. Builders of the thousands of Beaux-Arts urban monuments from the Gilded Age and the Progressive Era, the previous high point of public sculpture in the United States, acted upon the venerable belief that a well-made portrayal of a political or military hero or a virtue expressed in an allegorical figure might inspire civic pride and responsibility in citizens. The builders of the Selena monument, by contrast, do not seem to have imagined her example as spurring the regeneration of civic life in Corpus Christi. One might hope that her transfiguration into "a role model all communities need for their youth," as Durrill's inscription reads, would steer young people onto a constructive path. "Selena wanted people to live a wholesome life free of fear, drugs, and gangs," the inscription elaborates. "She influenced admirers to get an education, attend church, and respect families."[10] Considering that Selena was a working-class figure as well as a Hispanic one, this modest message partly reveals the working-class sense of limitations observed by sociologists. Still, statues in public places, even those commemorating working-class or ethnic figures, usually impart pride and ambition more than the defensiveness and anxiety revealed by Durrill's inscription.

The dispute over the Selena monument brought together a jumble of attitudes, conflicts, and agendas: class and ethnic conflicts over urban space; competing perceptions of regional history; populist disaffection with experts and government; alienation of the fine arts from public taste; and mixed feelings over the sculpture's civic purpose in an era of socially fragmented and geographically spread-out cities. Even as they accustomed themselves to the Selena monument, Corpus Christians anticipated more controversies involving art, politics, and cultural conflict. For the city—and for numerous American cities— quarrels over monuments, murals, or sculptures had become as regular as mayoral elections, and often harder fought.

"The Real Piece of Art"

Late in 1997, a few months after dedication of the Mirador de la Flor, MAC chose six finalists for $215,000 that it had set aside to purchase work by an "internationally known" sculptor for the "Gateway," where Interstate 37 meets Shoreline Boulevard. Arts activists organized the competition so that both procedure and result would differ from those that had produced the Selena monument and, indeed, every other public artwork on the bayfront. The managed competition would engage the public but not pander to popular tastes. The "grand scale" work that resulted would overshadow other works in the vicinity. In theory, it would win over residents after initial resistance and educate them about contemporary sculpture and about the value of open-mindedness and circumspect procedure. "I'm waiting for the final decision to see how many pages of explanation the art will require," joked the columnist Bill Walraven, who for decades had enjoyed the role of populist gadfly in arts controversies. "The description, I predict, will be the real piece of art."[11]

The rows over sculpture in Corpus Christi illustrate the contentiousness that surrounded the new wave of urban public art that began in the 1960s. To be sure, urban monuments have always been contentious. In the early days of the republic, urban Americans quarreled over the content, style, financing, and control of public sculpture; normal city dwellers often resisted proposed monuments as suspiciously European, a manifestation of the aristocratic pretentions of wealthy merchants and bankers.[12] Public sculpture first gained broad acceptance in the United States after the Civil War. Thousands of towns commissioned war monuments, and grieving families erected gravestones. The war thus gave a boost to sculpture studios, foundries, and related enterprises. In the North, the civic idealism inspired by the war eroded the old suspicion of monument building, and the Lost Cause mindset did the same in the South. Meanwhile, Beaux-Arts principles of art and architecture and City Beautiful ideas about urban design envisioned public buildings and places as elaborate compositions that integrated the visual arts—murals, glass, ceramics, and metalwork as well as reliefs and freestanding sculpture—into design programs with allegorical or didactic symbolism.[13]

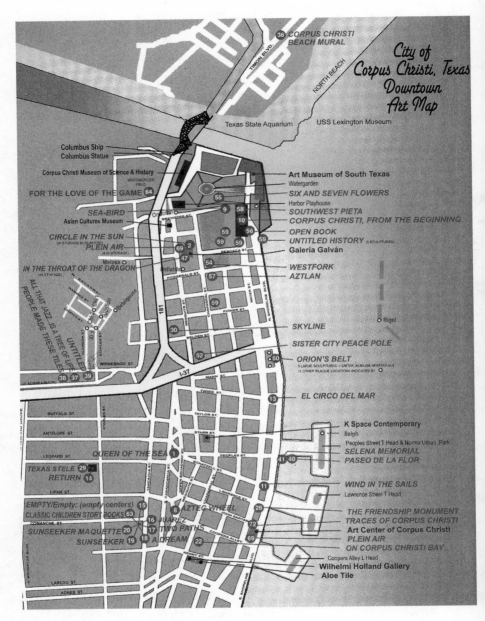

Figure 4.2. Public art in central Corpus Christi, 2009.
Courtesy of the City of Corpus Christi.

Early in the twentieth century, sculptors active in Texas, such as Elisabet Ney and Pompeo Coppini, were typical of their contemporaries in style and subject matter. They found steady work building monuments to the Texas Revolution as well as to the Confederacy. This first phase of Texas public sculpture bypassed Corpus Christi, with one revealing exception, Coppini's 1915 relief, *Queen of the Sea*. From around seventy-five total artworks in Corpus Christi's public inventory in 2009, including around thirty sculptures, only the Coppini relief dates from before the 1960s. The central city contains no other work of outdoor public art dating from before 1978.[14]

After World War I, arts professionals and laypeople developed an aversion to Beaux-Arts public sculpture, which they had adored only a few decades earlier. The genre's stylized approach had come to seem contrived, and its elaborate symbolism pedantic. In the 1920s, art deco entailed an exuberant celebration of decoration for its own sake, a far cry from Beaux-Arts refinement and didacticism. Then, at mid-century, the modernist emphasis on pure form won out. This mindset dismissed decoration as fakery. Public sculpture endured to some extent in the reliefs at New York's Rockefeller Center, in the grandiose schemes of Mount Rushmore sculptor Gutzon Borglum, and in ethnic commemoration projects such as Cleveland's Cultural Gardens.[15]

Public sculpture reemerged during the 1960s, by which time both art and cities had gone through vast transformations. Civic leaders, art patrons, and groups of citizens fought emotional battles in numerous cities, including places such as Corpus Christi, that had been remote and marginal during the Beaux-Arts and City Beautiful era. The quarreling that Walraven reviewed (and fueled) resulted largely from manifestly huge changes over the century in sculpture's form, aesthetics, and subject matter as well as in the arts professions and their public stance and reputation. Despite these changes, residents of cities such as Corpus Christi adhered to traditional beliefs about art and its power. People still believed—though often ambivalently, as the Selena inscriptions suggest—that sculpture could educate and uplift and generate civic consciousness. Sculpture could define a city visually and shape its identity. The city's disputes over public art took on an angry edge because people attributed qualities and capabilities to art that went beyond aesthetic and intellectual appreciation.

Until the twentieth century, a rough consensus existed on the range of messages that public monuments could send and the artistic vocabulary available to send these messages. Quarrels over this or that monument took place more or less within boundaries marked out by the visual and symbolic language that had prevailed in Western art since the Renaissance. By the second half of the twentieth century, in the aftermath of modernist and then postmodernist attacks on traditional Western aesthetics, the range of messages that public art could convey seemed open-ended, as did the forms that monuments could take and their placement within cities. Residents of Corpus Christi and other cities frequently expressed dismay at evidence appearing around their towns of the aesthetic and symbolic lawlessness of twentieth-century public art. Yet this lack of limits was attractive to diverse groups competing to push the definition of the city in a particular direction.[16]

Corpus Christi's embrace of public sculpture starting in the 1970s contained an element of urban boosterism, as in other cities that based part of their public relations image on outdoor art made by prestigious artists. The city likewise took advantage of funding innovations favorable to public art, such as a percent-for-art program and a trust fund based on hotel-motel taxes. (The city made little use of another commonly cited catalyst for urban public art, federal funding from the National Endowment for the Arts and the General Services Administration.) A great deal of the recent advent of public sculpture in Corpus Christi stems the spread across the American West of a network of art museums, galleries, and university art programs. The institutional development of the arts from Texas to the Pacific Northwest gave rise to a cadre of arts professionals ambitious and even evangelical in their devotion to elevating cultural standards in the places where they lived and worked. Curators, dealers, critics, and artists chafed against the apparent determination of these places to remain regional—or depending on one's perspective, provincial—in mindset and taste, even if no longer in wealth or significance.

In 1909, the Cosmos Club, a women's civic club of the sort that frequently took the initiative in urban beautification during the Progressive Era, invited Pompeo Coppini, an Italian sculptor who had settled in San Antonio in 1901, to advise Corpus Christi on forming a City Beautiful movement. The Italian was smitten by the sweeping bay and the forty-foot bluff that loomed behind the waterfront. The scene reminded him of Naples, as it did many European visitors before the deepwater port and the seawall transformed the visual effect. The artist outlined ideas for making the place, still a coastal town of 8,222 people, into "the most beautifull town along the golf coast" [*sic*].[17] As a result, Coppini was named art director of the Corpus Christi Civic League, a group that did nothing discernible. In 1912, one of the clubwomen enquired whether Coppini would sketch a "simple" fountain, since the club had only $200. Coppini responded that the town would really benefit from "one great fire which would destroy all the rubbish which has been built on the water and another many years to pass so as to get rid of the mossback citizens, of which all Texas towns are full."[18]

The fountain idea passed to the Daughters of the Confederacy, one of Coppini's frequent patrons. Since completing the Texas Confederate monument (on the Capitol grounds in Austin) in 1901, Coppini had found steady work building Confederate monuments, southern counterparts of the Union monuments in northern towns that did so much to spur American sculpture. The Florence-trained artist acquired an incongruous reputation as Texas's sculptor of the southern cause.[19] By 1914, Roy Miller, Corpus Christi's progressive mayor, had embraced beautification of the bluff as the highlight of his public improvement program. A fountain on the bluff, the Daughters of the Confederacy reasoned, would offer "a fitting memorial to the noble Texans who gave their lives for the South." The Rotary Club helped raise $1,000, enough to decorate the fountain with a bas-relief cast in a cheap stone mixture that replicated granite. Coppini donated his labor, in part "to keep [him] busy" during a lull in commissions.[20]

In line with pre–World War I conventions, Coppini produced a figurative allegory. Unlike his dozens of other Confederate or Texas Revolution monuments, the Corpus Christi relief did not mourn the dead or evoke a vanished age of heroes. The monument called on residents to embrace their city's destiny. "Corpus Christi," Coppini explained, "is represented by a young women with the keys of success in her hand and receiving the blessing of Mother Earth on the one side and Father Neptune on the other." Around stood symbols of land and sea, sources of the wealth that Corpus Christians could use to fill their city with well-conceived art and well-designed public places and thereby make it indeed the jewel of the Gulf.[21]

Coppini had little success in infusing Corpus Christians with an enduring preference for urbane public art or City Beautiful–style public places. Even as Corpus Christi went on to fulfill much of Coppini's vision of economic success, its sculptors paid no attention to his aesthetic vision. They sought inspiration in stock themes of Texas lore—the world of rangers, ranchers, wilderness, and heroes—which Coppini's relief eschewed. Corpus Christi's first outdoor sculpture remained for a century the only one to take the city itself as its theme.

Rather than turn into a nucleus from which a majestic city would radiate, the Coppini relief suffered neglect, especially as Corpus Christi's visual focus shifted from the bluff to the seawall and then diffused

Figure 4.3. Father Neptune and Mother Earth crown Corpus Christi in Pompeo Coppini's *Queen of the Sea*, as restored in the early 2000s. Photo by Kenny Braun, 2014.

along roadways outward from the central city. The city's only outdoor sculpture other than church statues for sixty years, the relief became a moldy, cracked, faded piece. In the late 1980s, a history-minded architect, John Wright, worked to place the bluff improvement on the National Register and make its restoration a priority. Wright interested the local Rotary in contributing $10,000 to restore what it had raised $1,000 to build seventy-five years before. This sufficed to hire Ron Sullivan, a sculpture professor at Del Mar College, to remove mold and paint, fill cracks and holes, and reshape the surface. Rededicated with fanfare in April 1991, Coppini's *Queen* was more presentable than before but still lonely and rusting beneath the surface, a metaphor for central Corpus Christi overall.[22] In 1997, the Municipal Arts Commission found that the monument's substructure had deteriorated so badly that the only choice was to recast it entirely, which a St. Louis art-conservation firm did in the early 2000s.[23]

"I never received any token of gratitude" from Corpus Christi, Coppini recalled, "while someone else who went there, in after years, was far more honored by them than I was, just for talking loud and making false promises."[24] The rival who provoked Coppini's resentment was Gutzon Borglum, American sculpture's grandiose genius. As explained in chapter 2, when sketching early plans for what became the Corpus Christi seawall, Borglum envisioned it as the terminus of a boulevard to the Rio Grande, to be lined with statues celebrating Texas heritage from a triumphalist, Anglo-Texan perspective. Even had Borglum not feuded his way out of the seawall project, such a boulevard was beyond Corpus Christians' finances and ambitions. Commercial and civic leaders distanced themselves from nearly every aspect of the quarrelsome artist's sketch.

A partial exception was Borglum's proposal for a thirty-two-foot-tall Christ colossus in Corpus Christi Bay. No town booster with any gumption could resist such a scheme. Beyond the association with the place's name, a Christ stilling the waters would have served as a powerful symbol of the contemporary city, which owed its existence to coastal engineering. The new deepwater port catalyzed Corpus Christi's prosperity, and the seawall would protect it from hurricanes. A Christ colossus would have been neither an Anglo nor even a Texas regional symbol. It had a broad attraction, at least among Christians, except those Protestant fundamentalists who condemned it as a supposed manifestation of Catholic idolatry and liberal Protestant slackness. Even if Corpus Christians had overcome their divisions and authorized the project, it is unclear whether Borglum could have made good on his promise. He was notorious, to quote Coppini again, for "constantly promoting schemes which he himself alone could not carry out." After the artist died in 1941, his son Lincoln attempted without success to erect a version of the Christ colossus in Spearfish, South Dakota, home of a production of the Passion play.[25]

The notion of a monumental Christ in Corpus Christi Bay has such self-evident appeal that the idea reappeared at least four times over the next half century. In 1953–1954, a group made national news with a proposal for a statue forty feet taller than Rio de Janeiro's *Christ the Redeemer*. "The monument must be the tallest one in the world," one supporter remarked, "for this is Texas."[26] In 1971, two Mexican artists arrived in town with a model for a sixteen-story steel-and-marble colossus, envisioned as a bicentennial gift from Mexico. The editor who had invited the pair neglected to arrange a reception, so they were left to display their model at a local mall.[27] In August 1979, after rancorous debate, the city council rejected an eighteen-foot Christ by Sherman Coleman, a local surgeon and sculptor. This time, resistance came not from fundamentalist Protestants but from Jewish groups, which threatened to sue to prevent the figure from being erected on a city-owned spoil island.[28] In 1995, the First United Methodist Church installed the sculptor Kent Ullberg's fifteen-and-a-half-foot bronze of Christ stilling the waters on its own land along Shoreline Boulevard.[29] Ullberg's Christ became a landmark at the south corner of the bayfront, but it hardly fulfilled Borglum's vision. The Christ colossus in the bay prompted inquiries and occasional debate into the 2000s.

"A Complete Lack of Understanding"

Between 1930 and 1960, Corpus Christi's population swelled from about 28,000 to over 200,000, but the number of its public sculptures remained at one: Coppini's forlorn *Queen of the Sea*. Like much of the urban Southwest, the South Texas port was transformed into a city during decades when urban planners placed little emphasis on building squares with statues in them and when a gulf appeared between architects and sculptors. By the 1960s, American cities were taking an interest in public sculpture for the first time since the decline of Beaux-Arts and City Beautiful ideals in the 1920s. The broadest explanation for the public sculpture revival relates to the widespread feeling that unadorned, modernist architecture and urban design had left central cities drearier than ever and may have accelerated the unraveling of the urban fabric. The works of Isamu Noguchi, Alexander Calder, and their counterparts made sculpture seem viable as an urban renewal device, a way of softening modern urban space and livening up disheartening city centers. Cities developed devices for generating funds, such as municipal percent-for-art ordinances, which set aside 1–2 percent of the cost of a public building for artwork. Federal agencies such as the National Endowment for the Arts (NEA) and the General Services Administration created funding programs to supplement local, private, and corporate funds. Federal involvement furthered the revival of public art even in cities such as Corpus Christi, which relied little on such grants.

Corpus Christi meanwhile developed a set of cultural institutions and a cadre of arts advocates typical of those in other Texas and western cities amid the rapid urbanization of the mid-twentieth century.[30] These included the Corpus Christi Arts Council, an umbrella organization initially sponsored by the local Junior League, which also worked to transform the cramped art center in the Centennial Museum building in out-of-the-way South Bluff Park into the Art Museum of South Texas (AMST). Opened in 1972 at the dramatic point where the ship channel meets the bayfront, and housed in one of the most admired of the architect Philip Johnson's small museum buildings, AMST is the highlight of the cultural district known as the Bayfront Arts and Science Park. Around the same time, the State of Texas took over the University of Corpus Christi, the struggling Baptist school damaged by Hurricane Celia. That change laid the groundwork for Corpus Christi State University, which evolved into Texas A&M University–Corpus Christi. The university created an art program that attracted faculty members from around the country. This new resource added to ones already available to the city through Del Mar College and Texas A&I University (later Texas A&M–Kingsville).

By the 1970s, therefore, Corpus Christi had ambitious arts institutions and groups, several of which had a stake in embellishing the central city, along with a pronounced dedication to the education-and-uplift line in American arts activism. Determined to expose provincial Corpus Christi to contemporary art, the museum's leaders—helped by Johnson and his friends among New York's curators and gallery operators—put together attention-grabbing exhibitions in styles such as pop art and minimalism. Numerous Corpus Christians, however, dismissed Robert Rauschenberg found-object assemblies and Donald Judd plywood "box" sculptures as inaccessible and pretentious. Such shows, along with the stylish tone of the museum's social events, tarred the museum as an elite institution at a time when deference to commercial-civic elites was disintegrating throughout the Southwest. At the same time, local artist groups felt shoved aside and denigrated by the civic activists who had taken over the small museum where the artists had held classes and showed work for decades. South Texas artists and art scholars became divided, often to the point of barely speaking, between those who applauded AMST's cosmopolitan emphasis and those who felt that a regional museum should stress regional art. And until the 1980s, Hispanic civic leaders shied away from involvement in AMST, which still seemed a bastion of an entrenched Anglo leadership.

Within this acrimonious environment, public and private efforts to embellish the bayfront with sculpture took shape. In December 1966, the city council established the Municipal Arts Commission. MAC's initial mandate was to oversee planning of the Bayfront Arts and Science Park, which explains why founding members included Anne Vaky, the Junior League activist who helped form the Arts Council, and Patsy Dunn Singer, coordinator of the campaign for the Art Museum of South Texas and wife of the oilman Edwin Singer, head of the Foundation for Science and Arts, which oversaw the bayfront culture park. MAC also received responsibility for aesthetic matters throughout the city, but at first only in an advisory capacity. In 1970–1971, the commission expressed frustration with the city manager and city council for failing even to respond to its recommendations. Like most such agencies, MAC initially had no independent funding to commission public art; it vetted others' proposals and encouraged donations.

This responsibility included the awkward task of resisting unwanted gifts, such as a sculpture of welded auto parts by a twenty-year-old about to leave for Vietnam or a fifteen-foot concrete skyline that would sparkle to promote the tourist slogan "Sparkling City by the Sea."[31]

With MAC busy keeping unwanted pieces off municipal land, the Nueces County government had the first success since Coppini in placing sculpture on public property, albeit indoors. In 1975, art and history enthusiasts convinced the county commissioners to authorize a sculpture garden in the three-story atrium of the county courthouse under construction in Uptown. With history or environment as themes, jurors selected two semiabstract structures. One used a longhorn skull and horns to evoke ranching, while the other used a shrimp boat and gulls to evoke the sea. Gradually, history groups and the county surrounded these structures with bronzes that alluded to the distant South Texas past: a Karankawa; a Spanish king donated by Spain's consul general; Father José Nicholas Ballí, for whom Padre Island is named; and the town's founder, Henry Lawrence Kinney.[32]

The perception that MAC might be too "august" in social composition and outlook led city council members to appoint several community activists and local artists to the commission. The board thereby embraced within itself the city's tensions over art. By 1978, MAC had put together a few thousand dollars to purchase an outdoor sculpture for a triangle of land away from the bayfront, "a partially conspicuous place" in case MAC "didn't do good," recalls Margaret Walberg, one of the community activists appointed to open up MAC membership. The contest winner, *Aztec Wheel* by Craig Gibbs, was made of Cor-Ten steel, a widely used material meant to rust slightly, a fact not known by most of the public. Most Corpus Christians dismissed the first municipal public sculpture in the central city in over sixty years as "a pile of rusty junk," as Walberg put it.[33]

MAC, whose majority was still prominent in status and cosmopolitan in outlook, meanwhile set the goal of placing a large contemporary work by a prestigious artist outside the new Bayfront Convention Center, next to the Arts and Science Park. The plan was to use $50,000 from hotel-motel taxes to secure an NEA matching grant, for a substantial fund of $100,000. Proponents sensed they would have a fight. Years of wrangling had caused lines to harden: elite versus popular, abstract versus representational, outsider versus local. Proponents, however, took heart from celebrated recent cases such as the Chicago Picasso and the Grand Rapids Calder. In those instances, residents gradually embraced works at first deemed suspect.[34]

Patsy Singer helped persuade MAC to create a review panel consisting of herself; AMST's director, Cathleen Gallander; several of their local allies; and museum directors from Fort Worth and Austin. The selection panel settled on *Turn* by James Surls, a sort of pinecone or flower shape, thirty-five feet high and fifty-five feet long, of chiseled cypress logs held together by a steel pipe core. Surls, whose wood sculptures recall the East Texas landscape, later emerged as one of Texas's most popular contemporary artists. As with Donald Judd, whose box sculptures became targets of scorn during a 1974 AMST exhibition, local advocates of contemporary art had identified an artist who later became associated with Texas and admired by Texans. In 1979, however, proponents invited a quarrel in which the merits of Surls's work were lost. They had excluded vocal skeptics from the selection panel, accepted submissions from local artists and then not reviewed them, and discussed submissions in private, a recipe for a hostile reception.[35]

The convention center sculpture proposal brought to the surface accumulated resentment among local artists as well as residents. Six months later, critics within AMST stressed the episode as indicating a "lack of responsiveness to the needs, desires and suggestions of the community" when they pushed through the firing of longtime director Gallander, respected for her steady upgrading of the institution before and after the 1972 move to Johnson's bayfront museum. Several local artists claimed to admire Surls but charged that the selection panel was rigged and that the determination to force an outlandish work on the city would undermine support for all public art. The sculptor Kent Ullberg, angry over the brusque dismissal of his own proposal, insisted that a city with "next to nothing in public art" should start with something "recognizable." If arts professionals and institutions persisted in alienating people unnecessarily, Ullberg argued, the public would be "up in arms against art and artists and the city will be art dry."[36]

Critics further insisted that youths would vandalize the wooden posts and that the steel core would rust in the Gulf Coast's salt air.

Proponents countered that *Turn* would prove durable and that experience elsewhere indicated that vandalism would not be a problem. To no avail. The columnist Bill Walraven dwelled on the story as evidence of the arrogance and inaccessibility of AMST's leadership. The dispute prompted a slew of letters to the editor. "The decision to ignore our local talent and use an out of state modern or abstract sculptor," began one of the more polite missives, "show[s] a complete lack of understanding for and empathy with the local people." After a divided MAC approved the Surls sculpture, the city council rejected it in January 1980. The council instead authorized $25,000 for a more modest work. This time, MAC invited public participation in a direct way: it ran a newspaper ballot for three finalists selected by jurors. The winner, a semiabstract *Sea Bird* by San Antonio's Fernando Turegano, took its place outside the convention center, an unloved focus of dissatisfaction over the city's art politics.[37]

Though "very hurt" by the rejection, Surls and his wife, Charmaine Locke, returned to Corpus Christi in the 1990s, contributing work to Mariposa Park, an interminably scruffy sculpture garden organized by the South Texas artist Michael Manjarris in a vacant lot at the south end of the bluff.[38] A decade later, MAC's successor agency, the Arts and Cultural Commission, chose Manjarris to curate the percent-for-art segment of the convention center's expansion and construction of the American Bank Center arena. This project was so huge that the 1.25 percent mandated by the ordinance generated $500,000. Manjarris purchased works by well-known contemporary Texas and western artists, including a fiberglass *Southwest Pieta* by El Paso's Luis Jiménez and Locke's *Open Book*, a six-armed Mother Earth–type figure. The highlight of Manjarris's installation was a twenty-four-foot bronze-and-steel Surls work, *Six and Seven Flowers*, a few yards from the proposed 1980 site. The *Turn* episode barely came up, but many remembered it. The *Caller-Times* warned of another debate over "contemporary artwork" in a "conservative" downtown, but local outrage seemed to have been spent on the recent Gateway controversy. Accounts now emphasized Surls as a Texas artist, though he and Locke had relocated to Colorado, the center of American sculpture fabrication.[39]

Figure 4.4. James Surls, *Six and Seven Flowers,* outside the Bayfront Convention Center. Photo by Kenny Braun, 2014.

Sailfish and Median Strips

The convention center sculpture mess in 1980 brought attention to Kent Ullberg, a young artist who had recently bought a house on the Corpus Christi portion of Padre Island. The son of two struggling artists from Gothenburg on Sweden's west coast, Ullberg studied at Stockholm's State School of Art. Captivated since childhood by wildlife, Ullberg also learned taxidermy and animal anatomy at Sweden's Museum of Natural History. In 1967, he went to Botswana as a taxidermist and safari hunter and wound up as curator at the Botswana National Museum and Art Gallery. The director of the Denver Museum of Natural History met Ullberg on a safari and invited him to Colorado, where in 1974 he became curator of the African hall. He sculpted all along, especially wildlife encountered on his travels. In 1975, after a leopard sculpture he made won a prize from the National Academy of Design, he quit the Denver museum in the hopes of making a living as an artist.

Throughout his career, Ullberg maintained a Colorado studio in order to have access to the foundries around Loveland. He came to Corpus Christi in 1978 when scouting for a home by the sea. He and his Flemish wife, Veerle, liked the sound of the name and, like many Europeans, were enthralled by the crescent bay. The South Texas coast came to provide many of the subjects that won the artist a following among environmentalists as well as enthusiasts for wildlife art: marine fish and mammals and coastal birds. Admirers praised his ability to fuse knowledge of modern forms and materials with a grounding in anatomy and animal behavior to create work with both artistic credibility and popular appeal. By the 1980s, antidecorative forms of modernist architecture were giving way to the postmodern emphasis on historical references, lively designs, and varied artistic styles. This shift eased the way for Ullberg to win dozens of public commissions in North America and Europe, earning him renown outside the circle of western and wildlife artists.[40]

Ullberg built a reputation despite starting in the period of the twentieth century when arts professionals were most inclined to dismiss his animal sculptures as a waste of talent on an outmoded genre. Ullberg asserted that his emphasis on the grace and fragility of the environment was contemporary in spirit. His public art "celebrate[s] nature for itself," he explained, "without any connection to man." By contrast, artists in prior centuries, even the French romantic *animaliers*, who had inspired him as a student, portrayed wildlife "as commentary on man's culture," as allegories for human experiences or emotions, or as symbols for dynasties, cities, and the like. Given their struggle to win acceptance for nonrepresentational art, critics within Corpus Christi were inclined to accuse him of catering to existing taste. Ullberg responded that it was a worthy goal for public art to communicate in terms people could understand.[41] Even artists and curators who disliked Ullberg and his work praised his professionalism, especially his understanding of casting methods and his facility at translating models into outdoor works of monumental scale. Sculptors often find it difficult to adapt to the scale, complexity, and cost of public projects.

Art scholars who knew Ullberg remarked that he brought a "European" sense of public sculpture to South Texas, that is, he perceived that a profusion of public monuments could help orient local people even after the original, time-bound aesthetics and messages lost relevance. In Gothenburg, Ullberg recalled, grave equestrian statues of this or that king, known by irreverent nicknames, served as landmarks and gathering places over generations. One of his ambitions was to leave behind analogous landmarks in his adopted city.[42] Over time, he succeeded to a remarkable degree, becoming the artist who has most shaped Corpus Christi's visual identity. By the 2010s, at least fifteen of his works of public sculpture, several of them over twenty feet high, were on display in the city and surrounding towns.

Upon settling in Corpus Christi in 1978, Ullberg scouted for sites, of which there was no shortage, and patrons, who were harder to come by. A year later, insulted by the secretive selection panel's out-of-hand rejection of his submission for the convention center commission, Ullberg accused the "elite" in charge of the project of intimidating the public into accepting a sculpture with which normal people could not identify. With youthful overstatement, he asserted in the press, "Someone has to blow the whistle on these buggers." Ullberg, at the time new to the city, still unfamiliar with its art politics, explained that he meant to expose a rigged jury, not denigrate Surls's work or contemporary genres per se. Even so, for years afterward, advocates of *Turn* expressed anger at Ullberg for undermining them. The regional-local faction, however, was delighted to have an ally with the art history background and professional self-confidence to rebut the pro-Surls side point by point.[43]

Shortly after the Surls debacle, the city rejected Corpus Christi National Bank's offer to place an Ullberg sculpture of dolphins configured to form a "CC" on the median strip in front of the bank's new building on Shoreline Boulevard. The Municipal Arts Commission endorsed what would have been the first statue on the bayfront itself. Rival banks, however, complained that the dolphins would advertise the donor, since the bank's logo had a dolphin in it.[44] Ullberg placed a version of the dolphins in the bank's atrium, leaving the bayfront still without a sculpture. Edward Harte, publisher of the *Caller-Times*, then proposed to donate another Ullberg sculpture for the spot where the dolphins would have gone, in honor of the newspaper's centennial. A gradualist-reformist in art and much else, Harte wanted his city to have culture, but in a way that persuaded people that they wanted it themselves.[45] Ullberg's combination of skill and popularity presented a formula for finally winning acceptance of a bayfront sculpture.

For the biggest commission of his career to date, Ullberg produced a soaring, spiraling design, twenty-three feet high including the base, of two huge sailfish, in the artist's mind the most striking Gulf of Mexico fish. Ullberg named the statue *Wind in the Sails*, as a Swedish good-luck wish to his adopted hometown: "May you always have wind in the sails." With Harte's backing and MAC's endorsement, *Wind in the Sails* in 1983 became the first public art on public land along Corpus Christi Bay. For decades, it remained the only one placed there without a ruckus.[46] Even Ullberg's detractors admitted to liking it. The sculpture, which won the National Sculpture Society's Gold Medal in 1983, helped establish him as a designer of public art. His list of commissions came to include the *Whooping Cranes* fountain, installed in 1989 at the National Wildlife Federation in Washington, and Fort Lauderdale's enormous fountain, *Sailfish in Three Stages of Ascending*, installed 1991. Between 2002 and 2009, his *Spirit of Nebraska's Wilderness* took shape over six blocks in downtown Omaha. The world's largest wildlife monument consists of fifty-eight sculptures of flying geese—many atop specially designed traffic poles—arrayed as though

Figure 4.5. The sculptor Kent Ullberg installing *Wind in the Sails* along the Corpus Christi Bayfront, 1983. *Corpus Christi Caller-Times*, reprinted by permission.

they were taking off from fountains or flying through atriums, shifting in material from bronze to steel to represent movement through time. Accompanying the geese on the ground were a stampeding herd of Ullberg's bison, apparently set in motion by Blair Buswell and Edward Fraughton's equally epic wagon train in Pioneer Courage Park.[47]

In the 2000s, the sculptor's early nemesis, the Art Museum of South Texas, held a retrospective exhibition, named a gallery for him, and commissioned one of his bison for its front lawn. With that, Ullberg had four major public sculptures near or on the bayfront and two more across the ship channel on the grounds of the Texas State Aquarium. Of these, the first, *Wind in the Sails*, an evocation of the awesome Gulf, came closest to providing a symbol for the city. From an urban-design standpoint, however, Ullberg may have had more success in Omaha or Fort Lauderdale in leaving behind landmarks and rendezvous points. Like much recent urban public sculpture, Ullberg's Corpus Christi statues are frequently in median strips and other places that people drive past. People rarely linger enough for them to become fixtures in the consciousness. In 2005, Padre Island residents, with support from the Arts and Cultural Commission and a local foundation, erected *The Journey's End*—a nine-foot group depicting the Kemp's ridley sea turtles that nest nearby—as the highlight of Ullberg Park, near his house, a landmark for a neighborhood but not for the city overall.[48]

If, in 1997, the city council had ignored motorists' outcry and stuck by its approval of Dusty Durrill's proposal for rerouting Shoreline Boulevard, *Wind in the Sails* would no longer stand isolated on a median strip. Couples who met beneath Ullberg's sailfish might live to tell grandchildren about it. At that point, people preferred a clear view of the bay from their cars to the contemplation of sculpture. In 2004, the city council approved—and voters authorized start-up funds for—a modified plan to reroute Shoreline Boulevard and to make the bayfront more pedestrian friendly. This rerouting, however, began at the Gateway, five blocks north of *Wind in the Sails*. In 2008 voters approved a realignment to South Shoreline Boulevard that would end at Cooper's Alley, three blocks to the south of the bronze sailfish, again left high and dry on the median. Ullberg used soaring forms to compensate for the fact that most people would see his sculpture from moving cars.

Still, public sculpture may succeed better in providing the "cultural continuum" the artist remembered from Gothenburg when it is installed in cities oriented around squares filled with statues, and not along roads dotted with them.[49]

"An Art's-a-Poppin' Kind of Place"

Corpus Christi "got lucky" with the widely liked *Wind in the Sails*, a local arts writer observed. The town reverted to form when a group offered to donate a fountain composed of four pelicans, designed by Buddy Tatum—later the sculptor of the Selena monument—for the entrance to the new convention center. Robert Zion, an associate of Philip Johnson hired to construct a water garden in the Bayfront Arts and Science Park, pointedly left Tatum's pelican fountain out of the landscaping plan he submitted in 1982. Tatum produced a scaled-back design—no fountain and two pelicans—for the entrance to the Corpus Christi Museum of Science and History. Zion and his supporters saw this as an intrusion as well. In 1985, MAC finally placed *El Circo del Mar*, a sculpture intended for children, on a forlorn median along Shoreline Boulevard in the shadow of a high-rise hotel.[50]

Fed up with such disarray and bickering, the city government determined to "get things under control," as Mic Raasch, the city planner responsible for cultural programs, recalled.[51] In 1982, the city council set aside part of its hotel-motel tax for the Permanent Art Trust Fund, which MAC could spend on large public art projects. In 1986, the city hired Jerry Allen, the director of Dallas's Department of Cultural Affairs and a formulator of Seattle's acclaimed Art in Public Places program, to help draft a public art ordinance, one that would have review procedures for both purchases and donations. Allen explained that well-run reviews could insulate the city council by letting MAC "serve as the 'lightning rod' in rendering aesthetic decisions." Though the ordinance mandated that MAC not favor "any particular school, style, taste or medium," supporters hoped that by reserving two of four voting slots on review panels for arts professionals, the plan would limit the ability of opponents to block contemporary works.[52]

Allen's plan also included what would be the second percent-for-art provision adopted in Texas, with 1.25 percent of the cost of municipal construction projects to be spent on artwork.[53] The city manager's office questioned the wisdom and legality of Allen's preferred arrangement, which would have diverted funds even from bonds for streets, sewage treatment plants, and such. The city reworked the ordinance so that the 1.25 percent would apply only to the cost of buildings and would have to be spent at the site for which the bond was passed. This would drastically lessen the funds available, Allen predicted, and it would compel MAC to contract for art in fire stations and similar places that not many people visit. Moreover, the ordinance made it difficult to contract with an artist until the final cost had been determined, which meant that art would be added onto already-designed buildings rather than integrated into the architecture from the start.[54]

Nevertheless, the *Caller-Times* remarked, even the "drastically scaled-down" art ordinance approved in March 1987 would be "a step toward shaking Corpus Christi's sleepy-fishing-village legacy." In providing MAC the authority to commission works using accumulated hotel-motel taxes, along with oversight of the percent-for-art program, the city council had in fact given the Corpus Christi board powers denied to analogous commissions in many bigger cities. Even the venerable Art Commission of the City of New York reviewed proposals from other agencies or private donors, but could not initiate projects and controlled almost no revenue.[55]

The public-art ordinance indeed encouraged the spread of smaller sculptures and murals, costing from $1,100 to $8,000, to neighborhood parks, senior centers, and branch libraries. In the decade after the ordinance was passed, Corpus Christi's public art collection jumped from eight to twenty-nine works and the number of sculptures from six to sixteen, but few municipal purchases were designated for prestigious spots. One exception was the city's first work by the renowned sculptor Jesús Moroles, a native Corpus Christian with a studio in nearby Rockport. In 1992, percent-for-art funds generated $39,000 for a ninety-two-inch pink granite monolith, *Texas Stele*, relatively small by Moroles's standards but appropriate for a niche in the atrium of the new city hall. In 1989, the city acquired its first large outdoor work under the percent-for-art ordinance, *Sunseeker* by Danny O'Dowdy, a tile-and-concrete plant form at the entrance to the new public library in Uptown.[56]

The spread of new work around town, one reporter noted, had made Corpus Christi "an art's-a-poppin' kind of place" by the early 1990s.[57] Still, the notion that a public-art ordinance could insulate art from city politics, and vice versa, never worked out. The city council reserved for itself final approval of purchases and donations, which made the process inescapably political. Also, by the mid-1980s ethnic identity had joined the mix of class, cultural, aesthetic, bureaucratic, and professional disagreements that had made public art a source of wrangling for years.

Orgullo

When, in the early 1980s, the Westside Business Association began fixing the neglected triangle where Agnes and Laredo Streets meet, the WBA decided to place a monument there to Captain Alonso Álvarez de Pineda, the Spanish explorer who in 1519 mapped the Gulf of Mexico. The Spanish consulate made a vague offer of a statue, but the WBA felt safer in commissioning Sherman Coleman, a local physician and sculptor, to design an eight-foot bronze, the city's first outdoor statue to a historical figure. The WBA gathered funds and support with relative ease. The city spent $44,000 to construct the plaza. The Municipal Arts Commission approved the statue and gave $10,000 toward it. WBA members built the foundation and pedestal themselves, using donated materials and machinery. Though done in a conservative manner by a local amateur, the statue raised little of the typical aesthetic controversy surrounding public art. "We weren't bothering anybody" so far from the bayfront, recalled Oscar Flores, the WBA officer who oversaw the project.[58]

As recounted earlier, the WBA agreed to use the word "legend" on the monument's inscription in reference to Álvarez de Pineda's alleged discovery and naming of Corpus Christi Bay. Whatever the provenance and plausibility of the story, many Mexican American Corpus Christians expressed a belief in it. These included Flores, who imagined the explorer saying to himself that he had come upon "the most beautiful bay I have ever seen." In the end, undocumentable aspects of the Álvarez de Pineda story mattered less to Flores than the undeniable fact that the 1519 voyage provided a starting point for narratives of South Texas that emphasized and validated the Hispanic presence. According to Flores, the Pineda monument built *"orgullo,"* or pride, in barrio children. "You can get up there and hug [Pineda's statue] and say, 'This is ours. This man was an Hispanic like me.'"[59]

For Pineda Plaza, the WBA secured help from the Spanish consul but attracted little Mexican interest, a reflection of Mexican and Mexican American ambivalence about Spanish-heritage projects. As also discussed earlier, critics charged that Spanish heritage conjured a romantic past that downgraded the Mexican and Tejano roots of the region's Hispanics and that downplayed Anglo-Mexican conflict as a force in regional history. Spanish-heritage projects such as Pineda Plaza did have some of the distracting effects that bothered their critics. But as Flores suggested, groups such as the WBA were attracted to them anyway as an assertion of Hispanic priority and legitimacy in a city whose street layout, public works and places, and building styles created a mainly Anglo-American visual identity.

In 1988, such considerations prompted the WBA to seek to place on Shoreline Boulevard a thirteen-foot equestrian statue of Blas María de la Garza Falcón, who in the 1760s led the Mexican expedition that settled Nueces County, a well-recorded event of undeniable significance. WBA president Flores recalled that the group wanted an "impressive" monument in the city's "living room." "There's no way," Flores remembered being warned, given the years of quarrels over public sculpture on the Corpus Christi Bayfront.[60] Adept at maneuvering through city politics, the WBA lined up support in the city manager's office before presenting the statue to the Municipal Arts Commission, which, under the recent public-art ordinance, was to review donations before their acceptance.

For the Falcón statue, the WBA again turned to Sherman Coleman, a choice that reveals a gap in perspective between the civic activists in the WBA and the arts activists on MAC. The art professors and curators who served on MAC's review panels doubted Coleman's ability to produce a first-rate historical monument on the scale that the WBA planned. Among local sculptors in figurative genres, only Ullberg and Roberto García, a young University of Texas–trained artist with a studio near Kingsville, had the requisite professional background in large monuments. As several tense exchanges revealed, the WBA treated MAC as a manifestation of an Anglo establishment that still meant to reserve the symbolic heart of the city for itself. The arts commissioners, meanwhile, reacted to WBA members as well-connected businessmen pulling strings to put a statue of less than the "highest aesthetic standard" on the bayfront.[61]

The mutual suspicions of MAC and the WBA provided a South Texas variant on a pattern evident since the late 1800s, when ethnic heritage monuments emerged as a genre in American cities. Sometimes with reason and sometimes not, ethnic organizations have perceived municipal arts-review panels as condescending to them and as scheming to consign their monuments to inferior or peripheral sites. For their part, arts reviewers have complained about such organizations' defensiveness with regard to even well-intended advice and their manipulation of political connections to seize sites that may not be appropriate for a particular monument. From the ethnic organizations' perspective, the point of proposing a monument was visibility and respect. This attitude inclined such groups toward works of conventionality, even predictability, as though each group needed a normal statue to affirm its presence. Arts review organizations frequently responded by asserting that a particular design could be more distinctive or imaginative. This was a formula for mutual frustration, even when—as in the case of the WBA's Falcón proposal—the expert reviewers agreed with the proposers' rationale for honoring a historical figure in a prominent place.[62]

The arts commissioners indeed reacted with frustration when the Falcón monument came to them in the spring of 1989. MAC charged that by securing prior backing from the city manager's office, the WBA had subverted the 1987 art ordinance during one of its first serious tests. The WBA meant for MAC to "rubber-stamp" Coleman's Falcón, not review it, recalled the artist Barbara McDowell, then chair of MAC's Visual Arts Committee. MAC referred the proposal to a review panel anyway. The reviewers decided that an equestrian statue would be a proper way to memorialize the colonizer, but Coleman's maquette lacked "vitality, movement, and proper perspective" and would not translate to monumental scale. The WBA and Coleman refused to incorporate suggestions offered by a sculpture professor on the review panel to make the design less "static."[63] The arts commissioners proposed a delay until there was a master plan for public art along the bayfront. The WBA refused to wait for a plan that might use some aesthetic or planning principle to exclude them. MAC claimed not to want to "mix and match" on the bayfront, Flores recalled, to which he responded that Falcón "has got it over 150,000 fish that you could put there." Boxed in, MAC approved Coleman's Falcón in May 1989.[64]

The WBA covered most of the cost of the $130,000 statue by selling bronze miniatures of it. The nearly equal cost of the base and landscaping proved more elusive until Dusty Durrill joined the fund-raising campaign. As with Pineda Plaza, the WBA attracted more interest from Spanish than Mexican authorities. The Spanish embassy contributed $15,000. The city helped arrange for Flores and his associates to travel to Spain to promote the project. Decades of heated discussion among Mexican Americans rendered groups such as the WBA self-conscious about celebrating Spanish ancestors who may have subdued or displaced native peoples in their background. Flores and Coleman took pains to represent Falcón as a pioneer of whom Hispanics could be proud, and not as an oppressive conquistador. The officer's right hand carried not a sword but a hat, raised in a gesture of greeting. The statue, on the Shoreline Boulevard median strip a block south of *Wind in the Sails*, bore the name *Friendship Monument*. No evidence survives regarding clashes between Falcón and native peoples, Flores explained. "He was a good, kind man," the WBA leader said. "We're proud of him."[65]

Given this Hispanic interest in historical monuments, it was almost inevitable that the first personality in the city's modern history to receive a statue would be the civil rights leader Hector P. García. In 1993, an ad hoc group launched a drive to build a monument to García, then nearly eighty and ailing, perhaps at the Corpus Christi airport or in Sherrill Park, a square on the bayfront dedicated to veterans. Texas A&M University–Corpus Christi, which held García's papers, proposed a García Plaza in front of its library, beneath its special-collections reading room.[66] Though this site, at the southeastern corner of the city, promised less visibility than the bayfront, the monument's promoters readily agreed to the proposal. The university could provide professional fund-raisers capable of securing the needed $500,000. The university also offered relative freedom from the political and administrative hurdles that faced a sculpture project on municipal land. Furthermore, the site conformed to the mindset of García himself.

Figure 4.6. Friendship Monument, with Sherman Coleman's equestrian statue of the colonizer Blas María de la Garza Falcón, installed in 1992 along the Corpus Christi Bayfront. Richard Colley's Marina Hotel (discussed in chapter 5) is in the background. Photo by Kenny Braun, 2014.

Firmly Mexican American in his approach, García stressed citizenship and integration, with education as a vehicle toward those goals. A plaza in the shadow of the university library that housed his papers seemed an appropriate tribute.

Rather than make the monument grand and dramatic, the university sought a "quiet, hushed" haven in the middle of the campus. The university landscape designer placed García's statue on a small base in a fountain and surrounded the plaza with gardens and a tall semicircular wall. Bright colors, tile work, and tropical plants loosely recalled "the ambience of old Mexico." To sculpt the civil rights leader, sponsors chose Roberto García, the young artist bypassed in the Falcón competition. A Laredo native and former assistant to Charles Umlauf, a revered sculpture teacher at the University of Texas, García had recently gained critical praise for his lively portrait of Christopher Columbus at the Port of Corpus Christi, another Spanish-heritage project, commissioned for the 1992 quincentenary.[67] (The Columbus statue did draw protests from Native American groups, who were not usually a presence in such disputes in this part of Texas.)

Roberto García explained that he sought to express the universal character of a speaker, an advocate for his people. His goal was for the monument to remain relevant after direct memories of Hector García had faded.[68] For the time being, however, the statue seemed to humanize and historicize a figure who, even while alive, had taken on attributes of a paragon and legend. The monument project brought forth a slew of "Dr. Hector" anecdotes: amusing ones having to do with García's withering bursts of temper, grateful ones having to do with the free medical care he provided from his Westside office long after he became renowned.

Until the García monument, most of Corpus Christi's public sculptures illustrated the extent to which residents of all ethnic groups persisted in identifying local history with a preurban age of explorers and heroes. Hector García, of course, was a hero in his own time as well as a person. Still, his peaceful, subtle monument suggested—just as, in a noisier way, the Selena memorial completed a year later had done— that in the last years of the twentieth century, Corpus Christians had begun to view the city around them and its life and drama as worthy of contemplation and commemoration through public art.

Figure 4.7. Roberto García's portrait of Hector García in the Hector Garcia Plaza, Texas A&M University–Corpus Christi. The university library's Special Collections and Archives, which houses the massive García Collection, is on the second story in the background. Photo by Kenny Braun, 2014.

"A Salutary Few Moments of Beauty and Bewilderment"

Cooperation between Hispanic civic groups and arts professionals on Hector García Plaza pointed to a possible solution of at least one strand in Corpus Christi's tangled quarrels over public art. In 1989, when seeking approval for the Falcón monument, the Westside Business Association, distrusting the arts review process, used political influence to circumvent MAC. The WBA presupposed that MAC would not appreciate the importance of a heritage project on the bayfront. The WBA assumed as well that MAC would try to impose its own aesthetic standards on the project, even if that meant delaying or scuttling the Falcón monument. In such an atmosphere of miscommunication and resistance, an arts review process could not achieve its goal of sanctioning projects while encouraging improvements in them.

By this time, the Art Museum of South Texas, determined to overcome its reputation as rigid and out of touch, had undertaken conspicuous efforts to support regional arts, above all by collecting, documenting, and exhibiting Texas and northern Mexican art. As part of a merger in 1997 that created the South Texas Institute for the Arts, the museum, in conjunction with Texas A&M–Corpus Christi, absorbed the Center for Hispanic Arts, a WBA-sponsored enterprise on Agnes Street on the Westside. The WBA's motives for ceding control of what became the Antonio E. García Center—named for Corpus Christi's first widely known Hispanic artist, who died in 1997—were largely financial and organizational. Along with the commissioning of the architectural firm Legorreta + Legorreta to expand Philip Johnson's building, such moves signaled that the local arts institution with the greatest visibility and influence intended to participate as fully as possible in South Texas's multiethnic environment.

A tentative meeting of the minds between Hispanic civic leaders and arts professionals hardly guaranteed a citywide consensus about public art. The very existence of the Selena monument on the bayfront—let alone its style and iconography and its visceral connection to youthful fans—revealed differences over social class, popular culture, and taste and refinement among Hispanics as well as across ethnic groups.

In late 1997, MAC raised the possibility of an alternative vision of the interplay between the arts and South Texas Hispanics when it named Jesús Moroles, along with El Paso's Luis Jiménez, among six finalists for the $215,000 Gateway sculpture, underwritten by the Public Art Trust Fund. None of the other finalists—three Anglo-Americans and a Russian—had Texas connections. Typically, Jiménez proposed four larger than life regional archetypes made from fiberglass: a vaquero, a fisherman, an industrial worker, and a Tejano singer. Political leaders clearly hoped that MAC, renamed the Arts and Cultural Commission during these events, would select Moroles. The son of a Mexican immigrant who had prospered in an eyeglasses business, Moroles, though born in Corpus Christi, grew up largely in Dallas. He studied at the University of North Texas, apprenticed with Jiménez, and trained as well in Pietrasanta, a stone-carving town in northern Italy. The sculptor already had a dozen pieces around the state, including the *Houston Police Officers Memorial* (1991), but as yet no outdoor work in his hometown, only *Texas Stele* in the city hall atrium. Moroles intended his work to evoke Texas and the Southwest, but he addressed international themes in contemporary sculpture as well. As a personality and artist, he crossed the aesthetic as well as ethnic divides that had rankled the city. In keeping with his characteristic approach of presenting granite as though it had been torn along its natural grain, the artist proposed for the Gateway three monoliths made of pink Texas granite—between twelve and fourteen feet high—with sheets of water streaming down them.[69]

Throughout 1998, the arts commission endeavored to generate support through public presentations by the six finalists. Yet even well-publicized appearances by Moroles and Jiménez attracted audiences mainly of art enthusiasts already well disposed to the project. In October 1999, to the surprise of many, the arts commissioners bypassed Moroles in favor of *Orion's Belt*, a kinetic sculpture by the New York artist Robert Perless. The three steel weathervane shapes, fifty-five-feet long on twenty-foot piers, would shift with the wind direction, "making the winds that surround us really visible" in the seafaring city, as the artist explained. Beyond representing the wind and a constellation associated with navigation, Perless's giant structures also could symbolize aeronautics, the navy, and even ocean birds. The steel structures, the arts commissioners reasoned, would hold up well in the humid Gulf air, though residents worried that they might become projectiles during hurricanes, as did the General Services Administration, responsible for the new federal courthouse across Shoreline Boulevard. In the years after their installation in 2002, the Gulf of Mexico did not test Perless's insistence that the steel vanes could be readily secured as a storm approached. Within the first year, however, the sculpture did require rust treatment.[70]

A decisive factor, emphasized in public and private by the selection panel and the arts commission, was the location in a median strip at the juncture of a highway and a multilane boulevard. Moroles's fountain made of three granite monoliths would stand out in a pedestrian square but would prove underscaled for "vehicular approach," as commission chair Chuck Anastos explained. Whereas with *Orion's Belt*, "friends, family, and visitors" would be protected "from having to cross Shoreline Boulevard to admire or engage with" it. "You can see [Perless's] sculpture from a mile and a half away," arts commissioner Victor Martinez told the *Caller-Times*, "where Mr. Moroles' would have required viewing from across the street and then getting up on the median to really appreciate it." Anastos envisioned drivers having "a salutary few moments of beauty and bewilderment" as they rolled by.[71]

Neither city manager David Garcia nor Mayor Loyd Neal anticipated difficulty. *Orion's Belt* would "appeal to a wide segment of our population," Neal remarked, adding that the arts commission "did an excellent job looking for community input."[72] At its next meeting, the city council voted to reject the sculpture. "They went through three years of deliberation," Perless retorted when opponents on the council suggested that the public had had "not enough input." With decades of hassles in mind, the *Caller-Times* rated the Gateway project's prospects as "slim," adding that "matching the public's sense with artistic values is not as tight as the proverbial camel through the proverbial needle's eye, but there's not much give either." Yet in contrast with its predecessor's actions during the Surls disaster two decades earlier, the arts commission regrouped. After displaying Perless's model alongside Moroles's in city hall for nearly two months, the commissioners returned to the council, which this time voted 8–1 in favor. Three council members, however, including two of four Hispanics, specified that they would have preferred Moroles's work.[73]

Corpus Christians might not know much about art, the newspaper reflected, "but we certainly know how to have a good fight about it."

Figure 4.8. Robert Perless, *Orion's Belt*, at the Gateway intersection along Shoreline Boulevard. Photo by Kenny Braun, 2014.

The arts commission's victory might finally have inculcated respect for the process outlined in the 1987 public-art ordinance, which was intended to balance "public sentiments with the perspective of art expertise."[74] In its relatively disciplined campaign to sell *Orion's Belt*, the Arts and Cultural Commission avoided pronouncements about the work's potential for cultivating art appreciation and overcoming provincialism. The commission confined itself to claims about public relations and tourism. But rationales based in urban identity and civic betterment remained implicit. Such arguments justified, for example, defense of the Public Art Trust Fund when in 1998 the city council considered diverting the carefully saved money into a cause such as minority business development.[75]

Moroles's fountain could have offered aesthetic education, along with a lesson in the complexities of cultural interaction in Texas and the borderlands. Yet as the arts commissioners recognized, Moroles's work would have captured people's attention and served public art's civic-betterment purpose only in a central city of squares and lingering pedestrians, not in a diffuse city that people experience in automobiles at thirty miles an hour. Perhaps public sculpture cannot hope to foster urbanity and civic patriotism in a spread-out, linear, southwestern-style city such as Corpus Christi. Especially since the publication of *Learning from Las Vegas* (1972), public art advocates, as well as architects and urban planners, have wrestled with the problem that confronted Corpus Christi's Arts and Cultural Commission during the Gateway competition. Aesthetics based upon contemplation falters in cities based upon movement.[76]

The notion of public sculpture as the focal point for civic consciousness, which Ullberg brought to South Texas from Gothenburg, could not easily translate to a city with no stopping points for everyone. Ullberg, after all, could not gather his audience into a square, as his teachers could in Sweden. He needed to create swirling shapes that would perhaps catch people's eyes as they drove distractedly past. Two projects discussed in this chapter that did succeed as gathering places were exceptions that proved the rule. The Selena monument became a tourist draw in an accessible pavilion on the seawall. García Plaza offered a friendly spot for students to read, talk, or hold events in a place closed to traffic nine miles from the center of town.

The mingling of history, heritage, and Texas saga in many of Corpus Christi's public sculptures gives credence to concerns that monuments may block appreciation of history as often as they encourage it. "Reality disappears when art is put in its place," wrote a German critic of public art as a device for commemorating the dreadful episodes of his country's past.[77] Though not all monument builders were as grandiose as Gutzon Borglum, almost by definition they responded more to picturesque, grand legends than to inconclusive history. Tejano as well as Anglo Corpus Christians identified with legend, intrepidity, and adventure. When Mexican American groups began to insist that Corpus Christi should pay more attention to their history in its public art, they perhaps really wanted more regard for their grandeur. Residents of Texas cities such as Corpus Christi had long perceived the wilderness past as grand, but had found little romance in the urban present. Given this mindset, it makes sense that they have filled their city with monuments to many things other than their own city. Nonetheless, amid all their competing agendas, groups supporting sculpture projects accepted the venerable yet vague notion that public art can have civic utility, that sculpture can bring a community together and enlighten its people.

Chapter 5

A MATTER OF
LITTLE IMPORT

∽

"Ah, *young love*," sighed the *Caller-Times* columnist Leanne Libby concerning the greeting afforded Destination Bayfront, a group of civic and business figures formed in the winter of 2010 to revitalize the southern portion of the Corpus Christi Bayfront. "Think Houston's Discovery Green. San Diego's Balboa Park. Heart going pitter-patter yet?"[1] Destination Bayfront targeted the central city's most prominent troubled area: two dozen acres of vacant land and deserted auto dealerships surrounding the abandoned Memorial Coliseum. Pointing to waterfront revitalizations across the country, Destination Bayfront described the coliseum's impending demolition as an "identity-creating, game-changing opportunity."[2]

Determined to avoid the corporate control and theme-park tawdriness that alienated residents from earlier bayfront schemes, the group commissioned New York's Project for Public Spaces, a planning and design group whose emphasis on participation and access might counter the distrust that surrounded planning for the central city, an atmosphere exacerbated by a five-year quarrel over whether to preserve or demolish the coliseum.[3] Familiar with Corpus Christi from a transit station it had helped design, PPS worked with Destination Bayfront to organize dozens of public meetings. Volunteers devoted around 3,000 hours to gathering over 1,000 ideas from the public. A fifty-slide Pow-erPoint presentation to the city council in June 2010 was followed by an eighty-five-page report in November. "Whatever we put there," the PPS consultant Fred Kent told one of the public meetings, "has to be something that you will own and celebrate and come to on a regular basis." PPS's preliminary plan—whose implementation was assigned to Hargreaves Associates, another firm that worked on Discovery Green—fused marketing to tourists with attentiveness to locals. Rec-reation, shopping, restaurants, promenades, and concert places would extend along the bayfront from a square given the regionalist name zocalo.[4]

As if to validate Libby's sense of déjà vu, Destination Bayfront's website listed recent forerunners, including a 2008 Downtown Vision Plan (forty-three PowerPoint slides) and a 2007 Bayfront Master Plan Update (forty-seven PowerPoint slides). These were follow-ups to the Shoreline Boulevard Master Plan (fifty PowerPoint slides), present-ed in June 2004. Much of the impetus for these studies came from a Corpus Christi architectural firm, Raymond Gignac and Associates, whose work on the American Bank Center—the north bayfront build-ing that made Memorial Coliseum redundant—deepened its expertise concerning central Corpus Christi. Like PPS and Destination Bay-front, Gignac and his out-of-town associates, Boston's Sasaki Asso-ciates and Miami's Arquitectonica, envisioned a mixture of tourism, parks, pedestrian zones, recreation, culture, and housing. These plans also sought an atmosphere geared to the city's geography and mindset, along with a sense of ownership and civic pride.[5]

Gignac emerged as coordinator of bayfront renewal plans in the wake of a thirteen-hour charette in October 2003. This session—or-ganized after public opposition forced the city to back away from a plan to lease the marina to Landry's, a Houston-based restaurant and entertainment company—involved nearly every South Texas architect with an interest in the central city. The *Caller-Times* reviewed bayfront schemes going back to Gutzon Borglum's ill-fated 1928 proposal. "Bayfront plans keep coming around again," proclaimed the headline. The city planning office noted that it could document thirty-seven plans over a half-century that dealt at least in part with the bayfront. "We've probably got more," remarked the planner Robert Payne.[6]

Among this profusion was a 1974 plan by Sasaki, which sought "a blend of growth and protection" that would "exploit" without "destroying" the "magnificent waterfront."[7] The official bayfront plan, adopted in 1982, repeated Sasaki's priorities and even its wording. The municipal South Central Area Plan, as revised in 2004, promised "a mix of tourist, retail, entertainment, residential, and civic uses in the Bayfront and Downtown Business District," and "pedestrian friendly retail, restaurant, and entertainment uses along street frontages combined with multi-family residential, hotel, office uses and parking garages on aboveground levels." Two years later, the citizen-run Downtown Redevelopment Committee called for "multiple traffic generators," walkability, "anchor projects," "broad public-private investment," "strong, adjacent residential districts" (perhaps "upscale"), and a downtown "beloved by citizenry" enough that people would argue constantly about it.[8]

"We seem to have the brainstorming process down," Libby observed wearily. "Our completion track record stinks." Another exasperated journalist, Nick Jimenez, remarked, "The downtown bayfront is where development ideas go to die."[9] By November 2013, Destination Bayfront seemed headed for that fate, victim of an off-year bond election held amid resentment over a street-user fee tacked onto utility bills. "Do we need a $40 million park now," summarized one letter to the editor, "when there is an urgent need to repair and restore almost all of our city streets?" Supporters countered that the south bayfront park, a free-admission nonprofit public-private venture, would attract tourists and businesses, generating much-needed revenue for municipal services. Since it was to be built on central-city land, Destination Bayfront would require few utilities extensions, and an endowment and assessments on adjacent property would pay for operations and maintenance. Such claims evoked memories of promises made a dozen years earlier regarding another recreation-related infrastructure project, Packery Channel, discussed in chapter 6. Insisted a letter writer who drew the connection: "The voters cannot trust the City to honor the promises made in its bond proposition." Bonds for the south bayfront project lost 2–1 among the 25,000 residents who turned out to vote, despite supporters having raised twenty-six times as much money as opponents.[10]

This chapter traces the central city's emergence as a site of dissatisfaction. It reviews strategies for revitalization and looks at obstacles to a flourishing downtown, problems epitomized by the south bayfront's struggles even as cultural institutions and meeting and entertainment venues enlivened the north bayfront. The chapter then discusses historic preservation in central Corpus Christi, most efforts at which have ended in disappointment, for many of the same reasons that hampered central-city revitalization overall.

The restoration and reuse of historic buildings is both a redevelopment strategy and a commentary on the present. In Corpus Christi, the central city's fragmentation and bickering over its conditions seemed indicative of the city's lost opportunities and directionless politics. A half century earlier, the city had a reputation for coherent planning and effective implementation, albeit under an "elitist, unaccountable, and undemocratic" business and civic leadership, as Jimenez reminded Corpus Christians.[11] When, back in 1950, the chamber of commerce formed the Area Development Committee to oversee planning and public works, the self-perpetuating panel saw no reason to downplay the prominence and wealth of the people who sat on it. Even when calling for hefty tax increases to finance public works, buildings, and parks, the ADC, like commercial-civic movements in other southwestern cities, was confident that it represented the entire public and understood how Corpus Christi could "realize [its] potential as one of the most progressive industrial and agricultural areas in the country." This confidence stemmed from members' prominence in enterprises that had caused the city to multiply ten times in population since the 1920s: the port, commercial agriculture, land development, oil and petrochemicals, and utilities. Implementation of ADC-sponsored plans would make "all citizens . . . proud of their City and enjoy living and working here."[12]

In 1953, the ADC published the last comprehensive plan adopted as official by the city council, a three-year study by the St. Louis planning firm Harland Bartholomew and Associates (HBA).[13] HBA did not produce a separate study of the bayfront and the central business district (CBD), in part because planners remained convinced that the CBD's "importance" was "well understood" and that Corpus Christians would support improvements to ensure its "dominant position in the trade area." Also, for midcentury planners, a comprehensive plan required a citywide perspective—"the whole picture," as ADC chair Lon C. Hill Jr. put it. This meant treating even the CBD as a component of the overall urban system.[14]

The Bartholomew plan praised a 1944 report by the Kansas City consultants Hare and Hare and chastised the city for allowing private uses to intrude as landscaping of the new Corpus Christi seawall began after World War II. The plans of Hare and Hare and HBA illustrated the confidence of the midcentury elite in their disinclination to use the bayfront for tourist marketing, though the ADC appreciated tourism as a business and as a way to attract attention. Planners defined the bayfront as a "community asset" to be "reserved for public purposes." "Impressive public building groups" should line Shoreline Boulevard, in the modernist spirit of the architect Richard Colley's new civic center, of which Memorial Coliseum was a component. The plan called for an arts commission more formidable than the agency that was in fact formed (discussed in chapter 4). The ADC's arts commission would have had authority "to determine the appropriateness and adequacy of all public buildings [throughout the city] and all buildings, both public and private, which face the Bayfront." Hotels and other commercial activities would be consigned to the margins; the closer to the center they were, the more discreet they would need to be. Gaudy or glitzy tourist construction would not be tolerated along the seawall.[15]

By 1966–1968, when HBA updated its plan, the ADC had lost faith in the city's ability to control its image and direction. Planners now assumed that a city hungry for investment needed to market the bayfront, which meant compromising its civic character. This shift formed the background to ensuing quarrels over who controlled the bayfront and to what end. Stagnation of the Coastal Bend economy eroded the unity, imagination, and effectiveness of the business and civic leadership represented by the ADC. Stagnation likewise fed attacks on the Anglo establishment from multiple directions, based on class, ethnicity, geography, and principle. Yet even in Texas and southwestern cities that shared the dynamism of the Sunbelt era, upper-class governing alliances were facing increased opposition by the late 1960s. Visions for central cities fragmented as urban politics grew more fractious and urban life more diffuse.[16]

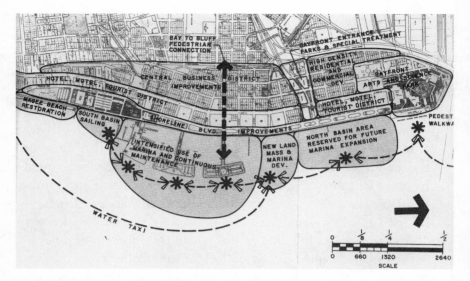

Figure 5.1. The city's 1982 Bayfront Plan, based on Sasaki's 1974 study, illustrates the abandonment of the Area Development Committee's earlier vision of the bayfront as civic space. Although pushed to the margins earlier, tourist uses could now line Shoreline Boulevard. From "Bayfront Plan: Corpus Christi, Texas," December 1982, revised March 1984.

In this way, nostalgia for the age of downtowns—for the cohesive urban form and vibrant urban life that downtown supposedly represented—took hold in Corpus Christi. Such yearnings animated preservation and revitalization movements throughout the United States, even in southwestern cities like Corpus Christi that had grown because of petroleum and around internal combustion engines.[17] Corpus Christi's status as an economic laggard in Sunbelt Texas generated a self-consciousness about matters such as redevelopment and preservation. Local perceptions of a city especially prone to incompetence or shortsightedness in such matters, however, were more apparent than real.

"Internal Problems of Access and Circulation"

Because of the timing of the city's growth, central Corpus Christi is more or less coincident with the historic city. Until World War II, Corpus Christi encompassed around twelve square miles. The built-up area stretched from North Beach to middle-class Anglo neighborhoods such as South Bluff Park, the Furman and Morgan areas, and some of the current Del Mar. Little development had occurred beyond Louisiana Avenue, less than a mile south of the seawall, or Port Avenue, about a mile west of the Corpus Christi Bluff. A fraction of the subsequent area, this was still generous territory, even for a city whose population quintupled to over 50,000 between 1910 and 1950. Prewar Corpus Christi was never tightly woven; its neighborhoods rambled loosely in proximity to the port or in a semicircle around the business district that straddled the bluff. Then during the 1940s, the city began to explode in area as its population nearly doubled. By 1950, the municipal limits encompassed around twenty-two square miles, stretching southwest to Gollihar Road and southeast to Oso Bay. The city would expand to over one hundred square miles by the mid-1960s. Decentralization was so rapid that the 1953 Bartholomew report defined almost the entire prewar city as the CBD. Planning documents into the 2000s maintained this practice of identifying the central city with the pre–World War II city.[18]

Already in the 1930s, Harland Bartholomew, city planning director for St. Louis as well as operator of his own consulting firm, had begun to warn that decentralization of population and business—hitherto favored by planners as a cure for central-city overcrowding—might soon create more problems than it solved. Bartholomew and other planners long remained convinced, however, that within most metropolitan regions, CBDs did not need the reconstruction that became known as urban renewal, but could be shored up through civic centers, slum clearance, highways, and parking garages. This confidence applied even more to a southwestern city such as Corpus Christi, which at midcentury boasted a healthy, broad-based economy.[19]

Accordingly, HBA's 1953 plan proposed routing intercity traffic through the Westside along Leopard and Agnes Streets and then into the CBD. Intracity traffic from the Southside would move downtown along postwar thoroughfares such as Staples and Alameda. Nearly ten thousand new parking spaces could accommodate the anticipated influx of cars. Improved access and parking for automobiles would protect downtown as "the principal destination of city and Bay Area traffic." Only a few segments of this CBD-focused system materialized before Interstate 37, the Crosstown Expressway, and South Padre Island Drive combined to channel traffic around downtown as readily as through it. To offset the dispersal of retail trade from downtown while protecting the shoreline's accessibility and civic character, the 1953 plan concentrated public buildings in "an imposing, well-planned array." To balance Colley's municipal center along the south bayfront, HBA would have located a new county courthouse, a federal building, and state and federal courts at a "prominent and commanding position" along the north bayfront near the later Gateway, roughly where the federal government did open its new courthouse in 2001.[20] Beyond suiting the confident mood of the ADC, the assumption that public activities—as opposed to business or tourism—should occupy the most symbolic place adhered to the City Beautiful tradition, in which Bartholomew was trained.

The 1953 HBA plan "made a significant contribution toward guiding the rapid growth and development of the Community," the ADC summarized in 1958. Although the catalyst for Harbor Bridge, the Wesley Seale Dam, the Corpus Christi International Airport, and numerous other projects, the plan did little to stem dispersal from downtown and may even have accelerated it by encouraging annexation and service extensions to outlying areas.[21] Businessmen with central-city interests grew suspicious of colleagues investing in Southside subdivisions and shopping centers, including the oilman Guy Warren, the ADC's founder. When Warren refused in 1964 to take a public stance in favor of downtown revitalization, a long-standing collaborator, the real estate agent William Neyland, noted angrily that he "should have resigned" as ADC president. Warren's new Cullen Mall, at Alameda and Airline on the Southside, showed him to be "not interested in the down town or up town areas," only in "his own interests."[22]

Neyland turned his energies to a Central Business District Association, which in 1965 invited the Urban Land Institute to study "the relentless erosion of the strength and vitality of downtown" and to propose "realistic" new uses for the CBD. In contrast to the HBA report from a decade earlier, the ULI supported "motel construction along Shoreline Boulevard" in conjunction with other "tourist-oriented facilities" downtown. Instead of "After-Sundown-Lifelessness," the CBD should feature restaurants, hotels, a sports arena, "an aquatic show area," and similar attractions to prompt convention goers and prosperous vacationers to "come in larger numbers and stay for longer periods."[23] The ULI was acknowledging that competition from outlying shopping and office developments, along with the shift of beach tourism toward Padre and Mustang Islands, rendered a civic vision for the bayfront unviable. Up-to-date waterfront hotels, including Richard Colley's high-rise Sheraton Marina Inn across from the Lawrence Street T-Head pier and Holiday Inn's Emerald Beach Hotel to the south across Shoreline Boulevard from Memorial Coliseum, were intended to enhance the central city's attractiveness to vacationers and conventioneers.[24]

When the ADC and the city agreed in 1965 to cosponsor a new plan by HBA, the St. Louis planners recognized anxieties over the central city in Corpus Christi and nationally by examining the CBD's land use, property values, and office space in unprecedented detail. Like the Urban Land Institute report, HBA now highlighted the "inherent difficulties" of Corpus Christi's "dramatic" site. As Malcolm Drummond, who oversaw the revised plan published in 1967, recalled, the high bluff looming over the long bayfront created "one of the more unusual central areas I have seen." This topography, however, divided the CBD into three "loosely connected sub-centers": the financial and business center atop the bluff, a "weak" retail section below it, and hotels and office and public buildings along the seawall. In a CBD "spread . . . over much too large an area," these subcenters were interspersed with old residential areas, port-related businesses, and land-eating uses such as automobile dealers. To make matters worse, the spread of population and commerce to the Southside left the CBD in an "off-center location," making it inconvenient for routine errands.[25]

HBA recommended pulling public activities from Shoreline Boulevard and concentrating them in a government center beneath the bluff at the CBD's midpoint. By massing constantly used buildings at the point where the Uptown office center connected with the lower CBD, the planners sought to "overcome" the "obstacle" of the bluff, countering "internal problems of access and circulation" created by topography. A government center might protect the retail businesses that remained along Chaparral and Mesquite a few blocks south. In the mid-1960s, central Corpus Christi still contained 30 percent of the city's retail space, of which only 15 percent was then vacant, despite competition from twenty-three shopping centers. The 1967 plan also proposed a pedestrian mall along Chaparral; at the time, this seemed like a plausible device for luring shoppers back to the center. HBA also sketched in apartments and townhouses as well as new office developments as ways of filling central Corpus Christi's gaps. In retrospect, Drummond observed, there was "just not that much cultural and civic stuff you can put in" such a diffuse area to offset the outward movement of residences and offices.[26]

HBA insisted on the central city's "fundamental importance" to the metropolitan area and on the need for "even the most drastic or unusual public actions" to protect its role in retail and services. The planners pleaded that public indifference was "mistaken," but nonetheless conceded: "To the average citizen of Corpus Christi, the condition of the central area of the city may seem a matter of little import. What difference does it make to him whether or not the central area declines

Figure 5.2. This aerial view from the 1980s reveals both the "dramatic" topography of central Corpus Christi and what the 1967 comprehensive plan termed its "inherent difficulties," above all the unlikelihood that activities could be woven together effectively along the bayfront, which stretches two miles from Harbor Bridge (*upper right*) to Memorial Coliseum (*lower left*) and then inland up the Corpus Christi Bluff (*left center*). KZTV-10 publicity photo, courtesy of the Kenneth L. Anthony Collection, Special Collections and Archives, Bell Library, Texas A&M University–Corpus Christi. Reprinted by permission.

or prospers? He does not own any of the buildings; operate any of the stores; he may be employed in an outlying industry and may not even go downtown often. If the central area deteriorates, he will simply take his business elsewhere."[27]

Like the Urban Land Institute, HBA also proposed accepting the bayfront as "tourist and recreational" space. The plan envisioned balancing the Bayfront Arts and Science Park, then under development at the north, with a convention center at the south, connected to Memorial Coliseum, around which Shoreline Boulevard would be rerouted. The site for the new center set off a "long argument," as the *Corpus Christi Times* recalled. When the Bayfront Convention Center opened in 1981, after a political quarrel marked by three bond elections and a convoluted lawsuit, it was located adjacent to the Bayfront Arts and Science Park.[28] This strengthened the northern CBD, but it left the southern CBD with no specific function. And then in quick succession came decisions to site the new Nueces County Courthouse and the new city hall in Uptown, rather than in a civic center beneath the bluff. Central Corpus Christi continued to evolve in the scattered, fragmentary way that worried the HBA planners, and successes in revitalizing some of its segments had little effect on other areas.

Culture as an Anchor

About two miles north to south and one and a half miles east to west, downtown Corpus Christi amounts to a first-rate example of why it has proved excruciatingly difficult to reverse central-city abandonment as retail trade, services, the professions, and residences dispersed across auto-oriented metropolises. By the 1960s and 1970s, most American CBDs simply contained more area and buildings than were required for the narrower purposes that downtowns had come to serve. The plights of northeastern and midwestern downtowns attracted the most attention, but southwestern cities such as Phoenix struggled to reverse downtown decline as well.[29]

To compensate for central Corpus Christi's expansive, fragmentary layout, planners from the 1960s to the 2000s envisioned subcenters that might sustain themselves, even if other parts of downtown remained stagnant. If functions and activities envisioned for up and down the bayfront—government, businesses, residences, cultural venues, a convention center, tourism, and recreation—took root, they might then gradually spread together and nurture a vibrant downtown, a "single, vigorous center" as the 1967 HBA plan put it. In its reliance on culture, recreation, and tourism to underpin central-city redevelopment, Corpus Christi pursued a fairly consistent "anchor" strategy. The idea is that cultural and tourist attractions, developed by the public sector or through partnerships with cultural organizations, nonprofit groups, and private enterprise, would provide dependable anchors around which private development could grow.[30] This strategy's accomplishments became most visible at the northern end of the CBD, emanating from the Bayfront Arts and Science Park. Destination Bayfront hoped to apply this strategy to the southern CBD.

The notion of a cultural district in the northern CBD took shape in the early 1960s when organizations in the Corpus Christi Arts Council began looking for permanent homes. The Junior League and the city's Parks and Recreation Board worked with a University of Texas architecture professor on a design competition. The winning entry placed the cultural district on a man-made peninsula in Corpus Christi Bay, one of many visions offered during the 1950s–1970s for building in the bay. Beyond its "educational and cultural value," emphasized the UT professor, the proposal sought "to counteract the flight of business from the city's central business district" and shore up land values and tax revenue.[31] The city council and the arts council agreed instead on the central city's northeast corner, where the Corpus Christi Ship Channel meets the bayfront. The site—"one of the city's most picturesque," in the words of the *Caller-Times* publisher, Edward Harte—did not raise as many safety and environmental issues as did a peninsula in the bay. Moreover, eight of the fifteen acres were already in public hands. In addition to an Army Corps of Engineers building, the area included an abandoned school, rundown apartments, and miscellaneous businesses, such as a marine supply company and a taxicab fleet.[32]

The Centennial Museum, the South Bluff Park forerunner of the Art Museum of South Texas, underscored the Bayfront Arts and Science Park's relation to contemporary trends by bringing to town an American Institute of Architects exhibition on new culture centers, ranging from Lincoln Center and the Sydney Opera House to suburban art centers in Maryland and California. The waterfront location also followed worldwide trends. Changes in shipping methods and technologies had caused ports and related businesses to move from cramped inner harbors to large sites around bays and ship channels. As waterfront businesses left, public attitudes shifted from dismissing inner harbors as rough and seedy to celebrating their aesthetic, residential, and recreational potential. Moreover, port authorities perceived an opportunity to diversify into waterfront real estate development and recreational and tourist activities, if only to make use of abandoned port and industrial property.[33] Until the 1990s, the Port of Corpus Christi Authority was not very active in projects to reuse docks, warehouses, and industrial sites; its abandonment problems were not as acute as, say, San Francisco's. The City of Corpus Christi, by contrast, had both the motive and the opportunity to put together an ample cultural district in a beautiful location.

Once the culture park moved from concept to development, initiative shifted from women active in the Junior League and the arts council to male business and civic leaders, who organized the Foundation for Science and Arts to ease land acquisitions and manage the private side of the venture. This group's chair, Edwin Singer, a New York–born petrochemicals entrepreneur and investor in communications and other industries, was a good example of the well-connected oil industry figures who sponsored civic and cultural initiatives in Corpus Christi and across urban Texas. In addition to the Arts and Science Park, he and his wife, Patsy Dunn Singer, who came from a well-known South Texas ranching family, became the main sponsors of the Art Museum of South Texas and worked to build up the Corpus Christi Symphony, which ended up with a home in the cultural district.[34]

Edwin Singer first proposed not a culture park but a science and recreation complex, with a marine science institute, an aquarium, and a planetarium, along with water sports and restaurants. "Industry," he presciently analyzed, "will be harder to attract here in the 60s and 70s than in the 40s and 50s," because oil and gas discoveries were diminishing. The bayfront redevelopment might offer a "way to get Corpus Christi into the marine science age."[35] Over the next years of land acquisition, planning, and fund-raising, the project reverted to the museums-and-performance-space concept promoted all along by the Junior League and the arts council. Elements of Singer's vision did materialize, though not at his Bayfront Arts and Science Park. The Texas State Aquarium was built over the ship channel on Corpus Christi Beach. The University of Texas never took up the offer to expand its Marine Science Institute from Port Aransas into the city. But eventually Texas A&M University–Corpus Christi created its own centers for coastal and gulf research.

While Singer's foundation and the city shared condemnation costs for the site, the city alone built the Corpus Christi Museum of Science and History, the culture park's first occupant, which opened in the 1968. Wariness over asking taxpayers for another museum building helped persuade Singer to finance the art museum with private donations, leading to a variant on the commonplace American practice of developing art museums through public-private partnerships. In the most familiar approach—following a precedent set in an 1871 deal between New York's Tammany Hall political machine and the upper-class founders of the Metropolitan Museum of Art—a foundation owns the collection and operates the museum, but the city acquires the land and builds and maintains the building. In Corpus Christi, the city took title to the Art Museum of South Texas and agreed to maintain it, but only after private backers engaged an architect and oversaw design and construction. The Houston art collectors John and Dominique de Menil referred the Singers to Philip Johnson, who designed the Menil's house, along with the University of St. Thomas, of which they were patrons. Fort Worth's Amon Carter Museum had already familiarized Texas art patrons with Johnson's skills as a museum designer. Johnson and his partner, the Chicago architect John Burgee, poured thought and energy into the unusual commission for a waterfront museum, producing a light-filled, white concrete building of juxtaposed geometric shapes, the attention generator that the Singers had hoped for.[36]

A celebrity persona comfortable with the press, Johnson gained a soapbox wherever he went. In Corpus Christi, he urged residents to envision the museum as an element in a vibrant central city. In 1969, he presented a sketch for a "mini-fair" in the Bayfront Arts and Science Park, with a planetarium, an aviary, a dance floor shaped like Texas, and a beer garden. Such a "mixture of culture and beer and pretzels" might ensure its use and connect the cultural center on the CBD's northern edge to the city's life.[37] Johnson "volunteered his time to help plan the entire bayfront complex," Edwin Singer recalled, but "he might have been a little rich for [the city council's] blood." The idea of the museum as part of a "coherent urban design," Singer explained, became so neglected that in 1975 the Singers barely managed to prevent the city from constructing the Bayfront (later Selena) Auditorium so that its blank back wall would loom over and dwarf the art museum.[38] Finally, in the 1980s, Singer's foundation split with the city the cost of hiring Johnson's associate, the New Jersey landscape architect Robert Zion, to construct a water garden as the centerpiece of the culture park.

By this time, the auditorium and convention center had ratified the practice of concentrating cultural institutions and related anchor facilities around the original Bayfront Arts and Science Park site. This precedent more or less became policy when the city's 1982 Bayfront Plan redefined the Arts and Science Park to include the convention center and auditorium complex, Heritage Park (discussed below), and a swath of adjacent land.[39] The original culture park ultimately featured Harbor Playhouse along with its two museums and water garden. The Asian Cultural Museum as well as Heritage Park appeared to the south. Opened in 2004 and with more than twice the capacity of the abandoned Memorial Coliseum, American Bank Center provided an 8,000-seat venue for conventions, concerts, basketball, and (of all things) minor league ice hockey. In spring 2005, a Texas League baseball team owned in part by Nolan Ryan began playing in Whataburger Field on port authority land to the west. Designed by the firm responsible for Globe Life Park in Arlington, home of the Texas Rangers, the stadium, following the fashion set by Baltimore's Camden Yards, took on "the look of an old cotton warehouse" to recall what once stood on the site.[40] Between the ballpark and the Harbor Bridge, a water park named Hurricane Alley opened in 2012. This attraction, developed by Dusty Durrill's son Bill, broadened the north bayfront's appeal to Texas families, Corpus Christi's tourist base. It added to the younger Durrill's credibility as a contractor for the Corpus Christi Museum when the city decided to lease it, for reasons already described. The north bayfront anchors reinforced the city's two most popular attractions,

Figure 5.3. Postcard of the Lichtenstein Building on Chaparral Street, late 1940s, then the heart of the downtown retail district. Courtesy of the Dan Kilgore Collection, Special Collections and Archives, Bell Library, Texas A&M University–Corpus Christi.

both on Corpus Christi Beach across the ship channel, the Texas State Aquarium and the USS *Lexington*, a World War II aircraft carrier. In 2008, the aquarium ranked as the nineteenth most popular attraction in Texas, and the aircraft carrier twenty-first. The only area site that came close was Port Aransas on Mustang Island, thirty-third.[41]

As HBA and other planners foresaw, anchor attractions straddling the ship channel did not reverse the patchwork character of most of downtown. High-rise hotels and skyscrapers that lined Shoreline Boulevard during the 1980s sustained restaurants a block or two to the west. In 1983, Brad Lomax, a Houston restaurant manager with a love of surfing, founded Water Street Oyster Bar in a vacant transmission shop surrounded by topless bars and a flophouse on Water Street between Lawrence and William. Working with the New Jersey investor who owned the site, Lomax added a second Water Street restaurant and the Executive Surf Club, a first-rate venue for Texas-style music. Lomax's ventures became the core of the Water Street Market district.[42] Bars and restaurants spilled south across William and west onto Chaparral, but the energy dissipated within two blocks. In 1988, the last operator closed the city's best-known retail building, the Lichtenstein Department Store at Lawrence and Chaparral. The city tried repeatedly to line up an investor to convert the sleek 1941 structure into shops and apartments. By 2011, the building was suffering from "rusted rebar, gaping holes in concrete floors and walls and [other] structural defects." The city finally accepted a proposal from an Austin developer to demolish the old store and replace it with a residential and retail project called the Cosmopolitan, one of several developments occurring amid the South Texas shale-oil boom that revived hopes for downtown.[43]

"Some Buildings Worth Saving"

Water Street Market provided Corpus Christians with an example of the reuse of old buildings in downtown revitalization, though these workaday structures raised few issues of historic preservation for Lomax and his partners. Lichtenstein's, whose architecture and associations would have qualified it for the National Register of Historic

Places, illustrated the difficulty of this enterprise. So did the dreary condition of the city's oldest commercial building, the 1891 Lovenskiold Building on Mesquite Street, whose distinctive cast-iron finish remained hidden behind an ill-applied plaster facade. There were exceptions, such as the brick-sided 1914 McDonald Building on People's Street, used for law offices after being restored by the Downtown Management District, the CBD's improvement district, which had intended it for its headquarters.[44] But the dispersal of commerce and the professions to the Southside combined with consolidation of the oil business in Houston and other major cities to create an abundance of business structures from 1910–1940, half vacant or worse, uptown atop the bluff as well as downtown below it.

The drawn-out dispute over Memorial Coliseum, which touched upon both revitalization and preservation, evoked a torrent of condemnation for Corpus Christi's "backwater" approach to history and culture, in the words of Janet Rice, who had frustration to vent. In the 1980s, Rice campaigned in vain to save Richard Colley's companion structure, the 1952 city hall. Then as chair of the Quincentenary Commission, she tried in vain to stave off the Columbus fleet debacle. San Antonio, Rice wrote, had turned an old cement plant into the Alamo Quarry Market; the San Antonio Museum of Art was in the old Lone Star Brewery, and San Antonio's armory now housed a corporation. "If the Alamo had been in Corpus Christi," she charged, "it would not be standing today."[45]

Compared to other Texas cities, Corpus Christi had a record in preservation that was indeed meager, and in revitalization disappointing. Yet the culprit may not have been South Texans' defects of character and taste. Advocates of building and neighborhood preservation in Corpus Christi looked with envy at San Antonio and Galveston, where a combination of circumstances had yielded apparent success. More aware of the accomplishments of those cities than of their quarrels and setbacks, pro-preservation Corpus Christians came to disdain what they saw as their city's stubborn and even philistine streak. But circumstances that worked for preservation in related Texas cities worked against it in Corpus Christi.[46]

As already discussed, Corpus Christi is mainly a post–World War I city in a region whose historical lore and sensibility is focused on the eighteenth and nineteenth centuries. Many cities exhibit a similar disjuncture between preconceptions of what counts as historic and the history embodied in actual buildings. Urbanization during the twentieth century meant that a huge portion of the world's urban fabric was constructed between the 1920s and the 1980s. Only at the end of the twentieth century did a movement for appreciating and preserving modernist structures appear; until then, the recent past was taken for granted and rarely treated as historic.

Moreover, preservation as an accepted element in urban policy had become so familiar by the early 2000s that one could forget how recent and conditional the mindset is. In Europe and the Americas, sustained efforts to analyze, catalogue, and protect historic structures date only to the nineteenth century. North American cities that produced vigorous preservation movements before World War II, such as Boston, New Orleans, and San Antonio, had a profusion of undeniably valuable structures, along with cultural, economic, or political motives to impose then-unusual protections. Nearly everywhere else, the principles and practices of preservation took shape in the 1960s and 1970s. Preservation efforts thus appeared in Corpus Christi around the same time as in most American cities, especially midsized regional ones. Exceptions among midsized cities, such as Charleston and Galveston, proved the rule. Both inherited an architectural heritage with tourism potential. Just as importantly, modern commerce more or less bypassed both cities, which is why they retained so many remnants of their former glory days.

Prodded by groups such as the San Antonio Conservation Society, the State of Texas had a legal and institutional framework for preservation by the time of the National Historic Preservation Act of 1966, which provided understandable guidelines and procedures, along with creating the National Register of Historic Places. Federal and state historical agencies, working in tandem with a new group of preservation professionals and organizations, pushed government at all levels to revise tax and building codes, along with planning, zoning, and permit processes, to make awareness of history a feature of urban construction and reconstruction.[47]

Far from being exceptional, Corpus Christi shared in and illustrated a widespread shift in attitude. Memorial Coliseum seemed worth preserving in the 2000s because it represented the mindset of the 1950s, when the municipal government turned to an innovative young architect to give form to the future. Midcentury Corpus Christi typified urban culture in the Southwest and the country overall in assuming that the future counted more than the past. Until the last third of the twentieth century, buildings and neighborhoods survived only when they continued to serve some contemporary purpose or when development and commercial trends had so bypassed them that replacing them was not worth the effort, as in the case of Lomax's abandoned transmission shop (or most of central Galveston or Charleston). But by the 1970s, myriad cities besides Corpus Christi were experiencing the drift and disappointment that encouraged people to look hopefully upon aging buildings and places that represented more vibrant, aesthetically pleasing eras, which in turn encouraged history to be seen as a revitalization tool. It became common for urban dwellers to express a hankering for the past rather than faith in the future as far as the physical city was concerned. The entire mindset would have struck the 1950s Area Development Committee as lacking in vision and gumption.[48]

Until late in the twentieth century, Corpus Christians tended to assume that their city had few historic buildings, defined for the most part as pre-1920 structures. Preservationists and officials often cited hurricanes as the reason that "saving a historic home in Corpus is a little like saving an endangered species." In 1987, the city planning director, Larry Wenger, concurred that the South Texas port could not match San Antonio's fabric of "historical homes or buildings" because "most of them were wiped out by the 1919 storm."[49] The 1919 hurricane swept away all but three structures on North Beach and destroyed an estimated 900 homes below the bluff. Yet debris from the storm surge barricaded low-lying areas more than two or three blocks inland, similar to the way that debris limited the destruction of historic Galveston in the great storm of 1900. And residents of sections beyond the Corpus Christi Bluff recalled not being aware of the catastrophe until the next morning. By the time of Corpus Christi's next direct hit, Hurricane Celia in 1970, the seawall protected the central city against storm surges; Celia killed eleven people in the Corpus Christi area and did around a half-billion dollars worth of damage, but mainly through wind and rain.[50]

Flood, then, did rob Corpus Christi of historic structures. Fire, earthquake, war, and social and economic collapse caused greater disruption to urban cores elsewhere. Studies in the 1970s and 1980s identified dozens of structures in Corpus Christi from the 1870s to 1920, though these buildings were generally too "widely scattered" to satisfy preconceptions of a historic neighborhood. Outside the central city, there were intact residential neighborhoods that dated from the city's burst of growth in the 1920s–1940s, though many of these areas had declined into sections of houses converted into marginal apartments and offices.[51] Corpus Christians paid little attention to such neighborhoods until the century's last decade, when they grew more inclined to regard the interwar decades as historic, and its houses and neighborhoods as attractive. In sum, Corpus Christi's seeming lack of a historic atmosphere resulted less from a pernicious combination of Gulf storms and residents' shortsightedness than from the central city's odd physical layout and the timing of the city's growth.

As Corpus Christi burgeoned in population, expanded in area, and decentralized in activity, residential property in the pre–World War I town came under threat of redevelopment for business use. Or older houses faced decay because they were located in areas abandoned by middle-class residents and also bypassed by commercial development. People noticed when "another landmark on the skyline of Corpus Christi" lost out to new construction. The press regretted that these landmarks were "falling to progress," which is how the *Caller-Times*'s described its own building expansion in 1956, which displaced the house of E. B. Cole, the developer of early Southside projects such as Six Points, Del Mar, and Cole Park.[52] The Meuly House on Chaparral Street, constructed in 1852, the year of Corpus Christi's incorporation, had been an outpost of urbanity in the isolated town, with wrought iron and interior wood imported from New Orleans. In 1919 it survived ten feet of water. In the 1950s, it gave way, with minimal outcry, to a grocery store parking lot.[53] Likewise, as office buildings spread along Upper Broadway starting in the 1920s, residents regretted but did little to halt the disappearance of the town residences of South Texas ranching families that once lined the Corpus Christi Bluff.

In 1963, a group of civic leaders, including Edward Harte of the *Caller-Times* and Mamie Searcy Kleberg of the King Ranch family, formed the Corpus Christi Area Heritage Society to acquire and restore the city's oldest surviving house, Centennial House, which was begun in 1849 and was adjacent to Corpus Christi Cathedral on Upper Broadway. Also known as the Britton-Evans House, this building was identified with several early families; Forbes Britton bought the lot from town founder Henry Lawrence Kinney. From the 1930s to the 1960s, it served as headquarters for the Southern Minerals Corporation, whose founder, Maston Nixon, had developed the Nixon Building two blocks to the north, the first of the tall office buildings that transformed the bluff. In the late 1970s and early 1980s, the heritage society acquired its only other project, the rural homestead of the McGloins, one of the Irish families behind the Mexican-era San Patricio settlement.[54]

The heritage society's success with Centennial House validated the idea, as Harte remarked in 1974, that preservation was not only "okay for New Orleans or San Antonio."[55] Perhaps the most influential local figure to take up the cause was Cecil Burney, a lawyer and Democratic official who served as president of the Texas Historical Foundation and chair of the Texas Historical Commission. In 1974, Burney helped persuade the city council to pass a historic zoning ordinance whose preamble reasonably attributed the "increased demolition of these landmarks" to "rapid change in population, economic functions, and land-use activities." The ordinance created the Landmark Commission, whose membership was drawn from history, art, business, and real estate groups, as well as from the American Institute of Architects, the Mexican Chamber of Commerce, and the Junior League.[56]

In 1976 the Landmark Commission produced the city's first municipal preservation survey and plan. In 1981, Nueces County used Texas Historical Commission and federal funds to hire the Chicago planner Robert Grossman, assisted by the local architect James Rome, to survey historical sites. Grossman had served as HBA's on-site coordinator for the 1967 comprehensive plan, which had forcefully articulated the central city's difficulties. Grossman, Rome, and their team identified Old Irishtown at the northeastern end of the CBD as having the most potential as a historic district. Running roughly along Mesquite and Chaparral east of the approach to the Harbor Bridge and south of the ship channel, this section took its name from Irish settlers who established port-related artisan and merchant businesses there during the 1800s. Around sixty noteworthy structures remained into the 1980s, many dating to 1870–1900. According to the consultants' report, Old Irishtown featured "some of the [city's] best examples of late nineteenth-century wood frame houses."[57] This low-lying neighborhood's survival as Corpus Christi's most plausible historic district belied the notion that hurricanes were to blame for a paucity of older buildings, though no one remarked on the contradiction.

The consultants drew attention to a possible historic district in a north-south line atop the bluff, beyond a reasonable walk for most people from Old Irishtown. The proposed Blucherville and South Upper Broadway districts were even farther, across visual and practical obstacles. None of these areas had more than four or five historic structures in proximity, so they qualified as historic districts only marginally. The heart of downtown featured "a number of interesting buildings," but in a "thin" pattern, "with insufficient significant structures to support an historic district classification."[58]

Central Corpus Christi's geography and developmental history, therefore, go far toward explaining why historic districts never took hold there, despite the examples of San Antonio and Galveston, whose cultural and tourist strategies the South Texas port sought

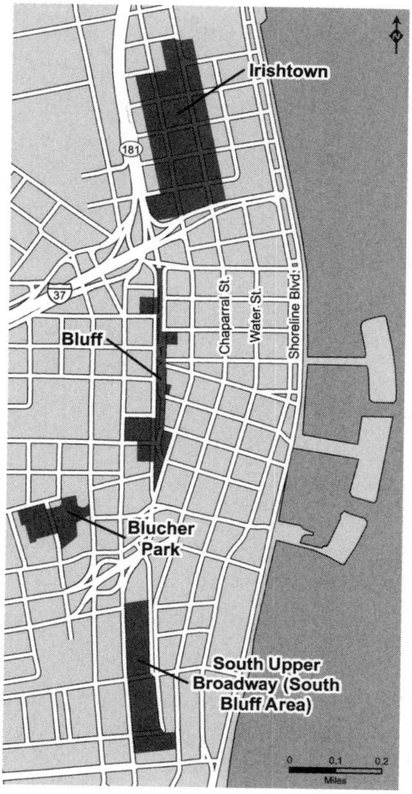

Figure 5.4. This map, based on one in the 1982 preservation plan sponsored by Nueces County, illustrates the scattered, "thin" quality of potential historic districts in central Corpus Christi, other than the Old Irishtown site to the north. By Crystal K. Williams, GEOMAP, Illinois State University, based on *Historical-Architectural Preservation Plan, Nueces County, Texas* (Northbrook, Ill.: Associated Planners, 1982), 43.

to emulate. During the last decades of the twentieth century, as the historic-district movement spread to cities in many countries, Corpus Christi real estate interests and progrowth public officials, the usual suspects, resisted the designation of historic districts, with their perceived constraints. Yet the physical city itself did not present a case powerful enough to overcome property-owner resistance and official skepticism.

Grossman and Rome argued that if Corpus Christians would expand their understanding of South Texas history forward to encompass the interwar years, the city would look more historic to them. The survey recommended that "'close-in' areas developed from approximately 1910 to 1940" receive "conservation" status. On the near Southside, they emphasized neighborhoods that illustrated Anglo-American residential decentralization starting around World War I: South Bluff Park, Furman Avenue, and especially the Cole Park–Del Mar area. This last was an "exceedingly good neighborhood," with blocks of pre–World War II bungalows as well as the Cape Cod, Colonial, and ranch houses that epitomized middle-class housing in interwar Texas.[59]

"Building Zoo"

Grossman and Rome also called for the conservation of 1930s–1950s areas west and northwest of the CBD that had become more Hispanic or black with the encroachment of the port, petrochemicals, and highways. They did not call for conservation of the Northside, kept intact by racial discrimination in housing and not by historical sensibility. In an illustration of white popular hostility in the Southwest to federally funded urban programs—even those backed by the white political and business establishment—voters in 1959 and 1966 overwhelmingly defeated ADC-backed urban renewal proposals for the area. Into the twenty-first century, blocks of rickety cottages attested to housing conditions once ubiquitous among local blacks. The Northside's churches, the Solomon Coles School, and perhaps the Harlem Theatre fit conventional definitions of historic sites. As discussed in chapter 3, a determined movement saved the Coles school by persuading the Corpus Christi Independent School District to find a new use for it as an alternative high school.[60]

The 1990s saw attempts to protect the D. N. Leathers Housing Project. In the early 1950s, Richard Colley designed the Leathers II addition to the project, the first phase of which dated to the New Deal era. Colley's Leathers II project was intended as attractive, though still segregated housing to replace Northside cottages targeted for urban renewal. But Leathers II occupied a floodplain near an oil refinery's storage facility. A flood in 1994 led to its abandonment and eventual demolition, after which soil studies revealed the area to be too contaminated for new residential construction. Documented and alleged instances of contamination from nearby refineries and chemical plants exacerbated the Northside's reputation as a place to leave behind.[61] In 1986, the city sponsored the move of the area's best-known historic home, the Littles-Martin House, to Heritage Park. Restored by the NAACP for its headquarters, it endured as an exiled relic of the Northside in the same way that other Heritage Park houses represented central-city neighborhoods that had disappeared, decayed, or been built over.

By gathering houses in Heritage Park, the city conceded that the central city's historic character would be difficult to maintain. The area—two blocks bounded by Fitzgerald, Chaparral, Hughes, and Mesquite Streets—amounted to the northern segment of the Old Irishtown historic district as sketched in the Grossman and Rome report. Even this area almost did not survive, since during the 1970s it had been among the sites proposed for the Bayfront Convention Center. Working with Cecil Burney, the preservationist lawyer, and preservation-minded architects such as Lee John Govatos, the Junior League raised funds to acquire and restore three houses threatened by the convention center. The Colonial Revival Lichtenstein House and the Victorian Gugenheim House, both built in 1905, were identified with Jewish merchant families. The Sidbury House, a Victorian with Queen Anne elements, dated from 1893. None of the buildings was originally located in the 1600 block of Chaparral Street, where they now stood; a property investor had moved all three there in the 1920s and divided them into apartments. The Sidbury House originally came from the portion of the bluff taken over by office towers, and the Lichtenstein House had occupied a site later taken by a downtown movie theater. The Gugenheim House was originally built on Chaparral, but five blocks closer to downtown.[62]

The city agreed to acquire and maintain the houses if private groups took the lead in raising funds for restoration so that they could be used by nonprofit groups. The Junior League won a National Trust award in 1979 for overseeing the project that provided headquarters for itself in the Sidbury House, the Creative Arts Center in the Lichtenstein House, and the Camp Fire Girls in the Gugenheim House, which in the process was moved again, a few hundred feet closer to the others. The three buildings entered the National Register in 1983. As Tom Utter, the city's longtime redevelopment coordinator, noted, for "miniscule cost," Corpus Christi could start an area that might eventually compare to San Antonio's La Villita.[63]

The Grossman-Rome report praised these efforts but admonished against treating Old Irishtown as a preservation zone to which buildings could simply be moved. The National Register resisted accepting districts of relocated houses, even ones with undoubted historic and architectural value.[64] Yet Corpus Christi officials continued to buy or arrange for the donation of historic houses and to move them to the preservation site. Between 1982 and 1987 the city gained title to and moved the 1851 Merriman-Bobys House, the second-oldest survivor after Centennial House and a fixture on the South Bluff, as well as two houses from Uptown associated with Mexican American history and discussed in chapter 3, the French-Galván House and the Grande-Grossman House. The city opened the Multicultural Center in the French-Galván building, and the League of United Latin American Citizens (LULAC) occupied the Grande-Grossman House. In addition to the Littles-Martin house from the Northside, two houses came from unprotected blocks in Old Irishtown. The 1905 Jalufka-Govatos House, which had both Czech and Greek associations, became headquarters for a Czech heritage group; for the Ward-McCampbell House, the city made a similar arrangement with a local Irish group.[65]

By the time the four-acre Heritage Park officially opened in 1985, the city and private groups had devoted around $3 million to it. The name embodied the association that emerged between the project and the city's ethnic heritage, which in turn became a rationale for public expenditure on historic buildings. The breach of the original-site principle irked preservationists, such as an architectural historian for the Texas Historical Commission, who chastised the city for creating a

Figures 5.5a & 5.5b. Map of the preservation zone at Heritage Park, from a city parks department guide, 2003. Looking south along Chaparral Street from near the Merriman-Bobys House (*front right*). Photo by Kenny Braun, 2014.

"building zoo." In the view of Utter and other city officials, it was better to have the houses cared for and used in an accessible district than to leave them decrepit and vulnerable in scattered locations that no one visited.[66]

Numerous proposals for adding land and buildings to Heritage Park appeared over the next two decades. The first significant addition came in 1999, when the Lawrence House, a pioneer family house dating from 1892, was moved by barge from the buffer zone for a gas recovery plant on the city's outskirts.[67] Plans fell through for this to become the headquarters of the Hispanic Chamber of Commerce, a reflection of recurring problems with relying on civic groups as partners. In 1990, the Corpus Christi Arts Council left the Merriman-Bobys House for free space in a bank building, because it needed "relief" from maintenance costs and restoration loan payments. In 1991, the city forgave back debts accumulated by the Czech and Irish heritage societies, the NAACP, and LULAC (which meanwhile also left the park). The city converted loans for groups remaining at Heritage Park into lease payments. Ultimately, the chamber of commerce took over the Irish society's Ward-McCampbell House, and a foundation sought to place a Hispanic civil rights museum in the Grande-Grossman House. Several times, the city rented the Merriman-Bobys house to a restaurant or deli in vain hopes of sparking "a mix of boutiques, shops, restaurants, and office space," indeed similar to La Villita.[68] Heritage Park endured as a city-supported zone for arts and civic groups and as a quiet, attractive place for residents and tourists.

In 2007, the area became a refuge for the Steamboat House from 1890, nicknamed for its double-decker round porches, which resembled the front of a steamboat. This house's checkered history illustrates downtown's diffuse geography, investment trends, and competing policy priorities. The house's builder, Captain W. T. Ropes, was the brother of Elihu Ropes, the New Jersey promoter whose schemes for Corpus Christi collapsed amid the Panic of 1893. The house was originally located near the current Ropes Park along Ocean Drive, in the vicinity of the ill-fated Alta Vista Hotel. In 1920, tractors moved it to Carancahua Street, a block from the Corpus Christi Bluff. There, divided into apartments, it rotted from neglect. Grossman and Rome's report in 1982 identified it as a landmark for their proposed South

Upper Broadway historic district. The Steamboat House stood around the corner from Furman Avenue, a first-rate residential street from the early twentieth century whose own restoration movement never won historic-district status.

The Steamboat House lot, along with several lots on Furman Avenue, fell within the site of a large apartment complex developed in the mid-2000s by a Houston corporation. In this situation, residential opportunities in downtown trumped preservation. The property for the apartment complex was available because over several decades, Morris Lichtenstein Jr.—of the department store family—had bought Steamboat House along with most of the two blocks around it. One of the Houston developers had grown up in Corpus Christi. This partner purchased the Steamboat House from the Lichtenstein Foundation and donated it to the city, which spent nearly $50,000 to move it to Heritage Park. The developer also arranged with a contractor to move all but ten or so structures on the apartment complex site. "I couldn't just demolish them," remarked the contractor, who planned to take one for his own use at Lake Corpus Christi, nearly forty miles northwest. This "ultimate recycling job" further dimmed prospects for a historic district in the Furman Avenue vicinity.[69]

Preservationists never conceded that restoration of old houses would take place only in the safe haven of Heritage Park. In the 1990s, the Junior League helped put together a $1 million renovation of three houses in Blucherville, southwest of the bluff. These houses were associated with the Bluchers, a German family involved in the original surveying of southern Texas and later prominent in conservation. The effort resulted in an Audubon Nature Center and a bed-and-breakfast on a street overlooking Blucher Park, a famous stopover for migratory songbirds. The Junior League occupied the third house. Blucherville offered a contrast to the city's "unremarkable record in historic preservation and adaptive re-use," remarked Lee John Govatos. "One of the irrefutable values of the Blucher houses," the preservationist architect continued, "is that they stand where originally built."[70] In the late 2000s, the Junior League sold its house to a law firm because even it could not afford the maintenance of a historic structure. "We loved the house," a spokesperson told the *Caller-Times*, but "as a volunteer organization it was hard to see fundraising dollars going to [upkeep]."[71]

"Acropolis of Our City"

/The protracted misery of the old Nueces County Courthouse largely explains the reluctance of Corpus Christi and Nueces County officials to take risks on behalf of historic buildings and neighborhoods. Like many Texas county courthouses, the 1914 structure was designed to express urbanity. Over decades, the building's inadequacy for the area's increasing level of business intertwined with the public-sector vice of deferred maintenance and with changes in architectural fashion to send the structure and its reputation into a downward spiral. The courthouse was in dismal condition by 1977, when its functions were moved to the new county courthouse in Uptown. For the next thirty years, a melodrama of failed restoration efforts consigned it to long-term vacancy, a hard fate for a building. In Corpus Christi, preservation became synonymous with the old courthouse, for which preservationism paid a price.

Designed by the San Antonio architect Harvey Page in the Greek Revival style and built for $250,000, the six-story courthouse—the county's third—occupied a prominent spot along Mesquite Street three blocks from the old shoreline at Water Street. Decorated with marble and terra-cotta and outfitted with up-to-date plumbing, electricity, and soundproofing, the courthouse testified that the frontier region along the Texas Gulf Coast "has come into its own." Offices, courtrooms, and public areas occupied the lower stories, while the upper two floors featured a prison with a hospital and a death cell, which was "secluded" to spare the condemned "humiliation."[72] "No County in the great State of Texas can boast a finer or more ornate building," a Commercial Club pamphlet from the mid-1910s proclaimed.[73] The building entered hurricane lore when hundreds of residents found shelter there during the 1919 storm. For decades, the county treated the courthouse and its award-winning landscaping as a credit to the area.

By the 1990s, old county courthouses would become treasured relics of a bygone form of civic spirit. Texas—with over 230 historic courthouses—responded to this sentiment by creating a substantial preservation program. Admirers of these buildings usually overlooked the reasons that they had fallen from favor in the first place: they had become dysfunctional and unpleasant for people who worked there.

Figures 5.6a & 5.6b. The Greek Revival Nueces County Courthouse as a showcase for urbanity in the decades after its 1914 opening and as an abandoned, decayed embarrassment in the early 2000s. a. Courtesy of the Dan Kilgore Collection, Special Collections and Archives, Bell Library, Texas A&M University–Corpus Christi; b. Photo by Kenny Braun, 2014.

Even the Texas Capitol, now a cherished Gilded Age landmark, had a well-deserved reputation as a cramped, miserable firetrap before its overhaul in the 1980s and early 1990s. Page, a former student of the Library of Congress's architect, J. L. Smithmeyer, had experience with large, complex projects.[74] Yet the ambitions of county officials may have outrun their resources and certainly their forethought. By the 1950s, the courthouse's shortcomings had become undeniable: cramped courtrooms, dreary offices, and no storage areas. Experience showed the top two floors to have been an eccentric location for the jail. Residents—some attracted to the romantic shabbiness—recalled lawyers and judges, county officials, and the public mingling in humid halls, with desks and file cabinets arranged every which way. Those same lawyers, judges, officials, and clerks longed for a modern, spacious, and practical building.

In the 1950s and 1960s, studies repeatedly called for replacing the courthouse. "Inadequate for present needs," the Harland Bartholomew firm assessed in 1953. "Out-dated and in poor condition," HBA reiterated in 1967, calling attention to "the location of the jail on the top floors, wasted space between floors [a consequence of Page's soundproofing], and the [dys]functional arrangement of offices."[75] Admittedly, HBA's reports for numerous cities called for replacing old county courthouses, among other forms of downtown surgery that cities came to regret. But in the Nueces case, the evidence was strong that the county needed a new courthouse and that renovating the historic building for a new use would be expensive.

Planners in the 1950s–1960s tended to site the proposed new county courthouse either along the bayfront or inland a few blocks. The government center beneath the Corpus Christi Bluff envisioned in the 1967 HBA report offered an example of the reasoning. Cheap land was an important consideration for county officials in their decision to move instead to Uptown. Evidence of frugality would reassure bond-election voters that a new courthouse was a wiser investment than "patch[ing] our present decaying, crowded, obsolete courthouse," as bond election ads contended. Some preservationists came to believe that their misfortunes with the old courthouse started in the campaign for a $14.5 million bond issue for a new one. Margaret Walberg, for decades a leader of the effort to preserve the courthouse, recalled people joking at the time that Nueces County judge Robert Barnes had ordered maintenance workers to push small pieces off the courthouse "so he could say that the building was substandard, and he could get a bond issue passed for the new courthouse." The 1914 courthouse was beyond redemption, bond supporters contended: "Early this year the outer facing of the north wall collapsed, hurling tons of bricks to the grounds below." Wooden passageways were needed to lead people into the building while protecting them from debris. "Inside, structural cracks, fallen plaster, leaking pipes, worn-out plumbing, and a jail resembling a dungeon underline the need for action—NOW!" Against this, bond opponents could only offer dubious estimates that the new courthouse would cost more than Dallas's new county courthouse and that county commissioners had selected a "bad location." Opponents made only feeble attempts to counter supporters' contention that the existing courthouse was "unsafe, unsightly, and obsolete."[76]

Nueces County won the September 1972 bond election. As the new building rose, Barnes and other county officials tried to avoid any commitment to the old building, partly protected under a Texas law requiring six months' notice to the Texas Historical Commission before demolition, leasing, or sale of a county courthouse. Dismissing prospects for restoration and reuse, Barnes remarked in September 1976, "People have known we were going to move for two years, and we still don't have a concrete proposal." The best course would be to "accumulate all the information that anyone would ever need from a historical standpoint, and then tear it down."[77] Such comments provoked outrage from the old building's supporters. "It was all right to bad-mouth the old courthouse during the bond election. Nueces County had far outgrown the building," retorted one prominent resident, who insisted that Page's structure was "sound," adding, "For many years it has stood as the Acropolis of our city."[78]

With the county signaling its intention to demolish the 1914 courthouse as soon as the law allowed, the preservationist attorney Cecil Burney used his position on the Texas Historical Commission to have the building quickly and quietly placed on the National Register of Historic Places, the first Corpus Christi building so designated. National designation did not ensure the courthouse's salvation, but it complicated demolition and made restoration projects eligible for federal funds. Preservationists' maneuvers seemed to increase the hostility of the *Caller-Times*, whose publisher, Ed Harte, shared the disdain of lawyers and county officials for the "white elephant." "Margaret, that's the ugliest building I've ever seen," Walberg recalled Harte remarking after a personal tour designed to evoke the opposite response. The reporter and columnist Nick Jimenez continually poked fun at the "old hag" and its admirers. Like Harte, Jimenez told Walberg that it was "the most terrible building I've ever been in." His youth in San Antonio had left him with an appreciation of preservation, Jimenez recalled, but the courthouse seemed an "extravagance" in the absence of a viable reuse plan. "Everyone can agree in principle that old buildings should be saved," the paper insisted. Still, preservation was "not feasible, or even desirable" in this case, "and let's face it, the old courthouse isn't all that beautiful, inside or out."[79]

After the county left in June 1977, preservationists organized a nonprofit corporation, Friends of the Courthouse, with officers including Burney, the architect Lee John Govatos, and Margaret Ramage and Margaret Walberg, two familiar personalities in cultural and historical groups.[80] This group secured a federal matching grant for a feasibility study by Grossman's Chicago firm along with an Austin planning firm. The study called for "restoration and rehabilitation," perhaps into a cultural center that might include shops; a gallery; a restaurant in the sixth-floor jail; offices for public agencies, nonprofit groups, and businesses; and space for the public library, Del Mar College, or the local public television station. Since the county "wants to be relieved of all maintenance and operational responsibilities as soon as possible," the study proposed that Friends of the Courthouse or a similar organization pursue federal or state grants to buy or lease the building and oversee its restoration. Rentals, Grossman's report argued, could cover an estimated $170,000 in annual operating and maintenance costs.[81] "Not a single investor or prospective tenant has come forward with money in hand," the *Caller-Times* remarked, making the study a "catalogue of dreams." The paper's reporters, one columnist revealed, had contrived their own list of reuse proposals. These included using it as a bat house and then harvesting the guano or turning it into a storage site for downtown and courthouse studies. Last but not least on their list: "Fill it up with historians and seal it off."[82]

Figure 5.7. The 1970s Nueces County Courthouse in Uptown.
Photo by Kenny Braun, 2014.

Skeptics cited a 1977 General Services Administration estimate of $7 million for turning the building into a federal courthouse. In 1994, the GSA rejected a second offer of the National Register building, again citing inadequate court space and an outmoded arrangement of rooms, as well as daunting renovation costs. The federal government preferred to build an entirely new courthouse, which opened in 2001 a few hundred yards in front of the abandoned county building at the Gateway intersection.[83]

Meanwhile, Judge Barnes seemed to waver in his determination to destroy the building. When an auction in August 1977 failed to attract the minimum bid of $500,000, Barnes remarked that the county might accept a lease if a "public-spirited group" would assume maintenance costs. The county then assigned twenty-three workers under the federal CETA (Comprehensive Employment and Training Act) program to undertake repairs.[84] Walberg speculates that in the end Barnes "didn't want to be the villain to tear it down." The judge, however, was one of two Nueces County commissioners who voted no in May 1978 when the commission voted 3–2 to accept a covenant demanded by the Texas Historical Commission that would prevent the building's destruction until 2018. This covenant enabled a group of local lawyers acting on behalf of the Friends of the Courthouse to use $100,000 in federal grant money toward the $200,000 now requested by the county to turn over title. Editorialized the *Corpus Christi Caller*, "We can only wish the Friends and their angels good luck."[85]

Concerns over any appearance of conflict of interest dissuaded Cecil Burney from putting his own money into the courthouse. He instead oversaw the purchase by the attorneys' group and then the resale to Charles Bennett, an ambitious developer of seaside condominiums. Rumors circulated that Bennett paid up to $500,000. Burney insisted that the real price was closer to $250,000, still a profit of $150,000 on the attorney group's investment, which had been backed by a federal matching grant.[86] Dubious aspects of the resale would have caused little consternation had Bennett followed through on promises to put around $6 million into transforming the courthouse into restaurant and office space, according to plans supplied by a Boston firm of historical architects. As Tom Utter, city redevelopment coordinator, remarked, the building "sat and sat and sat and sat" until it became a target for vandals and a haven for the homeless and drug users. "Wino Hilton," jeered the *Caller-Times* columnist Bill Walraven. Bennett never gave a full account of what went amiss, but apparently his overstretched business became mired in the Texas oil bust of the 1980s. Even as the city threatened to condemn the building or seize it for back taxes, Bennett announced plans for a 400-room high-rise hotel behind the restored courthouse while he was attempting to work out a bond guarantee with the city. By decade's end, Bennett had relocated to Dallas and later moved to Florida. The courthouse owner became so uncommunicative that the city had difficulty locating him for delinquent tax notices and legal papers.[87]

In hindsight, one might conclude that the *Corpus Christi Caller* had been correct all along in placing the courthouse's prospects in the "slim-to-none category."[88] But the movement to save the courthouse had drifted into this impasse. A moment of decision or a chance to cut losses never presented itself until the investment of time, emotion, and credibility had become too great to allow its backers to accept defeat easily. In the 1970s and 1980s, appreciation of urban buildings in once-denigrated styles was on the upswing. The tear-it-down mentality seemed small-minded and uncivilized. Preservationists in other cities had saved and restored buildings in worse shape, and less significant, than the 1914 courthouse. Why not us?

Years later, Walberg recalled the effort to engage private investors as one that sent the project in an unpromising direction even before the messy association with Bennett. As soon as the county departed the building, for example, Friends of the Courthouse began lining up non-profit organizations to rent offices cheaply, in order to keep the place in daily use. For insurance reasons and to avoid commitments that might hamper restoration, Burney's group of investors and later Bennett's discouraged such rentals, which meant that apart from the Friends' own office, the massive building was open only for tours and special occasions. Even that diminished during the 1980s as city inspectors became anxious about safety. Given the physical and political damage done by prolonged vacancy, the preservationists' inclination to keep the courthouse occupied made sense. In Walberg's view, if investors had "allowed [nonprofit groups] to move in and pay rent, that would have given us a better start."[89]

As the stalemate dragged on, preservationists adamantly defended the building, organizing an annual "preservation celebration," along with other commemorations. Preservationists and the Texas Historical Commission left no doubt that they would sue to enforce the 1978 preservation covenant should the city move ahead with condemnation threats. Courthouse supporters expressed dismay at the lack of support they received from city officials. Walberg, for example, asserted that Utter repeatedly tried "to prove that it was in worse shape than it was." Utter countered that by the 1990s, when he was assistant city manager, he had "turned on" the courthouse because in the absence of a viable reuse plan, it seemed to him a hopeless blight in a prestigious location.[90]

After another round of condemnation threats in 1992, the county and the city worked out a complex deal that enabled the history-minded philanthropist Dusty Durrill to buy the building for around $300,000 in back taxes. Though he lacked the resources for a full restoration, Durrill took steps to stop the deterioration, clean the grounds, restore utilities, protect the building from vandalism, and install spotlights. The *Caller-Times* applauded: "At least the building, with the grounds spiffed up and signs of activity around, looks like a work in progress rather than a study in dilapidation." Durrill off and on had difficult relations with Friends of the Courthouse, which continued to conduct tours and do everything possible to keep the courthouse's plight before city residents and state officials, including helping put the building in shape for a public-television documentary that aired in April 1992.[91] Durrill proposed turning the courthouse into a community correctional center for nonviolent offenders. When that notion went nowhere, a new miscellany of reuse ideas appeared—for example, a downtown campus for Texas A&M University–Corpus Christi or a visitor center and museum for transportation. In 1994, one city council member denounced the building as an outhouse at the city's front door and suggested offering it to a Hollywood studio to blow up for an action movie. The stalemate remained, as the *Caller-Times* remarked, "with no developer racing to renovate the deteriorated structure and the Texas Historical Commission vowing to block any attempts to raze" it until the forty-year covenant expired in 2018.[92]

After assuming office as county judge in 1995, Richard Borchard took a more optimistic stance than his predecessor, Barnes, who rued not tearing down the county's old home when he had a chance. Borchard consulted with Friends of the Courthouse and supported grant applications to the Texas Historical Commission and the Texas Department of Transportation. He allowed the National Guard to destroy a 1961 annex that undermined the building's historic status. Sustaining this more favorable outlook was the appearance of a new generation of local preservationists, some with training in restoration techniques. Examples included John Wright, who in the 1990s oversaw restoration of the Bluff Balustrade and the Corpus Christi Cathedral; Patrick McGloin, a younger member of the old-line San Patricio family; and his wife and partner, Brooke Sween-McGloin, who made downtown and the courthouse her cause.[93] Even with new people taking initiative, Walberg and other veterans of the struggle persevered. They lobbied for state Historic Courthouse Preservation Program funds and organized matching-grant campaigns and even an "Annex Asbestos Angels" campaign to underwrite the clean-up that would enable demolition of the 1961 annex. "Pray for the Old Courthouse," proclaimed the monthly newsletter of the Nueces County Historical Society, which used Lee John Govatos's print of the building as its symbol.[94]

Still, Borchard remained daunted by restoration costs, which had reached an estimated $18.5 million–$25 million. In 2000, the county worked out a complicated deal to acquire the property back from Durrill. Ownership enabled the county to gain around $2.9 million in state and private funding for a "Phase 1" restoration, under Sween-McGloin's supervision: waterproofing the building and making a start on repairs to terra-cotta, brick, and other architectural details. A downside, for some, was the state's insistence on extending its covenant to 2027. Then, after Borchard left office in 2003, the county partially reverted to its earlier wariness. In August 2005, county commissioners refused even to second a motion to accept the Texas Historical Commission's offer of a $1.76 million matching grant to continue Sween-McGloin's work. "This is a setback, but not the end," the restoration project manager remarked.[95] The McGloins eventually relocated to California, where Sween-McGloin worked on restorations and other public projects for the City of Santa Monica.

In 2010, a Nueces County–sponsored study estimated that restoration costs had risen to around $40 million, while demolition would cost $3 million. This prompted county commissioners to negotiate with the

Texas Historical Commission to lift the deed restriction protecting the building. "We can either try to move forward or stand here for the next 15 years and watch the building crumble brick by brick," remarked the county commissioner coordinating the issue. Such moves and statements sparked a new round of argument, recrimination, and accusations of bad faith. The city council, bolstered by its success in pushing through the demolition of Memorial Coliseum, voted unanimously to back county efforts to rid itself of the old courthouse. "Would we miss the structure?" asked one council member. "Yes, but it's time to move on."[96]

Given the courthouse's status as a symbol of Corpus Christi's transition from town to city, the principled arguments for saving it were strong indeed. Still, this dreary story raised questions of the price of persistence in the face of forgone opportunities and lost credibility. Preservation by definition entails devoting money and effort to fixing up neglected, rundown buildings. When does neglect become too much and the necessary money and effort excessive? In Corpus Christi, the dilapidated shell of the Nueces County Courthouse came to stand for a movement that was sincere and energetic but that might not have known how to move on from a worthy but lost cause.

The Quonset Hut of Sisyphus

"We can't make up our minds on what to do with the Columbus ships. We have problems with the old courthouse. And now we can't decide what to do with the Coliseum," observed a dot-connecting letter writer to the *Caller-Times* on Veteran's Day in 2009. Compared to the 1914 courthouse, Memorial Coliseum did not have the advantage of being in a back-in-fashion style surrounded by romance and regret. In the early 2000s, it took a connoisseur's appreciation of midcentury modernism to grasp why architectural writers in the 1950s had insisted on praising its "successful merger of beauty and functionality."[97] But as important, the building suffered because it provoked over-familiar quarrels, a storyline of which many residents had grown thoroughly tired. As American Bank Center neared completion in 2004, the city council's impulse was not to wait to tear down the coliseum, which even supporters described as neglected and dilapidated. Revitalization proposals for the south bayfront site, however, became mired in uncertainty over direction, feasibility, and funding. This enabled pro-coliseum sentiment to grow strong enough to throw obstacles in front of demolition but not strong enough to rally support for an indefinite wait until a viable plan to save the building materialized. Which is to say, the very stalemate loomed that the city council had hoped to avoid.

Usually supportive civic figures made clear that they had no stomach for this struggle. Dusty Durrill, who had devoted time and money to numerous downtown projects, including the jinxed Columbus fleet and the vexatious Nueces County Courthouse, left no doubt that his priority was 4.4 acres that he owned in the coliseum's vicinity, where another "morass of inactivity" would serve no purpose. Durrill complained bluntly, "People who don't know a thing about it are giving input, and these conversations don't go anywhere."[98] Likewise, the *Corpus Christi Caller-Times* history columnist, Murphy Givens, responded in scathing terms to the impasse over the coliseum. Givens wistfully recounted the brusqueness with which the city had once rid itself of derelict buildings: "Maybe in a backroom with a shot of whiskey and a seegar," leaders of former times "would have made the decision to fix it up or tear it down, and we would have moved on." "We have become like Sisyphus," the journalist chided. The coliseum was "our colossal stone," punishment from the gods for a chronic "inability to make decisions."[99]

The building that put Givens in mind of an ancient allegory of futility was a long, low-slung barrel vault with lamella steel arches set upon concrete buttresses to create an impressive 224-foot span. World War II veterans whom it honored returned the favor by labeling it the "Quonset hut." More than its artistry, the coliseum's engineering ranked it among the "sentinel buildings of the 20th Century," in the words of the local architect who had it placed on Preservation Texas's endangered list. It was a fixture in the memories of generations of residents. Although an Elvis Presley concert in 1956 prompted restrictions on rock and roll, the coliseum eventually hosted Bob Dylan, Willie Nelson, and other stars, along with rodeos, graduations, craft shows, and similar events. Designed to withstand hurricanes, with footings driven into the seabed through the landfill on which it sat, the coliseum was a physical fixture as well, as federal officials recognized when housing evacuees from Hurricane Katrina there in September 2005. Along with Harbor Bridge, another 1950s engineering feat threatened with obsolescence, the coliseum's "gentle arced roof" framed the skyline.[100]

From a preservationist perspective, the coliseum had National Register value as the last surviving structure in Richard Colley's vanished civic center. A Fort Worth native, Colley (1910–1983) had worked in Mexico before establishing a practice in Corpus Christi. He started by designing Spanish Revival houses and churches but gradually became fascinated by modernist forms and technologies. In the mid-1940s, Colley served as city planning director, after which he had a long collaboration with O'Neil Ford, the great San Antonio architect, renowned for Trinity University, among many other Texas projects. Their best-known project together, the Texas Instruments Semiconductor Building outside Dallas (1956–1958), ranks among the masterpieces of twentieth-century industrial architecture. With Ford and

Figure 5.8. Aerial-view postcard of Memorial Coliseum, "the largest Quonset hut in the United States." Of the other components of the architect Richard Colley's bayfront civic center, the Exhibition Hall is visible adjacent to the coliseum, and city hall was beyond the parking lot to the right. Courtesy of the Dan Kilgore Collection, Special Collections and Archives, Bell Library, Texas A&M University–Corpus Christi.

on his own, Colley continued to design for Texas Instruments both in Texas and around the world as TI went multinational.[101]

For his civic center, Colley used ideas that he worked on with Ford and on his own. He intended the grouping of coliseum, exhibition hall, and city hall to represent a "fresh approach to the design of civic buildings," appropriate for a confident, growing city. The civic center's "greatest significance," Colley added, was that the progress-minded city could create a "broad, long-range city-planning program" around this ensemble. Throughout the 1950s, the coliseum in particular and the civic center in general attracted attention from architecture publications for its simplicity, durability, and adaptation to a difficult site and environment.[102]

When, starting in the 1960s and partly by accident, the city arrived at the policy of concentrating cultural, convention, and auditorium facilities around the Bayfront Arts and Science Park, the south bayfront languished as an afterthought. After Colley's exhibition hall gave way to a parking lot in 1985 and his city hall disappeared three years later, the city and the *Caller-Times* insisted that demolition of two-thirds of the once-lauded civic center had opened up "Corpus Christi's most valuable real estate" to development, a rationale revealed as wishful thinking by the city's repeated inability to interest investors in the site. In response to Janet Rice and others who argued for protecting the bayfront city hall, the city council member and later mayor Mary Rhodes regretted to *Texas Architect* magazine that only a "very, very small group" cared. The saga of the Nueces County Courthouse had by this point so disenchanted residents that Rhodes recounted being booed in a public meeting merely for expressing a favorable view of it.[103]

Including his bayfront hotel, numerous Colley buildings survived in his hometown into the twenty-first century. His chamber of commerce building along Shoreline Boulevard, similar to the civic center in design and technology, gave way in 2011, when the chamber left for Heritage Park, and the federal government, which owned the site, determined that repairs would cost too much.[104] But Colley was still represented by a prosperous Southside shopping center, high-rise Ocean Drive apartments, a high school, a Catholic church in a Mexican style that he designed to be built by the parishioners themselves, and perhaps seventy-five private houses in regionalist and modernist styles.

Even so, Memorial Coliseum remained the lonely remnant of an ensemble that embodied the pride and dynamism of the mid-twentieth century, when a cosmopolitan-minded business and civic elite imagined Corpus Christi as a leader in sophisticated planning and design, a place to be emulated. In January 2010, one architectural historian made a last-ditch case by stressing favorable accounts of the coliseum in Spanish and French publications and a photograph displayed at the 1958 Brussels World's Fair.[105] The historian was recalling a thwarted glory. Who emulated Corpus Christi anymore?

Plans that the city considered for reusing or replacing the coliseum seemed to illustrate a decline in imagination, sophistication, and ambition. In 2006, the city council accepted a proposal to turn the area into a fairground and entertainment center, with a Ferris wheel possibly replacing the coliseum as the south bayfront's visual landmark. The development company, TRT Associates, was affiliated with the Corpus Christi native Robert Rowling, owner of the Omni hotel chain. In the late 1990s, Rowling's move of his operation to Dallas offered disheartening evidence of the city's difficulty in retaining corporate headquarters, but his firms still owned almost one-fourth of the property within the Downtown Management District. The company explained that low occupancy rates at Omni's hotels along Shoreline Boulevard largely inspired its proposal. The city "needs some type of activity that makes people want to come to Corpus and the downtown area, or if they do come, to stay an extra day," a TRT vice president told the *Caller-Times*, repeating a theme of downtown renewal efforts going back to the 1960s. "We also wanted something to draw local residents," TRT officials added, alluding to the tension between attractiveness to outsiders and accessibility to locals that had pervaded decades of arguments over redevelopment, the arts, heritage, and preservation, all dependent on sales taxes and hotel-motel taxes, and thus on tourism.[106]

In that context, TRT's notion that a Ferris wheel might take Memorial Coliseum's place on the skyline was a public relations mistake. In 2003, the Houston entertainment company Landry's had included a Ferris wheel in its ill-fated proposal to lease the marina for a waterfront entertainment center. Ferris wheels thenceforth took their place as a loathed symbol of privatization and hucksterism along the bayfront.

As with the Landry's proposal, opposition and funding uncertainties stymied TRT's plan, which was withdrawn early in 2007. Attendees at public meetings then offered dozens of alternative ideas. Most accepted that tourist development was appropriate for the south bayfront so long as the city recognized that the coliseum was "more than just a building," as one resident remarked. A navy veteran who had settled in Corpus Christi recalled that when he first saw the town from the air in 1957, the pilot made sure to point out "the largest Quonset hut in the United States." "I don't want them to tear it down," the veteran continued. "It's where my kids graduated and where I took my wife on our second date."[107]

"It's not going to be demolished and the land is not going to be given away," promised the city council member overseeing public review. Arguments, concepts, proposals, and reports kept the impasse going through 2009. That fall, the city council attempted to strike a deal with a San Antonio developer to renovate the coliseum into a rink for the minor league hockey team, which bore the gloriously oxymoronic name IceRays. The developer would gain the right to build apartments, shops, and restaurants on the south bayfront, an aspect of the proposal that contributed to its failure, in part because local real estate interests resisted a municipal grant of advantages to an out-of-town competitor. The city then began steps toward demolition, even as the council kept discussing reuse proposals. In January 2010, an architect who had been an outspoken proponent of preservation offered a beyond-last-ditch idea for restoring the distinctive vaulted roof into an open-air pavilion. The architect "came up with a large, pretty picture, but not a dollar amount," remarked the new mayor, Joe Adame, himself a downtown property investor.[108] Even as the Destination Bayfront group organized and solicited ideas for the site, the city council invited demolition bids that left open the prospect of retaining at least the roof, in case of another change of heart. "Nothing in the City Charter says that [the council] must fish or cut bait," Murphy Givens taunted.[109]

Adame, who won election in the spring of 2009 based on his success as a developer and on promises not to tolerate such stalemates, led Corpus Christi into defying its reputation for irresolution. In February 2010, the council ended six years of discussion with a 7–2 vote to demolish the coliseum. "In order to bring [the south bayfront] back to life, it needs a clean slate," insisted the mayor. The city then implemented the council vote "swiftly and efficiently," an impressed *Caller-Times* remarked. Desperate, the coliseum's friends sought outside intervention, taking advantage of provisions of Texas preservation law that allowed them to file suit in Austin rather than locally. An Austin court spared the structure from March until May, when city attorney Carlos Valdez persuaded an appeals court to reverse the injunction. "It's a great day," the mayor told the press.[110]

Within hours, wrecking crews were at their tasks. The city intended to damage the structure as much as possible to render pointless a National Register application scheduled to come before the Texas Historical Commission on May 15, 2010. In 1976, Nueces County had failed to block a similar application on behalf of the 1914 courthouse, a lesson the city took to heart. After listening while preservationists vilified city officials as, in the *Caller-Times*'s words, "a bunch of weasels," the state commission unanimously approved the nomination. Within days, the commission backed away on the grounds that the building had been irreversibly compromised. The coliseum was "a loss to the City of Corpus Christi, the State of Texas, and the nation," the state historic preservation officer chastised Mayor Adame. Neither Texas nor the federal government could protect a building that Corpus Christi was "determined to demolish." Valdez then pursued claims for legal fees and demolition overruns against the preservationists, a type of human not known for having excess money. The coliseum was mostly gone by July, though crews continued to clean debris and break the foundation into the fall. Two-and-a-half years later, in November 2012, a district court ordered Friends of the Coliseum to pay the city $30,000.[111]

To the west behind the old courthouse, wedged between the Northside and the downtown highway interchange, is a half-maintained historical site whose users engage in no recriminations and file no lawsuits. Corpus Christi's founder, Henry Lawrence Kinney, set aside the land for what became Old Bayview Cemetery in September 1845, when the U.S. Army needed a place to bury soldiers who had died in a steamboat explosion during General Zachary Taylor's encampment in the lead-up to the Mexican War. Catholics and Jews acquired their own cemetery sites in the 1860s and 1870s, and the town laid out another cemetery in the 1880s. Burials continued steadily until 1914 and in a limited way until the 1980s.[112]

A graveyard for prominent as well as humble settlers in the town's early decades, Old Bayview Cemetery has long attracted interest, both of those imbued with a traditional, founding-family approach to local history and of devotees of the social-history mindset that became popular in the 1960s and 1970s. Poor record keeping along with reinterments meant that the number of extant graves remained uncertain. But a local protection movement in the late twentieth century managed to trace over 550 of the estimated 660 people buried there. Volunteers documented people from every level of society, from fourteen countries and twenty-one states, including veterans of six wars as well as "victims of yellow fever and other epidemics, tropical storms, and bandit raids." Other types of human violence helped fill the graveyard: "Some are murder victims, other died at their own hands because of the stresses of those days."

The preservationists documented concern over the cemetery's condition dating to the 1870s and 1880s, when a newspaper described it as a "public disgrace" with "tumble-down" fences that let in "ruminating cows [and] inquisitive hogs." Starting in the 1910s, the *Corpus Christi Caller*'s editor Eli T. Merriman looked after the graveyard to the point of personally paying the sexton. After Merriman's death in 1941, it suffered the ills of neglected cemeteries, including deteriorated and vandalized gravestones. The Grossman-Rome report of 1982 noted that the approach road to Harbor Bridge blocked a linkage between the cemetery and their proposed Old Irishtown historic district. In any case, the consultants concluded, Old Bayview featured neither enough grave sites of prominent people nor sufficiently distinctive burial monuments to meet National Register criteria. The cemetery's supporters did win state and city landmark recognition.

The cemetery endured through decades of neglect, spruced up during interludes of appreciation, because none of the conditions applied to it caused ambition and argument to coalesce around other segments of the central city. Even in the downtown's heyday, the cemetery lay outside paths of development, and it was never envisioned as hampering or helping any redevelopment scheme. No one proposed that the cemetery could increase property values or yield revenues derived from tourists. No political dispute or engineering crisis happened over it. The time to do something or move on never came. The cemetery illustrates the urban historian's axiom that amid the flux of a living city, history has better survival prospects in places that are bypassed and overlooked than in places that matter and are visible. Heritage Park, the equivocal preservation success recounted in this chapter, also illustrates history's dependence on the living city. Corpus Christi's so-called building zoo compromised preservationism's principles, but it accommodated the central city's shifting geography and changing functions.

Ultimately, preservation means no more to buildings than it does to residents of a cemetery. The redevelopment of older parts of towns that have fallen on hard times supports the living city. The appropriate mix of old and new in redevelopment—when to construct new buildings and places and when to restore and reuse old ones—belongs within the realm of city politics and not above it. The demolition of Memorial Coliseum and then the failed campaign for Destination Bayfront left the south bayfront emptier than before. Still, Corpus Christi's government devoted years, to the point of seeming vacillating and ineffective, to letting preservationists, veterans, other residents, civic-space advocates, developers, and others articulate their agendas for this highly visible, troubled space. Advocates of history and heritage usually start from the assumption that they act from the highest principles. For all of preservation's flaws—particularly all the ways it can intertwine with the profit motive and elevate some people's understandings of and romances with history over others—attentiveness to historic places probably does provide people with a fuller, more varied, and more thought-provoking urban environment than do heedless demolition and redevelopment and may even enhance civic pride and responsibility. Yet in any dispute over a historic place, one cannot start by assuming that advocates of clearing away the old to make way for the new are "exhibiting the uninformed thinking of the grossly unenlightened," as one pro–Memorial Coliseum architect insisted.[113]

To their misfortune, preservation and heritage groups in Corpus Christi invested hope, time, and resources in highly visible projects that for one reason or other did not pan out. Those failures fed a conviction that the city was negligent with its history, excessively inclined toward the "wrecking ball mentality," in comparison with San Antonio or Galveston, where, seemingly, preservation and heritage progressed smoothly. "Texas has a history of discarding history," Dusty Durrill lamented to the *New Yorker* in 2000, "of saying we can build it bigger and better and newer." Of course, civic and political leaders imbued with that break-with-the-past spirit commissioned Page for the 1914 courthouse and Colley in the 1950s for the south bayfront civic center.[114] Given Corpus Christi's perception of itself as Sunbelt Texas's disappointment, it is not at all paradoxical that people sought to recapture a past of entrepreneurship and innovation.

The Harland Bartholomew firm began Corpus Christi's era of downtown renewal plans by worrying whether anyone would care. In a distended, multicentered, automobile-oriented metropolis, would "the condition of the central area" seem "a matter of little import?" A gaggle of plans and interminable quarrels demonstrated that numerous residents cared a great deal about the central city's character, appearance, and role in local life. While often troubled and in places sick, central Corpus Christi was not ready for Old Bayview. That, in turn, meant rounds and rounds of visions and studies and enough "small-group roundtables" to leave a newspaper columnist "woozy" in the July heat.[115]

Chapter 6

A DYNAMIC & PROGRESSIVE CITY

∾

E *ven my own kids say,* 'I don't want to come back to Corpus Christi,'"
Ruben Bonilla Jr. told a forum in 2005. Chair of the Port Authority of Corpus Christi for three terms, former national president of the
League of United Latin American Citizens, lawyer and businessman
from a successful family, Bonilla would seem like an argument for his
hometown. But, he asserted, led by a complacent elite, "we decided we
were going to be a community of no growth." Even the port, Bonilla insisted with hyperbole, "just sat on petroleum while everybody else was
building container terminals." The place seemed "parochial" to young
people with ambition, especially young Hispanics. The city, concurred
Leon Loeb, offered little to attract "a young person in Houston or
in Agua Dulce"—a nearby town—"to invest [his or her] intellectual
and social capital." A commercial real estate operator from a fourth-
generation family, Loeb noted that only one of his three children had
returned: "One is in Chicago, and one is in Santa Monica."[1]

The forum where Bonilla and Loeb spoke was part of a project to
focus attention on the city's difficulties in retaining college-educated
youth. Since the 1960s, Corpus Christi had suffered a net outmigration
of young people, especially those with education and skills. Census
Bureau figures indicated that between 1995 and 2000, the population

of college-educated single people between the ages of 25 and 34 shrank by 7.3 percent. Bonilla had often chastised the local establishment as inward looking and arrogant. Yet he knew that the city had displayed not complacency in the face of its troubles, but distress, confusion, and acrimony. Evidence that the city had lost "control over its destiny," as a 1978 study put it, sparked bitter debate, with sides accusing one another of blocking innovation and of not appreciating the depth of the city's problems. "We could have been doing things years ago that would have bolstered the economy now," ran a typical complaint, this from a developer in 1986 when multisided opposition scuttled his downtown resort proposal.[2] That Corpus Christians as visible as Bonilla and Loeb articulated such misgivings about their own city leads to an overarching theme of Corpus Christi history and politics in the late twentieth and early twenty-first centuries: the sense that the city was in danger because it had let decades of opportunities slip amid the Sunbelt-style success of Texas's other metropolises.

Doubt and recrimination over the city's prospects took place in the context of political changes that had parallels in Texas and southwestern cities whose economies remained solid. Since 1964, when Tony Bonilla's election as state representative broke the Hispanic exclusion from major local offices, the Bonilla brothers had remained prominent among a generation of civic activists—black and Anglo as well as Hispanic—who pushed for a more pluralistic political system than had prevailed in the post–World War II decades. A turning point came with the 1979 election of a multiracial slate led by Colonel Luther Jones, a retired commander of the Corpus Christi Army Depot, whose candidacy for mayor had been encouraged by the powerbroker Hayden Head as an alternative to the antiestablishment conservatism of 1970s mayor Jason Luby. Over four terms, Mayor Jones oversaw the implementation of a court-ordered shift from an at-large council to a system that mixed single-member districts with an at-large system, a final blow to the Anglo commercial-civic regime that Head had helped organize after World War II. As in Henry Cisneros's San Antonio or in Houston under the string of Democratic mayors that started with Kathy Whitmire in 1981, Corpus Christi replaced the midcentury elite with loose centrist coalitions that remained mainly progrowth in policy. Commercial, real estate, and financial interests found that they could work more easily with ethnic politicians and even liberal professionals than with segments of the Anglo middle class. The ethnic movements, after all, favored an active, development-minded public sector; they mostly sought a full voice in policy and a shift in emphasis toward jobs, education, housing, and public services. Residents of outlying Anglo sections such as Calallen or Flour Bluff suspected the establishment of pursuing the pet projects of well-connected developers at the expense of them and their neighborhoods.[3]

The common enemy of the centrist progrowth coalitions became the Corpus Christi Taxpayers Association, an entrenched force starting in the 1980s. Critics accused this organization of being the local manifestation of Texas-style "aginner" sentiment, so-called because its agenda seemed to involve stopping whatever someone else proposed, a mindset that one city council member labeled, "Bay Area Residents Against Virtually Everything."[4] The mutual suspicion that ensued—the impulse to write off critics as self-serving if they were for a project, or small-minded if they were opposed—gave a sour tone, into the 2010s, to debates over bonds and public works and indeed to all proposals for a public-sector or public-private attack on the city's stagnation.

After the 1970s, Corpus Christi politics became more fractious and less efficient than it was at the height of commercial-civic rule. But this was true in cities across Texas and the Southwest. A loss of cohesion in politics and policy was an inevitable consequence of a more open, competitive municipal politics, which by the 1970s, establishment figures such as Head had accepted as inevitable and maybe desirable. Already in 1971, when the Area Development Committee, a crumbling bastion of the establishment, sought to rejuvenate and broaden itself by "bring[ing] in minority group representation and other elements of the community," the Caller-Times remarked, "The day seems gone when a few people can meet in a room and decide what is going to happen."[5]

Corpus Christi diverged from other large Texas cities less in its political tendencies than in its economic and geographic situation. As in Dallas or Phoenix, the credibility of Corpus Christi's midcentury commercial-civic leadership was founded on success. In the 1950s, a thriving private sector and an innovative public sector stood as evidence for the claim of Guy Warren, Lon Hill Jr., and their colleagues to represent the "progressive citizens" of a "dynamic" city.[6] Thirty or forty years later, few sought a return to the oligarchic methods of the midcentury elite, but they did mourn the loss of the dynamic atmosphere of that earlier period and the progressive reputation the city had earned. The second-tier or satellite status into which the city had drifted created practical problems, but also problems of mindset and image. People feared that "satellite" meant "vulnerable" and that "second-tier" equated to "second-rate."

At times, critics accused Corpus Christi's business and civic leaders not of being ossified and complacent—as Bonilla charged—but of manipulating worries over slow growth and of hankering for glamorous schemes that belonged in Dallas or Houston, big-city solutions to a medium city's problems. Yet whatever the merits of this or that expensive proposal to attack the city's problems, proponents did not, for the most part, simplistically assert that matching other Texas metropolises in growth rate or atmosphere was the key to prosperity and livability. The problem was not size and growth rate per se, but the city's autonomy and the opportunities it could offer. Other midsized cities seemed more effective at developing new sectors and networks and building reputations as places to settle and not to leave. In the same 2005 publication that included Bonilla's and Loeb's complaints, the developer Joe Adame, the future mayor, recounted a study he had organized a few years earlier when he chaired the Regional Economic Development Corporation, a nonprofit partly supported by the city and the port authority. The study focused on Boise, Idaho; Lafayette, Louisiana; and Fort Collins and Colorado Springs in Colorado, second-tier cities with populations similar to Corpus Christi's, but better outlooks. To Adame's dismay, none of the study's recommended innovations were implemented. "Young people aren't going to want to stay," Adame lamented, if the city continued doing "things the same way they've always been done."[7]

"Understand Who You Are"

Through all the distrust, frustration, and acrimony, Corpus Christians did in general exhibit an understanding that the city needed to redirect and rebuild. In 2003–2005, the Regional Economic Development

Corporation sought advice on strategies for midsized cities from renowned urban affairs consultants. The proposed solutions contradicted one another, as expert advice will, but the upshot was that Corpus Christi had options. The most prominent visiting expert was the
planner and economist Richard Florida, an articulate proponent of the
view that cities needed to attract talented young entrepreneurs and
professionals, the so-called creative class at the center of the postindus-
trial, knowledge-based economy. In Corpus Christi, Florida argued
against "fairly standard large-scale development projects," including
the new arena then under construction. The planner cited as "a truly
smart investment" the new Harte Research Institute at Texas A&M
University–Corpus Christi, one of the university's four institutes devoted to Gulf of Mexico and coastal issues, along with at least eight
specialized laboratories and a handful of graduate programs. Regionally distinctive, yet with international implications, environmental and
marine sciences could do for Corpus Christi what aviation, electronics,
and computers had done for Dallas–Fort Worth or Austin: provide a
creative-class activity that could "attract people from all over." The
consultant added that embrace of ethnic diversity was "everything,"
especially in smaller cities, which needed to multiply their connections
and magnify their innovative potential.[8]

"You have to understand who you are," countered the geographer
Joel Kotkin. "Don't follow the lemmings who want to be the next
Boston or San Francisco." A persistent critic of Richard Florida, Kotkin contended that hype over the information age had overshadowed
the continuing value of midlevel industrial and commercial cities. To
Kotkin, there was a "huge pent-up demand" for cities such as Corpus
Christi, which combined low housing prices with a Gulf Coast life-
style, all accessible to middle-class and working-class families. Kotkin urged Corpus Christi to combine nuts-and-bolts improvements to
public services and education with beautification projects that would
build civic spirit. From that standpoint, the Corpus Christi Bayfront
was "key," an example of the unique or "sacred" places that, as Kotkin
explained, had inspired city dwellers over the centuries to identify with
a city and devote themselves to it.[9]

Florida—with his emphasis on ambition and innovation—and
Kotkin—with his stress on decent housing, sound public services, and

civic pride—were updating old debates about how cities grow, prosper, and attract migrants and investors. Despite their differences, both consultants addressed basic issues of human capital, the local pool of skills and talents, and social capital, people's organizational networks and resources for working together. These issues worried a range of Corpus Christians around the turn of the twenty-first century. "We need more of these young, smart people" summarized the *Caller-Times* columnist Nick Jimenez in 2010. They "enliven a city, drive its economy, become leaders, and have a stake in the future." Echoing Kotkin, the journalist added that Gulf Coast life could feel like "vacation every day" and that the city "didn't go crazy on house prices like the rest of the country." Still, Corpus Christi needed "to have a positive reputation for creating something other than what God already put here, the sand and the sea."[10]

The underlying concern, which Richard Florida caught in his comments on the Harte Institute, was that Corpus Christi had never found an alternative to the resource-extraction economy that had driven Texas urbanization for the first two-thirds of the twentieth century. By the mid-1960s, oil-and-gas production and the petrochemicals industry together accounted for two-thirds of regional income. In 1967, the Harland Bartholomew firm began a study commissioned by the Coastal Bend Regional Planning Commission by insisting that it was "imperative" that this portion of South Texas "broaden its economic base" beyond oil and gas and the military.[11] The oil bust of the 1980s clarified the matter for those not previously paying attention. Upswings in oil-and-gas prices generated optimism, but each oil-and-gas cycle left the region weaker relative to Houston and Dallas–Fort Worth, where authority and technical skill in petrochemicals was concentrated, even as those cities diversified into other sectors.[12] In the 2010s, the Eagle Ford shale oil field west of Corpus Christi promised to create over 35,000 jobs in the region, jobs likely to endure for a generation, catalyzing further hiring in services as well as industry. Amid the region's first caution-to-the-wind phase in thirty years, the *Caller-Times* off and on sounded a note drawn from hard experience: "For all the local benefits, Eagle Ford is a boom driven by outside forces."[13]

Especially compared to midwestern industrial cities such as Akron, Youngstown, or Toledo, Corpus Christi remained diverse and durable.

The area "has not grown much," but other areas "have had rapidly declining economies," conceded one study intended to wake up those not yet worried.[14] The Port of Corpus Christi and its network of industries were generating an estimated $2.7 billion a year in direct and indirect revenue and $2.2 billion in wages and salaries even before Eagle Ford. From 1970 to 2010, the population of metropolitan Corpus Christi increased about 46 percent, from around 285,000 people to over 428,000. A State of Texas study in 2002 noted that from 1970 to 2000, real personal income in the Coastal Bend region from Victoria to Corpus Christi had risen by perhaps 80 percent. Even so, the state report stressed, other regions of Texas had grown faster by almost any economic measure.[15]

After making its run at metropolitan status in the mid-twentieth century, the South Texas port seemed stuck, ever more dependent financially and culturally on Houston, Dallas–Fort Worth, San Antonio, and (gallingly) Austin, which Corpus Christi had rivaled in population as recently as 1970. The city had to break partially from the Texas and southwestern urban network and nurture new patterns of commerce and exchange. But into the twenty-first century, initiatives to foster new patterns of innovation, finance, commerce, and industry yielded disappointing results. Corpus Christi's experience suggests that the more pessimistic hypotheses of authorities such as Richard Florida have merit. Opportunities for satellite cities to reposition and reinvent themselves, rare to begin with, may have become rarer as population, jobs, and technical skill have become concentrated in the "hub cities" of urban megaregions. Houston's predominance in energy production stood as a major example of Florida's point.[16]

It requires a mental leap to analyze a Texas or southwestern city in terms of stagnation and vulnerability. In popular discussion and urban studies writing, growth is the theme in the urban Southwest during the post–World War II decades. Discussions of urban political culture in the Southwest presume that residents saw their cities as growing with no end in sight, even when groups of residents were skeptical of unremitting growth or when they perceived growth's benefits as deplorably distributed. Such experiences and attitudes also characterized portions of the Southeast from Nashville and Charlotte through Atlanta to Miami, cities also identified with Sunbelt-style urbanization. The growth-oriented, probusiness coalitions that dominated urban politics in Texas and the Southwest during the 1940s–1950s had frayed by the early 1970s.[17] Still, throughout the Sunbelt era, the drive for growth and responses to growth so pervade southwestern urban history that it is jarring to encounter Corpus Christi's intense, even overstated awareness of falling behind.

Decrepitude, exploitation, and poverty pervaded many southwestern cities, but in the Sunbelt period this was not associated with decline. It was, instead, a by-product of the region's route to prosperity. The success of every southwestern city—large, medium, and small—from Los Angeles through the maquiladora towns of the Mexico-U.S. borderlands and up to Houston—hinged on a pool of low-wage labor, generally Hispanic or black. Indeed, into the 1980s, economic studies of Corpus Christi often made the explicit argument that low-skilled, nonunion workers, especially Hispanics and women, could serve as a selling point to potential investors. By the 2000s, even business-supported studies often switched to depicting a low-wage labor market as a trap, arguing instead for raising the region's skill and wage levels. Cities do not remain "dynamic," one such report explained, by promoting themselves as "any type of employment" places.[18]

In the Northeast and the Midwest (and in some southern cities, for example, New Orleans), the public as well as urban affairs scholars accepted that stagnation needed to take a central role in accounts of recent history and prescriptions for the future. Accordingly, researchers studying the urban Northeast and Midwest developed methods and concepts for examining stagnation or decline in secondary or satellite cities as well as in large cities.[19] To some degree, the perception that rapid growth counts as the overriding reality of the Southwest's recent urban history is a side effect of the way that both experts and the public take large cities as archetypes and extrapolate their experiences to smaller cities. From Fresno to Beaumont, the Southwest was dotted by medium-size, secondary cities where, as in Corpus Christi, the sense prevailed that the Sunbelt had bypassed them. Second-tier cities in the Southwest experienced such struggles not in common with larger neighbors but in a vexing contrast with them and without terms for discussing and tools for analyzing their situation.

In the post–World War II decades, the large cities of Texas and the

Southwest emerged as metropolises of continental, even worldwide influence. From Houston to Las Vegas, Phoenix, and San Diego, growth was indeed the story, albeit with interruptions such as that caused by the Texas oil bust of the 1980s. The financial crisis of 2008–2009 may compel a partial change in the Southwest's self-perception as home to perpetually growing cities. Richard Florida was the most noteworthy observer who suggested that the recession exposed the narrow foundations of some of the region's cities, Phoenix and Las Vegas above all, and marked the start of a period when the fortunes of large southwestern cities would diverge from one another.[20]

San Antonio, Corpus Christi's famous neighbor, offers a partial exception to the presumption of growth among large Texas and southwestern cities. From 1930 to 1980, San Antonio's metropolitan population tripled from 321,458 to 1,072,000. The city shared in Texas's general urbanization and wrestled like its counterparts with infrastructure, environmental, political, and social problems associated with demographic and geographic expansion. But San Antonio, the state's largest city as recently as 1920, fell behind Dallas–Fort Worth, Houston, and Austin in the conversion of petrochemical wealth into financial, commercial, technological, and industrial enterprises. Writers on San Antonio often blame this lost ground on "a remarkable lack of entrepreneurial aggressiveness" on the part of the commercial-civic elite, a contrast with the relentless booster ethic of the other Texas metropolises, including Corpus Christi from the 1910s to the 1960s. The city's secure situation as the commercial hub of south-central Texas, along with the military's preference for it as a site for large bases, meant that San Antonio lacked the occasion or incentive to develop "an indigenous promotional spirit."[21]

San Antonio business, asserts one expert, "had no imaginative responses to the changing economic structure of the state and region." Having let the opportunity presented by oil and gas slip past, the Anglo commercial-civic elite "adopted the more conservative strategy of enhancing San Antonio's role as a center for defense, tourism, and regional services." Local historians depict the city's midcentury leadership as complacent as well about ethnic and class divisions. Racial and ethnic division and oppression weighed upon all Texas cities, but historians of San Antonio place considerable emphasis on the burden created by substandard housing, infrastructure, and public services in Mexican American and African American neighborhoods and on the malign neglect of education, public health, and social welfare in those same neighborhoods. As an older polity than its counterparts, San Antonio also struggled with a heritage of machine-style politics.[22] By contrast, Dallas and, to a lesser degree, Houston developed their political traditions during the Progressive Era and the 1920s. This meant that machine-style politics was weak there, while commercial-civic politics was strong—though to be sure, Dallas-style good-government regimes also displayed continual neglect of conditions in ethnic and poor neighborhoods.

Themes on which San Antonio writers dwell have parallels with Corpus Christi's discussions of its recent struggles. An important difference was that Corpus Christi did produce a Dallas-style commercial-civic movement. From the late 1940s to the early 1970s, this progrowth regime oversaw the city with "tenacity and a strong sense of civic pride," as a retrospective in the *Caller-Times* put it.[23] Comparisons between San Antonio and Corpus Christi are also limited by the fact that one was an established metropolis overtaken by upstart rivals, whereas the other had fallen short while making a run for metropolitan status. As Florida's models predicted, by the start of the twenty-first century, San Antonio's size and complexity had enabled it to multiply connections and magnify opportunities relative to its smaller neighbor to the southeast. San Antonio's diversity and critical mass of cultural institutions and activities gave it an advantage in attracting young entrepreneurs and professionals. Corpus Christi had fewer potential new directions to follow and fewer prospects that something would turn up through the back-and-forth of big-city life. It had to focus its energies, though its residents could not agree on what, and neither could experts such as Kotkin and Florida.

"Charmed Life"

By no means did Corpus Christi enter a downward spiral during the 1960s and 1970s. Still, disturbing demographic and economic trends took shape, of which the shift from importing to exporting people seemed especially worrisome. Net outmigration from Nueces County during the 1960s was estimated at over 28,000, about 12.7 percent of the 1960 population. By the late 1960s, the area suffered an outmigration of high school graduates of perhaps 50 percent. Over the next two decades, such statistics served as a persuasive argument for transforming the area's higher education institutions into the Texas A&M University campuses at Corpus Christi and Kingsville. Yet pouring resources into local colleges did not stop educated young people from pursuing their ambitions elsewhere. Overall, into the 2000s, population growth—natural increase plus or minus migration—hovered between around 0.7 and 1.4 percent a year. In Michigan or Ohio, a midsized city would have been content with this modest growth. In Texas, it was vexatious. Around the start of the new century, Texas's

Figure 6.1. Net migration between Corpus Christi and other areas of Texas, 1965–1970. After the mid-1960s, economic studies regularly attempted to document out-migration and other signs of economic lag and diminishing opportunities. Table based on *Corpus Christi Community Renewal Program*, March 1973, 27.

Area	Origin of In-migrants		Destination of Out-migrants		Net Migration
	Number	Percent*	Number	Percent*	
TOTAL	37,175	100.0	49,419	100.0	−12,244
Texas	20,938	56.3	30,619	62.0	−9,681
Area within Texas					
Houston	3,225	15.4	9,259	30.2	−6,034
Dallas–Ft. Worth	1,953	9.3	3,780	12.3	−1,827
Austin	729	3.5	1,781	5.8	−1,052
North Coastal Bend Region	3,327	15.9	4,079	13.3	−752
San Antonio	2,076	9.9	2,271	7.4	−195
Rio Grande Valley	2,065	9.9	1,155	3.8	+910
South Texas	2,458	11.7	1,868	6.1	+590

* Texas as a percentage of total. Areas as a percentage of Texas.
Source: U.S. Bureau of the Census. *1970 Census of Population PC(2)-2E. Migration between State Economic Areas.*

overall net in-migration approached 5 percent. Metropolises such as Dallas–Fort Worth at times attracted over 20 percent more people a year than left.[24]

Behind mediocre growth figures was the slowing of enterprises that had fed expansion from 1920 to 1960. Corpus Christi surged in that era because of the advent, in succession, of the deepwater port in the 1920s, petrochemicals in the 1920s–1930s, high-energy-consuming industries such as inorganic chemicals and aluminum in the 1930s–1950s, and military installations during World War II. Once these sectors ceased to expand, the region seemed capable of generating only low-wage service and retail jobs. By 1970, around three-fourths of local workers earned average or below-average incomes. Per capita income, which in the 1950s had been a source of boasting, was now around three-fourths of the national average. Regional unemployment in 1970 hovered around 4.3 percent, close to the average for the country's metropolitan regions but higher than the rate in fast-growing Texas cities such as Houston. Unemployment, concluded a Community Renewal study in 1973, "would have been much higher if other cities in Texas had not grown fast enough to absorb Corpus Christi's jobless."[25]

Despite warnings that oil and gas would sooner or later slow and even shrink and take the region with it, the industry seemed reliable enough until the 1980s. Offshore drilling, the refining of imported oil, and natural gas production offset the waning of exploration and production in South Texas itself. Petrochemicals' dominance was "clearly evident to even a first-time visitor," noted an economic study in 1982. Every aspect of the industry was present: "Along with the major platform fabricators, refineries, and chemical plants are dozens of small facilities making everything from drilling mud to hydraulic motors to meter provers."[26] That year, Texas oil prices crashed, falling from around $33 a barrel to $10 a barrel by 1986. Local unemployment peaked in 1983 at 11.6 percent before a slow recovery, with 6.9 percent still listed as out of work in 1990. The bust "chang[ed] forever Corpus Christi's base economy," in the words of the local historian Bill Walraven.[27]

The plight of Houston attracted national attention and an element of schadenfreude from Rustbelt cities. Outside Texas, few understood how the crisis's aftermath gradually benefited Houston at the expense of satellite petrochemical centers along the Gulf Coast. The crisis accelerated consolidation of the managerial and technical aspects of the business in cities with corporate headquarters: Houston, Dallas–Fort Worth, or Wichita, home of Koch Industries. San Antonio's role in the oil-and-gas business was less well known, but San Antonio corporations such as Valero and South Texas Drilling and Exploration came to own a huge portion of the Corpus Christi energy sector. By the late

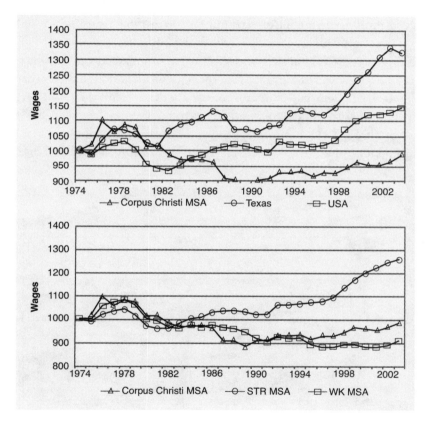

Figure 6.2. Corpus Christi wages in comparative perspective. The charts on which these are based appeared in a 2006 Regional Economic Development Corporation report among a mountain of documentation that Corpus Christi could no longer promise most workers an appropriate living standard. The charts depict inflation-adjusted ("CPI Factored") wages in Corpus Christi over thirty years as measured against the country overall, Texas, strong metropolitan statistical areas, and weak metropolitan statistical areas. Based on *Corpus Christi, Texas, Metropolitan Area: Historical, Comparative Economic Analysis* (Palm City, Fla.: Policom, 2006), sec. 2, 8.

1990s, numerous exploration, pipeline, and processing companies had moved or fallen under out-of-town ownership. Geological consulting, rig equipment supply, and other specialized services withered to shadows of their former selves. Supplied by imports and offshore rigs, the refineries that lined the Port of Corpus Christi returned to near-capacity production, and employment was slightly higher in 1990 than in 1985. But in the same half decade, employment in the extraction side of oil and gas fell from around 8,000 to under 4,000. Overall industrial employment fell from around 16,500 in 1980 to around 11,800 in 1990, roughly where it remained into the 2000s.[28]

For years, the region's oil-and-gas businesses reacted warily to upswings. "If they were to forget" the "overextension and high debt" that characterized them in 1982, one university study remarked in 1991, "financial institutions would quickly remind them." In early 2001, when high oil and gas prices brought demand for locally produced equipment to their "highest levels since the 1980s," a *Caller-Times*

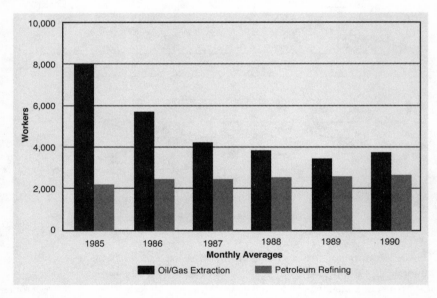

Figure 6.3. Energy-related employment, Corpus Christi MSA, 1985–1990. In the aftermath of the 1980s oil bust, employment in Corpus Christi's oil-and-gas-extraction sector fell by half, though refining remained stable. Based on *The Corpus Christi Bay Area Economy: Annual Report* (Corpus Christi: Center for Business Research, Corpus Christi State Univ., 1991), 13.

assessment ended with admonitions from industry figures. "The area is fortunate to have a heavy concentration of oil and gas interests" during prosperous periods, explained Chuck Cazalas, a local spokesperson for Houston-based Citgo. With "new monies . . . flowing into the local economy," it was "a good time to start the movement" from the current level of reliance on petrochemicals.[29]

In the 2010s, the Eagle Ford shale formation—"a vast underground network," according to the *Houston Chronicle*, of gas liquids and oil, 400 miles long and 50 miles wide, running between Corpus Christi and San Antonio—sparked the region's most intense investment in decades. Among Corpus Christi businesses quickly to notice the effects were auto dealers, who put the recession of 2008 into the past through sales to newly hired oil-and-gas workers. Petrochemical equipment suppliers anticipated a boom as well, but they understood that the initiative belonged not to upstart local enterprises but to multinationals, including Shell, BP, and China's CNOOC. Only firms on that scale had millions of dollars to invest in the high-pressure hydraulic-fracturing equipment needed to make deep, dense shale deposits profitable. The Port of Corpus Christi recognized this in February 2011 when it agreed to divide the former Naval Station Ingleside site between Houston's Canyon Supply and Logistics and Flint Hills Resources, a subsidiary of Koch Industries, which invested with Eagle Ford in mind. With contracts for around $120 million from two out-of-town petrochemical firms, the port for good measure leased, for $87,000, a small portion of the closed navy base to Texas State Technical College for a wind-energy education center. Within a year, these deals became stuck over details and then fell through when Canyon ran into financial problems. The port turned to another multinational operator, Occidental Petroleum, which purchased the Ingleside site for $85 million in November 2012. With Eagle Ford having added over $25 billion to the Coastal Bend economy by 2011, the port understood that its real estate, which offered access to deep water and a network of oil and gas pipelines, was valuable as long as the shale boom continued.[30]

Energy extraction and processing, therefore, remained essential to the metropolitan economy, even though its potential for generating large, new local firms remained limited. The Port of Corpus Christi, dominated by oil, gas, and related products since the 1930s, usually ranked among the top six or seven ports in the country in tonnage handled and at times among the top twenty ports in the world. Even during the oil bust, tonnage at the port grew every year except 1982. Growth in tonnage and revenue continued through the 1990s and into the 2000s, when the city was a receiving point for imports from the Middle East, Nigeria, and Venezuela, as well as a staging ground for oil operations in the Gulf of Mexico.[31]

While the port was the city's most important asset and its major link to the world's urban and commercial networks, the area's "major, basic industrial employer" was the Corpus Christi Army Depot on Flour Bluff. Specializing in helicopter repair and overhaul, CCAD employed 4,400 civilians and boasted a payroll of $366.4 million in the early 1990s. U.S. Department of Defense realignments had caused these numbers to shrink to 2,700 employees and $162.6 million by 2007.[32] CCAD shared Flour Bluff with Naval Air Station Corpus Christi, which accounted for around 1,700 military personnel along with 500 civilian employees. In the 1990s, the military complex also contained a Coast Guard station, a U.S. Customs office, and a navy hospital. Nearby were two other large bases: the Naval Air Station at Kingsville, Texas, forty miles to the west, and Naval Station Ingleside, a deepwater port opened in 1992 in San Patricio County on the northern shore of Corpus Christi Bay. One study in 2001 estimated that the military accounted for 14 percent of jobs and 21 percent of wages in the metropolitan area.[33]

The scope and complexity of the oil-and-gas business meant that no one firm or entity could make a decision that would spell disaster for Corpus Christi. By contrast, all the military installations belong to one employer. What was a medium-size reshuffling from the Pentagon's perspective could have enormous consequences for military cities. The precariousness of Corpus Christi's reliance on the military was dramatized in 1959 when the previous occupant of the CCAD site, the Naval Air Station's Overhaul and Repair Department, closed, putting 4,000 people out of work for two years, until the army arrived in 1961. In the mid-1970s, as the Vietnam era ground to its inglorious end, a similar pullout did not materialize; if it had, a stagnating metropolitan economy would have deteriorated into a depressed one.[34]

As historians of San Antonio and other military cities have observed, a high level of dependence on the military may have unfortunate effects on local civic and political leadership. The federal government bestows bases; cities then endeavor to protect them. This is a conservative task, not an innovative or expansive one. Public officials and commercial organizations devote enormous time, thought, and money to lobbying to "protect area military bases" and to "benefit from any military base downsizing and/or closures" in other cities, in the words of a chamber of commerce report.[35] Government and business in military cities defend their bases by enshrouding them with arguments for the superiority of local facilities in comparison with those in other metropolitan areas, who claim the opposite with equal plausibility.

Intended as a home port and training station—functions that interacted with other area bases—Ingleside ended up as a headquarters for navy minesweepers. Since the Gulf of Mexico was unlikely to experience mine warfare any time soon, Ingleside quickly became vulnerable to the Defense Department's Base Realignment and Closure Commission (BRAC). The August 2005 vote to close Ingleside cost the area nearly 3,000 direct and indirect civilian jobs, and an estimated 1,260 more were lost through reductions at the Flour Bluff facilities. In the ensuing half decade, until the place became a focus of Eagle Ford–related development, officials cast about for and quarreled over alternative uses for the 483 acres and 70 buildings that the navy handed back to the port authority. "Local economic development leaders," the *Caller-Times* reported after the BRAC vote to close Ingleside, "have no plans to offset" the loss of civilian and military positions "because they have concentrated on saving those jobs from base closure." Through the previous rounds of base closings, the paper editorialized, the area had "led a charmed life," but "all that came to an end" with the Ingleside vote.[36]

The Ingleside closure shook the region, but the Coastal Bend was not out of luck or resources. Observers warned of Corpus Christi's limitations, but the port, petrochemicals, and the remaining military bases ensured that the sky never fell. Cautious commentators, such as Mexican consul Francisco González de Cossío (at one time his country's ambassador to Saudi Arabia and Jordan), admonished the city to "follow [Houston's] path" and diversify beyond petrochemicals, given their threatening "tendency for mergers into bigger conglomerates."

Citgo's Cazalas agreed that Corpus Christians were "overdue" for reorientation "in our attitudes and in the economy."[37] But no setback dramatic enough occurred to force this reassessment to take place.

Turn to the South?

The presence of an experienced diplomat such as González de Cossío as Mexico's consul reflected not just the large Mexican American population, which rose from around 40 percent in 1970 to over 54 percent in 2000. It also reflected a hope on both sides of the border that the South Texas port could develop into a productive partner for Coatzacoalcos and Veracruz. Those Mexican ports sought routes into the United States for Mexican-made cars, cut flowers, and a range of other goods, especially after the North American Free Trade Agreement (NAFTA) went into effect in 1994.[38] The enlargement of the Panama Canal in the early twenty-first century seemed further to enhance the city's potential connections to Mexico and Central America.

Proposed partnerships with Mexico amounted to a break with the city's twentieth-century orientation and character in favor of an older vision. In the 1830s–1840s, the city's founders, led by the Pennsylvania native Henry Lawrence Kinney, understood this northernmost harbor in the disputed territory south of the Nueces River as offering an excellent location for trade—legal and illegal—between Mexico and the Texas Republic. Promoters projected the city's first railroad line, the so-called Texas Mexican Railroad, completed in 1881, as a replacement for the oxcart trade with Laredo and beyond. Beginning in the 1870s, however, economic, social, and political trends turned Corpus Christi away from Mexico and wove the city into U.S. commercial and industrial networks.

Especially after the 1870s, when incidents such as the Nuecestown raid led to the tightening of Anglo control in the trans-Nueces region, Corpus Christi served much more frequently as a staging ground for Anglo colonization of the borderlands than as an exchange nexus between Mexico and the United States. The transformation of ranching into a sophisticated, modern enterprise and the subdivision of South Texas ranchland into commercial farms operated by midwestern migrants presumed a firm Anglo grip on Corpus Christi's hinterland. In their initiatives to develop Corpus Christi's institutions, commerce, and transportation from the 1870s through the 1926 opening of the port and beyond, landholding families such as the Kings, Klebergs, Kenedys, and Driscolls envisioned the city and its region as a resource for the United States. All the sectors that fed the city's expansion until the 1960s—the shipping of Texas cotton and oil, chemicals and metals manufacture, military bases, tourism—reinforced the city's ties to Anglo Texas and Anglo America.

Corpus Christi, therefore, took shape as a gateway into the borderland region between the Nueces River and the Rio Grande, but only peripherally as a gateway to Mexico itself. During the city's era of rapid development, its business, civic, and professional leadership tended to look northward toward Dallas, Kansas City, and even Chicago. This was not merely a function of distance. Like Corpus Christi, San Antonio sits around 150 miles from Laredo, to which the inland city also acquired a railroad connection in 1881. Yet San Antonio retained diverse commercial and cultural ties throughout the borderlands and into Mexico. This despite the fact that—as in most former Mexican towns colonized by the United States—initially flexible relations between Mexican and American merchants gave way to a lengthy period of control by an ethnically exclusive Anglo-American business class.[39]

Organizations linked to Corpus Christi's mid-twentieth-century Anglo establishment, such as the Better Government League and the Area Development Committee, often did not even bother to include token Hispanic or black representation. To cite a key example, during the years when the city and the ADC worked with the Harland Bartholomew firm on the landmark 1953 comprehensive plan, no member of the ADC or the planning commission had a Hispanic surname. Only two Hispanics were listed among over one hundred people who participated in one of the ADC's functional committees on housing, water, and so on.[40] The battle against the Parrs of Duval County and allegations of vote buying among residents of the old Hill barrio reinforced the elite's tendency to associate Hispanic political involvement with the paternalism of the old Anglo ranching families and with machine-style manipulation of uneducated Hispanic voters. These were relics of provincial backwardness, and the midcentury generation of business and professional leaders were inveterate modernizers and good-government reformers. The post–World War II Mexican American generation of professionals, businesspeople, and labor leaders shared much of this modernizing, reformist outlook, but the Anglo establishment was painfully slow to realize this. Until the 1970s, the Anglo leadership did little to include Hispanic or black civic leaders in discussions of the port, transportation, the central city, and similar issues. They could not imagine that Hispanic and African American residents had much interest in such matters or much to say about them.

The business and professional structure of Hispanic Corpus Christi long reflected these circumstances. As recounted in chapter 3, almost all promotional, economic, tourist, and historical accounts of Corpus Christi through the 1950s perpetuated stereotypes of the Mexican and Mexican American population as providing unskilled or semiskilled labor for Anglo-controlled enterprises and as adding an element of romance to the region. Recurring scenes of farmworkers pouring into Corpus Christi on Saturday night to spend their meager earnings were demeaning in their depiction of the supposed childlike profligacy of South Texas Tejanos. Even so, this imagery built upon the reality that enterprises catering to Coastal Bend Hispanics were concentrated in Corpus Christi. The city's Hispanic business and professional sector, which organized the first Mexican chamber of commerce in the late 1930s, grew around the provision of goods, services, and entertainment to those who labored on farms and ranches, along with the city's own Mexican American working class. This was a typical pattern for ethnic-based commerce and professions in U.S. cities. But orientation toward a disproportionately poor, regional customer base reinforced other factors—including discrimination and lack of access to capital— that kept the Hispanic business and professional sector mostly small in scale and local in scope. Groups such as the Westside Business Association embodied in their names the reality that most Hispanic-owned businesses were proprietorships, partnerships, or small corporations that provided goods and services mainly to a Hispanic clientele.

Nevertheless, as throughout the Southwest, by the 1970s, the Mexican American middle class was growing in size, resources, and ambitions. The aging Anglo leadership began making overtures to Hispanics and, to a lesser degree, African Americans. In 1974, for example, the board of directors of the Corpus Christi Chamber of Commerce featured J. A. "Tony" Canales, Hector P. García's nephew and an attorney with manifold political and business connections, in addition to former state representative and future LULAC national president Tony Bonilla.[41] Even after the partial adoption of single-member districts in the 1980s and the shift to a Hispanic-majority population in the 1990s, however, the move of Hispanics into political office was fitful. Until the election of Joe Adame in 2009, the only Hispanic mayor, Gabe Lozano, had served on an interim basis in 1978–1979, when Jason Luby resigned to run for Congress. Not until the late 1990s did voters place a Hispanic majority on the city council, a situation that lasted only one term and did not recur for over a decade. Many observers felt that this lag resulted in part from factionalism within local Hispanic politics. Extended family groups off and on engaged in intense competition, and Corpus Christi–based figures competed with politicians identified with outlying Hispanic-majority towns, especially Robstown.

Hispanics gradually attained key positions with economic development implications. For the two decades that began with the appointment of Juan Garza in 1988, Corpus Christi's city manager remained, with a few interruptions, a Hispanic public-administration professional with experience in several southwestern cities. In 1994, Richard Borchard, who had a mixed ethnic background but was identified with Robstown's Hispanic politics, won the first of two terms as Nueces County judge. In 2001, the banker Yolanda Olivarez became the first Hispanic port commission chair, a post held from 2002 to 2010 by Ruben Bonilla Jr. By the 1990s, the city's state legislative delegation usually included one or two Hispanic professionals with prestigious educational backgrounds, for whom the position promised to be a stepping-stone to a career of regional or statewide scope. Carlos Truan, long the area's most prominent legislator, stood as an exception to this use of the state legislature as a stepping-stone. Until his retirement in 2001, Truan served twenty-five years in the Texas Senate after eight in the state's House of Representatives.[42]

Despite enhanced Hispanic visibility in political, professional, and business affairs, a view of the Hispanic business sector as a resource for building connections with Mexico and Central America took hold in only gradual and limited ways. Until the late 1980s, analysts tended to discuss the city's distance from major U.S. markets rather than its proximity to Mexican ones. Studies warned that the city's peripheral location within the United States represented "a significant transportation penalty" for American firms contemplating building a plant or office, a "distinct disadvantage" that Mexico's nearness only partly offset.[43] This tentativeness about the vast potential hinterland within five hours by truck resulted in part from obstacles inherent in trade with Mexico before the ratification of NAFTA. Also important, for a very long time Anglo commercial-civic leaders appeared reluctant, to say the least, to give up the presumption that Hispanic entrepreneurs were not ready to manage large, highly capitalized operations. Hispanic leaders repaid this dismissal with lingering suspicion of Anglo-controlled enterprises and organizations.

The founding generation of Hispanic entrepreneurs—often the children of laborers and farmworkers—necessarily concentrated on small- and medium-size businesses in retail and services. By the time they had left the scene in the 1980s–1990s, the midcentury Mexican American–minded cohort had built connections and accumulated investments that provided the foundation for efforts by the next generation to operate on a larger scale. Still, judging at least by the membership of the Hispanic Chamber of Commerce in the early 2010s, Hispanic-owned businesses remained mainly local in orientation.

In 2011, the Hispanic chamber featured members in around 200 different categories. The chamber included businesses with a multi-ethnic or citywide clientele. The organization also included Hispanic officials from petrochemical companies, utilities, banks, health-care providers, and similar enterprises, signs of the move into once-closed areas. Yet none of the 200 categories specifically involved commercial ties with Mexico, the Caribbean, or Latin America. I was not able to trace a single firm from among hundreds of members that emphasized such ties. More visible were firms in civil and environmental engineering, petrochemical equipment and services, and commercial construction that were either owned by Hispanics or had a large Mexican American presence in management. Robert M. Viera, the chamber's chair in 2011, for example, was the V in LNV Engineering, a Corpus Christi–based civil engineering firm with offices in San Antonio and Austin. These were the sorts of South Texas firms positioned to benefit from the Eagle Ford discovery, even though the field's development was mainly in the hands of multinational enterprises.

The seven newsletters published by the Hispanic chamber from December 2009 through the summer of 2010 contained much evidence of a Hispanic presence in South Texas's energy and engineering sectors. The newsletters dwelled on small-business promotion, aid with government contracting, and liaisons with analogous groups in San Antonio and other Texas cities, activities typical of chambers of commerce, whatever their ethnic composition. The publications gave no emphasis at all to Latin America.[44] In effect, Corpus Christi Hispanics with business and professional ambitions seemed to perceive more opportunities in South Texas's customary sectors than in any presumed advantages that language or culture might bring them in dealings south of the Rio Grande.

The reality was that even after NAFTA, Corpus Christi's potential as a gateway into Mexico remained unclear. That doubt contrasted with the city's established commercial ties to the Caribbean more broadly, on account of the port's role in oil refining, metals manufacturing, and similar products dependent on raw materials from the larger region. The city's business and political leaders discussed opportunities in Mexico but seemed uncertain about how much effort and risk the pursuit of Mexican markets was worth.

Even before the ratification of NAFTA, intense local discussion began concerning improved communications, transport, and institutional links to northern Mexico and beyond, even though Corpus Christi lay outside the section of the borderlands that generated the maquiladora economy of the 1980s.[45] The port and the visitors bureau shared with Laredo a trade and tourism office in Monterrey. Port officials held conferences with representatives from such distant Mexican states as Morelos and Chiapas and negotiated with port officials from Coatzacoalcos and Veracruz, one of Corpus Christi's designated sister cities. The port's 100,000-square-foot cold-storage warehouse, constructed in the early 2000s, seemed inviting to Mexican officials seeking outlets for produce. But through 2007, by which time the cold-storage project's revenues had fallen nearly $21 million below investments, no significant Mexican exporter counted among the operation's customers, though a shipper of Guatemalan melons did.[46]

Several years into the NAFTA era, estimates were that half of the imports from Mexico and a third of the exports into it passed through southern Texas, but this included goods transported via Interstate 35 between Laredo and San Antonio. No freeway crossed the 140 miles from Laredo to Corpus Christi, where officials worried that truck traffic from Mexico would continue to bypass them for Houston, with its enormous container facilities. The first tenant secured for La Quinta Terminal, planned as a multipurpose dock and container facility in San Patricio County across Corpus Christi Bay, was a thirty-acre cotton compress operation that exported Texas cotton to Mexico and Asia. La Quinta's potential as an alternative to Houston would remain limited as long as "the most direct connection" between Laredo and Corpus Christi—as the Texas Department of Transportation stressed in 2006—was "a combination of U.S. and state highways through mostly rural and business districts," at speeds as low as thirty miles an hour.[47]

The *Caller-Times* even fretted that Congressman Solomon Ortiz paid too much attention to Brownsville, whose port handled one-twentieth as much cargo as Corpus Christi's. South-to-north tourism offered a tangible connection across the border; the city profited considerably from the estimated $900 million spent by the three million Mexicans who came to Texas each year for business, vacation, shopping, medical care, or personal visits. In fact, Corpus Christi benefited despite having no direct air service to Mexico as of 2013.[48] Port officials and commercial and political leaders regularly discussed trying to expand tourist traffic by going into competition with Galveston as a starting point for Gulf of Mexico cruises. Offsetting Corpus Christi's proximity to Mexico, however, was Galveston's access to Houston, Dallas, and other cities of the southern plains states.

Though fitful in attention and ambiguous in results, this contemplation of the south as a field of opportunity—rather than as a source of cheap labor, staple crops, or raw materials—entailed breaking with patterns of thought and activity, and with social and ethnic relations, that had shaped the city for over a century. Like cities throughout the southwestern border regions, Corpus Christi wrestled with the challenge of ceasing to be an endpoint of United States urban networks and resuming an older, once violently repudiated role as gateway between two countries and their peoples.

"Set Up Pretty Well"

To sum up so far, despite four decades of concern, argument, proposals, and effort, Corpus Christi had by the early 2000s made no break with its customary emphases and had embarked on no clearly new direction. Initiatives that achieved the most results built on existing functions. As in 1960, the city's most reliable asset remained its port, deeply intertwined with the oil-and-gas sector. A magnificent work of civil engineering and an impressively sophisticated institution, the port nonetheless worried about keeping pace with Houston, which also loomed over South Texas petrochemicals. Corpus Christi functioned also as a center for the military and for regional services such as government, health care, and retailing. Despite frequent feuding over public-sector support for cultural institutions and visitor-oriented attractions, the city had managed to reinforce its position as a major tourist destination and as a second-tier convention center, in large measure through the reshaping of downtown. "Is Corpus Christi dying and is anyone trying to save it?" asked a widely cited *Texas Monthly* article in 1978.[49] The answers were surely no and yes, whatever cynics quipped. But until Eagle Ford changed the mood, and perhaps the equation, in the 2010s, the city experienced frustratingly slow growth, mainly as an offshoot of vigorous development elsewhere in Texas and along the Gulf Coast.

The port continued to upgrade and expand, despite the mixed results of efforts to diversify beyond petrochemicals and to improve connections with Mexico. The Port of Houston overshadowed all ports along the Intracoastal Waterway from Florida to Brownsville, with the exception of southern Louisiana, an outlet in the 2000s as in the days of the Louisiana Purchase for grain from the Mississippi Valley. Houston's twenty-five-mile ship channel, which received 7,700 vessels in 2009, consistently ranked first in imports and second in exports to the Louisiana ports. It handled three-fourths of the container traffic on the Gulf of Mexico and, with over 150 industrial employers, boasted the world's second-largest concentration of petrochemical plants and refineries. Beaumont, about seventy-five miles northeast of Houston, also in some years outranked Corpus Christi, mainly because it served as an embarkation point for U.S. military cargo. While such neighbors garnered more attention, the Port of Corpus Christi was still a stunning complex of ship channels, docks, and industrial operations stretching over thirty-four nautical miles from the Gulf of Mexico. In tonnage, it rivaled such vaunted operations as the Port of Long Beach, though it did so on account of petrochemicals—habitually 70–80 percent of the activity at Corpus Christi—and not because of the container imports on which the Southern California ports concentrated.[50]

During the early 2000s, ill-tempered struggles occurred over representation on the port authority commission. These struggles involved confusing alliances of Hispanic and Anglo business and political figures and were accompanied by charges of excessive politicizing of appointments and conflicts of interest involving commissioners with ties to port-related businesses. A lengthy quarrel with county judge Borchard led Senator Truan to push legislation to shift the balance of power away from the Nueces County government, which had traditionally appointed four of the seven commissioners. Partly as a result, San

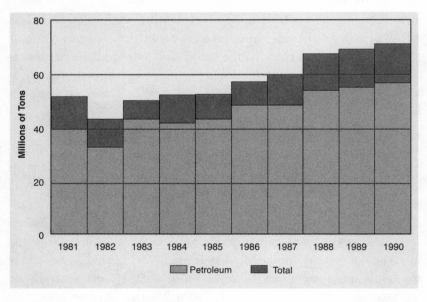

Figure 6.4. Cargo tonnage, Port of Corpus Christi, 1981–1990. Petrochemicals prevailed at the Port of Corpus Christi through the 1980s oil bust and then continued to dominate, despite decades of diversification efforts until the 2010s, when the Eagle Ford shale-oil boom undermined scruples about overconcentration, at least temporarily. Based on *The Corpus Christi Bay Area Economy: Annual Report* (1991), 17.

Patricio County gained a representative at Nueces County's expense.[51] The fact that prominent Hispanic politicians and businesspeople lined up on both sides of these quarrels illustrated the complexity of Corpus Christi–area politics. Struggles over seats on the port commission continued for years afterward, illustrating the port's absolute economic and political centrality. When Borchard reentered public life in 2009 after a seven-year interval, his office was county representative on the port commission.

The Port of Corpus Christi Authority strove to remain attractive to petrochemical operations while broadening its base. The 1970s oil crisis gave rise to a plan for a supertanker port dredged to seventy-two feet, which would have been by far the deepest channel on the Gulf. A coalition of conservationists, residents of seacoast towns, and antitax and antigrowth groups tied up this project into the 1980s, when enthusiasm for supertankers dissipated amid the Texas oil bust. Meanwhile, the ship channel was dredged in stages to forty-five feet. By the late 1980s, Corpus Christi boasted of having the Gulf's deepest port.[52] As an Army Corps of Engineers' survey in the early 2000s (that is, before the shale oil boom) revealed, at least twenty of around thirty-five privately run wharves, docks, dry docks, and other facilities along the port had a direct connection to oil-and-gas production or processing or to the offshore oil industry. This was in addition to the dozen oil docks operated by the port authority itself, let alone the refineries and other petrochemical plants operating on port authority land.[53]

To encourage more manufacturing, the port implemented a foreign trade zone in 1985, which allowed industries to avoid duties on imported raw materials, especially oil, until finished goods were shipped to domestic markets; reexports were not taxed. Diverse projects such the cold-storage warehouse and a conference center, along with the free-trade zone, gave the port director, John LaRue, confidence, as he remarked in 2000: "We're set up pretty well for the next 10 years to help this community grow." By 2008, Corpus Christi had become the preferred entry point for imported turbines for Texas's wind-energy sector, an industry that thrived quietly amid the hullabaloo over shale oil. The port expanded open-storage yards that received turbine components, though with the expiration of federal wind-energy tax credits in 2012, the business ground to a halt, at least temporarily. Efforts to lure container facilities made inconsistent progress. The port's expansion across Corpus Christi Bay into the 1,100-acre La Quinta Terminal site included the goal of creating a 1,250-container wharf to compete with nine existing container ports on the Gulf. Through 2010, La Quinta's most substantial development deal remained its cotton compress operation, the port's most traditional enterprise.[54]

For the most part, the port's diversification efforts did not involve a large move into commercial or residential real estate or waterfront recreation, as had become common among port authorities from Tampa to San Francisco. Starting in the 1980s, the port authority off and on considered a festival market or another project similar to Baltimore's Harborplace as a way of reusing the cotton warehouse at Cargo Docks One and Two west of the Harbor Bridge. But even with the concentration of cultural and tourist attractions and events facilities at the nearby Bayfront Arts and Science Park, the port could never demonstrate that the project would draw enough customers to justify the investment. A version of the proposal published in 1987 would have connected a "People's Project" at the cotton warehouse via water taxi to an "Old Town Corpus Christi" near the Texas State Aquarium, north of the ship channel. "Opportunities for the Port Authority," proclaimed a 1987 strategic plan, "are limited only by our imagination and our willingness to commit to an entrepreneur dedicated to the *people* business." In June 1987, the port commission unceremoniously "mothballed" the proposal after receiving a negative market study. The commission chair, James C. Storm (after whom the port later named a pavilion for rental events at the old cargo dock site), told the *Corpus Christi Caller* that he "would rather receive a negative report in advance of the project than negative results after it was built."[55]

In the 2000s, after renovating the old docks into a meeting and events center named for Congressman Ortiz, who helped secure a federal grant for the renovation, the port continued to discuss putting a cruise terminal there. But in the end, most of the Corpus Christi Ship Channel remained given over to shipping and industry. The ship channel's durability as a working port contrasted with the fate of the inner harbors of Baltimore and San Francisco. Far from venturing into condominium and office development, the port authority spent much time working with refineries and petrochemical plants to buy out homeowners and create a buffer zone, on account of consternation over air and ground contamination. When all its vast territory was taken into account, the port authority had plenty of land for state-of-the-art harbor facilities and enough of a task just in keeping pace with Houston or Beaumont. It played mostly a supporting role in the municipality's network of attractions in the northern central business district—for example, by providing the site for the Whataburger Field baseball stadium. The port reserved downtown property for development in case the opportunity comes.

"America's Birdiest City"

By the late twentieth century, cities of all sizes resorted, like Corpus Christi, to downtown redevelopment and to aggregations of anchor attractions as generators of new businesses and jobs when commerce and industry seemed stymied. In the scramble to increase the number of visitors and persuade them to stay longer and spend more, Corpus Christi had regional and historical advantages. Travelers from outside Texas knew San Antonio, Galveston, and South Padre Island, but for Texans themselves, Corpus Christi had long served as an accessible vacation destination. By the 2000s, consultants estimated that around 80 percent of Corpus Christi visitors came from within Texas, compared with an average of 63 percent for other destinations in the state. The average distance traveled to Corpus Christi in 2008 was 361 miles, which is less than the city's distance to Dallas. Corpus Christi's popularity among Texans has been enough at times to make it the second- or third-leading tourist destination in Texas, always behind San Antonio. A study in 2009 ranked the city sixth in Texas, noting that an estimated 7.2 million visitors generated over $1 billion. Tourist-related businesses employed nearly 13,000 people in the metropolitan area, though that included bars, restaurants, and other venues used only in part by visitors. Directly or indirectly, tourism may have accounted for around 11 percent of regional employment; only health care employed more people. Tourism could not generate the high-skilled, high-salary jobs associated with the port and its industries, but its entrepreneurial, labor-intensive character made it attractive to cities worried about slow employment growth.[56]

Figure 6.5. Pelicans and other shorebirds in Oso Bay, which was spared from resort development and made into the Hans and Pat Suter Wildlife Refuge, a popular urban bird-watching site. Texas A&M University–Corpus Christi is on Ward Island in the background. Author photo, 2013.

Corpus Christi boosters have seen promise in tourism since the Ropes Boom of the 1890s. As with Elihu Ropes's failed deepwater port, the city took shape more or less as the promoter had imagined, but too slowly for him to benefit. By the 1910s, hotels, railroads, and commercial groups advertised the Naples of the Gulf as "the ideal place for the restoration of health and for outdoor activities and diversion." Railroads brought "the most delightful" winter climate on the continent "within reach of the traveling public."[57] The Splash Day festival promoted the city starting in the late 1910s, giving way in 1938 to Buccaneer Days. Over time, festivals were dispersed around the calendar to emphasize year-round accessibility for oceanfront vacations.

The downside of Corpus Christi's popularity among Texans for weekend vacations and regional conventions was its reputation as inexpensive and not especially classy, a place of cluttered signs for shrimp houses and beachfront motels, with little to offer travelers in sophisticated or self-improving moods. The Urban Land Institute's 1965 study of downtown—discussed in the last chapter—made the case frankly that the city should direct more effort to attracting well-heeled travelers. "The automobile vacationer who enjoys the simple life and who pulls a trailer," the ULI remarked, would not "add materially to the economic base of the city."[58] Changing the mix of visitors and the ways in which they used the city emerged as a rationale for decades of planning for the bayfront and downtown, though residents and civic leaders evinced wariness about conceding too much of the bayfront to tourist-oriented uses.

One could make protourism arguments in an unalloyed way with regard to North Beach on Rincon Peninsula across the ship channel. Even as freeways channeled traffic toward Padre and Mustang Islands, this area, renamed Corpus Christi Beach during the 1950s, became the subject of numerous revitalization schemes. All presumed that the area would remain focused on recreation and perhaps condominiums and high-rise apartments. Hurricanes Beulah in 1967, Celia in 1970, and Allen in 1980 all damaged the area and evoked disturbing memories of the hundreds who died there in the storm surge of 1919. The opening in 1990 of the Texas State Aquarium and the aircraft carrier *Lexington* museum in 1992—soon to rank first and second among local attractions—promised steady tourist traffic north of the ship channel for the first time in decades. A municipal plan adopted that year summarized notions of how the run-down resort might become "a uniquely attractive atmosphere for small and large scale tourist attractions and services." The plan called for diverse recreational and resort options along a pedestrian promenade that would run the length of the beach. As a "partner and active participant," the city would provide convenient, well-designed amenities while discouraging billboards, RV parks, and other distractions. New "visual/scenic corridors" might make people forget Corpus Christi Beach's decades of decrepitude.[59]

Beginning in the 1970s with the prolonged battle over the Bayfront Convention Center, public funding for entertainment and tourist anchors downtown became a target of neighborhood, antitax, and antigrowth sentiment, identified first with Mayor Jason Luby and later with the Corpus Christi Taxpayers Association. As in much of urban America, ethnic minorities and the white upper-middle class seemed pushed into a progrowth alliance. In the final convention center bond election, in 1976, the city's wealthiest and poorest precincts voted 70 percent or more for the bonds, while voters in mainly Anglo, recently annexed areas voted no by nearly the same margin.[60]

Commercial and civic leaders came regularly to express the fear that a segment of the Corpus Christi population was infected with shortsighted obstructionism. This perception fed a tendency among the commercial and civic elite to dismiss criticism of their schemes, even when that criticism had merit. Especially in the 1990s and early 2000s, a string of controversies and hard-fought bond elections pushed growth-minded civic and political leaders into unreflective, at times petulant support for proposals that in a calmer climate might have been rejected as ill considered or modified to satisfy objections.

The battle in 2003 over the city's plan to lease the downtown marina to the Houston firm Landry's prompted charges and countercharges along these lines. Anti-Landry's residents argued that the city government was far too willing to concede an indispensable segment of the bayfront to an out-of-town corporation with an arrogant reputation and a penchant for "upscale carnival." Proponents countered that the community was behaving small-mindedly. "We've had a lot of opportunities to do things in this town, and they've all been turned down," one resident complained after the Landry's deal collapsed. "I think the people who turn it down want to keep Corpus small."[61] Even widely embraced projects such as Whataburger Field prompted such observations. The *San Antonio Express-News* noted the care with which Nolan Ryan and his sons lined up support and personally answered critics at public meetings. In the absence of someone with Ryan's credibility, Corpus Christi seemed to dance around "progress as if it were a poisonous beast."[62] The dramatic defeat in a November 2013 bond election of Destination Bayfront, which proponents saw as clearly beneficial but critics saw as a giveaway to developers, repeated and reinforced this pattern. "Complainers and naysayers" had earned Corpus Christi recognition as "the city that doesn't do anything," lamented Dusty Durrill, a south bayfront property owner, but one whose decades of contributions to downtown made him hard to write off as self-serving. "Don't ever make the mistake," Durrill added, "of thinking that they will quit being roadblocks, stopping good projects."[63]

The most successful strategy for expanding Corpus Christi's tourist reputation and appeal was remarkably simple and inexpensive and prompted none of the recrimination associated with the downtown anchor strategy. From the whooping cranes of Aransas National Wildlife Refuge to the spoonbills, white pelicans, and stilts of Oso Bay, the Coastal Bend featured one of the continent's most stunning aggregations of shorebirds. In addition, the area served as a funnel for migratory birds—from thousands of broad-winged hawks to swarms of ruby-throated hummingbirds—en route between the Mississippi Valley and Mexico. During the spring and fall migrations, any visitor to the four-acre Blucher Park in central Corpus Christi could see an unforgettable assortment of songbirds. Assisted by local Audubon societies and other conservation groups, and encouraged by avian authorities such as Roger Tory Peterson, the region's towns began perceiving wetlands and other habitats as tourist assets, promoted through events such as the Texas HummerBird Festival in Rockport every fall. By the early 1990s, the Texas Parks and Wildlife Department and the state Department of Transportation coordinated these efforts into the Great Texas Coastal Birding Trail, which included over 300 identified birding sites up and down the coast from Corpus Christi, proclaimed "America's Birdiest City." No one knew how many visitors came for the birds. By the 2000s, an estimated 28 percent of tourism was nature oriented in one way or other, though that figure may have grouped birders with other sorts of visitors. Twenty percent of visitors claimed sightseeing as their goal, while another 11 percent came for the area's vaunted hunting and fishing.[64]

"An Ill-Conceived Project"

Harland Bartholomew and Associates had prosperous tourists in mind in 1967 when it proposed that Corpus Christi spend $100 million to construct a Florida Keys–style offshore highway extending across four man-made islands in Corpus Christi Bay. Thirteen miles of new shoreline might support 3,750 new hotel rooms and generate over 10,000 jobs. The highway would have ended at a resort in Oso Bay near the naval air station and the University of Corpus Christi. "Cayo del Oso is a birdwatcher's paradise," HBA's report tersely observed. "Birds will leave this area as soon as development takes place." This scheme helped galvanize the wetlands protection movement that made possible the Great Texas Coastal Birding Trail. The wetland itself later became the Hans and Pat Suter Wildlife Refuge; an industrial chemist, Suter had emerged during the 1960s–1970s as the area's most prominent environmentalist, largely on account of his drawing attention to threatened bays and wetlands. His wife, Pat, a chemistry teacher at Del Mar College, carried on their shared commitment to wetlands and bird habitats for years after her husband's death, in 1984.[65]

Because HBA's plan abetted "dredge and fill" coastal development and took no account of environmentalist sentiment, it would be easy to dismiss it as out of tune with the times.[66] From Bali (in Indonesia) to Antalya (Turkey) to Malaga (Spain), the reshaping of coastal environments for multimillion-dollar resorts, catering to well-heeled travelers as well as package-deal ones, accelerated during the late twentieth century. For resort developers, the entire Gulf of Mexico coast could appear to be a zone of opportunity, the Corpus Christi area included.

Part of HBA's miscalculation related to location. After the 1960s, hotel and resort promotion shifted from Corpus Christi Bay to North Padre and Mustang Islands. The barrier islands had caught developers' attention upon the opening in 1950 of the four-mile causeway across Laguna Madre. But for years little private development took place to supplement the Padre Island National Seashore and the Nueces County beaches popular with college students on spring break. Only 134 permanent residents, along with a few hotels and condominiums, had appeared on the islands by 1970.[67] The Padre Island Investment Corporation, formed in 1965, was by the early 1970s touting plans for 2,400 house lots on 683 acres, with hundreds of lots having access to Laguna Madre along twenty-four miles of dredged canals. The project, which followed in style and intent similar oceanfront and barrier-island projects on South Padre Island, along the Florida coast, and off the Carolinas, attracted investment from around the United States and from Europe. Compared to coastal development elsewhere, North Padre sputtered along; in 1990, fewer than 3,000 people lived on portions of the islands annexed to the municipality during the 1980s.[68]

In August 1980, the Gulf of Mexico sent a reminder—forgotten swiftly enough—of the hazards of barrier-island development in the form of Hurricane Allen and its seventeen-foot storm tides. In 1986, the Padre Island Investment Corporation, weak from years of disappointing growth and shaken by the real estate slump that plagued Texas after the oil bust, fell into bankruptcy and was besieged by lawsuits from over 1,500 lot owners scattered around the world, some of whom had bought marsh property not yet filled in. The project fell into the hands of Pittsburgh's Westinghouse Credit Corporation, which sold it to Texas investors led by Paul Schexnailder, a politically connected Austin-based entrepreneur.[69]

With fresh capital and strategic support from the state and metropolitan governments, subdivision and construction revived on North Padre Island. Population had reached nearly 6,500 by 2000, with projections for over 16,700 by 2010. (The real figure ended up being closer to 10,000.) Estimates for the price of new housing began to range from $164,000 for modest townhouses to over $2 million for lavish dwellings. Less wealthy buyers from the islands' slow-growth periods worried that soaring property taxes would drive them from what promoters claimed to be the last substantial stretch of developable coastline from Virginia to the Mexican border. Inflation of the island's beachfront lots, whose prices climbed to as high as $650,000 by mid-2007, invited speculators, whom real estate agents accused of slowing construction in prime subdivisions.[70]

Figure 6.6. On North Padre Island by the 1990s, houses, in subdivisions sketched decades earlier, had finally come to line dredged canals with access to Laguna Madre. Author photo 2011.

Island developers' political connections became a source of consternation during the 1990s when the county and city governments started to pay close attention to a decades-old proposal to dredge Packery Channel, the almost invisible border boundary between North Padre and Mustang Islands. Named for the hide-and-tallow operations that ranchers set up there before railroads transformed the South Texas cattle industry, the shallow, shifting channel underwent several attempts at dredging for ocean traffic, including Elihu Ropes's disastrous Port Ropes plan of the 1880s–1890s. The channel silted decisively in the 1920s, probably a side effect of construction of the Corpus Christi Ship Channel off Port Aransas at Mustang Island's north end. Hurricanes periodically reopened it more effectively than the Texas Game and Fish Commission, which used everything from a dredge to blasting powder in futile efforts to maintain a fish pass there in the 1930s–1950s.[71]

When the idea of reopening the channel reappeared in the 1980s, the main purpose was recreation and resort development. Environmentalists and coastal preservationists formed an awkward coalition with antitax and antigrowth groups to fight the plan. In part to gain Army Corps of Engineers' sanction and federal subsidies, proponents claimed that the channel would provide environmental benefits such as improved conditions for marine life in Laguna Madre and better flood control. One might be tempted to dismiss these claims as a rationalization, but some close observers of the coastal waterways agreed that improved water flow would benefit marine life in the lagoon. Environmental groups such as the Sierra Club disputed such arguments; they countercharged that the channel would displace the habitat of endangered shorebirds and hasten flooding during a hurricane. "For government officials to encourage population increases on the islands," asserted the geologist Henry Berryhill in a letter to Nueces County judge Richard Borchard in 1995, "is irresponsible and courts potential disaster."[72]

Until the inevitable hurricane, Berryhill continued, the beneficiaries of Packery Channel would be developers "and those who buy a residential lot with a boat slip."[73] Contradictory environmental information, the geologist implied, obscured Packery Channel's real goals: a convenient route between Laguna Madre and the Gulf of Mexico for recreational boating, along with thousands of feet of semiprotected shorefront property. Supporters insisted that Packery Channel would spark $677 million in condominium, hotel, and recreational development, generate between 3,500 and 4,450 new jobs, and pump at least $42 million a year into the South Texas economy. Such figures overcame objections that the dredging was "a chance for Schexnailder and insiders to get rich while a beautiful barrier island is despoiled," as the San Antonio Express-News remarked. When, in August 2000, the Corpus Christi city council authorized a tax increment financing (TIF) district to pay for the city's portion of dredging costs, opponents forced a referendum for April 2001. Opposition flyers ridiculed the notion that "we're all going to get rich . . . when we dig this ditch." Opponents argued that the dredging would increase beach erosion, pollution, and the threat of storm surges. The TIF approach's promise that the channel would pay for itself by attracting outside capital and increasing property values helped voters overcome their mistrust of municipal involvement in tourist-oriented public works. The channel dredging referendum won by a 3–2 margin; the 22 percent turnout was heavy for a city bond election. Voters seemingly heeded the Caller-Times's plea not "to let an opportunity for more jobs and a better quality of life pass them by again."[74]

Figure 6.7. Packery Channel during dredging. Author photo, 2005

Under the name "North Padre Island Storm Damage Reduction and Environmental Restoration," Packery Channel received around $20 million in federal funds, about two-thirds of the total cost. While alluding to the environmental benefits of water exchanges between the Gulf and Laguna Madre, city documents noted that the channel's main purpose was to provide "a convenient recreational water passage," the focal point of "a world-class multipurpose development unique to the Texas Coast with the potential to attract tourists from all over the state and nation."[75] Environmentalists won partial vindication in 2003 when the Army Corps of Engineers instructed the city to set aside $1.25 million to create a new bird habitat to replace that lost to dredging.[76] In November 2006, weeks after the channel's opening, surfers and beachgoers exacted revenge on Schexnailder by voting down proposed limitations near Packery Channel on driving on the beach. For many Texans, "the perceived right to spin wheels on the beach," the *Texas Observer* remarked, stood "there with God, Mom, and Apple Pie," despite being loathed by environmentalists as well as resort developers. Unless voters approved the driving ban, Schexnailder threatened to back out of the planned resort, now estimated to cost $1.5 billion.[77]

Through the next half decade, Schexnailder held on to most of his island property, even as construction on the barrier islands ran dramatically short of projections. "Ditch digging goes platinum," proclaimed a *Caller-Times* headline in 2005. By 2007, construction permits on the Corpus Christi portions of the barrier islands had tumbled to 119, about half the level of a few years before. Permits fell further after the onset of the recession of 2008; only 49 permits were issued for the islands in 2010. Between 2003 and 2010, about half the permits were for single-family houses, with the rest divided between commercial construction, duplexes, and condominiums. This belied predictions that the channel would set off waves of expensive resort development.[78]

Searching for some accommodation with residents, Schexnailder in 2008 hired a consulting firm connected with the Disney Corporation. The consultants planned to engage in a "story jam" with residents in order to reenvision "this marvelous thing we're going to build," as the firm's "chief story-telling officer" remarked. Resorts along Packery Channel remained just stories in 2011. As of that summer, construction was evident as one sailed the channel west of the Route 361 bridge. From the bridge east to the Gulf, one saw an impressive expanse of empty waterfront property. Still, enough money had accumulated in the TIF district account to underwrite improvements even after the city's construction bonds were paid. Around $2.9 million was designated for amenities promised when the channel was put before voters in 2001. When an advisory committee that included Schexnailder proposed diverting much of that money into street and utility projects that might entice developers, residents pressured the city council to stick with the original plan. "Provid[ing] a shortcut for pleasure boats to the Gulf of Mexico" was supposed to "cause Padre Island development to explode," conceded the *Caller-Times*. "Enticements" might help, but "the city [needs] to keep its word to voters."[79]

As property values collapsed in early 2009 and foreclosures multiplied, Richard Florida decried as "giant Ponzi schemes" the real-estate-driven booms of southwestern cities such as Phoenix and Las Vegas. In much of the Sunbelt, he argued, civic and business leaders had imagined that "development itself" could substitute for "sustainable, scalable, highly productive industries or services."[80] In the 1990s–2000s, Texas cities, including Corpus Christi, mostly avoided bubbles in real estate that outran underlying growth. The barrier islands, however, presented a temptation to the public-sector-supported property speculation that Florida and other urban economists deplored.

At the time of the Packery Channel referendum, the *Express-News* reporter could barely maintain an air of neutrality about what "environmentalists, scientists, and concerned residents . . . view . . . as an ill-conceived project that would benefit only a handful of wealthy residents." The San Antonio paper nevertheless urged readers elsewhere in Texas to empathize with the "allure" of ocean resorts for a city "that sees itself as trailing the economic boom of other communities." As a secondary city in the Texas system, Corpus Christi was limited in its ability to redirect commerce and industry to its advantage. Tourism and resort projects such as Packery Channel gave such cities something to do when other options ran into frustration.[81] In 2012, Schexnailder and New Braunfels's Schlitterbahn company completed a deal to build a sixty-five-acre water park on the island. The city council voted for $117 million in tax incentives in the hope of spurring the barrier-island boom that Packery Channel was supposed to spark. "Corpus Christi needs a win," explained Toby Futrell, the city official who negotiated the agreement.[82]

As the *Packery Channel* or Destination Bayfront cases underscored, projects for which a case could be made on both sides came to generate acrimony so repetitive that it could seem a stylized distraction from any proposal's merits and defects, risks and benefits. In June 2007, to cite another example, the head of the chamber of commerce, Terry Carter, remarked, "We may be hungry for growth, but we're not starving at the well." Carter was arguing for delaying an offer of tax credits for a new $300 million shopping mall on the Westside. Given other cities' hard experiences with retail overdevelopment, prolonged deliberation over such a proposal might make sense. (In fact, construction never began on the Crosstown Commons before the recession put it "on hold," as its developer conceded in 2009.) Carter's remarks generated not second thoughts but angry charges, in this case with an undercurrent of distrust on account of the mall's location in a largely Hispanic part of the city. In the words of the *Caller-Times* editor Libby Averyt, the "comfortable" Carter was defending "older, wealthy businessmen who own retail centers," who were brazenly "protecting themselves at the expense of those less fortunate." Averyt quoted an "appalled" activist, Abel Alonzo: "Well maybe where he lives this community is not hungry." "Where has everyone been?" asked Nancy Vera, a LULAC council president. Commercial and civic leaders, Vera felt, needed to support "everything we can do to bring [Corpus Christi] out of the hole it's in."[83]

Amid nervousness over stagnation and fierce debates over development, the city's residents struggled to remember that their problems were relative. Corpus Christi was sluggish compared to the city during its 1910–1960 burst of growth and to cities such as Austin and Dallas–Fort Worth. Yet the South Texas port avoided the severe decay evident in some places in the Southwest and in many northeastern and midwestern cities. Until the recession of 2008–2009 and the Texas budget crisis that followed it, sectors such as government, retail sales, and health care had grown more or less steadily for decades, highlighting the city's role as a service center for southern Texas. By the late 1990s, two health-care systems—Christus Spohn and Columbia—employed 4,500 and 2,882 people respectively and ranked second and seventh among area employers. (Government and the military accounted for the rest of the top seven.) These hospital systems, as well as Driscoll

Children's Hospital, served patients from as far away as the Rio Grande Valley.[84] Urban economists doubt whether regional services such as health care can reinvigorate a stagnant urban economy, but they provide a stable floor under it.

The expansion of Texas A&M University–Corpus Christi, a small commuter campus until the 1990s, illustrated the city's ability to reinforce its centrality in South Texas while seeking new areas of activity. In 2002, after a decade that saw thirty-six buildings constructed and student and faculty growth to match, the university claimed that in addition to the 26 percent of students drawn from out of town, around 45 percent of students were locals who might have gone elsewhere had the university not existed. The university tried to set a dollar figure on its value to the city, but more important was its role in offsetting the out-migration of educated youth.[85] The university emphasized research and education devoted to South Texas regional issues and to coastal, wetlands, and environmental matters. This mission was a frank attempt to balance service to the metropolitan area with research and development connections around the Gulf Coast and indeed along all the North American coasts.

The city's vulnerability had been evident since the mid-1960s, but Corpus Christi managed to avoid disaster in its military sector, upgrade its port, retain a significant (though no longer self-directed) presence in oil and gas, build step-by-step an attractive network of cultural institutions and recreational facilities, and nurture stabilizing activities such as the hospitals and the university. Perhaps this capacity to endure and adapt itself inhibited residents from taking seriously enough the disappearance of the city's pre-1960 dynamism. Some urban affairs scholars suggest that secondary or regional cities seem to confront their problems thoroughly only when faced with disaster, not prolonged sluggishness. Examples might include Omaha or Allentown, both of which reoriented themselves around high-skilled, high-wage enterprises after the collapse of meatpacking in Omaha's case and steel in Allentown's. Yet for every Omaha or Allentown, a Youngstown or Rockford remained stuck in a dreary spiral despite considerable local effort. The divergent experiences of secondary cities in regaining dynamism further suggests to experts that some geographic or economic circumstance has to emerge to present new opportunities; then social and political conditions have to enable the city to perceive and take advantage of these novel prospects.[86] The message to Corpus Christi from comparable places is ambivalent, though far from despairing. Such observations do make one wonder how much of the flood of money from Eagle Ford will flow into the still-necessary quest for alternatives to oil and gas.

Starting in the 1980s, urban scholars anticipated that as the Sunbelt era wound down, southwestern cities would face political and social challenges similar to those confronted by cities in other regions with slowing rates of urbanization and rigid, brittle economies. Corpus Christi represented an early example of a southwestern city faced with this type of urban maturity. Its anxieties, arguments, false starts, grasps at straws, and successes offer lessons for other southwestern cities that have lost their dynamism and confidence in their progressiveness.

CONCLUSION

〜

E arly in the book, I asserted that in the booster phrase borrowed for
a title, "Where Texas Meets the Sea," Corpus Christi's accent has
been upon Texas. Every phase of Corpus Christi's history has derived
from and reinforced the city's ties to its South Texas hinterland, the
Mexico-U.S. borderlands, the Southwest, and especially the urban
system centered on the Texas Triangle of Houston, San Antonio, and
Dallas–Fort Worth. Even though the town's founder, Henry Lawrence
Kinney, marketed the town as the Naples of the Gulf, his ambitions for
the place and himself hinged on his ability to manipulate connections
to the Texas Republic and later to the United States, along with factions in Mexico, without fatally alienating any of them. As the failure
of his 1852 Lone Star Fair illustrated, Corpus Christi's prospects in
its early period remained limited by its distance from the heartland of
Texas, despite its proximity to the sea.

When Corpus Christi began to thrive, gradually after the 1870s
but especially after construction of the deepwater port in the 1920s,
it was because enterprises synonymous with modern Texas perceived
Corpus Christi Bay as a useful place for a port city. Corpus Christi became integral to the South Texas ranching families as they transformed
cattle raising into a sophisticated business while subdividing lands for

commercial farmers. Although Corpus Christi became an oil-and-gas port, cotton had provided much of the original rationale for dredging the Corpus Christi Ship Channel through the shallow bay. The satellite towns that surround Corpus Christi, its railroads and port, and its financial, political, and cultural institutions all took shape as urban extensions of the operations of the ranching families, whose townhouses for decades dominated the Corpus Christi Bluff. Uriah Lott, who oversaw the region's railroad network, and Roy Miller, the mayor and *Corpus Christi Caller* editor who modernized the city's appearance and public works and then lobbied for the port and the Intracoastal Canal, were both protégés of the Klebergs of the King Ranch. Indeed, Robert Kleberg Sr. recruited Miller to South Texas to do public relations for Lott's Brownsville railroad.

The ranch families envisioned Corpus Christi as both a port and a service town for the Coastal Bend and the lower Nueces basin. In the 2000s, this regional service role was epitomized by a network of hospitals, including Christus Spohn Hospital, which the Klebergs initially underwrote. After the 1919 storm destroyed the Spohn Hospital building on North Beach, the institution moved temporarily to the Kenedys' mansion on the bluff before building on land donated by Henrietta King, Richard King's widow.[1] Clara Driscoll's will provided for what became the renowned Driscoll Children's Hospital.

From the 1930s to the 1950s, oil-and-gas production, petrochemical processing and shipping, and energy-consuming metal and chemical manufacturing made the Port of Corpus Christi into a civil-engineering marvel and Corpus Christi into a dynamic city, a place of opportunity for the ambitious. These enterprises created the generation of Anglo business and civic leaders—coherent in their vision and proud to the point of arrogance—who looked toward Houston and, especially, Dallas as models for professional urban governance and a sophisticated and attractive city. If their plans had worked out, figures like Guy Warren of the Area Development Committee, the architect Richard Colley, and the lawyer and powerbroker Hayden Head might have caused Houston and Dallas to look toward Corpus Christi as well.

Petrochemicals enriched Corpus Christi but also constrained it. As the midcentury generation passed from the scene, as the oil-and-gas business became consolidated in the largest Texas metropolises, and as other Texas cities used earnings from oil and gas to expand into aeronautics, electronics, and other innovative enterprises, Corpus Christi slipped into its uncomfortable role of being a satellite city in Sunbelt Texas. Songwriters based in Austin reinforced Corpus Christi's image as a relaxed beach town for Texas's faster-moving cities, an adored place that had its tacky and even dissolute sides. Ever since Congressman Richard M. Kleberg helped secure the naval air station for the area, Texas politicians have cooperated in local efforts to protect Corpus Christi's military installations, which heighten the extent to which the city's fortunes depend on decisions made elsewhere, in the Pentagon as well as in Houston or Dallas office towers.

Perhaps in the twenty-first century the sea might take equal or greater precedence. Marine and environmental science institutes could place Corpus Christi in communication with Tampa–St. Petersburg or New Orleans on matters that have no reason to pass through Dallas, Austin, or San Antonio. Expansion of the Panama Canal could supplement NAFTA in making Veracruz's status as a sister city practical as well as ceremonial. In the 2010s, the Eagle Ford shale field sparked enthusiasm and activity not seen in Corpus Christi since the early 1980s. Shale oil, however, reinforced the Coastal Bend's reliance on outside capital and its dependence on cities in Texas and elsewhere where petrochemical corporations have their headquarters. Still, enough profit from Eagle Ford might remain in South Texas to allow Corpus Christi to diversify into a range of enterprises beyond resource extraction, should the city's business and finance adopt the attitude that their counterparts in Dallas–Fort Worth and Houston displayed decades earlier.

The city's political and economic history hinges on its ethnic history. Corpus Christi was a key gateway into southern Texas for Anglo-Americans, a staging ground for Anglo colonization, and with it, subordination of the Tejano homeland that had been taking shape before 1836. In 1845–1846, the town served as a literal staging ground for the U.S. conquest of the disputed region. The suppression of Tejano resistance and the pacification of Corpus Christi's turmoil-filled hinterland were preconditions for the developments that wove the city and the region into Texas and the United States. Anglo-led agriculture and commerce, in turn, drew Mexican settlers back to the Nueces region as migration from the south accelerated with the outbreak of the Mexican Revolution in 1910.

From the earliest phases of this migration, a portion of Mexicans and Tejanos moved into South Texas's cities, especially San Antonio but also Corpus Christi, where they worked along the waterfront and in construction; in rail yards, warehouses, and factories; and increasingly in shops and offices. Tejano Corpus Christi remained continuously and consciously intertwined with Tejano South Texas. Extending across space and over time, memories of displacement in the nineteenth century and grinding, oppressive conditions in the twentieth century animated the Mexican American movements that Corpus Christi generated, beginning with LULAC in the 1920s. Similar processes molded African American Corpus Christi, although black migrants to South Texas more often moved directly into towns and urban occupations.

Corpus Christi ended up as a satellite of Houston, Dallas–Fort Worth, and San Antonio, their port and outpost on Texas's southern Gulf Coast and one of their main leisure-time outlets. Still, the core of Texas took the direction it did because of conditions and events in its extensions and peripheries. The South Texas hinterland and Corpus Christi made each other, and so did the Texas coast and Central Texas. This book will achieve one of its main goals if readers—especially those in Corpus Christi and similar satellite or secondary cities—take away an understanding that modern urban regions such as Greater Texas need and depend upon them, as well as the reverse.

As this book has stressed, Corpus Christi and Texas defined and shaped one other through heritage and lore as well as through geography, resources, economics, and politics. Both of the frontier sagas that underpin Texans' sense of history—the Anglo-American drama that moves from east to west and the Mexican American story extending south to north—run through Corpus Christi and the lower Nueces region. These epics can act as myths in the negative sense of the word. That is to say, simplifications and distractions can overshadow the elements of documentable reality that they contain. Even so, readers will have noticed that I never asserted that the city's people should surrender the Texas epics and their role in them entirely. Lore can draw attention to realities that systematic history might overlook.

If one began Corpus Christi's modern story with the port's opening in 1926 or even with the Nuecestown raid in 1875, one would distort the city's past and significance. From the ship channel and seawall at the north of the crescent-shaped city to the naval air station on Flour Bluff—indeed from Choke Canyon Dam and the Lake Texana pipeline to the Padre Island Causeway and Packery Channel—the modern city hinges upon technologies, structures, institutions, and arrangements unimaginable to Blas María de la Garza Falcón in the 1760s or to Henry Lawrence Kinney in the 1840s. Despite all that, explorers and *empresarios*; traders, land dealers, ranchers, and rangers; and settlers from Mexico, Ireland, the United States and many other places created the foundation on which modern urban life in South Texas took shape.

Corpus Christi's epics—its Gulf Coast, borderlands, and Texas sagas—serve the functions of epics and myths in numerous societies, including the capacity of such stories to symbolize conflicts, frayed edges, and injustices. Given the ethnic tensions and moral rough edges inherent in Corpus Christi's Texas sagas, Tejano and Texan heroics from the eighteenth and nineteenth centuries act as allegories, as tacitly agreed-upon vehicles for discussing and disputing the place and its problems.

A review of local authors reveals numerous ways that Corpus Christians have mixed Texas lore with regional history to converse about the city's meaning overall and significance to different people. The Spanish-heritage writings and activities of Hector García's sister Clotilde, explained in chapter 3, typified the pattern. So did the writings and activities of Laura Lou "Dee" Woods (1896-1984). After moving to Corpus Christi with her husband in 1933, Woods devoted herself to regionalist writing about Corpus Christi and its portion of South Texas. She worked along lines championed by the Texas folklorist J. Frank Dobie, mentor to another figure discussed in chapter 3, the educator and folklorist Jovita González. Woods was intrigued by the imaginative and expressive power of Anglo South Texas's east-to-west epic in the same way that González engaged the region's Hispanic south-to-north heritage intellectually as well as imaginatively.

Woods's newspaper and magazine articles on early Corpus Christi figures such as Kinney, "King of the Wild Horse Desert," and on episodes such as the post–Civil War yellow fever epidemics set the tone for later journalist-historians such as Bill Walraven and Murphy Givens. Through a group that Woods helped organize, the Corpus Christi Byliners, she supported other aspiring writers. The Southwest Writers'

Conference, a Corpus Christi event that she founded in 1944 and directed for nearly two decades, enabled aspiring writers to participate in workshops with Texas literary and scholarly figures such as Dobie, Walter Prescott Webb, and Carlos E. Castañeda. Woods's circle was preoccupied with the South Texas environment as well as its lore and legend, after the manner of her 1942 book, *Blaze of Gold: Treasure Tales of the Texas Coast, Mostly of Gold That Is Buried and Ghosts Which Are Not.*[2]

Woods was one of the first Anglo South Texans to write about a miserable event that, transposed into legend, became a vehicle for discussing Hispanic dispossession and its consequences: the 1863 hanging in San Patricio County of Josefa (Chipita) Rodríguez, convicted of robbery and murder in a questionable trial presided over by district judge Benjamin Neal, who in 1852 had been Corpus Christi's first mayor. During the twentieth century, local writers and artists found in the Chipita Rodríguez story a drama that concentrated the region's foundational injustices and durable conflicts. In the 1940s, Rachel Bluntzer Hebert, a Spanish teacher and author from a family of early Catholic settlers, worked with the artist Antonio García on an illustrated epic poem. In the 1980s, professors at the local state university collaborated on an opera, a genre that by its nature infuses subjects with legendary qualities.[3]

Two other representative Coastal Bend writers, Vernon Smylie and Keith Guthrie, published books about the Chipita Rodríguez story. Smylie, a former reporter who owned a public relations firm, produced works with titles such as *The Secrets of Padre Island, Taming of the Texas Coast,* and *Conquistadors and Cannibals,* the last a "comprehensive" twenty-four-page history of Padre Island to 1845. Guthrie was a newspaper editor in San Patricio County, whose official history he wrote. His books included such Gulf Coast–oriented Texana as *Raw Frontier: Armed Conflict along the Texas Coastal Bend; Raw Frontier: Survival to Prosperity on the Texas Coastal Bend;* and three volumes of *Texas Forgotten Ports.* Lost ports such as Indianola on Matagorda Bay, abandoned after hurricanes in 1875 and 1886, amount to a Gulf Coast variant of the frontier town and ghost town themes in western writing.[4]

Most writers associated with Corpus Christi remained regional in reputation, and most writings set in or around the city drew an audience of locals and tourists. But Edna Ferber, a Michigan-born professional author of Hungarian Jewish descent, made the epic of South Texas relevant internationally with *Giant*. This 1952 novel, set in the plains west of the city, featured characters and situations that recalled the King Ranch, the Driscolls, and other family enterprises that mixed Texas identity with multinational business. Written in the clipped, earnest style of mid-twentieth-century popular novels, *Giant* offers an intense evocation of a harsh environment known for harsh events. Anglo characters struggle to maintain their heritage while facing the dark sides of their history, especially the expropriation and exploitation of the region's Mexicans, with whom they are more intertwined than they care to admit. Modernity, especially in the form of the oil business, erodes local traditions, the good and the bad. Through the eyes of an outsider, Leslie, the Virginia-born wife of the rancher Bick Benedict, readers encounter the miserable poverty and casual denigration of small-town and rural Tejanos. *Giant*'s descriptions of the housing and health conditions of South Texas Mexicans and the deplorable state of their schools revealed the influence of Hector García, with whom Ferber traveled for weeks.[5] Fictionalized as Dr. Guerra, the civil rights activist inspires the Benedicts' son, who, in defiance of his father, marries a Tejana and abandons ranching for medicine and public service.

Corpus Christi itself stays mostly in the background in *Giant*, sometimes referred to by name, while also fictionalized as Vientecito, "Wind City," a "thriving little city, perched as it was on a high bluff overlooking Vientecito Bay." Leslie, like newcomers since the 1700s, was "amazed at the natural beauty" of the site, even though she was vexed by the wind. She notices that few people walk along the bayfront, preferring to drive "briskly by, staring at the brilliant expanse of rolling waters as at some strange and unapproachable phenomenon of nature." She observes an elaborate fiesta, similar to Buccaneer Days, with Anglos dressed in "Spanish costumes, Mexican costumes; charro costumes, vaquero costumes, señoritas, ruffled long-skirted dancers, grandees, pirates, conquistadores, toreros, Spanish music, Mexican music . . . all about Spain and Mexico and old Texas." The city's actual Hispanics hold a "real Mexican Fiesta over in the Mexican part of town," where Dr. Guerra also has his practice.[6]

George Stevens's 1956 movie of *Giant* stripped Ferber's plot in ways that heightened the vividness of the setting and the mythic grandeur of the story. For better or worse, the easiest way to begin to explain the Corpus Christi region when one is outside the United States is to allude to *Giant*.

Decades later, another widely known author used one of western civilization's archetypal epics to infuse Corpus Christi with mythic stature. Terrence McNally, who grew up in the city, structured his 1997 *Corpus Christi* as a passion play, with the twist that Jesus and his apostles are gay men living in Texas. McNally intended the play as a provocative fable of gay rights, which is how his livid detractors also perceived it. The setting is not the city he had known but a mixture of the ancient and contemporary worlds, an experience more than a place.[7]

Ferber and McNally employed grand imagery to infuse the Corpus Christi region with universal lessons. In a 2004 collection of stories, also entitled *Corpus Christi*, Bret Anthony Johnston, another author who grew up in the city, took the opposite approach. The only exaggerated feature of the book is the frequency of hurricanes. "Named storms" do not hit anywhere close to "four and five times a season," as Johnston suggests. The threat of hurricanes, which is constant, serves in the book as a motif of human vulnerability and persistence, the "concerted and admirable effort to weather storm after storm" that the city exhibits, as Johnston told an interviewer.[8] Johnston's goal was to make the place special yet universal, its people's experiences normal yet meaningful. The stories shift between a middle-class world of refinery supervisors, engineers, chamber of commerce officials, and small-city lawyers, and a working-class environment split between the naval air station and the ship channel. Johnston depicts Corpus Christi's prosperous neighborhoods, rambling and pleasant, yet often pervaded by a sad atmosphere, as though one can feel the disappointments of the inhabitants of the low-slung ranch houses. In tracts of rickety frame dwellings, working-class Corpus Christians scramble to keep their lives and families together. One NAS worker destroys himself and his family when he burns down the Portland house he cannot afford in an attempt to make the arson appear to be an electrical fire. Convoluted ethnic interactions take place against a background of personal moral failure and amid an undercurrent of threatened violence.

The Corpus Christians in Johnston's stories associate their aspirations with leaving behind their present situation and often with leaving town altogether. One recurring character, a directionless history teacher who has returned from St. Louis to nurse his dying mother, "seemed never to have unpacked his bags." He pines for a flamboyant ex-girlfriend now working with a dance company in London. Her "wispy clothes smelled of marijuana and incense—pungent teases of her other, more alluring life." When she flies home, too late for his mother's funeral, he realizes that her phase of cosmopolitan adventure amounts to little more than the melodramatic nervousness of a woman whose reach exceeds her grasp. "If she [later] remembered" the night they were then spending together, "the memory would be fleetingly sad, a lost example of who she thought she'd become" before a mundane "trajectory" took her over.[9]

"Corpus Christi is a beautiful, beautiful city, and as complex as almost any place I've known," remarked the author.[10] Johnston's absorption of his town proved a resource in building a career as a writer and university teacher. The fact that he did so first in California and eventually at Harvard University might reinforce the fears of marginality, limited potential, and limited attractiveness that pervaded Corpus Christi's discussions of itself from the 1960s into the 2000s.

During 1999, a year that invited summing up, the *Caller-Times* worked with historians, preservationists, civic and business figures, and others on retrospective supplements that used the previous two centuries to mull over the city's prospects. The "Celebrate 2000" format encouraged its share of generic fluff. For example, the first page of the first issue proclaimed: "Corpus Christi has heralded the future ever since the winds whipping off the bay found little more than a rough-and-tumble trading village struggling to lure ships and settlers." What city could not claim to have "sometimes stumbled on its path but never stopped chasing its vision"? But two pages later, the editors raised the level by presenting an effective account of failed visions from the past and the circumstances that generated them. Over the year, the paper took readers step-by-step through environment, geography, transportation, industry, business, education, tourism and recreation, politics, ethnicity, and much else. A supplement on architecture offered a platform for ruminating on the city's cultural self-consciousness, its lack of a "defining" style and penchant for allowing the past to be "razed in the name of progress." When Murphy Givens compiled several sections of historical photographs, the columnist made sure to emphasize "the era between the opening of the port in 1926 and the opening of the Harbor Bridge in 1959," when "Corpus Christi went from being a small to a large city." He arranged photos to illustrate the city's geographic logic, beginning with the "high bluff overlooking the bay," the reason for "the city's location." He took readers through eras and phases of the city's growth, as this book has done, while presenting individual and group photos that illustrated the variety of people and activities.[11]

Givens titled his set of photo essays "The Light of Other Days." He explained that his research had caused him to ponder how old photos amounted to "a brief flash of light preserved for the future long after the people shown have died."[12] At the head of the column was his own present-day picture, a man tangibly older than the business journalist whose photo accompanied columns two decades before. In a photograph or in a book, people remain unchanging, ever present for those who come later, even though life and the city move relentlessly on. All the evidence that a city's people leave behind, all their attempts to express their experiences of a place, all their wrestling with its myths, history, arguments, and prospects, its grandeur and its disappointments, all these make that city endure and its people matter.

ACKNOWLEDGMENTS

T he errors in this book, as the disclaimer goes, are mine, and so, I would assert, are many of its virtues. But the idea came from Char Miller, formerly of Trinity University and now of Pomona College. During a Texas State Historical Association meeting in 2003 in El Paso (a city that would deny that it ought to belong to New Mexico, as historians and geographers sometimes assert), Char suggested that I collect into one volume, accessible to a South Texas audience, scattered academic articles that I had written about Corpus Christi. Char then arranged for a visiting scholar's position at Trinity in 2005 to push the project to completion, or so we thought. For reasons sketched in the introduction, I discarded the idea of an efficient revision of existing work and wrote a new book, supported mostly by new research and drawing on those earlier essays where they still seemed to help. That took eight more years, after which Char read a sprawling draft and saved me from various irrelevancies and one important gap. Benjamin Johnson of Loyola University Chicago also commented thoughtfully on the unexpurgated manuscript and came up with that rarest of useful advice to authors: a practical approach to cutting the book to a better size. I am especially grateful to the Corpus Christi historian Mary Jo O'Rear, who read everything as I wrote it with an eye toward clarity, accuracy, and relevance.

The person who most influenced this book other than myself is Tom Kreneck, head of special collections at Texas A&M University–Corpus Christi for over two decades, an extraordinary figure in shaping historical research on his native region. Materials that Tom oversaw and collected (and in a few cases that we collected together) form the foundation of this book; his knowledge and sensibilities pervade it. Over the years, Grace Charles, Ceil Venable, Jan Weaver, and the late Norm Zimmerman treated me as an honorary member of the A&M–Corpus Christi archives staff. I also received help and advice from Don Zuris, former curator at the Corpus Christi Museum of Science and History; Bob Payne and Mic Raasch of the Corpus Christi Planning Department; and the staff of the Local History Room at the Corpus Christi Public Library.

At A&M–Corpus Christi, I had the good fortune to work with one of this generation's most respected professionals among Texas historians, Robert Wooster, who from the start understood why I wanted to place Corpus Christi within Texas lore as well as within the state's modern, urban history. He and Catherine Cox have remained friends and supporters. My debts to former colleagues at A&M-CC who have written about related issues, Pat Carroll, Anthony Quiroz, and Ignacio García, is partly evident from the footnotes. Though he came to Corpus Christi after I left, David Blanke has shared with me ideas about doing urban history there. At Del Mar College, Liz Flores arranged a large, enthusiastic audience to hear me out in 2011 as I completed the first draft; Liz understands why I adored her father-in-law, Oscar Flores. Other friends from South Texas days shared their homes on research trips and gave of themselves in good times and bad: Dorothy McClellan and Nikola Knez, Barbra Riley and Roger Steinberg, Carol and Peter DeRuiter, and Veerle and Kent Ullberg. I would also thank the people mentioned in the book who provided interviews, documents, knowledge, and ideas. And I would honor Corpus Christi mentors, collaborators, and personalities who died before this appeared: Oscar Flores, Joe B. Frantz, Jim McClellan, Geraldine McGloin, and Mike Zepeda.

From 1995, when as an assistant professor I gave my first conference paper on Corpus Christi, the two established Texas urban historians on that panel, David McComb and Bob Fairbanks, encouraged me to cast my work in dialogue with their own. Chapter 6 began with a paper presented in 2007 at the Small Cities Conference at Ball State University's Middletown Center. The center's director, James J. Connolly, a prized collaborator in two separate fields of research, then edited and published an essay based on that paper, which gave me a chance publicly to test arguments that I intended to place at this book's heart. In a long-running conversation, Walter Nugent affirmed my sense of how the lower Nueces River and Corpus Christi Bay figure in the epic of Texas, the Southwest, and northern Mexico. Cam Cocks taught me how to read and use the source materials generated by tourist cities. At a key moment, Amy Wood pressed me to stick to my purposes. Scott Henderson, Ted Kohn, and Axel Schäfer have endured throughout as friends and intellectual compatriots.

Beyond providing research and writing time, including a sabbatical in 2005, along with funding for maps, index, and travel, colleagues at Illinois State University showed enthusiasm for the book's substance and agenda as these changed and grew. My PhD adviser, Ron Walters, has redirected my life several times with seemingly offhand comments; in 1992, he pointed me toward a job ad at then–Corpus Christi State University with an understated, "This might interest you." Thomas Welskopp, a colleague and friend since our Johns Hopkins years, arranged a visiting professorship at the Bielefeld Graduate School for History and Sociology during 2010–2011, where I completed the first draft, and then another visit during summer 2012, when I finished the second draft. Bielefeld's Anna-Lisa Müller, now at the University of Bremen, shared her research on the international context of Corpus Christi's recent debates over its character and direction.

Robert Devens of the University of Texas Press showed why an editor who grasps a book's spirit is more valuable to an author than the fabled treasure of Padre Island. He, his assistant Sarah Rosen, and their colleagues took exquisite care in crafting the book as historical writing and as a physical work of art. Designer Lindsay Starr made the book look like what it is trying to say. Kip Keller, a freelance copy editor, vastly reduced the number of gaps, typos, errors, and infelicities. Kaila Wyllys and the production staff scrutinized maps, charts, photos, and other illustrations with much-appreciated taste and skepticism. The press recruited Kenny Braun, a wonderful photographer of the Texas coast, to ensure that the photos came out as I had envisioned them. Crystal Williams of GEOMAP at Illinois State University did the same for the maps. Nancy Bryan of UT Press's marketing department, a warts-and-all lover of Corpus Christi, understood right away why and how this book would appeal to urban Texans. My former student Dave Varel, now at the University of Colorado, helped right at the end with indexing and proofreading.

I first sketched some ideas that appear in chapter 1 in "Corpus Christi: A Regional City for South Texas," *Touchstone* 15 (1996): 51–70. Some themes in chapters 2–3 began with "A Texas City and the Texas Myth: Urban Historical Identity in Corpus Christi," *Southwestern Historical Quarterly* 100 (Jan. 1997): 305–329. Thanks to the Texas State Historical Association for permission to draw upon this material. Chapter 4 is a revised and updated version of "Public Sculpture in Corpus Christi: A Tangled Struggle to Define the Character and Shape the Agenda of One Texas City," *Journal of Urban History* 26 (Jan. 2000): 190–223. Portions of chapter 6 first appeared in "Corpus Christi, 1965–2005: A Secondary City's Search for a New Direction," *Journal of Urban History* 35 (Nov. 2008): 108–33, a special issue on satellite and peripheral cities compiled by James J. Connolly. Thanks to the journal's editor, David Goldfield, and Sage Publications for permission to draw upon that material.

On a personal note, David Naour, Pramern Sriratana, and Sabrina Peterson and her colleagues kept me focused on the final draft while they ferried me across rough waters. Mineke Reinders shares with me the way of seeing and feeling cities that I have tried to convey in this book. Most of all, Corpus Christi gave us Audrey Lessoff, for whom the boats will always dance on the water.

NOTES

∾

INTRODUCTION

1. By the 2000s, initiatives had arisen to encourage research on small and medium cities and what they reveal about urban regions, for example, the Center for Middletown Studies at Ball State University in Muncie, Indiana. See James J. Connolly, "Decentering Urban History: Peripheral Cities in the Modern World," *Journal of Urban History* 35 (Nov. 2008): 3–14; Connolly, ed., *After the Factory: Reinventing America's Industrial Small Cities* (Lanham, Md.: Lexington, 2010).

2. David G. McComb, *Travels with Joe, 1917–1993: The Life Story of a Historian from Texas* (Austin: Texas State Historical Association, 2001), 77.

3. Frank Goodwyn, *Lone-Star Land: Twentieth-Century Texas in Perspective* (New York: Knopf, 1955), 165. Goodwyn was a poet and Spanish scholar whose father had been a manager on the King Ranch, an experience recounted in Frank Goodwyn, *Life on the King Ranch* (1951; repr., College Station: Texas A&M University Press, 1993).

4. "What Germany Offers the World," *Economist*, Apr. 12, 2012.

CHAPTER 1: A CITY OVER SPACE AND ACROSS TIME

1. Texas's incorporated municipalities larger than Corpus Christi in 2010 included Dallas, Fort Worth, and Arlington, all part of the Dallas–Fort Worth MSA, the state's largest urban conglomeration, with 6.4 million people. The municipal and MSA populations of Houston, San Antonio, Austin, and El Paso exceeded those of Corpus Christi, too. Also larger than metropolitan Corpus Christi

was the McAllen-Edinburgh-Mission MSA in the Rio Grande Valley, which had around 775,000 people in 2010. The string of midsized cities and their surrounding towns from Laredo in the west to the Brownsville-Harlingen MSA in the east added up to an urbanized population about three times that of Corpus Christi. When one adds in the twinned Mexican cities south of the river from Nuevo Laredo to Matamoros, the Lower Rio Grande Valley amounts to a huge, diffuse urban region. The 2010 census is available at www.census.gov/2010census. Metropolitan data comes from CPH-1, tables 9–16.

2. No summary book exists on Texas urban history. Introductory essays include Char Miller and David R. Johnson, "The Rise of Urban Texas," in *Urban Texas: Politics and Development*, ed. Char Miller and Heywood T. Sanders (College Station: Texas A&M University Press, 1990), 3–29; and Christopher S. Davies, "Life at the Edge: Urban and Industrial Evolution of Texas, Frontier Wilderness—Frontier Space," *Southwestern Historical Quarterly* 89 (Apr. 1986): 443–554.

3. This discrepancy between the top ten MSAs and municipalities results from San Antonio's aggressive use of Texas's favorable annexation laws; by 2010, the city's core municipality accounted for over 60 percent of the 2.14 million people of a metropolitan area stretching to New Braunfels. The figure for Houston, also historically aggressive about annexation, was closer to 35 percent of a metropolitan area of 5.95 million. Given variations in municipal governance and laws in different parts of the United States, MSAs are the more sensible comparative tool. By that measure, metropolitan San Antonio did not rank among the top twenty in 2010.

4. Carl Abbott, *How Cities Won the West: Four Centuries of Urban Change in Western North America* (Albuquerque: University of New Mexico Press, 2008), ch. 15; D. W. Meinig, *Imperial Texas: An Interpretive Essay in Cultural Geography* (Austin: University of Texas Press, 1969).

5. For explanations of the Texas Triangle, see Regional Planning Association, "America 2050" project, www.america2050.org/texas_triangle.html (accessed Dec. 18, 2013); and the Center for Sustainable Development, University of Texas School of Architecture, "Texas Triangle," www.soa.utexas.edu/csd/research /texas-triangle (accessed Dec. 18, 2013).

6. Readers may notice that I omit El Paso, the largest Texas city outside the triangle. Closer to San Diego than to Houston, El Paso is so linked to the Southwest that its leading historian concludes that it "is in Texas but should be in New Mexico"; see W. H. Timmons, *El Paso: A Borderlands History* (El Paso: Texas Western Press, 1990), 307. See also Bradford Luckingham, *The Urban Southwest: A Profile History of Albuquerque, El Paso, Phoenix, and Tucson* (El Paso: Texas Western Press, 1982).

7. Richard V. Francaviglia, *The Shape of Texas: Maps as Metaphors* (College Station: Texas A&M University Press, 1995).

8. Char Miller, "Water Conservation in Texas," address to the Texas State Historical Association, Mar. 1, 2013; Miller, "Running Dry: Water and Development in San Antonio," *Journal of the West* 44 (Summer 2005): 44–51; Miller, ed., *On the Border: An Environmental History of San Antonio* (Pittsburgh: University of Pittsburgh Press, 2001), esp. chs. 1, 7–9.

9. Martin Associates, *The Local and Regional Economic Impacts of the Port of Corpus Christi* (Lancaster, Pa.: Martin Associates, 2004), 18–19; see also the websites of the Port of Corpus Christi (www.portofcorpuschristi.com) and the Port of Houston (www.portofhouston.com).

10. Carl Abbott, *The Metropolitan Frontier: Cities in the Modern American West* (Tucson: University of Arizona Press, 1993), 56.

11. Corpus Christi Regional Economic Development Corporation, *Economic Development Plan, Corpus Christi Metropolitan Area* (Corpus Christi, 2006), draft in author's possession, 1; CCREDC, "It's about Prosperity for All! Strategic Plan for Action, 2007–2012" (Corpus Christi, 2007), 4 (emphasis in the original).

12. *Corpus Christi Caller-Times*, Jan. 16, 1996, May 27, 2001, Apr. 5, 2009 (hereafter cited as *Caller-Times*).

13. Murphy Givens and Jim Moloney, *Corpus Christi: A History* (Corpus Christi: Nueces Press, 2011), 1–2.

14. On the spread of Spanish urban forms into southern Texas, see the following works: Gilbert R. Cruz, *Let There Be Towns: Spanish Municipal Origins in the American Southwest* (College Station: Texas A&M University Press, 1988); Daniel D. Arreola, *Tejano South Texas: A Mexican American Cultural Province* (Austin: University of Texas Press, 2002), chs. 5–7; Arreola, "Plaza Towns of South Texas," *Geographic Review* 82 (Jan. 1992): 56–73; Gilberto M. Hinojosa, *A Borderlands Town in Transition: Laredo, 1755–1870* (College Station: Texas A&M University Press, 1983); Jesús de la Teja, *San Antonio de Bexar: A Community on New Spain's Northern Frontier* (Albuquerque: University of New Mexico Press, 1995). See also Armando Alonzo, *Tejano Legacy: Rancheros and Settlers in South Texas, 1734–1900* (Albuquerque: University of New Mexico Press, 1998); David J. Weber, *The Spanish Frontier in North America* (New Haven, Conn.: Yale University Press, 1993), 320–326.

15. People overemphasize grid plans as relics of the material interests of town promoters, since rectangular lots are easier to market. To Anglo-Americans, grids also represented the spread of an orderly civilization across the irregular wilderness. See John W. Reps, *Cities of the American West: A History of Frontier Urban Planning* (Princeton, N.J.: Princeton University Press, 1979); David Hamer, *New Towns in the New World: Images and Perceptions of the Nineteenth-Century Urban Frontier* (New York: Columbia University Press, 1990).

16. "'The Naples of the Gulf': What Corpus Christi Is Doing to Tempt the Summer Visitor," *Texas Weekly Review*, Aug. 1917; "vision of heaven": Mary A. Sutherland, *The Story of Corpus Christi* (Corpus Christi, Tex.: Daughters of the

Confederacy, 1916), 49; see also Mary Jo O'Rear, *Storm over the Bay: The People of Corpus Christi and Their Port* (College Station: Texas A&M University Press, 2009), chs. 1–3. For accessible accounts of the founding of Corpus Christi, see Bill Walraven, *Corpus Christi: The History of a Texas Seaport* (Sun Valley, Calif.: American Historical Press, 1997), chs. 1–3, and Givens and Moloney, *Corpus Christi*, ch. 1; a detailed and documented version is in Eugenia Reynolds Briscoe, *City by the Sea: A History of Corpus Christi, Texas, 1519–1875* (New York: Vantage, 1985), chs. 3–4.

17. Hortense Warner Ward, "The First State Fair of Texas," *Southwestern Historical Quarterly* 57 (Oct. 1953): 166.

18. Quotations: John Willet, "Take Notice, Capital," *Gulf Messenger*, June 1893, 164; *Deep Water and Corpus Christi*, pamphlet, c. 1892, Kilgore Collection 6235 (this collection hereafter cited as Kilgore), Special Collections and Archives, Texas A&M University–Corpus Christi (this archive hereafter cited as TAMU-CC). See also William E. Kent, "Ropes Pass, Texas," *Engineering Magazine*, June 1892, 340–349; Coleman McCampbell, *Texas Seaport: The Story of Corpus Christi and the Coastal Bend Area* (New York: Exposition, 1952), 65.

19. *Deep Water and Corpus Christi*.

20. *Corpus Christi, Texas: Sea—Sunshine—Soil*, c. 1916, Kilgore 6258.

21. "Brief of the City of Corpus Christi and the Corpus Christi Commercial Association, submitted to the Board of Engineers . . . ," 1920, Kilgore 6205.

22. Corpus Christi Chamber of Commerce, *Corpus Christi: Where Texas Meets the Sea*, c. 1935, Kilgore 2149.2; also *The Port of Corpus Christi: Where Texas Meets the Sea, Opens to the World*, commemorative booklet, 1926, Kilgore 2150.

23. *Corpus Christi: Port of Play and Profit*, chamber of commerce brochures, Kilgore 6252; Gerald D. Nash, *The American West Transformed: The Impact of World War II* (Bloomington: Indiana University Press, 1985); Roger Lotchin, *The Bad City in the Good War: San Francisco, Los Angeles, Oakland, and San Diego* (Bloomington: Indiana University Press, 2003).

24. Corpus Christi Industrial Commission, *It's a Good Move to the Sparkling City by the Sea*, booklet, c. 1976, Kilgore 4865. An expanded version of this booklet in the author's possession, Corpus Christi Industrial Commission, *It's a Good Move to the Sparkling City by the Sea, Corpus Christi, Texas*, study, c. 1976 (copy in author's possession), includes tables on wage rates, labor laws, and strikes in order to demonstrate that the "fair and equitable labor laws of Texas combine with the attitudes of South Texas workers to yield a stable labor environment," with few "crippling strikes and other unrest." In the 1960s–1970s, southern and southwestern cities often advertised in this fashion. They promoted Sunbelt-style amenities to technicians and managers while promising a low-cost, weakly unionized labor pool for positions where workers could be readily replaced; see Ann Markusen, Peter Hall, Scott Campbell, and Sabina Deitrick, *The Rise of the Gunbelt: The Military Remapping of Industrial America* (New York: Oxford University Press, 1991), 108–117.

25. Lynn M. Alperin, *History of the Gulf Intracoastal Waterway* (Washington, D.C.: U.S. Army Water Resources Support Center, 1983), 57; Mary Jo O'Rear, "A Ditch of a Dream: Bringing the Gulf Intracoastal Waterway to South Texas," unpublished presentation to Harte Research Institute, 2011.

26. Walter Prescott Webb, *The Great Plains* (Boston: Ginn, 1931); Abbott, *Metropolitan Frontier*, xiv; Glen Sample Ely, *Where the West Begins: Debating Texas Identity* (Lubbock: Texas Tech University Press, 2011), esp. ch. 1.

27. Within Corpus Christi's MSA, Portland, Aransas Pass, and Robstown all had over 10,000 people in 2010, and Ingleside and Rockport both exceeded 8,000. Of these, all but Robstown are along the coast. This reinforces Webb's notion of a sparse hinterland.

28. Walter Prescott Webb, "The American West: Perpetual Mirage," *Harper's Magazine*, May 1957, 25–31; Abbott, *Metropolitan Frontier*, 131.

29. Quotation: *Corpus Christi's History of Water*, pamphlet, c. 1958, Kilgore 4115; C. Alan Berkebile, Karen K. Dodson, Rick Hay, and James A. Dodson, "The Present and Future Status of Water in the Coastal Bend Area," in *Water for Texas*, ed. Jim Norwine, John R. Giardino, and Sushma Krishnamurthy (College Station: Texas A&M University Press, 2005), 92.

30. *Corpus Christi's History of Water*; *Corpus Christi: Area Resources for Industry* (Austin: Center for Business Research, University of Texas, 1961), 141–145; Mary Jo O'Rear, "The Sculpture, the Statue, the Dame, and the Dam—And the Elusive Corpus Christi Seawall," presentation to the Texas State Historical Association, Fort Worth, Mar. 2013.

31. Area Development Committee minutes, Sept. 26, 1951, file 13.23, and "Proposed New Storage Dam on the Nueces River," file 13.52, William M. Neyland Papers, TAMU-CC (hereafter cited as Neyland Papers); W. W. Horner to Harland Bartholomew, Aug. 10 and Nov. 16, 1950; William Anderson to Bartholomew, Jan. 22, 1951; Bartholomew to Harry Alexander, Feb. 4, 1951, correspondence reel 8, series 5, Harland Bartholomew and Associates Papers, University Archives, Washington University, St. Louis (hereafter cited as Bartholomew Papers); Harland Bartholomew and Associates, *Comprehensive Plan for the Corpus Christi Area* (St. Louis: Harland Bartholomew and Associates, 1953), ch. 13.

32. *Caller-Times*, Mar. 19, 1967; *Corpus Christi Caller*, Aug. 19, 1971; Atlee M. Cunningham, *Corpus Christi Water Supply: Documented History, 1852–1997* (Corpus Christi, 1998), ch. 12; "What Is the Future?," pro–Three Rivers dam pamphlet, 1950s (undated), TAMU-CC; water supply flyers, Kilgore 2711; Berkebile et al., "Water in the Coastal Bend Area," 92.

33. *Caller-Times*, May 16, 1965.

34. Harland Bartholomew and Associates, *Preliminary Report on Water and Sewer Facilities, Coastal Bend Region, Texas* (St. Louis: Harland Bartholomew and Associates, 1968), 31, 35; *Caller-Times*, May 14, 1967; Cunningham, *Corpus Christi Water Supply*, ch. 12; "Third and Final Report of A.D.C. Subcommittee

on Coastal Bend Water Development Plan," Jan. 23, 1971, copy in Local History Room, Corpus Christi Public Library.

35. *Choke Canyon Headway*, June 1982, copy in author's possession; *Caller-Times*, Sept. 21, 1995, Sept. 27, 1995, Apr. 28, 2013; City of Corpus Christi Water Department, www.cctexas.com/government/water/index (accessed June 2, 2013); Nueces River Authority, www.nueces-ra.org (accessed June 2, 2013).

36. *Caller-Times*, Jan. 27 (1st quotation), Feb. 14 (3rd quotation), May 30, Dec. 22, 2013; 2nd quotation: Courtney Smith, "Drought Perspectives: Nueces River Authority," Texas Water Resources Institute, http://twri.tamu.edu/publications/drought/2011/september/drought-perspectives-nueces-river-authority (accessed June 2, 2013).

37. Robert Bruegmann explains shortcomings of the concept of sprawl in *Sprawl: A Compact History* (Chicago: University of Chicago Press, 2005).

38. Carl Abbott, "Southwestern Cityscapes: Approaches to an American Urban Environment," in *Essays on Sunbelt Cities and Recent Urban America*, ed. Robert Fairbanks and Kathleen Underwood (College Station: Texas A&M University Press, 1990), 77–78; Abbott, *Metropolitan Frontier*, 131, 134.

39. On the Nueces River and the Polk administration's Mexico policy, see Walter Nugent, *Habits of Empire: A History of American Expansion* (New York: Knopf, 2008), 194–197.

40. *Caller-Times*, Outlook: Industry section, July 25, 1998; see also *Caller-Times*, Dec. 14, 2003, Jan. 12, 2005, and Nov. 6, 10, 2005; *San Antonio Express-News*, Aug. 25, 2005.

41. *Corpus Christi: Area Resources for Industry*, 280–289; see also *Corpus Christi Industry*, Apr. 1965; DeWitt Morgan, "Industry in Corpus Christi," *You . . . in Corpus Christi*, Oct. 1961, 7–9.

42. Port of Corpus Christi, *Annual Report*, 1985; *Caller-Times*, Horizons: Industry section, Jan. 21, 1996; Outlook: Industry section, July 25, 1998; Outlook: "Energy to Expand" section, July 29, 2001.

43. Christopher Sellers, "Petropolis and Environmental Protest in Cross-National Perspective: Beaumont–Port Arthur, Texas, versus Minatitlan-Coatzacoalcos, Mexico," *Journal of American History* 99 (June 2012): 11–23; John W. Tunnell Jr. and Frank W. Judd, eds., *The Laguna Madre of Texas and Tamaulipas* (College Station: Texas A&M University Press, 2002), esp. chs. 9, 19.

44. *Caller-Times*, Horizons: Industry section, Jan. 21, 1996; *Caller-Times*, Outlook: Industry section, July 26, 1998; *Caller-Times*, Mar. 6, 2010. For a comparison, see Hugh S. Gorman, "The Houston Ship Channel and the Changing Landscape of Industrial Pollution," in *Energy Metropolis: An Environmental History of Houston and the Gulf Coast*, ed. Martin V. Melosi and Joseph A. Pratt (Pittsburgh: University of Pittsburgh Press, 2007), 52–68.

45. Jenny Strasburg, "The Northside: A Place in History," *Caller-Times*, Feb. 8, 1998; Margaret Wead, "Rooting through the Cultures II: Blacks," *Corpus Christi Magazine*, Aug. 1982, 67–71.

46. Harland Bartholomew, *Comprehensive Plan*, 1953, 11–16.

47. See the Molina Packet, Alan Lessoff Collection, TAMU-CC (hereafter cited as Lessoff Collection). Noyola, a combative figure who made several runs for local office, went on to serve as principal of Corpus Christi's Miller High School, which at the time was about 95 percent Hispanic. See also *Caller-Times*, Oct. 17, 1991, Oct. 19, 1994, Sept. 27, 1996, June 28, 1997, Aug. 10, 1997, Sept. 28, 1999, June 24, 2006.

48. *Washington Post*, national weekly edition, Apr. 9–15, 2004.

49. Myers and Noyes, consulting engineers, "Corpus Christi Bayfront Project," Dec. 1942, copy in author's possession; *Corpus Christi: A History and Guide* (*Corpus Christi Caller-Times*, 1942), 214–218; *Caller-Times*, Jan. 25, 1998.

50. *Corpus Christi, Texas: Sea—Sunshine—Soil.*

51. *Caller-Times*, Apr. 19, 1994.

52. Ibid., Apr. 22, Oct. 19–22, Nov. 11, Dec. 14–15, 1999.

53. Quotations: Port of Corpus Christi, *Fiftieth Anniversary Port Book, 1976,* (Corpus Christi, Tex.: Port of Corpus Christi, 1976), 34; Murphy Givens, "City Won't Be the Same without Napoleon's Hat," *Caller-Times*, Nov. 22, 2006; Port of Corpus Christi Authority, *Project 2001* (Corpus Christi, 1987), 26; *Corpus Christi Times*, Oct. 23, 1959; *Caller-Times*, May 9, 1998, May 18, 2007, Aug. 10, Oct. 28, 2011, May 14, 2013; Caller.com, "Corpus Christi Harbor Bridge: Special Report," www.caller.com/harbor-bridge (accessed Dec. 21, 2013).

54. Gignac and Associates, "Shoreline Boulevard Master Plan," presented June 29, 2004; City of Corpus Christi, *South Central Area Development Plan*, revised July 2004, 50–53; *Caller-Times*, July 21, 1997, July 27, 1997, July 30, 1997, Oct. 1, 1997, Nov. 6–12, 1997, Oct. 23, 2003, Oct. 25, 2003, Apr. 14, 2004, July 27, 2004, Nov. 6, 2005.

55. *Caller-Times*, May 30, 1999; Murphy Givens, "Religious Roots," *Caller-Times*, Aug. 16, 2001; Margaret Lasater Clark, *On This Bluff: Centennial History, 1867–1967* (Corpus Christi, Tex.: First Presbyterian Church, 1967), 61–62; Spohn Hospital, *In the Footsteps of Christ, the Divine Healer*, booklet dated 1955, Kilgore 4268.

56. *Caller-Times*, Aug. 6, 1950, Oct. 28, 1999, Nov. 25, 2001; Joshua Thomas, "The Bluff Improvements: A Focal Point of Downtown Corpus Christi," *Texas Historian*, Sept. 1986, 11–13.

57. Alan Lessoff, "Harland Bartholomew and Corpus Christi: The Faltering Pursuit of Comprehensive Planning in South Texas," *Planning Perspectives* 18 (Apr. 2003): 218–222.

58. *Corpus Christi: A History and Guide*, 156–159; Murphy Givens, "Landmark of a Town Down on Its Luck," *Caller-Times*, June 7, 2000; Murphy D. Givens, ed., *Old Corpus Christi: The Past in Photographs* (Corpus Christi, Tex.: Caller-Times, 2002), 23.

59. John R. Dykema Jr., "Corpus Christi's Ocean Drive: The Continuing Evolution of an Urban Identity," *Texas Architect* 31 (Sept.–Oct. 1981): 30–37.

60. Jenny Strasburg, "Stripping a Mall," *Caller-Times*, Oct. 19, 1997; see also, *Caller-Times*, Aug. 28, 2008.

61. Briscoe, *City by the Sea*, 70.

62. *The Year Book: U.S. Naval Air Station Corpus Christi, 1940–1941*, copy in TAMU-CC; clippings and correspondence in Neyland Papers, file 13.49, and Naval Air Station packet, Lessoff Collection.

63. *The Navy in Corpus Christi, 1968: Unofficial Guide* (Lubbock: Boone, 1968), 7–8, Kilgore 5624; *Caller-Times*, Horizons: Military supplement, Jan. 29, 1995; *Caller-Times*, Aug. 25, 2005; *San Antonio Express-News*, May 14–15, Aug. 25, 2005.

64. *A Great University for a Great City*, 1947, pamphlet in TAMU-CC; Board of Trustees, University of Corpus Christi, minute books, vol. 1, Dec. 16, 1946–Dec. 9, 1948, and clippings books, University of Corpus Christi archives, TAMU-CC; "Eight Eventful Years: The Story of the Development of the University of Corpus Christi," 1954, Kilgore 3100; Carl R. Wrotenbery, *Baptist Island College: An Interpretive History of the University of Corpus Christi* (Austin: Eakin, 1998), 16–61.

65. *A Decade of Change and Growth, 1992–2002* (Corpus Christi: Texas A&M Univ.–Corpus Christi, 2002); *Brain Gain: How Corpus Christi Can Attract and Keep More Educated Young Professionals?* (Corpus Christi, Tex.: CorpusBeat, 2005), 36–39.

66. *Corpus Christi Times*, May 1, 1979.

67. Vernon Smylie, *The Secrets of Padre Island* (Corpus Christi, Tex.: Texas News Syndicate Press, 1964), 21–25; *Padre Island News*, Mar. 1951.

68. *Corpus Christi: Area Resources for Industry*, 350–354; *Corpus Christi Times*, Sept. 12, 1966, June 1, 1969; *Caller-Times*, July 11, 1969.

69. Ben D. Marks, "Padre Island: Fitting Development to the Environment," *Urban Land*, July–Aug. 1972, 8–14; W. Armstrong Price, "Environmental Impact of Padre Isles Development, South Texas," *Shore and Beach* 39 (Oct. 1971): 4–10; *Caller-Times*, Nov. 16, 1980, June 28, 1985; Robert A. Morton, Orrin H. Pilkey Jr., Orrin H. Pilkey Sr., and William J. Neal, *Living with the Texas Shore* (Durham, N.C.: Duke University Press, 1983); Tunnell and Judd, *Laguna Madre of Texas*.

70. *Caller-Times*, Mar. 27, 1983, Oct. 9, 1983, May 27, 1984, Sept. 26, 1999, Jan. 30, 2005; City of Corpus Christi Planning Department, *Mustang–Padre Island Area Development Plan*, rev. Nov. 1988; City of Corpus Christi, Department of Development Services, *Mustang–Padre Island Development Plan*, 2004, 4.

71. Jim Lee, "The Economic Significance of Tourism and Nature Tourism in Corpus Christi," Corpus Christi Convention and Visitors Bureau, Apr. 2009, iii; *Caller-Times*, Sept. 30, 1998; *Caller-Times*, "Celebrate 2000" supplement, Apr. 25, 1999.

72. Tom Utter, interview by the author, Corpus Christi City Hall, Nov. 30,

2005; City of Corpus Christi, Department of Development Services, "Island Action Group: Capital Improvements Priority Report," Sept. 2005, with accompanying PowerPoint display, in author's possession.

73. *Corpus Christi, Texas: Sea—Sunshine—Soil*; Corpus Christi Industrial Commission, *It's a Good Move*, 1st unnumbered page.

74. *Caller-Times*, "Celebrate 2000" supplement, Apr. 25, 1999.

75. Coleman McCampbell, *Saga of a Frontier Seaport* (Dallas: South-West Press, 1934), 1–2; *Corpus Christi: A History and Guide*, iii, 11.

76. On western towns as spearheads of the frontier, see Richard C. Wade, *The Urban Frontier: Pioneer Life in Early Pittsburgh, Cincinnati, Lexington, Louisville and St. Louis* (1959; repr., Urbana: University of Illinois Press, 1996), 1.

77. John M. Richards, *Corpus Christi: The Critical Years* (Corpus Christi: Corpus Christi State University, 1978), 3.

78. J. W. Wilbarger quoted in Briscoe, *City by the Sea*, 73–74; Tom Lea quoted in Walraven, *Corpus Christi: Texas Seaport*, 44; Clotilde P. García, *Captain Enrique Villarreal and Rincon del Oso Land Grant* (Corpus Christi, Tex.: Grunwald, 1986).

79. Briscoe, *City by the Sea*, 115ff; Walraven, *Corpus Christi: Texas Seaport*, 37–45; McCampbell, *Texas Seaport*, 30–44; Ward, "First State Fair of Texas"; Murphy Givens, "Kinney's Great Fair Was a Great Failure," *Caller-Times*, Dec. 11, 2003.

80. Briscoe, *City by the Sea*, 123–124, 180, 289; Walraven, *Corpus Christi: Texas Seaport*, 45, 64, 73; O'Rear, *Storm over the Bay*, 18; Bill Walraven, "The Port of Corpus Christi, 1500–1926," *Nueces County Historical Commission Bulletin* 4–5 (Nov. 1997): 6.

81. Briscoe, *City by the Sea*, chs. 6–8; Walraven, *Corpus Christi: Texas Seaport*, ch. 4; McCampbell, *Texas Seaport*, 51, chs. 11–15; Norman C. Delaney, "Corpus Christi: The Vicksburg of Texas," *Civil War Times Illustrated* 16 (July 1977): 4–9, 44–48.

82. Randolph Campbell, "Reconstruction in Nueces County, Texas, 1865–76," *Houston Review* 16, no. 1 (1994): 3–26; Briscoe, *City by the Sea*, 182–191, 250–281; Murphy Givens, "The 'Devil' in the Governor's Office," *Caller-Times*, Jan. 9, 2008.

83. Paul Schuster Taylor, *An Anglo-Mexican Frontier: Nueces County, Texas* (Chapel Hill: University of North Carolina Press, 1934), ch. 9 (1st quotation, 54); *Corpus Christi Caller*, Aug. 24–25, 1939; Walraven, *Corpus Christi: Texas Seaport*, 55–57; 2nd quotation: "Nuecestown Raid of 1875," *Handbook of Texas Online*, www.tshaonline.org/handbook/online/articles/jcnnt (accessed Mar. 6, 2013); William Hager, "The Nuecestown Raid of 1875: A Border Incident," *Arizona and the West* 1 (Autumn 1959): 258–270; David Montejano, *Anglos and Mexicans in the Making of Texas, 1836–1986* (Austin: University of Texas Press, 1987), chs. 2–3.

84. Dan E. Kilgore, "Corpus Christi: A Quarter Century of Development, 1900–1925," *Southwestern Historical Quarterly* 66 (Apr. 1972): 434; McCampbell, *Saga of a Frontier Seaport*, ch. 45; *The Driscolls: Benefactors of South Texas* (Corpus Christi, Tex.: Driscoll Foundation, 1979), Kilgore 533; *Centennial Journey: Corpus Christi Caller* (Corpus Christi, Tex.: Caller-Times, 1983).

85. McCampbell, *Texas Seaport*, 57–58; Briscoe, *City by the Sea*, 278; O'Rear, *Storm over the Bay*, chs. 2–3; Walraven, *Corpus Christi: Texas Seaport*, 57–76; Alonzo, *Tejano Legacy*, 104. Montejano, *Anglos and Mexicans in Texas*, ch. 5.

86. Richard A. Laune, "The Political Struggle for the Port of Corpus Christi," *Journal of South Texas* 18 (Spring 2005): 91–112; O'Rear, *Storm over the Bay*, ch. 8; Walraven, *Corpus Christi: Texas Seaport*, 73–75.

87. On towns in the Midland-Odessa region, see Robert L. Martin, *The City Moves West: Economic and Industrial Growth in Central West Texas* (Austin: University of Texas Press, 1969). Eugene Moehring documents strings of medium towns throughout the West as well as regions dominated by a regional metropolis in *Urbanism and Empire in the Far West, 1840–1890* (Reno: University of Nevada Press, 2004).

88. "Brief of the City of Corpus Christi and the Corpus Christi Commercial Association . . . ," Sept. 20, 1920, 6, Kilgore 6205.

89. William C. Barnett, "A Tale of Two Texas Cities: Houston, the Industrial Metropolis, and Galveston, the Island Gateway," in Melosi and Pratt, *Energy Metropolis*, 192; see also David G. McComb, *Galveston: A History* (Austin: University of Texas Press, 1986), chs. 4–5; Patricia Bellis Bixel and Elizabeth Hayes Turner, *Galveston and the 1900 Storm* (Austin: University of Texas Press, 2000), chs. 3–4.

90. "Brief of the City of Corpus Christi and the Corpus Christi Commercial Association . . . ," Sept. 20, 1920, 7–8.

91. Kilgore, "Corpus Christi: A Quarter Century of Development"; Murphy Givens, "Women Couldn't Vote, But They Won an Election," *Caller-Times*, Aug. 26, 1998; Montejano, *Anglos and Mexicans in Texas*, pt. 2; Evan Anders, *Boss Rule in South Texas: The Progressive Era* (Austin: University of Texas, Press 1982).

92. Benjamin Johnson, "The Plan de San Diego Uprising and the Making of the Modern Texas-Mexican Borderlands," in *Continental Crossroads: Remapping U.S.-Mexico Borderlands History*, ed. Samuel Truett and Elliott Young (Durham, N.C.: Duke University Press, 2004), 273–298.

93. Quotation: "The Naples of the Gulf," *Texas Weekly Review*, Apr. 7, 1917, 3; Kilgore, "Corpus Christi: A Quarter Century of Development," 438; "Newsmakers of the Century," *Caller-Times*, Jan. 2, 2000; O'Rear, *Storm over the Bay*, chs. 7–8.

94. Miller quotation: *Centennial Journey*, 16; documents on the Storm Stricken Area Committee and the Deep Water Harbor Association are in the W. E. Pope Papers, 81.7, TAMU-CC, copies in port packet, Lessoff Collection; O'Rear,

Storm over the Bay, chs. 9–12; Laune, "Struggle for the Port of Corpus Christi."

95. Quoted in Bill Walraven and Marjorie Walraven, *Wooden Rigs, Iron Men: The Story of Oil and Gas in South Texas* (Corpus Christi, Tex.: Corpus Christi Geological Society, 2005), 51; see also *South Texas Blowout*, 1951, 17–18, Kilgore 4224.

96. *Corpus Christi Commerce*, Nov. 1937; see also *Centennial Journey*, 89; Richard Alan Laune, "Battle for Prominence: The Port of Corpus Christi, 1840–2001" (MA thesis, Texas A&M University–Kingsville, 2002), ch. 4.

97. *Caller-Times*, Oct. 26, 1934; "Industrial Banquet, Plaza Hotel, Corpus Christi," Oct. 26, 1934, program in Southern Alkali packet, Lessoff Collection.

98. "Corpus Christi," *Monthly Business Review: Federal Reserve Bank of Dallas* 36 (Nov. 1951), repr. in Kilgore 5545.

99. 1st and 2nd quotations: *Caller-Times*, Oct. 1, 2011; 3rd quotation: *Caller-Times*, "Outlook: Energy to Expand" supplement, July 29, 2001; see also, *Caller-Times*, "Horizons—Industry" supplement, Jan. 21, 1996.

100. Ron George, "A City in Transition," in Walraven, *Corpus Christi: Texas Seaport*, 123–124.

CHAPTER 2: A TEXAS SEAPORT IN TEXAS LORE

1. Char Miller and David R. Johnson, "The Rise of Urban Texas," in *Urban Texas: Politics and Development*, ed. Char Miller and Heywood T. Sanders (College Station: Texas A&M University Press, 1990), 3; Char Miller, "Sunbelt Texas," in *Texas through Time: Evolving Interpretations*, ed. Walter L. Buenger and Robert A. Calvert (College Station: Texas A&M University Press, 1991), 303–309.

2. Murphy Givens, "Seawall: Our Eighth Wonder of the World," *Caller-Times*, July 11, 2007; Givens, "Seawall Was Built to Hold Back Ocean," *Caller-Times*, Oct. 21, 1999; Bill Walraven, "Seawall May Be Standing on Last Leg," *Corpus Christi Caller*, Jan. 14, 1985; see also the *Caller-Times*, July 5, 1998, Feb. 17, 1999, and Feb. 21, 1999. For a description written shortly after the seawall's dedication, see *Corpus Christi: A History and Guide* (Corpus Christi, Tex.: *Caller-Times*, 1942), 214–218.

3. For a profile of Durrill, see the *Caller-Times*, Jan. 1, 2011; Ron George, "A City in Transition," in Bill Walraven, *Corpus Christi: The History of a Texas Seaport* (Sun Valley, Calif.: American Historical Press, 1997), 121–122; Vivienne Heines and Scott Williams, *Corpus Christi and the Texas Coastal Bend* (Guilford, Conn.: Insiders' Guide, 2001), 9.

4. Howard Shaff and Audrey Karl Shaff, *Six Wars at a Time: The Life and Times of Gutzon Borglum, Sculptor of Mount Rushmore* (Sioux Falls, S.D.: Center for Western Studies, 1985), 248, 291; Robin Borglum Carter, *Gutzon Borglum: His Life and Work* (Austin: Eakin, 1998), 79–81; John Taliaferro, *Great White*

Fathers: The Story of the Obsessive Quest to Create Mount Rushmore (New York: PublicAffairs Press, 2002), 232–233; Robert J. Casey and Mary Borglum, draft of "Give the Man Room: The Story of Gutzon Borglum," in possession of Robin Borglum Carter; *Corpus Christi Caller,* Oct. 12, Nov. 28, 1927, Mar. 14, 1928.

5. *Corpus Christi: Where Texas Meets the Sea,* 1928, pamphlet, Local History Room, Corpus Christi Public Library; "Final Report of the Bayfront Improvement Committee," Mar. 13, 1928, in possession of Robin Borglum Carter.

6. Quotations: *Corpus Christi: Where Texas Meets the Sea*; Bill Walraven, "Ambitious Artist Had Colossal Plans for South Texas," *Corpus Christi Caller,* Nov. 6, 1987; on Borglum's vision of American history as the conquest of wilderness, see Simon Schama, *Landscape and Memory* (New York: Knopf, 1995), 385–402.

7. *Corpus Christi Caller,* Mar. 16, 1928.

8. *Corpus Christi Times,* Oct. 13, 15, 1928; Gutzon Borglum to Charles W. Gibson, Nov. 13, 1930, Dec. 19, 1930, Sept. 5, 1934 (1st quotation), W. M. Neyland Papers, file 17.10, Special Collections and Archives, Texas A&M University–Corpus Christi (this archive hereafter cited as TAMU-CC); also file 13.32. "Facts about the Bayfront Protection Plan," typescript in W. E. Pope Papers, file 166.17, TAMU-CC (2nd quotation). C. W. Gibson to Mayor Schaffer and the City Council, with attached exhibits; John L. Tompkins to Gutzon Borglum, Aug. 28, 1940; and Borglum to Tompkins, Aug. 31, 1940, all in possession of Robin Carter Borglum. Mary Jo O'Rear, "The Sculpture, the Statue, the Dame, and the Dam—And the Elusive Corpus Christi Seawall," presentation to the Texas State Historical Association, Fort Worth, Mar. 2013.

9. David G. McComb, "Galveston as a Tourist City," *Southwestern Historical Quarterly* 100 (Jan. 1997): 355–360; McComb, *Galveston: A History* (Austin: University of Texas Press, 1986), ch. 6; David Hamer, *History in Urban Places: The Historic Districts of the United States* (Columbus: Ohio State University Press, 1998), chs. 1–3.

10. Robert Fairbanks, *For the City as a Whole: Planning, Politics, and the Public Interest in Dallas, Texas, 1900–1965* (Columbus: Ohio State University Press, 1998), 6; see also, Amy Bridges, *Morning Glories: Municipal Reform in the Southwest* (Princeton, N.J.: Princeton University Press, 1998); Anthony M. Orum, *Power, Money, and the People: The Making of Modern Austin* (Austin: Texas Monthly Press, 1987).

11. Miller and Sanders, *Urban Texas,* illustrates how the Sunbelt idea was applied to Texas urban history during the 1980s. In *The New Urban America: Growth and Politics in Sunbelt Cities,* rev. ed. (Chapel Hill: University of North Carolina Press, 1987), Carl Abbott tried to give coherence to the notion of the Sunbelt by seeking themes and qualities common across the urban South, Southwest, and West. But by the 1990s, many experts had become skeptical whether the Sunbelt counted as a meaningful entity; see Raymond A. Mohl, ed., *Searching for*

the Sunbelt: Historical Perspectives on a Region (Knoxville: University of Tennessee Press, 1990). A case for the term's continued usefulness can be found in Michelle Nickerson and Darren Dochuk, eds., *Sunbelt Rising: The Politics of Place, Space, and Region* (Philadelphia: University of Pennsylvania Press, 2011).

12. McComb, *Galveston*; Martin V. Melosi and Joseph A. Pratt, eds., *Energy Metropolis: An Environmental History of Houston and the Gulf Coast* (Pittsburgh: University of Pittsburgh Press, 2007); Char Miller, ed., *On the Border: An Environmental History of San Antonio* (Pittsburgh: University of Pittsburgh Press, 2001); William Scott Swearingen Jr., *Environmental City: People, Place, Politics, and the Meaning of Modern Austin* (Austin: University of Texas Press, 2010).

13. Walter Buenger, "The Story of Texas? The Texas State History Museum and Memories of the Past," *Southwestern Historical Quarterly* 105 (Jan. 2002): 481–493.

14. Harvey J. Graff, *The Dallas Myth: The Making and Unmaking of an American City* (Minneapolis: University of Minnesota Press, 2008), 50–51.

15. Ibid., 51.

16. McComb, "Galveston as a Tourist City," 345; McComb, *Galveston*, 180.

17. 1st quotation: *This Month in Corpus Christi and the Texas Tropical Coast*, May 1957, photocopy in Buccaneer Days packet, Alan Lessoff Collection, TAMU-CC; 2nd quotation: *Caller-Times*, Buccaneer Days supplement, May 28, 1939.

18. 1st quotation: *Padre Island News*, Mar. 1951, copy in author's possession; remaining quotations: Writer's Round Table, *Padre Island* (San Antonio: Naylor, 1950), 101; see also, William Mahan, *Padre Island: Treasure Kingdom of the World* (Waco, Tex.: Texian, 1967), ch. 27; Vernon Smylie, *The Secrets of Padre Island* (Corpus Christi, Tex.: Texas News Syndicate Press, 1964); Stephen Harrigan, *The Eye of the Mammoth: Selected Essays* (Austin: University of Texas Press, 2013), 70–72.

19. Bret Anthony Johnston, *Corpus Christi: Stories* (repr., New York: Random House, 2005), 8–11.

20. *Corpus Christi: 100 Years* (Corpus Christi, Tex.: *Corpus Christi Caller-Times*, 1952), 19.

21. Robert S. Weddle, *Spanish Sea: The Gulf of Mexico in North American Discovery, 1500–1685* (College Station: Texas A&M University Press, 1985), ch. 6; Donald E. Chipman, "Alonso Alvarez de Pineda and the Rio de las Palmas: Scholars and the Mislocation of a River," *Southwestern Historical Quarterly* 98 (Jan. 1995): 370–383; Carlos E. Castañeda, *Our Spanish Heritage in Texas*, vol. 1, *Mission Era: The Finding of Texas, 1519–1693* (1936; repr., New York: Arno, 1976), ch. 1.

22. "Official Program of the Celebration of the Completion and Opening of the Port of Corpus Christi," Sept. 14–15, 1926, photocopy in Port packet, Lessoff Collection. For another early instance of the Pineda legend, see P. J. R. MacIntosh,

"The Port of Corpus Christi," *Bunker's Monthly*, 1928, 750, undated copy, Kilgore Collection 6256 (this collection hereafter cited as Kilgore), TAMU-CC. On the Anglo penchant for Spanish colonial heritage and the Mission Revival style, see Lawrence A. Herzog, *From Aztec to High Tech: Architecture and Landscape across the Mexico–United States Border* (Baltimore: Johns Hopkins University Press, 1999), 105–112; William Deverell, *Whitewashed Adobe: The Rise of Los Angeles and the Remaking of Its Mexican Past* (Berkeley: University of California Press, 2004), chs. 2, 6; Phoebe Kropp, *California Vieja: Culture and Memory in a Modern American Place* (Berkeley: University of California Press, 2006).

23. Coleman McCampbell, *Texas Seaport: The Story of the Growth of Corpus Christi and the Coastal Bend Area* (New York: Exposition, 1952), 15; *Caller-Times*, Apr. 15, 1954, quoted in Herb Canales, "¡Viva el Rey Alonso! The Legend of Who Discovered and Named Corpus Christi Bay," *Journal of South Texas* 24 (Fall 2011): 56–57.

24. Quoted in "Corpus Beach Hotel," c. 1915, Kilgore 6234; Mary A. Sutherland, *The Story of Corpus Christi* (Corpus Christi, Tex.: Daughters of the Confederacy, 1916), 1.

25. Dan E. Kilgore, *Nueces County, Texas, 1750–1800: A Bicentennial Memoir* (Corpus Christi, Tex.: Friends of the Corpus Christi Museum, 1975), 1–5; Eugenia Reynolds Briscoe, *City by the Sea: A History of Corpus Christi, Texas, 1519–1875* (New York: Vantage, 1985), 17–24. On the Spanish response to the La Salle expedition, see Robert S. Weddle, *Wilderness Manhunt: The Spanish Search for La Salle* (Austin: University of Texas Press, 1973).

26. "The History of Corpus Christi," typescript dated Feb. 1969, in Chamber of Commerce vertical file, Local History Room, Corpus Christi Public Library.

27. Kilgore quoted in *Caller-Times*, June 8, 1969; see also, Nueces County Historical Society, *History of Nueces County* (Austin: Jenkins, 1972), ch. 3.

28. Canales, "¡Viva el Rey Alonso!," 67.

29. See Walraven, *Corpus Christi: Texas Seaport*, ch. 2; Briscoe, *City by the Sea*, ch. 2.

30. Dan E. Kilgore, *How Did Davy Die?* (1978), enlarged by James E. Crisp (College Station: Texas A&M University Press, 2010); quotations: Harrigan, *Eye of the Mammoth*, 235–236. On Kilgore, see the memorial by Thomas H. Kreneck, *Southwestern Historical Quarterly* 99 (Apr. 1996): 552–555.

31. Clare V. McKanna, *Homicide, Race, and Justice in the American West, 1880–1920* (Tucson: University of Arizona Press, 1997); David T. Courtwright, *Violent Land: Single Men and Social Disorder from the Frontier to the Inner City* (Cambridge, Mass.: Harvard University Press, 1996), esp. chs. 3–6; Richard Maxwell Brown, *Strain of Violence: Historical Studies of American Violence and Vigilantism* (New York: Oxford University Press, 1975); Brown, "Violence," in *Oxford History of the American West*, ed. Clyde A. Milner II et al. (New York: Oxford University Press, 1994), 393–425. For reconsiderations of violence in frontier

and ranching Texas: Jacqueline M. Moore, "'Them's Fighting Words': Violence, Masculinity, and the Texas Cowboy in the Late Nineteenth Century," *Journal of the Gilded Age and Progressive Era* 13 (Jan. 2014): 28–55; Ty Cashion, "(Gun) Smoke Gets in Your Eyes: A Revisionist Look at 'Violent' Fort Griffin," *Southwestern Historical Quarterly* 99 (July 1995): 81–94. On urban violence as a product of urban conditions, rather than frontier ones, in the 1800s, see Eric Monkkonen, "A Disorderly People: Urban Order in the Nineteenth and Twentieth Centuries," *Journal of American History* 68 (Dec. 1981): 539–559; Jeffrey Adler, *First in Violence, Deepest in Dirt: Homicide in Chicago, 1875–1920* (Cambridge, Mass.: Harvard University Press, 2006); Roger Lane, *Murder in America: A History* (Columbus: Ohio State University Press, 1997).

32. Brown, "Violence," 422. On the Civil War as a catalyst for Texas strife, see Richard B. McCaslin, *Tainted Breeze: The Great Hanging at Gainesville, Texas, 1862* (Baton Rouge: Louisiana State University Press, 1994). On ethnic dimensions of Central Texas violence, see William D. Carrigan, *The Making of a Lynching Culture: Violence and Vigilantism in Central Texas, 1836–1916* (Urbana: University of Illinois Press, 2006).

33. Dan E. Kilgore, "The Story of Three Pioneers," in *Centennial Journey: Corpus Christi Caller* (Corpus Christi, Tex.: *Caller-Times*, 1983), 41, 58–60 (quotation).

34. *Corpus Christi Caller*, July 24, 1918, quoted in Paul Schuster Taylor, *An American-Mexican Frontier: Nueces County, Texas* (Chapel Hill: University of North Carolina Press, 1934), 234; Murphy Givens, "Women Couldn't Vote, but They Won an Election," *Caller-Times*, Aug. 26, 1998; Dan E. Kilgore, "Corpus Christi: A Quarter Century of Development, 1900–1925," *Southwestern Historical Quarterly* 66 (Apr. 1972): 439–442; Mary Jo O'Rear, *Storm over the Bay: The People of Corpus Christi and Their Port* (College Station: Texas A&M University Press, 2009), esp. ch. 6; David Montejano, *Anglos and Mexicans in the Making of Texas, 1836–1986* (Austin: University of Texas Press, 1987), chs. 5–6.

35. C. W. Carpenter, "Klan Activities Fostered Gun-Toting, Cross Burnings," in *Centennial Journey*, 54–55; quotation: Dan E. Kilgore, "50 Years Ago: Shootout at Bessie Miller's," *Corpus Christi Caller*, June 29, 1975.

36. *Corpus Christi: A History and Guide*, 16.

37. Quotations: McCampbell, *Texas Seaport*, 28, 47; *Corpus Christi: 100 Years*, 29; Dee Woods, "King of the Wild Horse Desert," *West*, Mar. 1967, clipping in Kilgore 4124; Walraven, *Corpus Christi: Texas Seaport*, 39; Coleman McCampbell, "H. L. Kinney and Daniel Webster in Illinois in the 1830's," *Journal of the Illinois State Historical Society* 47 (Spring 1954): 35–44; Hortense Warner Ward, "The First State Fair of Texas," *Southwestern Historical Quarterly* 57 (Oct. 1953): 163–174; Briscoe, *City by the Sea*, chs. 3–4.

38. Quotation: Corpus Christi Board of Realtors, *A Guide to Corpus Christi, 1988–89*, Kilgore 2806; Bill Walraven, *El Rincon: A History of Corpus Christi*

Beach (Corpus Christi, Tex.: Texas State Aquarium, 1990), 15; Taylor, *American-Mexican Frontier*, chs. 3–4, 27; Montejano, *Anglos and Mexicans in Texas*, 39–43, 52.

39. Walraven, *Corpus Christi: Texas Seaport*, ch. 4; Briscoe, *City by the Sea*, chs. 6–8.

40. Quotation: Briscoe, *City by the Sea*, 160; Montejano, *Anglos and Mexicans in Texas*, ch. 2; Taylor, *American-Mexican Frontier*, ch. 7; Arnoldo De León, *Mexican Americans in Texas: A Brief History*, 3rd. ed. (Wheeling, Ill.: Harlan Davidson, 2009), 42–43.

41. Frank Wagner, *Fires and Hard Times* (Corpus Christi, Tex.: Friends of the Corpus Christi Museum Occasional Papers, 1982), 3 (1st quotation); Nueces County Historical Society, *History of Nueces County*, 77, 82 (2nd quotation); Sutherland, *Story of Corpus Christi*, 38, 123–127; McCampbell, *Texas Seaport*, 52–56; Walraven, *Corpus Christi: Texas Seaport*, 55–57; Taylor, *American-Mexican Frontier*, ch. 9; Randolph B. Campbell, "Reconstruction in Nueces County, 1865–1876," *Houston Review* 16, no. 1 (1994): 3–26; Campbell, "Carpetbagger Rule in Reconstruction Texas: An Enduring Myth," *Southwestern Historical Quarterly* 97 (Apr. 1994): 587–596.

42. *Corpus Christi: 100 Years*, 93; McCampbell, *Texas Seaport*, 50.

43. *Centennial Journey*, 2.

44. Ibid., 4, 79, 82, 87–89, quotation on 88. On Richard M. Kleberg and the naval air station, see the correspondence between Kleberg and William M. Neyland in Neyland Papers. McCampbell, *Texas Seaport*, 133–143; *Corpus Christi: 100 Years*, 97–105, 137–144; Nueces County Historical Society, *History of Nueces County*, 167–168; Margaret Lasater Clark, *On This Bluff: Centennial History, 1867–1967* (Corpus Christi, Tex.: First Presbyterian Church, 1967), 18–19, 109–110; Mary Xavier Holworthy, "History of the Diocese of Corpus Christi, Texas" (MA thesis, St. Mary's University of San Antonio, 1939), 121; Spohn Hospital, *In the Footsteps of Christ, the Divine Healer*, booklet dated 1955, Kilgore 4268; John Cypher, *Bob Kleberg and the King Ranch: A Worldwide Sea of Grass* (Austin: University of Texas Press, 1995); Martha Anne Turner, *Clara Driscoll: An American Tradition* (Austin: Madrona, 1979), chs. 7, 11.

45. 1st and 2nd quotations: *The Driscolls: Benefactors of South Texas* (Corpus Christi, Tex.: Driscoll Foundation, 1979), 27, Kilgore 533; 3rd and 4th quotations: Turner, *Clara Driscoll*, 110–112.

46. *Caller-Times*, Aug. 16, 1998.

47. Quotation: Walraven, *Corpus Christi: Texas Seaport*, 75.

48. Quotations: McCampbell, *Texas Seaport*, 65, 67; Walraven, *Corpus Christi: Texas Seaport*, 75.

49. Walraven, *Corpus Christi: Texas Seaport*, 39.

50. Quoted in J. L. Allhands, *Uriah Lott* (San Antonio: Naylor, 1949), 172; see also, *Centennial Journey*, 14.

51. 1st quotation: Walraven, *Corpus Christi: Texas Seaport*, 75; 2nd quotation: Sutherland, *Story of Corpus Christi*, 54.

52. Walraven, *Corpus Christi: Texas Seaport*, 44, 64.

53. Graff, *Dallas Myth*, 57; Patricia Evridge Hill, *Dallas: The Making of a Modern City* (Austin: University of Texas Press, 1996), xxii.

54. John M. Richards, *Corpus Christi: The Critical Years* (Corpus Christi, Tex.: Corpus Christi State University, 1978), 6. In *For the City as a Whole*, Fairbanks details the role of progrowth policy and planning and commercial-civic rule in Dallas's expansion; critiques of Fairbanks in antibooster works such as Graff, *Dallas Myth* (see esp. 118–120, 172–173), have a shoot-the-messenger quality. For a review of how aggressive promotion enabled Houston to improve upon advantages offered by geography and politics, see William D. Angel Jr., "To Make a City: Entrepreneurship on the Urban Frontier," in *The Rise of Sunbelt Cities*, ed. David C. Perry and Alfred J. Watkins (Beverly Hills, Calif.: Sage, 1977), 109–128. San Antonio writers, by contrast, insist that desultory boosterism was a factor in their city's relatively slow growth; see, for example, David R. Johnson, "San Antonio: The Vicissitudes of Boosterism," in *Sunbelt Cities: Politics and Growth since World War II*, ed. Richard M. Bernard and Bradley Rice (Austin: University of Texas Press, 1982), 235–254; and Johnson, "Frugal and Sparing: Interest Groups, Politics, and City Building in San Antonio, 1870–85," in Miller and Sanders, *Urban Texas*, 33–57. On boosterism and city growth in the United States overall and the U.S. West in particular, see David Hamer, *New Towns in the New World* (New York: Columbia University Press, 1990), chs. 2, 5; Bridges, *Morning Glories*, chs. 1–2. Eric H. Monkkonen, *America Becomes Urban: The Development of U.S. Cities and Towns* (Berkeley: University of California Press, 1988), chs. 5–6; Carl Abbott, *Boosters and Businessmen: Popular Economic Thought and Urban Growth in the Antebellum Middle West* (Westport, Conn.: Greenwood, 1981).

55. *Corpus Christi: 100 Years*, 43; Woods, "Wild Horse Desert"; Ward, "First State Fair of Texas"; Murphy Givens, "Kinney's Great Fair Was a Great Failure," *Caller-Times*, Dec. 11, 2003; McCampbell, "H. L. Kinney and Daniel Webster"; McCampbell, *Texas Seaport*, 24–44; Walraven, *Corpus Christi: Texas Seaport*, 37–47.

56. Allhands, *Uriah Lott*, 170–171; Norman Rozeff, "The Man Who Brought the Valley into the Twentieth Century—Uriah Lott," *Valley Morning Star*, Nov. 22, 2008; *Centennial Journey*, 82; McCampbell, *Texas Seaport*, 49–50; Walraven, *Corpus Christi: Texas Seaport*, 61–63; Montejano, *Anglos and Mexicans in Texas*, 96–99.

57. This paragraph and the next: quotations from *Deep Water at Last*, flyer in Kilgore 6237; *Deep Water and Corpus Christi*, pamphlet in Kilgore 6235 (emphasis in the original); see also Lee C. Harby, "At Corpus Christi," *Frank Leslie's Monthly*, Feb. 13, 1892, typescript in Kilgore 4109; William Kent, "Ropes Pass, Texas," *Engineering Magazine* 3 (June 1892): 340–349, copy in Kilgore

409; McCampbell, *Texas Seaport*, 65; *Centennial Journey*, 6–8; Walraven, *Corpus Christi: Texas Seaport*, 74–75; Evans Wyatt, ed., *The Building of Corpus Christi* (Corpus Christi, Tex.: Charter Savings and Loan Assoc., 1977), 16–17; Jamie Ritter, "Elihu Harrison Ropes: A Man of Vision," *Nueces County Historical Commission Bulletin* 4–5 (Nov. 1997): 33–34.

58. 1st quotation: McCampbell, *Texas Seaport*, 65; 2nd quotation: *Corpus Christi: A History and Guide*, 158.

59. Sutherland, *Story of Corpus Christi*, 55.

60. Ibid., 76.

61. "Newsmakers of the Century," *Caller-Times*, Jan. 2, 2000; "Roy Miller," *Nueces County Historical Commission Bulletin*, 4–5 (Nov. 1997): 3; Port of Corpus Christi, *Fiftieth Anniversary Port Book, 1976* (Corpus Christi, Tex.: Port of Corpus Christi, 1976), 16; O'Rear, *Storm over the Bay*, esp. chs. 7–8; Evan Anders, *Boss Rule in South Texas: The Progressive Era* (Austin: University of Texas Press, 1982).

62. Quotation: "The Port of Corpus Christi, Where Texas Meets the Sea, Opens to World Commerce," commemorative program, Sept. 1926, Kilgore 2150; documents on the Storm Stricken Area committee and the Deep Water Harbor Association, box 81, W. E. Pope Collection, TAMU-CC; Port of Corpus Christi, *Fiftieth Anniversary Port Book*, 16–17; O'Rear, *Storm over the Bay*, chs. 8–12; Richard A. Laune, "The Political Struggle for the Port of Corpus Christi, 1900–1926," *Journal of South Texas* 18 (Spring 2005): 91–112.

63. Quotation: "Industrial Banquet, Plaza Hotel, Corpus Christi," Oct. 26, 1934, program in Southern Alkali packet, Lessoff Collection; *Corpus Christi Times*, Apr. 27, 1931; *Caller-Times*, Oct. 26, 1934.

64. *Centennial Journey*, 57, 89; *Corpus Christi: A History and Guide*, 187–189; Bill Walraven and Marjorie K. Walraven, *Wooden Rigs, Iron Men: The Story of Oil and Gas in South Texas* (Corpus Christi, Tex.: Corpus Christi Geological Society, 2005), 105–108.

65. On Warren, see the *Corpus Christi Caller*, Oct. 12, 1952, Oct. 14, 1956, Feb. 13, 1984; on Lon C. Hill Jr., see the *Corpus Christi Caller*, Nov. 23, 1983; *Caller-Times*, Oct. 6, 1997; *CPL 60th Anniversary: From Ice to Atoms*, booklet, c. 1976, TAMU-CC.

66. *Caller-Times*, Apr. 6, 1980.

67. *Corpus Christi Press*, Mar. 6, 1946; *Corpus Christi Caller*, Jan. 1, Jan. 3, Jan. 9, Mar. 6, 1946; *Caller-Times*, Jan. 9, 1946.

68. *Caller-Times*, Apr. 6, 1980; Kaye Northcott, "Corpus Delicti," *Texas Monthly*, Jan. 1978, 110, 116, 118.

69. Northcott, "Corpus Delicti," 116; see also, *Caller-Times*, July 26, 1987, Oct. 6, 1997, Nov. 13, 2005.

70. *Caller-Times*, Oct. 6, 7, 12, 1997.

71. Murphy Givens and Jim Moloney, *Corpus Christi: A History* (Corpus

Christi, Tex.: Nueces Press, 2011), illustrates the balance in Givens's columns, of which the book is an elaboration. The authors enter the twentieth century on page 151 of a 274-page book.

72. Murphy D. Givens, ed., *Old Corpus Christi: The Past in Photographs* (Corpus Christi, Tex.: *Caller-Times*, 2002); Bill Walraven and Marjorie K. Walraven, *Gift of the Wind: The Corpus Christi Bayfront* (Corpus Christi, Tex.: Javelina, 1997); see also, Walraven and Walraven, *Wooden Rigs, Iron Men*, and George, "City in Transition"; *Caller-Times*, "Celebrate 2000," period supplements, Jan. 31–Nov. 28, 1999; *Caller-Times*, "The Light of Other Days: Corpus Christi History in Photos," sections L–N, July 18, 1999.

CHAPTER 3: CITY ON A FRONTIER OF PEOPLES

1. Nick Jimenez, interview by the author, Caller-Times Building, Nov. 29, 2005.

2. Daniel Arreola, *Tejano South Texas: A Mexican American Cultural Province* (Austin: University of Texas Press, 2002), 131–149. On the Spanish heritage in San Antonio architecture, preservation, imagery, and pageantry, see Lewis F. Fisher, *Saving San Antonio: The Precarious Preservation of a Heritage* (Lubbock: Texas Tech University Press, 1996), chs. 5–6; Laura Hernández-Ehrisman, *Inventing the Fiesta City: Heritage and Carnival in San Antonio* (Albuquerque: University of New Mexico Press, 2008).

3. Arreola, *Tejano South Texas*, 170–175; see also Daniel D. Arreola, "The Mexican-US Borderlands through Two Decades," *Journal of Cultural Geography* 27 (Oct. 2010): 331–351; Arreola and James R. Curtis, *The Mexican Border Cities: Landscape Anatomy and Place Personality* (Tucson: University of Arizona Press, 1993).

4. This paragraph and the preceding three: Arreola, *Tejano South Texas*, ch. 4, esp. 45; Arnoldo De León, *Mexican Americans in Texas: A Brief History*, 3rd. ed. (Wheeling, Ill.: Harlan Davidson, 2009), chs. 4–8, esp. 74, 122; U.S. Bureau of the Census, *1970 Census of Population*, vol. 1, pt. 45, sec. 2: Texas, ch. D: Detailed Characteristics (Washington, D.C.: Government Printing Office, 1973), tables 140–141. See also Benjamin Heber Johnson, *Revolution in Texas: How a Forgotten Rebellion and Its Bloody Suppression turned Mexicans into Americans* (New Haven, Conn.: Yale University Press, 2003); Cynthia E. Orozco, *No Mexicans, Women, or Dogs Allowed: The Rise of the Mexican American Civil Rights Movement* (Austin: University of Texas Press, 2009).

5. Arreola, *Tejano South Texas*, 54–56; David Montejano, *Anglos and Mexicans in the Making of Texas, 1836–1986* (Austin: University of Texas Press, 1987), pt. 3; Emilio Zamora, *The World of the Mexican Worker in Texas* (College Station: Texas A&M University Press, 1993), esp. chs. 1–3. On Mexican migration to the Corpus Christi region, see Patrick J. Carroll, *Felix Longoria's Wake: Bereavement,*

Racism, and the Rise of Mexican American Activism (Austin: University of Texas Press, 2003), ch. 1; Emilio Zamora, *Claiming Rights and Righting Wrongs in Texas: Mexican Workers and Job Politics during World War II* (College Station: Texas A&M University Press, 2009), esp. chs. 2, 7; Neil Foley, "Mexicans, Mechanization, and the Growth of Corporate Cotton Culture in South Texas: The Taft Ranch, 1900–1930," *Journal of Southern History* 62 (May 1996): 275–302; Paul Schuster Taylor, *An American-Mexican Frontier: Nueces County, Texas* (Chapel Hill: University of North Carolina Press, 1934), esp. chs. 11–14.

6. Timothy Mahoney, "What Is a Spatial Narrative," in *Gilded Age Plains City: The Great Sheedy Murder Trial and the Booster Ethos of Lincoln, Nebraska*, Center for Digital Research in the Humanities, University of Nebraska–Lincoln, http://gildedage.unl.edu; James J. Connolly, "Bringing the City Back In: Space and Place in the Urban History of the Gilded Age and Progressive Era," *Journal of the Gilded Age and Progressive Era* 1 (July 2002): 258–278. These offer entry into a complex, international theoretical discussion over the manifold ways that people conceptualize and live in cities as "places" and "spaces."

7. Jimenez interview.

8. Elise Nakhnikian, "Weil's Tales," *Corpus Christi Magazine*, Mar. 1983, 69–70, 124; Natalie Ornish, *Pioneer Jewish Texans: Their Impact on Texas and American History for Four Hundred Years, 1590–1990* (Dallas: Texas Heritage, 1989), 78–80; Sidney A. Wolf and Helen K. Wilk, *Our Golden Years: A History of Temple Beth El, Corpus Christi, Texas* (Corpus Christi, 1983), 9–10.

9. Quotations: Oscar Flores Sr., interview by the author and Thomas H. Kreneck, King Furniture, Dec. 23, 1997; "Dedication of Statue of Capitan Alonso Álvarez de Pineda," June 24, 1984, copy in author's possession; Clotilde García, *Captain Alonso Alvarez de Pineda and the Exploration of the Texas Coast and the Gulf of Mexico* (Austin: Jenkins, 1982), 27. On Clotilde García and the Pineda story, see Herb Canales, "¡Viva el Rey Alonso! The Legend of Who Discovered and Named Corpus Christi Bay," *Journal of South Texas* 24 (Fall 2011): 54–75; Spencer Pearson, "Who Named the Bay," *Caller-Times*, "Hispanic Heritage" supplement, Sept. 25, 1988.

10. Joe B. Frantz, letter on behalf of Oscar Flores, Sept. 26, 1989, Westside Business Association / Oscar Flores Papers (hereafter cited as WBA/Flores Papers), Special Collections and Archives, Texas A&M University–Corpus Christi (this archive hereafter cited as TAMU-CC).

11. Coleman McCampbell, *Saga of a Frontier Seaport* (Dallas: South-West Press, 1934), 29–38, 50–51, 578, 66–67, 96–98; Mary A. Sutherland, *The Story of Corpus Christi* (Corpus Christi, Tex.: Daughters of the Confederacy, 1916), 44, 82–85.

12. *Corpus Christi: A History and Guide* (Corpus Christi, Tex.: *Caller-Times*, 1942), 20–24.

13. Phoebe S. Kropp, *California Vieja: Culture and Memory in a Modern American Place* (Berkeley: University of California Press, 2006), 239.

14. *Corpus Christi Times*, May 23, 1969.

15. On the dispute over Spanish heritage among Mexican Americans, see Phillip B. Gonzales, "The Political Construction of Latino Nomenclatures in Twentieth Century New Mexico," *Journal of the Southwest* 35 (Summer 1993): 158–185; F. Arturo Rosales, "Shifting Self-Perceptions and Ethnic Consciousness among Mexicans in Houston, 1908–1946," *Aztlan* 16 (1985): 71–94; Joseph A. Rodríguez, "Becoming Latinos: Mexican Americans, Chicanos, and the Spanish Myth in the Urban Southwest," *Western Historical Quarterly* 29 (Summer 1998): 165–185; Richard A. García, *Rise of the Mexican American Middle Class: San Antonio, 1929–1941* (College Station: Texas A&M University Press, 1991), 42–43, 138–139; Richard A. Buitron Jr., *The Quest for Tejano Identity in San Antonio, 1913–2000* (New York: Routledge, 2004). On the Spanish heritage theme in Mexican American historical writing, see Mario T. García, "Carlos E. Castañeda and the Mexican American Generation," *Renato Rosaldo Lecture Series* 4 (1988): 1–19; Mario T. García, *Mexican Americans: Leadership, Ideology, and Identity, 1930–1960* (New Haven, Conn.: Yale University Press, 1989), ch. 9; Félix D. Almaráz, *Knight without Armor: Carlos Eduardo Castañeda, 1896–1958* (College Station: Texas A&M University Press, 1999).

16. Quotations: Benjamin H. Johnson, "The Cosmic Race in Texas: Racial Fusion, White Supremacy, and Civil Rights Politics," *Journal of American History* 98 (Sept. 2011): 410, 413; see also Orozco, *No Mexicans, Women, or Dogs*, chs. 2–4.

17. M. García, *Mexican Americans*; Juan Gómez-Quiñones, *Chicano Politics: Reality and Promise, 1940–1990* (Albuquerque: University of New Mexico Press, 1990), esp. chs. 1–2; David G. Gutiérrez, *Walls and Mirrors: Mexican Americans, Mexican Immigrants, and the Politics of Ethnicity* (Berkeley: University of California Press, 1995), esp. chs. 4–6; Anthony Quiroz, *Claiming Citizenship: Mexican Americans in Victoria, Texas* (College Station: Texas A&M University Press, 2005).

18. Orozco, *No Mexicans, Women, or Dogs*, 62; Orm Øverland, *Immigrant Minds, American Identities: Making the United States Home, 1870–1920* (Urbana: University of Illinois Press, 2000), 56–57, 187–191.

19. Chris Wilson, *The Myth of Santa Fe: Creating a Modern Regional Heritage* (Albuquerque: University of New Mexico Press, 1997); Charles Montgomery, *The Spanish Redemption: Heritage, Power, and Loss on New Mexico's Upper Rio Grande* (Berkeley: University of California Press, 2002); Judy Mattivi Morley, *Historic Preservation and the Imagined West: Albuquerque, Denver, and Seattle* (Lawrence: University Press of Kansas, 2006), ch. 1; William Deverell, *Whitewashed Adobe: The Rise of Los Angeles and the Remaking of Its Mexican Past* (Berkeley: University of California Press, 2004), ch. 2; Kropp, *California Vieja*, ch. 4.

20. R. García, *Mexican American Middle Class*; Thomas E. Sheridan, *Los Tucsonenses: The Mexican Community in Tucson, 1854–1941* (Tucson: University of Arizona Press, 1986); Arnoldo De León, *Ethnicity in the Sunbelt: Mexican Americans*

in *Houston* (College Station: Texas A&M University Press, 2001); Thomas H. Kreneck, *Del Pueblo: A History of Houston's Hispanic Community* (College Station: Texas A&M University Press, 2012). On the Spanish background of various Texas cities, see Gilberto R. Cruz, *Let There Be Towns: Spanish Municipal Origins in the American Southwest, 1610–1810* (College Station: Texas A&M University Press, 1988); Gilberto M. Hinojosa, *A Borderlands Town in Transition: Laredo, 1755–1870* (College Station: Texas A&M University Press, 1983); Jesús F. de la Teja, *San Antonio de Béxar: A Community on New Spain's Northern Frontier* (Albuquerque: University of New Mexico Press, 1995); Gerald E. Poyo and Gilberto M. Hinojosa, eds., *Tejano Origins in Eighteenth-Century San Antonio* (Austin: University of Texas Press, 1991).

21. Clotilde P. García, *Captain Enrique Villarreal and the Rincon Del Oso Land Grant* (Corpus Christi, Tex.: Grunwald, 1986), 3; see also Clotilde P. García, *Captain Blas María de la Garza Falcón: Colonizer of South Texas*, 2nd ed. (Corpus Christi, Tex.: Grunwald, 1988); *Caller-Times*, "Hispanic Heritage" supplement, Sept. 26, 1988.

22. Andrés Tijerina, *Tejanos and Texas under the Mexican Flag, 1821–1836* (College Station: Texas A&M University Press, 1994); Tijerina, *Tejano Empire: Life on the South Texas Ranchos* (College Station: Texas A&M University Press, 1998); Andrés Sáenz, *Early Tejano Ranching: Daily Life at Ranchos San José and El Fresnillo* (College Station: Texas A&M University Press, 2001); Jane Clements Monday and Betty Bailey Colley, *Voice from the Wild Horse Desert: The Vaquero Families of the King and Kenedy Ranches* (Austin: University of Texas Press, 1997). On Tejano displacement in landholding, see Armando Alonzo, *Tejano Legacy: Rancheros and Settlers in South Texas, 1734–1900* (Albuquerque: University of New Mexico Press, 1998).

23. Nick Jimenez, "Helping Agnes Street Helps Corpus Christi," *Caller-Times*, July 21, 2013.

24. On Oscar Flores and the Westside Business Association, see Minority Small Business Advocate of the Year citation, 1991; Texas Senate Resolution 652, May 16, 1989; and other biographical documents in the WBA/Flores Papers; Flores interview; *Corpus Christi Caller*, Mar. 6, 1986; *Caller-Times*, Jan. 1, 2003. On the Center for Hispanic Arts, see *Caller-Times*, May 15, 1997; Antonio E. Garcia Arts and Education Center, garciacenter.tamucc.edu.

25. "Family-Owned King Furniture Nears 50-Year Mark," *South Texas Informer and Business Journal*, Sept. 1999, 6–7; "Ghosts of Galvans Past," *Caller-Times*, Apr. 8, 1990, copies in boxes 10–11, Galván Papers, TAMU-CC.

26. This paragraph and the previous: Quotation from *Emerida Fernandez Remembers Corpus Christi: The Early Years* (Rockport, Tex.: Magner, 2001), 133; biographical files, boxes 10–11, Galván Papers. David Louzon, "Corpus Christi's Galvan Ballroom: Music and Multiculturalism in the 1950s," *Journal of South Texas* 20 (Spring 2007): 213–236; Guadalupe San Miguel Jr., *Tejano Proud:*

Tex-Mex Music in the Twentieth Century (College Station: Texas A&M University Press, 2002), esp. 6, 56.

27. "Rafael Galvan," school name nomination and dedication program, Rafael Galvan Elementary School, Oct. 14, 1990, along with Multicultural Center documents and clippings, boxes 10–11, Galván Papers.

28. *Centennial Journey: Corpus Christi Caller* (Corpus Christi, Tex.: Caller-Times, 1983), 62; Leonard A. Nikoloric, "Bonillas: Good Guys or Bad Guys," *Corpus Christi Magazine*, Mar. 1983, 58–60, 121–122, quotations on 59, 122. The LULAC archives are at the Benson Latin American Collection, University of Texas at Austin. TAMU-CC has documents related to pre-LULAC *mutualistas* and Hispanic fraternal societies. On LULAC, Corpus Christi, and South Texas, see Carroll, *Felix Longoria's Wake*, 121–128; Guadalupe San Miguel Jr., *"Let All of Them Take Heed": Mexican Americans and the Campaign for Educational Equality in Texas, 1910–1981* (Austin: University of Texas Press, 1987), ch. 3; M. García, *Mexican Americans*, ch. 3; Orozco, *No Mexicans, Women, or Dogs*. See also Benjamin Márquez, *LULAC: The Evolution of a Mexican American Political Organization* (Austin: University of Texas Press, 1993); Craig Kaplowitz, *LULAC, Mexican Americans, and National Policy* (College Station: Texas A&M University Press, 2005).

29. *Caller-Times*, Mar. 19, 1996, Nov. 18, 2002, Nov. 7, 2004.

30. *Caller-Times*, Nov. 7, 2004; Jimenez interview; "Dr. Hector P. García Historical and Educational Center Project," Sept. 2005, booklet in TAMU-CC. See also posthumous folder, Hector P. García Papers, TAMU-CC (hereafter cited as Hector García Papers; Josh Hinojosa, interview by the author and Thomas H. Kreneck, Dec. 11, 1997.

31. *Caller-Times*, Oct. 8, 2004, Sept. 17, 2009, Oct. 9, 2011; Pamela F. Edwards, "Justice for My People: The Story of Dr. Hector P. Garcia," *Coastal Bend Medicine*, June–July 1998, 7–12.

32. *Caller-Times*, Jan. 17, 2004, June 12, 2005.

33. Biography sheets in Coll. 5: Biography, Hector García Papers; see also *Caller-Times*, Dr. Hector P. Garcia supplement, July 3, 1993.

34. García quotations: notarized report on personal inspection trip, Apr. 13, 1950, Hector García Papers, 13.47; "Preliminary Report on Mathis, Texas," Apr. 1948, Hector García Papers, 20.26. See also Carroll, *Felix Longoria's Wake*, chs. 1–2; Patrick J. Carroll, "Tejano Living and Educational Conditions in World War II South Texas," *South Texas Studies* 5 (1994): 82–99; Ignacío M. García, *Hector P. García: In Relentless Pursuit of Justice* (Houston: Arte Público, 2002), 75–88, 190–194.

35. Ignacío M. García, *Viva Kennedy: Mexican Americans in Search of Camelot* (College Station: Texas A&M University Press, 2000); Carl Allsup, *The American GI Forum: Its Origins and Evolution* (Austin: Center for Mexican American Studies, 1982).

36. Hector P. García, "Poll Tax Drives—Poll Taxes Dances—Poll Taxes," memo to GI Forum leadership, Jan. 5, 1951, semi-process area box 1951–53, Hector García Papers; Jimenez interview; I. García, *Hector P. García*, 89 (quotation), 152–154.

37. *Caller-Times*, "Dr. Hector P. Garcia, 1914–1996: A Remembrance" supplement, Aug. 11, 1996, 5; Jan. 2, 2000.

38. *Corpus Christi Caller*, Aug. 15, 1972.

39. Jose Cisneros quoted in the *Caller-Times*, Aug. 12, 1996.

40. Montemayor quoted in *Corpus Christi Times*, July 16, 1971, and *Corpus Christi Sun*, Feb. 16–22, 1978; see also *Corpus Christi Times*, Dec. 1, 1977, Aug. 8, 1978, *Corpus Christi Caller*, July 12, 1968, May 22, 1974, Sept. 6, 1982; Jimenez interview; accounts of the *Cisneros* case in Manuel Narvaez Papers, TAMU-CC (hereafter cited as Narvaez Papers); San Miguel, *"Let All of Them Take Heed,"* 176–181. In *Claiming Citizenship*, Quiroz argues that in Victoria the Mexican American civil rights agenda had a similar cross-class constituency. Zamora explains that during World War II, LULAC began working with labor unions on campaigns against employment discrimination in industrial plants along the port (*Claiming Rights*, ch. 7).

41. "Rafael Galvan: Submitted for Consideration as a Man Whose Name Would Lend Dignity and Honor to a School," box 11, Galván Papers; quotation: "Dedication Ceremony: Rafael Galvan Elementary School," Oct. 14, 1990, box 10, Galván Papers; see also Steve Zastrow, "Eddie, Blow Your Horn," *Corpus Christi Magazine*, Nov. 1984; *Caller-Times*, Feb. 27, 1996.

42. *Time*, Feb. 14, 1944; see also *Caller-Times*, Feb. 13, 1944; Harriett Denise Joseph, Alix Riviere, and Jordan Penner, "'Gente Decente': Tejanos Jovita González and Edmundo E. Mireles," in *This Corner of Canaan: Essays on Texas in Honor of Randolph B. Campbell* (Denton: University of North Texas Press, 2013), 361–382.

43. See, for example, *Caller-Times*, Feb. 5, 1950, Oct. 22, 1972.

44. *Caller-Times*, June 13, 1999; see also biographical files, Mireles Papers, TAMU-CC.

45. David Montejano, *Quixote's Soldiers: A Local History of the Chicano Movement, 1966–1981* (Austin: University of Texas Press, 2010), ch. 11.

46. On the Chicano movement in the Corpus Christi region, see Ignacio M. García, *United We Win: The Rise and Fall of La Raza Unida Party* (Tucson: Mexican American Studies and Resource Center, University of Arizona, 1989); and I. García, *Chicanismo: The Forging of a Militant Ethos among Mexican Americans* (Tucson: University of Arizona Press, 1997), esp. chs. 3, 5. Montejano summarizes Ramsey Muñiz's story (*Quixote's Soldiers*, 220–228). On tensions between the Mexican American and Chicano movements, see Gómez-Quiñones, *Chicano Politics*, esp. ch. 3; Kaplowitz, *LULAC*, esp. ch. 5.

47. 1st quotation: "USWA: A Union That Cares"; 2nd quotation: "A Real Success Story," draft script, both in Narvaez Papers.

48. Taylor, *American-Mexican Frontier*, 96–97; Foley, "Mexicans, Mechanization, and Cotton Culture," 282; Neil Foley, *The White Scourge: Mexicans, Blacks, and Poor Whites in Texas Cotton Culture* (Berkeley: University of California Press, 1997), ch. 5.

49. Rue Wood, "The Forging of the African American Community in Corpus Christi, Texas, 1865–1900," *Journal of South Texas* 12, no. 1 (1999): 34–75.

50. Quotation: "For a Man Once a Slave, Coles Left His Mark on City," *Centennial Journey*, 24; Edna Jordan, *Black Tracks to Texas: Solomon Melvin Coles—From Slave to Educator* (Corpus Christi, Tex.: Golden Banner, 1977); Margaret Wead, "Rooting through the Cultures II: Blacks," *Corpus Christi Magazine*, Aug. 1982, 67–71; Moses N. Moore Jr. and Yolanda Y. Smith, "Solomon M. Coles: Preacher, Teacher, and Former Slave—The First Black Student Officially Enrolled in Yale Divinity School" at "Been in the Storm So Long: Yale Divinity School and the Black Ministry," storm.yale.edu/about-us (accessed Aug. 23, 2013); Philip D. Fraissinet, "The Closing of Solomon Coles: A Case Study," Oct. 2006, conference paper in author's possession; *Caller-Times*, July 23, 2006; Bruce Glasrud, Mary Jo O'Rear, Gloria Randle Scott, Cecilia Gutierrez Venable, and Henry J. Williams, *African Americans in Corpus Christi* (Charleston, S.C.: Arcadia, 2012).

51. Quotations: Libby Averyt and Jenny Strasburg, "The Northside: An Uncertain Future—Looking Ahead," *Caller-Times*, Feb. 22, 1998; see also Jenny Strasburg, "The Northside: A Place in History—Forgotten Neighborhood," *Caller-Times*, Feb. 8, 1998; "H. Boyd Hall Led Fight on Segregation," *Centennial Journey*, 53; "Newsmakers of the Century," *Caller-Times*, Jan. 2, 2000.

52. *Caller-Times*, Feb. 15, 1998; Saint Matthew Missionary Baptist Church, *Centennial History, 1874–1974* (Corpus Christi, Tex., 1974).

53. *Caller-Times*, Dec. 2, 2012.

54. Lawrence A. Herzog, *From Aztec to High Tech: Architecture and Landscape across the Mexico-United States Border* (Baltimore: Johns Hopkins University Press, 1999), 121–139.

55. Associated Planners, *Historical-Architectural Preservation Plan—1982, Nueces County, Texas* (Northbrook, Ill.: Associated Planners, 1982), 17 (quotation), 22.

56. *Caller-Times*, Aug. 24, 1988, May 22, Dec. 31, 1989, Jan. 9, 2003.

57. Quotation: Spanish Embassy to U.S. Information Agency, memorandum, July 1991, copy in Aurelio Valdez / Westside Business Association (WBA) Collection, TAMU-CC; Janet F. Rice, chair, Corpus Christi Quincentenary Commission, chronology, Apr. 29, 1993, Valdez/WBA Collection; Corpus Christi Museum of Science and History, *Ships of Christopher Columbus*, flyer, in author's possession; "South Texas Life" supplement, *Caller Times*, June 27, 1993; *Caller Times*, Sept. 18, 1994, Aug. 23, 2000; Mark Singer, "Texas Shipwreck," *New Yorker*, Nov. 27, 2000, 78–83; Deborah Paredez, *Selenidad: Selena, Latinos, and the Performance of Memory* (Durham, N.C.: Duke University Press, 2009), ch. 3.

58. 1st quotation: Columbus Fleet Association, Executive Committee minutes, June 21, 1993, June 16, 1994; Board of Directors Minutes, Jan. 27, June 30, 1994; 2nd quotation: Rick Stryker to William H. Crook, Nov. 12, 1993; Stryker to Fleet Association Board, April 22, 1994, Valdez/WBA Collection; *Caller-Times*, Sept. 16, 18, Nov. 1, 1994.

59. This paragraph and the previous: 1st quotation: Fernando Moral Iglesias to Corpus Christi Bay Area Business Alliance, Oct. 28, 1994, Valdez/WBA Collection; 2nd quotation, Janet F. Rice to William H. Crook, Apr. 6, 1993, Valdez/WBA Collection; 3rd quotation, Rice, chronology, Apr. 29, 1993, copies with notations to Aurelio Valdez, Valdez/WBA Collection; see also Rice to Crook, Oct. 25, 1993, Valdez/WBA Collection; Quincentenary Commission minutes, Aug. 26, 1992; Los Barcos Columbus Ships Association minutes, Feb. 25, 1993; board of directors list, Mar. 15, 1993; and Rick Stryker to Aurelio Valdez, with board of directors list and slate, Apr. 11, 1994, all in Valdez/WBA Collection. In 2000, the Westside Business Association, stressing that it had been "instrumental in bringing the Columbus Fleet to Corpus Christi," unsuccessfully sought a Texas judicial inquiry into the fleet's troubles; see *Caller-Times*, Mar. 21 (quotation) and 24, 2000.

60. *Caller Times*, Sept, 18, 1994 (2nd quotation), Oct. 12, 1994 (1st quotation), Nov. 1, 1994, Dec. 21, 1994, Feb. 16, 1999, Mar. 15, 1999, Mar. 17, 1999, Apr. 26, 1999 (3rd quotation), Oct. 24, 1999.

61. *Caller-Times*, Apr. 26, May 12 (quotation), May 15, June 2, June 3, 1995; Judy Fort, "A Chronological History of the World of Discovery, Corpus Christi Museum of Science and History," copy in author's possession; museum flyers *The 1554 Collection* and *Seeds of Change*, in author's possession.

62. *Caller-Times*, Oct. 14, 1996, Aug. 8, 1997, Sept. 17, 1999, Oct. 11–13, 1999, Oct. 20, 1999, Nov. 5, 1999, Feb. 24–25, 2000, Apr. 23–24, 2000; Singer, "Texas Shipwreck."

63. *Caller-Times*, Oct. 13, 1999.

64. Quotations: *Caller-Times*, Apr. 24, 2000; Singer, "Texas Shipwreck," 79; see also *Caller-Times*, Jan. 9 and 13, 2000.

65. Singer, "Texas Shipwreck," 83; see also Paredez, *Selenidad*, 77.

66. *Caller Times*, Oct. 12, 1994.

67. Quotation: *Caller-Times*, Apr. 24, 2000; *San Antonio Express-News*, May 16, 2001; see also *Caller-Times*, Mar. 15, 1995, Mar. 17, 1995, Oct. 6, 2000, Apr. 18, 2001, Apr. 22, 2001, June 8, 2001.

68. *Caller-Times*, Apr. 24, 2000, July 21, 2005.

69. Ibid., May 4, 1996, Jan. 27, May 11, 2001.

70. Corpus Christi Museum of Science and History, revised mission statement, 2005, in author's possession; *Caller-Times*, July 21, Aug. 17, Sept. 2, Oct. 17, 2005.

71. *Caller-Times*, Aug. 21, 2012, June 23, 2013.

72. Ibid., Oct. 6, 2000.

73. Ibid., Apr. 26, 2013.

74. Vernon O. Elmore, *A Voyage of Faith: A History of the First Baptist Church of Corpus Christi, Texas* (Corpus Christi, Tex., 1994), 9–14; Mary Xavier, *Father Jaillet: Saddlebag Priest of the Nueces* (Corpus Christi, Tex.: Diocese of Corpus Christi, 1948); James Talmadge Moore, *Through Fire and Flood: The Catholic Church in Frontier Texas, 1836–1900* (College Station: Texas A&M University Press, 1992), 190–194; Margaret Lasater Clark, *On This Bluff: Centennial History, 1867–1967* (Corpus Christi, Tex.: First Presbyterian Church, 1967), 11–17, 31, 50–53.

75. These two paragraphs: D. B. South, "Our Fifteen Years in Corpus Christi and Area," pamphlet, c. 1953, Kilgore 2134, 19; Ed Gilpin and Wayne Pemberton, eds., *Calallen Baptist Church: July 4, 1874–1974*, Kilgore 4265, 24–26; Clark, *On This Bluff*, 40–42, 79, 119–120; Mary Xavier Holworthy, "History of the Diocese of Corpus Christi, Texas" (MA thesis, St. Mary's University of San Antonio, 1939), 57–62, 72, 122–127; Libby Averyt, "Cotton Fields to County Judge," *Caller-Times*, Jan. 1, 1995; Mary Lee Grant, "Leaving the Fold," *Caller-Times*, Apr. 12, 1998; Jimenez interview. On similar competition in El Paso, see Mario T. García, *Desert Immigrants: The Mexicans of El Paso, 1880–1920* (New Haven, Conn.: Yale University Press, 1981), 212–222; Camilo José Vergara, *How the Other Half Worships* (New Brunswick, N.J.: Rutgers University Press, 2005).

CHAPTER 4: PUBLIC SCULPTURE AND CIVIC IDENTITY

1. On imagery surrounding Selena, see Deborah Paredez, *Selenídad: Selena, Latinos, and the Performance of Memory* (Durham, N.C.: Duke University Press, 2009). On Tejano music and southern Texas, see Guadalupe San Miguel Jr., *Tejano Proud: Tex-Mex Music in the Twentieth Century* (College Station: Texas A&M University Press, 2002). For a *Caller-Times* archive, see "Remembering Selena," www.caller.com/news/entertainment/selena; for information from the family's production company, see Q Productions online, www.q-productions.com/home .html (both accessed Sept. 24, 2013).

2. *Caller-Times*, Aug. 20, 1995 (quotation), May 26, 1997.

3. *Caller-Times*, July 21, 23, 1998, June 2, 2000, July 20, 2000 (Quintanilla quotation), July 23, 2000 (Jimenez quotation). Jimenez is also quoted in Paredez, *Selenídad*, 86.

4. *Caller-Times*, June 22, 1997.

5. David G. McComb, personal communication, May 3, 1998; *Caller-Times*, Apr. 16, 1997.

6. Municipal Arts Commission minutes, Dec. 12, 1996, Feb. 6, 1997, Feb. 13, 1997; and Joseph Wilson to Mayor Mary Rhodes and the Corpus Christi City Council, Feb. 4, 1997 (quotations), Municipal Arts Commission minutes, Department of Parks and Recreation, Corpus Christi City Hall (hereafter cited as MAC minutes).

7. Aloe Tile, statement, MAC minutes, Feb. 13, 1997; see also the Aloe Tile Works website, www.aloetile.com (accessed Sept. 24, 2013).

8. H. W. "Buddy" Tatum, conversation with the author, Jan. 6, 1998. The statue and monument went through design changes, some at the last minute, in part because the original design for the mosaic on the pillar violated the family's religious beliefs. Like many South Texas Hispanics, the Quintanillas are Jehovah's Witnesses; see *Caller-Times*, April 16, 1997.

9. *Caller-Times*, June 22, 1997; Robert Hodder, "Redefining a Southern City's Heritage: Historic Preservation, Planning, Public Art, and Race in Richmond, Virginia," *Journal of Urban Affairs* 21 (Dec. 1999): 437–453; Sanford Levinson, *Written in Stone: Public Monuments in a Changing Society* (Durham, N.C.: Duke University Press, 1998), 39–41, 115–119. For those unfamiliar with the story, Richmond's Monument Avenue is a City Beautiful–style boulevard that features splendid statues of the leaders of the Confederacy—in effect, an artistically first-rate glorification of the southern cause in the Civil War. In the mid-1990s, Douglas Wilder, earlier Virginia's first African American governor and later his hometown's mayor, led an effort to have a twenty-four-foot monument to another renowned black native of Richmond, the athlete and humanitarian Arthur Ashe, placed on the avenue. Finding themselves in an awkward alliance with white southern traditionalists and Lost Cause romanticizers, preservationists and arts advocates unsuccessfully pressured the city's review board to reject the proposed design. Critics suggested that the monument had questionable artistic merit, which the Ashe statue's backers disputed, and that it undercut the avenue's aesthetic and historical coherence, which Wilder and his allies intended. At the time, the case seemed a textbook clash between aesthetics and historical integrity on one side and politics and ethics on the other in assessing public art.

10. Newspaper accounts also portrayed Selena as a "role model"; see the *Caller-Times*, May 26, 1997; Paredez, *Selenidad*, 82.

11. *Caller-Times*, Dec. 1, 11, 1997.

12. Mary P. Ryan, "Democracy Rising: The Monuments of Baltimore, 1809–1842," *Journal of Urban History* 36 (Mar. 2010): 127–150; Kirk Savage, *Monument Wars: Washington, D.C., the National Mall, and the Transformation of the Memorial Landscape* (Berkeley: University of California Press, 2009), chs. 1–2.

13. On Beaux-Arts public sculpture, see Michele Bogart, *Public Sculpture and the Civic Ideal in New York City* (Chicago: University of Chicago Press, 1989). On the aesthetics of the City Beautiful movement, see William H. Wilson, *The City Beautiful Movement* (Baltimore: Johns Hopkins University Press, 1989), ch. 4; see also, Savage, *Monument Wars*, chs. 2–5; Kirk Savage, *Standing Soldiers, Kneeling Slaves: Race, War, and Monument in Nineteenth-Century America* (Princeton, N.J.: Princeton University Press, 1997); Kathryn Allmong Jacob, *Testament to Union: Civil War Monuments in Washington, D.C.* (Baltimore: Johns Hopkins University Press, 1998); Bailey van Hook, *The Virgin and the Dynamo: Public Murals in American Architecture, 1893–1917* (Athens: Ohio University Press, 2003).

14. Inventory in MAC minutes, Jan. 1997; *City of Corpus Christi, Public Art Collection, 1914–2009*, brochure, in author's possession.

15. Bogart, *Public Sculpture and the Civic Ideal*, 309–316; John Bodnar, *Remaking America: Public Memory, Commemoration, and Patriotism in the Twentieth Century* (Princeton, N.J.: Princeton University Press, 1992), 97–103; Mark Tebeau, "Sculpted Landscapes: Art and Place in Cleveland's Cultural Gardens," *Journal of Social History* 44 (June 2010): 327–350.

16. The standard introduction to the new wave of urban public sculpture is Harriet F. Senie, *Contemporary Public Sculpture: Tradition, Transformation, and Controversy* (New York: Oxford University Press, 1992). For a sense of the variety of the new public art and the motives and interests behind it, see Erika Doss, *Spirit Poles and Flying Pigs: Public Art and Cultural Democracy in American Communities* (Washington, D.C.: Smithsonian Institution Press, 1995), ch. 2; Sarah Schrank, *Art and the City: Civic Imagination and Cultural Authority in Los Angeles* (Philadelphia: University of Pennsylvania Press, 2009). In *Here the Country Lies: Nationalism and the Arts in Twentieth-Century America* (Bloomington: Indiana University Press, 1980), Charles C. Alexander traces the history of the notion that art can and should be a useful feature of American society from before World War I through the aesthetic and critical upheavals of the 1950s and 1960s.

17. Quoted in John R. Wright, "Pompeo Coppini and Corpus Christi's First Experiment with Public Art," 7, unpublished study with documents, Local History Room, Corpus Christi Public Library; see also Jane Beckman, *Queen of the Sea: Corpus Christi's Historic Sculpture* (Corpus Christi, Tex.: Riviera Editions, 1995), 11–12.

18. Wright, "Pompeo Coppini," 7–8.

19. Carol Morris Little, *A Comprehensive Guide to Outdoor Sculpture in Texas* (Austin: University of Texas Press, 1997), 7–10.

20. 1st quotation: Mary A. Sutherland, *The Story of Corpus Christi* (Corpus Christi, Tex.: Daughters of the Confederacy, 1916), 141; 2nd quotation: Pompeo Coppini, *From Dawn to Sunset* (San Antonio: Naylor, 1949), 205–206; George Brown, speech to Corpus Christi Rotary Club at the rededication of *Queen of the Sea*, April 1991, typescript provided to the author by Ron Sullivan of Del Mar College; Beckman, *Queen of the Sea*, 41.

21. Quoted in Wright, "Pompeo Coppini," 15. The model for the figure of Corpus Christi, a local woman named Helen Leary McCauley, in 1921 became the first female lawyer to try a case in China. She defended an American sailor charged with murder for throwing a Chinese cobbler into the Yangtze River from a gunboat commanded by her husband. Beckman, *Queen of the Sea*, 27–35; *Corpus Christi Caller*, Dec. 2, 1985.

22. Ron Sullivan, interview by the author, Jan. 8, 1998; *The Restoration of the Queen of the Sea*, video in Del Mar College Library; Beckman, *Queen of the Sea*, 36–44; *Caller-Times*, Aug. 20, 1990, Apr. 12, 15, 1991.

23. MAC minutes, Mar. 13, May 8, 1997; Sullivan interview; *Caller-Times*, Oct. 28, 1999, Nov. 25, 2001.

24. Coppini, *From Dawn to Sunset*, 206.

25. *Corpus Christi Caller*, May 26, 1963, Feb. 19, 1979; Willadene Price, *Gutzon Borglum: The Man Who Carved a Mountain* (1983), 214–216; Coppini, *From Dawn to Sunset*, 348.

26. *San Antonio Express*, Mar. 7, 1954.

27. *Weekly Current*, Apr. 7, 1971; MAC minutes, Aug. 6, Sept. 14, 1971.

28. *Corpus Christi Caller*, Dec. 7, 25, 1977, May 11, 1978, Feb. 28, July 26, Aug. 9, 16, 1979.

29. Kent Ullberg, interview by the author, Dec. 23, 1997; *Caller-Times*, Apr. 3, 1994, Sept. 3, Oct. 21, 23, 1995.

30. Alan Lessoff, "An Art Museum for South Texas, 1944–1980," in William G. Otton, Amy Smith Kight, and Alan Lessoff, *Legacy: A History of the Art Museum of South Texas* (Corpus Christi, Tex.: Art Museum of South Texas, 1997), 25–53.

31. MAC minutes, May 2, 1967, May 16, 1967, Oct. 3, 1967, Nov. 7, 1967, Dec. 5, 1967, Feb. 11, 1969, Mar. 4, 1969, Apr. 16, 1969, June 3, 1969, Feb. 3, 1970, May 5, 1970, June 2, 1970, Aug. 16, 1971, Mar. 7, 1972; *Corpus Christi Caller*, Dec. 10, 1969.

32. Margaret Walberg and Susan Rees, interview by the author, Jan. 15, 1998; *Corpus Christi Caller*, Mar. 17, 1979, Jan. 9, 1980, Dec. 3, 1986; Bill Walraven, *Corpus Christi: The History of a Texas Seaport* (Sun Valley, Calif.: American Historical Press, 1997), 108–109, 179.

33. Quotations: Walberg and Rees interview; *Caller-Times*, Oct. 23, 1983. Gibbs was then on the faculty of Corpus Christi State University. Richard Serra's despised rusty wall at Federal Plaza in Manhattan, *Tilted Arc*, was made of Cor-Ten steel; see Senie, *Contemporary Public Sculpture*, 227–228; Doss, *Spirit Poles and Flying Pigs*, 32–33; Michael Kammen, *Visual Shock: A History of Art Controversies in American Culture* (New York: Knopf, 2006), 238–243.

34. *Corpus Christi Times*, Oct. 3, 1978.

35. *Corpus Christi Caller*, Sept. 28, 1979, Nov. 2, Jan. 5, 1980. *Corpus Christi Times*, Oct. 4, 1979. Walberg and Rees interview. On Surls, see Terrie Sultan, *James Surls: The Splendora Years, 1977–1997* (Austin: University of Texas Press, 2005); Patricia D. Hendricks and Becky Duval Reese, *A Century of Sculpture in Texas* (Austin: Archer M. Huntington Art Gallery, University of Texas, 1989), 101–103; James Surls's website, www.jamessurls.com (accessed Sept. 28, 2013).

36. 1st quotation: Art Auxiliary board minutes, June 3, 1980, in Auxiliary files, Art Museum of South Texas Papers, Special Collections and Archives, Texas A&M–Corpus Christi (this archive hereafter cited as TAMU-CC); 2nd quotation: *Corpus Christi Times*, Nov. 2, 1979; 3rd quotation: *Corpus Christi Caller*, Sept. 26, 1979; Ullberg interview.

37. *Corpus Christi Caller*, Sept. 28, 1979 (quotation), Jan. 19, 1980, Sept. 1, 1981, July 14, 1983; *Corpus Christi Times*, Jan. 11, 1980; *Caller-Times*, Jan. 5, 1980, July 27, 1986; Walberg and Rees interview.

38. *Corpus Christi Caller*, Mar. 8, 1990 (quotation); *Caller-Times*, June 17, 1992, Apr. 10, 1994.

39. *Caller-Times*, May 1, 2002 (quotation), June 5, 2008; Arts and Cultural Commission, Percent for Art PowerPoint and Bayfront Art Tour map, copies in author's possession.

40. Ullberg interview. On Ullberg's background, influences, and approach, see Todd Wilkinson, *Kent Ullberg: Monuments to Nature* (Scottsdale, Ariz.: International Graphics, 1998); *Kent Ullberg: Celebration of Nature* (Corpus Christi, Tex.: Art Museum of South Texas, 2001); *Kent Ullberg: Sculptures—An Overview* (Corpus Christi, Tex.: Art Museum of South Texas, 1985); Kent Ullberg's website, www.kentullberg.net (accessed Dec. 29, 2013); *Corpus Christi Times*, Nov. 24, 1978; *Caller-Times*, Jan. 13, 1985, June 16, 1991; *Dallas Times Herald*, June 12, 1984.

41. Ullberg interview (quotations); M. Stephen Doherty, "Kent Ullberg's Monumental Sculptures," *American Artist*, Nov. 1987, 48–53, esp. 49; Jacqueline M. Pontello, "Kent Ullberg," *Southwest Art*, May 1991, 92–99, 191, esp. 95; "The Icons of Our Time," *Focus/Santa Fe*, Jan.–Mar. 1995.

42. Ullberg interview; *Kent Ullberg: Sculptures*, 7; Jim Edwards, telephone conversation with the author, Dec. 18, 1997.

43. *Corpus Christi Caller*, Sept. 26, 1979 (quotation), Jan. 10, 1980, letters to the editor, Oct. 1, 2, 4, 1979; *Corpus Christi Times*, Oct. 4 and Nov. 2, 1979. Ullberg recalled that the committee returned his portfolio evidently without examining it; see Ullberg interview.

44. *Corpus Christi Times*, Sept. 17, 1980; *Corpus Christi Caller*, Dec. 16, 1980; Dolphin Sculpture (Shoreline Median) file, Director's Office Papers, Department of Parks and Recreation, Corpus Christi City Hall; Ullberg Interview.

45. Edward Harte, interview by the author, June 5, 1996.

46. Ullberg interview; *Corpus Christi Caller*, Apr. 7, 1982; *Caller-Times*, Jan. 13, 1983; Doherty, "Ullberg's Monumental Sculptures," 50.

47. Suzanne Smith, "Kent Ullberg: A Soaring Presence," *Sculpture Review* 52 (Spring 2003): 32–36; Kim Carpenter, "Fountains of Life / Allegories of Power: The Sculptures of Jean-Baptiste Tuby and Kent Ullberg," *Sculpture Review* 56 (Summer 2007): 8–15; Laura Zuckerman, "Kent Ullberg's Omaha Project: His Magnum Opus Is Complete," *Wildlife Art*, Nov.–Dec. 2007, 26–33; *An Epic in Bronze: The Omaha Sculptures*, DVD (Omaha: OmahaSculptures, 2011).

48. *Caller-Times*, Mar. 15, 2005; Community Support, Padre Island National Seashore, www.nps.gov/pais/naturescience/community_support.htm (accessed Sept. 28, 2013).

49. *Caller-Times*, July 20, 2004; Ullberg interview (quotation); Senie, *Contemporary Public Sculpture*, 157–158.

50. Walberg and Rees interview; Tatum conversation; *Corpus Christi Caller*, Apr. 21, 1982, Feb. 8, 1984; *Corpus Christi Times*, Dec. 3, 1980, Jan. 16, 1985; *Caller-Times*, Aug. 4, 1985, July 27, 1986 (quotation).

51. Mic Raasch, conversation with the author, Dec. 10, 1997.

52. Barbara McDowell, interview by the author, Jan. 19, 1998; MAC minutes, July 9, Oct. 6, 1986 (1st quotation); Corpus Christi Public Art Ordinance, Mar. 1987, Section 1.E.5, copy in author's possession (2nd quotation); draft letter to Patsy Singer, Dec. 1, 1986, Public Art Program file, Planning Department papers, Corpus Christi City Hall; *Caller-Times*, July 27, 1986; *Corpus Christi Times*, Sept. 10, 1986.

53. Austin was the first Texas city with such an ordinance. In 1959, Philadelphia adopted the country's first percent-for-art ordinance. By the mid-1980s, Corpus Christi could study over fifty such ordinances nationwide; see Public Art Program file; *Caller-Times*, Aug. 17 and Oct. 16, 1986; Senie, *Contemporary Public Sculpture*, 217–218.

54. Tom Utter, assistant city manager, to Hal George, city attorney, Oct. 1, 1986; Bill Hennings, assistant city manager, to the city council, Feb. 18, 1987; city council minutes, Dec. 16, 1986, excerpt; all in Public Art Program file.

55. *Corpus Christi Times*, Jan. 22, 1987; *Corpus Christi Caller*, Dec. 21, 1986, Feb. 1, 1987 (1st quotation), Mar. 17, 1987 (2nd quotation); Michele H. Bogart, *The Politics of Urban Beauty: New York and Its Art Commission* (Chicago: University of Chicago Press, 2006).

56. MAC minutes, Jan. 12, 1995, and inventory, Jan. 1997; objectives for 1987–1989, Aug. 11, 1987; annual report to the city manager, Jan. 14, 1988; Jesús Moroles file, MAC papers; *Corpus Christi Caller*, June 7, 1989, Jan. 14, 1990. On Moroles, see Little, *Outdoor Sculpture in Texas*, 31; Bonnie Gangelhoff, "Jesús Bautista Moroles," *Southwest Art*, Sept. 1997, 98–101, 116–117; Thomas McEvilley, *Art at the Gateway: Jesús Bautista Moroles* (Houston: Davis/McClain Gallery, 1990); *San Antonio Express-News*, Apr. 10, 2005; www.moroles.com (accessed Sept. 28, 2013).

57. *Caller-Times*, Jan. 27, 1991.

58. Oscar Flores Sr., interview by the author and Thomas H. Kreneck, Dec. 23, 1997 (quotation); WBA minutes for July 22, 1982; fund-raising pamphlet; and "Dedication of the Statue of Capitan Alonso Álvarez de Pineda," June 24, 1984, all in Westside Business Association / Oscar Flores Papers (hereafter cited as WBA/Flores Papers), TAMU-CC; *Corpus Christi Caller*, Aug. 6, Nov. 18, 1982.

59. Flores interview (quotations); *Caller-Times*, June 23, 1993.

60. Flores interview.

61. García submitted a proposal, but Coleman was able to contribute to fundraising, in part by producing small bronzes for sale; see the artist proposals in the Falcón file, WBA/Flores Papers; Flores interview; Art Review Panel Report [1989] (quotation), Falcón statue file, MAC Papers; *Caller-Times*, Mar. 31 and June 9, 1989; McDowell interview.

62. Bogart, *Politics of Urban Beauty*, esp. 101–131; Savage, *Monument Wars*, 203–210.

63. McDowell interview; Art Review Panel Report, Falcón file, MAC Papers; Greg Reuter, telephone conversation with the author, Dec. 31, 1997.

64. Flores interview.

65. Flores interview (quotation); *Caller-Times*, May 28, 1989, July 8, 1990, Sept. 7–8, 1992; Falcón monument files, WBA/Flores Papers. Flores's concerns over perceptions of Falcón were well placed. In the same period, El Paso and Santa Fe experienced quarrels over efforts to build statues to the conquistador Juan de Oñate, who earned a reputation for brutality during the 1599 Acoma uprising. In 1998, to protest 400th-anniversary commemorations of Spanish colonization, Indians from Acoma Pueblo symbolically sawed a foot from an Oñate statue in Española, New Mexico; see Chris Wilson, *The Myth of Santa Fe: Creating a Modern Regional Heritage* (Albuquerque: University of New Mexico Press, 1997), 318–319; Charles Montgomery, *The Spanish Redemption: Heritage, Power, and Loss on New Mexico's Upper Rio Grande* (Berkeley: University of California Press, 2002), 217–229; *Houston Chronicle*, May 24, 1998 (reference courtesy of David G. McComb).

66. *Caller-Times*, Apr. 22 and May 7, 1993; Josh Hinojosa, interview by the author and Thomas H. Kreneck, Dec. 11, 1997; Robert R. Furgason, university president, to Dr. Julio Vela, Apr. 23, 1993; Thomas Kreneck to Furgason, Apr. 30, 1993; Albert R. Huerta to Furgason, Apr. 30, 1993, García Plaza file, supplied to author by Thomas Kreneck.

67. A proposal to honor Dr. Hector P. García, 1994, typescript in Kreneck file (quotations), copy in author's possession; see also García project files, Office of Institutional Advancement, Texas A&M–Corpus Christi; *Caller-Times*, June 28, 1996. On Roberto García, see Artwork of Robert and Ana Garcia, www.garcia-art.com (accessed Sept. 29, 2013).

68. Roberto García, interview by the author and Thomas H. Kreneck, Feb. 4, 1998.

69. MAC minutes, Oct. 12, 1995, May 9, 1996; Arts and Cultural Commission, Bayfront Public Art Sculpture, Finalist Profiles, flyer in author's possession; *Caller-Times*, Dec. 1, 1997, Apr. 22, 1999. On Moroles, see the references in note 56 above.

70. *Caller-Times*, Oct. 19, 1999, Nov. 1, 1999, Dec. 14, 1999, Apr. 11, 2000, May 24, 2000, July 22, 2002, Aug. 9, 2002; *San Antonio Express-News*, Apr. 16, 2000 (Perless quotation).

71. Martinez quotation, *Caller-Times*, Oct. 19, 1999; Anastos quotations, *Caller-Times*, Nov. 1 and Dec. 14, 1999; Jim Edwards, conversation with the author, Oct. 19, 1999.

72. *Caller-Times*, Oct. 19, 1999.

73. Ibid., Oct. 20, 22, 24 (quotation), Dec. 14, 15, 1999.

74. Ibid., Dec. 15, 1999.

75. Ibid., Apr. 14–15, 1998.

76. Robert Venturi, Denise Scott Brown, and Steven Izenour, *Learning from Las Vegas* (Cambridge, Mass.: MIT Press, 1972); Carl Abbott, "Southwestern Cityscapes: Approaches to an American Urban Environment," in *Essays on Sunbelt Cities and Recent Urban America*, ed. Robert Fairbanks and Kathleen Underwood (College Station: Texas A&M University Press, 1990), 59–86; John M. Findlay, *Magic Lands: Western Cityscapes and American Culture after 1940* (Berkeley: University of California Press, 1992), ch. 6.

77. Quoted in Brian Ladd, *The Ghosts of Berlin: Confronting German History in the Urban Landscape* (Chicago: University of Chicago Press, 1997), 170–171.

CHAPTER 5: A MATTER OF LITTLE IMPORT

1. *Caller-Times*, Feb. 11, 2010.

2. Quotation: Destination Bayfront, www.destinationbayfront.org (accessed Oct. 3, 2013); *Caller-Times*, Jan. 25, 28, Feb. 7–8, 2010.

3. On the Project for Public Spaces, see its website, www.pps.org (accessed Oct. 2, 2013). PPS, whose Texas work includes Houston's Discovery Green, traces its origins to the sociologist William H. Whyte. Famous for *The Organization Man* (1956), Whyte spent decades devising methods for tracing of how people use urban space in their daily lives and for basing plans upon such studies; see William H. Whyte, *City: Rediscovering the Center* (New York: Doubleday, 1988), and Whyte, *The Social Life of Small Urban Spaces* (1980; New York: Project for Public Spaces, 2001).

4. Destination Bayfront presentations to the city council, June and Dec. 2010; "Placemaking at Destination Bayfront," Nov. 2010; "Bayfront Development Plan Phase 3," council presentation, Nov. 8, 2011; Hargreaves Associates, "Corpus Christi Destination Bayfront, Master Plan Implementation," Feb. 2013; *Caller-Times*, July 28 (quotation), Oct. 7, 2010, Oct. 13, 2010, Dec. 13, 2011.

5. Destination Bayfront, www.destinationbayfront.org/rfq.cfm (accessed Aug. 26, 2012; site later revised); website of Gignac & Associates, www.gignacarchitects.com (accessed Oct. 3, 2013); Sasaki Associates and Gignac & Associates, "Corpus Christi Downtown Vision Plan," Dec. 9, 2008; Arquitectonica, Gignac & Associates, and Sasaki Associates, "Bayfront Master Plan Update and Shoreline Realignment Phase 1," Oct. 30, 2007; Arquitectonica and Gignac & Associates, "Shoreline Boulevard Master Plan: Corpus Christi," June 29, 2004; "Bayfront Master Plan Update and Shoreline Realignment Phase 1," Oct. 30, 2007, slides 3–9; "Shoreline Boulevard Master Plan: Corpus Christi," June 29, 2004, slides 6–11; *Caller-Times*, May 3, 2001, May 13, 2001, Mar. 15, 2004, Apr. 14, 2004, Apr. 16, 2004, July 25, 2004, July 27, 2004, Aug. 6, 2004, Jan. 26, 2005.

6. *Caller-Times*, Oct. 22–25, 2003. Corpus Christi was hardly alone in generating a stream of downtown plans. Providence produced at least twenty between

1959 and 2000; see Brent D. Ryan, "Incomplete and Incremental Plan Implementation in Downtown Providence, Rhode Island, 1960–2000," *Journal of Planning History* 5 (Feb. 2006): 35–64.

7. Sasaki, Walker Associates, *Corpus Christi Bayfront Study*, Jan. 1974, 1–2.

8. "Bayfront Plan: Corpus Christi, Texas," Dec. 1982, revised Mar. 1984; City of Corpus Christi, "Executive Summary of the South Central Area Development Plan," Feb.–July 2004, 6, and full plan, 20–22; City of Corpus Christi, Downtown Redevelopment Committee, *Downtown Redevelopment Report*, Nov. 2006, 3.

9. *Caller-Times*, July 31, 2010 (Libby); Jan. 22, 2012 (Jimenez).

10. Opposition letters: *Caller-Times*, Sept. 28 and Oct. 1, 2013; see also *Caller-Times*, July 23, 2013, Aug. 25, 2013, Nov. 6, 2013, Jan. 18, 2014.

11. *Caller-Times*, Nov. 13, 2005.

12. 1st quotation: Harland Bartholomew and Associates, *Comprehensive Plan for the Corpus Christi Area* (St. Louis: Harland Bartholomew and Associates, 1953), chairman's message, v; 2nd quotation: "Corpus Christi's 25 Year Plan for Area Progress," supplement to *Corpus Christi Caller*, Industrial and Commercial Vertical File, Corpus Christi Public Library, cover.

13. For a detailed account, see Alan Lessoff, "Harland Bartholomew in Corpus Christi: The Faltering Pursuit of Comprehensive Planning in South Texas," *Planning Perspectives* 18 (Apr. 2003): 197–232.

14. Harland Bartholomew, *Comprehensive Plan*, 1953, v, 45; Robert B. Fairbanks, *For the City as a Whole: Planning, Politics, and the Public Interest in Dallas, Texas, 1900–1965* (Columbus: Ohio State University Press, 1998).

15. Harland Bartholomew, *Comprehensive Plan*, 1953, 65–69; Bill Walraven and Marjorie Walraven, *Gift of the Wind: The Corpus Christi Bayfront* (Corpus Christi, Tex.: Javelina, 1997), 74–75.

16. Amy Bridges, *Morning Glories: Muncipal Reform in the Southwest* (Princeton, N.J.: Princeton University Press, 1997), chs. 8–9; Carl Abbott, *The New Urban America: Growth and Politics in Sunbelt Cities*, rev. ed. (Chapel Hill: University of North Carolina Press, 1987), ch. 7–10; Abbott, *The Metropolitan Frontier: Cities in the Modern American West* (Tucson: University of Arizona Press, 1993), ch. 5.

17. Alison Isenberg, *Downtown America: A History of the Place and the People Who Made It* (Chicago: University of Chicago Press, 2004), esp. chs. 5–7.

18. *Corpus Christi: A History and Guide* (Corpus Christi, Tex.: *Corpus Christi Caller-Times*, 1942), maps and 11; "City of Corpus Christi, Texas, Annexation History by Decades," Planning Department map in author's possession; Harland Bartholomew, *Comprehensive Plan*, 1953, 6–10; City of Corpus Christi, "South Central Area Development Plan," July 2004, 9–16.

19. Carl Abbott, "Five Strategies for Downtown: Policy Discourse and Planning since 1943," in *Planning the Twentieth-Century American City*, ed. Mary Corbin Sies and Christopher Silver (Baltimore: Johns Hopkins University Press,

1996), 410–411; Jon C. Teaford, *The Rough Road to Renaissance: Urban Revitalization in America, 1940–1985* (Baltimore, Md.: Johns Hopkins University Press, 1990), ch. 1; Robert Fogelson, *Downtown: Its Rise and Fall, 1880–1950* (New Haven, Conn.: Yale University Press, 2001), esp. 243–245.

20. Harland Bartholomew, *Comprehensive Plan*, 1953, 43, 66.

21. ADC review committee to Guy Warren, May 21, 1958, accompanying Harland Bartholomew and Associates, "Accomplishments under the Comprehensive Plan," Jan. 1958, copy in author's possession.

22. Memorandum, Oct. 9, 1964, file 13.28, Neyland Papers, Special Collections and Archives, Texas A&M University–Corpus Christi (this archive hereafter cited as TAMU-CC).

23. Urban Land Institute, "A Report to the Central City Committee of Corpus Christi: Findings and Recommendations," June 1965, 4, 33–35; "Corpus Christi Central Business District, Advance Kit for Urban Land Institute Members," June 1965, 7, copies in author's possession; *Corpus Christi Today*, June 1965.

24. City of Corpus Christi, "Quarterly Progress Report," Nov. 1957, Kilgore 5551, TAMU-CC; "Corpus Christi Convention Climate," c. late 1960s, Kilgore 4961.

25. Harland Bartholomew and Associates, *The Comprehensive Plan: Corpus Christi* (St. Louis: Harland Bartholomew and Associates, 1967), pt. 2, 92; Malcolm Drummond, interview by the author, Parsons Harland Bartholomew offices, St. Louis, Aug. 31, 2001.

26. Harland Bartholomew, *Comprehensive Plan*, 1967, 2:95, 114–115; Drummond interview; *Corpus Christi Times*, Nov. 16, 1967; Margaret Wead, "Downtown: Looking Past the Present," *Corpus Christi Magazine*, Sept. 1981, 38–46.

27. Harland Bartholomew, *Comprehensive Plan*, 1967, 2:91–92.

28. *Corpus Christi Times*, June 22, 1976. Pamphlets, booklets, and press clippings tracing this debate can be found in the Convention Center and Bayfront Science Park vertical files, Local History Room, Corpus Christi Public Library.

29. Patricia Gober, *Metropolitan Phoenix: Place Making and Community Building in the Desert* (Philadelphia: University of Pennsylvania Press, 2006), ch. 6.

30. Harland Bartholomew, *Comprehensive Plan*, 1967, 2:91; Elizabeth Strom, "Cultural Policy as Development Policy: Evidence from the United States," *International Journal of Cultural Policy* 9 (Nov. 2003): 247–263; Strom, "Converting Pork into Porcelain: Cultural Institutions and Downtown Development," *Urban Affairs Review* 38 (Sept. 2002): 3–21.

31. Quotation: "A Student's Prize-Winning Design," *Texas Architect*, June 1960, 10–11.

32. Quotation: *Corpus Christi Times*, May 17, 1962; Corpus Christi Arts Council, *Bayfront Park and Civic Center*, brochure dated Dec. 1962, in author's possession; see also *Corpus Christi Caller*, May 17, 1962, Oct. 31, 1963.

33. "Arts and Cultural Centers," June 1962, exhibition files, Art Museum of

South Texas Papers, TAMU-CC. On this worldwide trend, start with Peter Hendee Brown, *America's Waterfront Revival: Port Authorities and Urban Redevelopment* (Philadelphia: University of Pennsylvania Press, 2009).

34. *Caller-Times*, Feb. 13, 2000; Edwin Singer, interview by the author, June 6, 1996; "Art Museum of South Texas" supplement, *Caller-Times*, Oct. 6, 1972.

35. *Corpus Christi Caller*, Oct. 31, 1963.

36. Alan Lessoff, "An Art Museum for South Texas, 1944–1980," in William G. Otton, Amy Smith Kight, and Alan Lessoff, *Legacy: A History of the Art Museum of South Texas* (Corpus Christi, Tex.: Art Museum of South Texas, 1997), 32–40; Frank D. Welch, *Philip Johnson and Texas* (Austin: University of Texas Press, 2000), ch. 4.

37. *Corpus Christi Caller*, May 16, 1968, Nov. 26, Dec. 10, 1969 (quotation), Dec. 14, 1971. Welch, *Philip Johnson and Texas*, 136–141.

38. Quotations: Welch, *Philip Johnson and Texas*, 148.

39. "Bayfront Plan: Corpus Christi, Texas," Dec. 1982, revised Mar. 1984.

40. Whataburger Field, http://cchooks.com/field (accessed Oct. 16, 2007).

41. Jim Lee, "The Economic Significance of Tourism and Nature Tourism in Corpus Christi, 2009 Update," Corpus Christi Convention and Visitors Bureau, Apr. 2009, 2.

42. *Corpus Christi Caller*, Nov. 29, 1987; *Caller-Times*, June 5, 1988, Apr. 13, 1997.

43. *Caller-Times*, Oct. 14, 2011, Dec. 30, 2011 (quotation), Jan. 1, 2014.

44. "A Culture and Heritage Tour of Downtown Corpus Christi," flyer, c. 2010, in author's possession.

45. *Caller-Times*, Feb. 7, 2006, Nov. 11, 2009; Ray Don Tilley, "Corpus Christi Set to Raze Colley's 1952 Civic Design," *Texas Architect* 38 (Mar.–Apr. 1988): 8–9; John Hutton, "Elusive Balance: Landscape, Architecture, and the Social Matrix," in *On the Border: An Environmental History of San Antonio*, ed. Char Miller (Pittsburgh: University of Pittsburgh Press, 2001), 222–238.

46. Lewis F. Fisher, *Saving San Antonio: The Precarious Preservation of a Heritage* (Lubbock: Texas Tech University Press, 1996); Fisher, "Preservation of San Antonio's Built Environment," in Miller, *On the Border*, 199–221; David G. McComb, *Galveston: A History* (Austin: University of Texas Press, 1986), ch. 6.

47. These three paragraphs: Norman Tyler, *Historic Preservation: An Introduction to Its History, Principles, and Practices* (New York: Norton, 2000), ch. 2; William J. Murtagh, *Keeping Time: The History and Theory of Preservation in America*, rev. ed. (New York: Wiley, 1997), chs. 2–5; Michael Holleran, *Boston's "Changeful Times": Origins of Preservation and Planning in America* (Baltimore: Johns Hopkins University Press, 1998); see also Daniel Bluestone, *Buildings, Landscapes, and Memory: Case Studies in Historic Preservation* (New York, Norton, 2011); Max Page and Randall Mason, eds., *Giving Preservation a History: Histories of Historic Preservation in the United States* (New York: Routledge,

2003). On the modernist preservation movement, see the National Trust for Historic Preservation, "Modernism and the Recent Past," www.preservationnation .org/information-center/saving-a-place/modernism-recent-past, and the International Committee for Documentation and Conservation of Buildings, Sites and Neighbourhoods of the Modern Movement, www.docomomo.com (both accessed Oct. 19, 2013).

48. Andrew Hurley, *Beyond Preservation: Using Public History to Revitalize Inner Cities* (Philadelphia: Temple University Press, 2010), ch. 1; David Hamer, *History in Urban Places: The Historic Districts of the United States* (Columbus: Ohio State University Press, 1998), esp. ch. 2; Judy Mattivi Morley, *Historic Preservation and the Imagined West: Albuquerque, Denver, and Seattle* (Lawrence: University Press of Kansas, 2006).

49. Margaret Ramage quoted in Nancy Goebel, "Surviving the Storm," *Texas Homes*, Nov. 1985, 22–23; Wenger quoted in Bill Walraven, "Corpus Christi Is Ripe for Message of Historic Preservation," *Corpus Christi Caller*, Oct. 2, 1987.

50. *Caller-Times*, Sept. 30, 1956; Terrell Bartlett, "The Tidal Storm at Corpus Christi and Its Effect on Engineering Structures," *Engineering News-Record*, Nov. 13–20, 1919, repr. in W. Armstrong Price, "Hurricanes Affect the Coast of Texas from Galveston to Rio Grande," 1956, Technical Memorandum 78, Beach Erosion Board, U.S. Army Corps of Engineers; Mary Jo O'Rear, *Storm over the Bay: The People of Corpus Christi and Their Port* (College Station: Texas A&M University Press, 2009), ch. 10.

51. Associated Planners, *Historical-Architectural Preservation Plan, Nueces County, Texas* (Northbrook, Ill.: Associated Planners, 1982), 80, 90.

52. *Corpus Christi Times*, July 4, 1946; *Caller-Times*, Sept. 16, 30, 1956.

53. *Corpus Christi: A History and Guide*, 209–211; Murphy Givens, "What Happened to the Old Meuly House," online response to reader query, Nov. 30, 2005, www.caller.com (accessed Feb. 27, 2010).

54. Corpus Christi Area Heritage Society, www.ccahs.com (accessed Oct. 17, 2013); "Generations of McGloins Have Left Their Mark on the Area," *Caller-Times*, Celebrate 2000 supplement, May 30, 1999.

55. *Corpus Christi Caller*, June 9, 1974.

56. Draft preservation ordinance, 1974, in author's possession; Cecil Burney, "A Place for the Past," *Corpus Christi Caller*, Sept. 15, 1974. On Burney, see the obituary and memorial, *Corpus Christi Caller*, June 12 and 15, 1989.

57. Quotation: Associated Planners, *Historical-Architectural Preservation Plan*, 42; Centennial House typescript roster of historic buildings, copy in author's possession; see also Landmark Commission, City of Corpus Christi, *Landmark Preservation Plan, Corpus Christi, Texas, 1976*; Murphy Givens, "Kinney's Immigrants Left Their Mark," *Caller-Times*, Nov. 3, 1999; *Corpus Christi Times*, Sept. 4, 1981.

58. Associated Planners, *Historical-Architectural Preservation Plan*, 90.

59. Ibid., 82.

60. *Caller-Times*, Feb. 22, 1998, June 13, 1999; Lessoff, "Harland Bartholomew and Corpus Christi," 212–213; Robert B. Fairbanks, "The Failure of Urban Renewal in the Southwest: From City Needs to Individual Rights," *Western Historical Quarterly* 37 (Autumn 2006): 303–325.

61. *Caller-Times*, Feb. 22, 1998, Sept. 17, 2009, Oct. 3, 2009, June 29, 2011; Robert B. Fairbanks, "Public Housing for the City as a Whole: The Texas Experience, 1934–55," *Southwestern Historical Quarterly* 103 (April 2000): 402–424.

62. Lee John Govatos, "Architectural Description of the Gugenheim and Lichtenstein Houses," typescript, c. 1975, in author's possession; *Corpus Christi Caller*, Jan. 21, 1974, Dec. 20, 1974, Jan. 17, 1976; *Corpus Christi Times*, Apr. 20, 1983.

63. *Corpus Christi Times*, June 13, 1977, Oct. 27, 1980, Apr. 20, 1983; *Corpus Christi Caller*, Feb. 15, 1977; *Caller-Times*, Feb. 17, 1985; Tom Utter, interview by the author, Corpus Christi City Hall, Nov. 30, 2005.

64. Associated Planners, *Historical-Architectural Preservation Plan*, 85.

65. *Caller-Times*, Feb. 17, 1985, May 8, 1986; *Heritage Gazette*, undated 1990s copy in author's possession; *Heritage Park Gazette*, vol. 11 (2003), in author's possession; Goebel, "Surviving the Storm."

66. Quotation from *Corpus Christi Caller*, undated clipping, c. 1983; see also *Corpus Christi Caller*, Sept. 13, 1983, June 20, 1984; *Caller-Times*, Feb. 17, 1985; Utter interview.

67. *Caller-Times*, Jan. 31, 1995, Sept. 1, 1998; *Heritage Park Gazette* 11 (2003).

68. *Corpus Christi Caller*, June 14, 1990, Dec. 3, 1991, Dec. 4, 1991; *Caller-Times*, June 28 and 29, 2005.

69. This paragraph and the preceding two: Potential Landmarks, Corpus Christi Landmark Commission, www.cclandmarks.org/landmarks.htm (accessed Feb. 4, 2012, later removed); *Heritage Park in Corpus Christi*, www.cctexas .com/Assets/Departments/Parks-and-Recreations/Files/Heritage Park History .pdf (accessed Oct. 19, 2013); *Caller-Times*, Dec. 7, 1998, Feb. 8, 2006, Feb. 24, 2006 (quotation), Nov. 23, 2007.

70. *Caller-Times*, June 2, 1995, May 12, 2000.

71. Ibid., Apr. 18, 2011.

72. Harvey L. Page, *Texas Truth: Nueces County Court House Number* (1915; repr., Corpus Christi, 1989), 2–5.

73. *Corpus Christi, Texas: Sea—Sunshine—Soil*, c. 1916, Kilgore 6258.

74. Christopher Long, "Page, Harvey Lindsley," *Handbook of Texas Online*, www.tshaonline.org/handbook/online/articles/fpa75 (accessed Mar. 9, 2010).

75. Harland Bartholomew, *Comprehensive Plan*, 1953, 65; Harland Bartholomew, *Comprehensive Plan*, 1967, 2:98, 119.

76. Advertisements about the Nueces County Courthouse bond election, 1972, in Nueces County Courthouse vertical file, Local History Room, Corpus Christi Public Library; Margaret Walberg, telephone interview by the author and Thomas Kreneck, Dec. 1, 2005.

77. *Corpus Christi Caller*, July 26, Sept. 22, Dec. 6, 1976.

78. Ibid., July 28, 1976.

79. Ibid., June 4, 1975, Mar. 24, 1976, July 26, 1976, Sept. 22, 1976, Oct. 12, 1976, Nov. 17, 1976, Feb. 6, 1977; *Corpus Christi Times*, Aug. 15, 1976; Walberg interview; Nick Jimenez, interview by the author, Caller-Times Building, Nov. 29, 2005.

80. On Friends of the Courthouse, see Bill Walraven, *Corpus Christi: The History of a Texas Seaport* (Sun Valley, Calif.: American Historical Press, 1997), 146–148.

81. "The Old Nueces County Courthouse, Corpus Christi, Texas," Mar. 1978, feasibility study, copy in author's possession, esp. 3, 20–21; *Corpus Christi Caller*, Oct. 10, 1976, Dec. 11, 1977; *Corpus Christi Times*, Mar. 20 and 21, 1978.

82. *Corpus Christi Times*, Mar. 18 and 23, 1978.

83. *Corpus Christi Caller*, June 1–2, 1977; *Caller-Times*, Sept. 24, 1994; Utter interview.

84. *Corpus Christi Times*, Aug. 26, 1977, Feb. 17, 1978; *Corpus Christi Caller*, Aug. 31, 1977, Mar. 14, 1978; Walberg interview.

85. Walberg interview; *Corpus Christi Caller*, June 16, June 18, July 7, 1978; *Corpus Christi Times*, May 16, May 18, July 6, 1978.

86. *Caller-Times*, Aug. 16, 1979, Aug. 17, 1979, Jan. 22, 1984; *Corpus Christi Caller*, Dec. 12, 20, 21, 1983.

87. Utter interview; Walraven quoted in Elise Nakhnikian, "A Case History," *Corpus Christi Magazine*, May 1983, 48; *Caller-Times*, Aug. 16, 1979, June 2, 1984, undated clipping, 1989, Jan. 18, 1992; *Corpus Christi Caller*, Apr. 25, 1980, June 6, 1984, June 10, 1985, Aug. 29, 1985, July 10, 1986, May 15, 1987, Aug. 24, 1987, Aug. 26, 1987, Dec. 22, 1987; *Corpus Christi Times*, Apr. 24, 1980, June 25, 1984, Oct. 11, 1984.

88. *Corpus Christi Caller*, Nov. 19, 1976.

89. Walberg interview.

90. Walberg interview; Utter interview; *Caller-Times*, May 19, 1992.

91. *Caller-Times*, Jan. 18, Jan. 24, May 10, May 19, May 25, May 26, June 27, July 9, July 18–23, Aug, 10, Sept. 2, Oct. 29, Oct. 31, 1992.

92. *Caller-Times*, Feb. 15, 1995.

93. Nueces County Historical Society newsletter, Sept. 2000, Feb. 2002; *Caller-Times*, May 30, 1999.

94. Walberg interview; Annex Asbestos Angel flyer, 2001, in author's possession; Nueces County Historical Society newsletter, Sept. 2000, Jan. 2001, Jan.–Sept. 2002.

95. Phase 1 Groundbreaking flyer, in author's possession; *Caller-Times*, Nov. 4, 1999, Jan. 13, 2000, Aug. 24, 2000, Oct. 31, 2001, July 22, 2002, July 23, 2002, Dec. 19, 2002, Jan. 24, 2003, Aug. 22, 2003, Dec. 11, 2003, Dec. 12, 2003, Feb. 14, 2004, Dec. 9, 2004, Mar. 29, 2005, Mar. 30, 2005, Aug. 25, 2005.

96. *Caller-Times*, Aug. 22–23, 2011.

97. *Caller-Times*, Nov. 11, 2009; Carol Wood, "Colley: Innovator in Architecture," *Caller-Times*, Jan. 10, 2010.

98. *Caller-Times*, Nov. 8, 2009.

99. Ibid., Nov. 18, 2009.

100. 1st quotation: George Clower, "Don't Let the City Tear Down Historic Memorial Coliseum," *Caller-Times*, Feb. 14, 2006; 2nd quotation: Johnny Cotten, "The Coliseum Could Last Another 50 Years," *Caller-Times*, Sept. 18, 2008.

101. Frank Wagner to Roy Barkley, Apr. 7, 1989, copy in "Colley, Richard" vertical file, Local History Room, Corpus Christi Public Library; Naomi Snyder, "Colley Left Strong, Durable Legacy," *Caller-Times*, Aug. 19, 2001; "Architect Designed Timeless Buildings," *Caller-Times*, undated clipping, c. 1989, in author's possession; Mary Carolyn Hollers George, *O'Neil Ford, Architect* (College Station: Texas A&M University Press, 1992), chs. 9–10; and George, "Colley, Richard Stewart," *Handbook of Texas Online*, www.tshaonline.org/handbook/on line/articles/fcoay (accessed Feb. 4, 2010). The Alexander Architectural Archive at the University of Texas holds a collection of drawings made by Colley's firm.

102. Richard S. Colley, "Civic Buildings: Corpus Christi," *Progressive Architecture* 34 (Feb. 1953): 83–92.

103. Quoted in Tilley, "Corpus Christi Set to Raze," 8–9.

104. *Caller-Times*, May 28, Oct. 10–11, 2011.

105. Wood, "Colley: Innovator in Architecture."

106. *Caller-Times*, Feb. 3, 2006.

107. Ibid., June 28 and July 12, 2007.

108. Ibid., Aug. 24, 2007 (1st quotation), Sept. 20, 2007, Nov. 6, 2007, Jan. 31, 2008, Apr. 29, 2008, Oct. 24, 2009, Nov. 11, 2009, Nov. 18, 2009, Dec. 2, 2009, Jan. 9, 2010, Jan. 16, 2010 (second quotation), June 27, 2010.

109. Ibid., Nov. 18, 2009 (quotation), Jan. 25, 2010, Feb. 10, 2010.

110. Ibid., Feb. 23 (1st quotation), Mar. 30, Mar. 31, Apr. 2, May 7 (3rd quotation), May 20, 2010 (2nd quotation).

111. 2nd quotation: Mark Wolfe, state historic preservation officer, to Mayor Joe Adame, June 3, 2010, copy at web.caller.com/2010/pdf/060710coliseum.pdf (accessed Oct. 23, 2013); *Caller-Times*, May 7, 15, 20 (1st quotation), June 7, July 23, Aug. 16, Sept. 30, 2010, Nov. 7, 2012.

112. This paragraph and the next two: quotations from Michael Howell, "Old Bayview: Not Just Another Cemetery," July 28, 2002, available at www.cclibrar ies.com/localhistory/oldbayview/index.php/history/145-old-bayview (accessed Oct. 24, 2013); Associated Planners, *Historical-Architectural Preservation Plan*, 39.

113. Quoted in the *Caller-Times*, Feb. 14, 2006.

114. Ibid., Feb. 18, 2008; Mark Singer, "Texas Shipwreck," *New Yorker*, Nov. 27, 2000, 79.

115. Harland Bartholomew, *Comprehensive Plan*, 1967, 2:91–92; *Caller-Times*, July 31, 2010.

1. *Brain Gain: How Corpus Christi Can Attract and Keep More Educated Young Professionals?* (Corpus Christi: CorpusBeat, 2005), 5–7.

2. John M. Richards, *Corpus Christi: The Critical Years* (Corpus Christi, Tex.: Corpus Christi State University, 1978), 6; *Brain Gain*, 3; Joe Gardner quoted in the *Caller-Times*, May 13, 2007.

3. On the decline of commercial-civic rule in Texas and southwestern cities, and the varieties of politics that have replaced it, see Amy Bridges, *Morning Glories: Municipal Reform in the Southwest* (Princeton, N.J.: Princeton University Press, 1997), ch. 8; Carl Abbott, *The New Urban America: Growth and Politics in Sunbelt Cities*, rev. ed. (Chapel Hill: University of North Carolina Press, 1987), chs. 9–10; Robert B. Fairbanks, *For the City as a Whole: Planning, Politics, and the Public Interest in Dallas, Texas, 1900–1965* (Columbus: Ohio State University Press, 1998), ch. 8; Michael Phillips, *White Metropolis: Race, Ethnicity, and Religion in Dallas, 1841–2001* (Austin: University of Texas Press, 2006), ch. 7; William Scott Swearingen, *Environmental City: People, Place, Politics and the Meaning of Modern Austin* (Austin: University of Texas Press, 2010); Philip VanderMeer, *Desert Visions and the Making of Phoenix, 1860–2009* (Albuquerque: University of New Mexico Press, 2010), chs. 8–10; Michael F. Logan, *Fighting Sprawl and City Hall: Resistance to Urban Growth in the Southwest* (Tucson: University of Arizona Press, 1995).

4. Kevin Kieschnick quoted in Sara Foley, "Is It Hard to Do Business in Corpus Christi?," *Caller-Times*, Apr. 16, 2011.

5. *Caller-Times*, Oct. 3, 1971.

6. "Corpus Christi's 25 Year Plan for Area Progress," supplement to *Corpus Christi Caller*, Industrial and Commercial Vertical File, Corpus Christi Public Library, unpaginated, cover and first sheet.

7. *Brain Gain*, 30. On medium cities in the recent American West, see Carl Abbott, *How Cities Won the West: Four Centuries of Urban Change in Western North America* (Albuquerque: University of New Mexico Press, 2008), chs. 14–15.

8. Quoted in *Brain Gain*, 19–20. Richard Florida came to public attention in the early 2000s with books such as *The Rise of the Creative Class* (New York: Basic Books, 2002); and *Cities and the Creative Class* (New York: Routledge, 2004).

9. Quoted in *Brain Gain*, 17–18. Kotkin was familiar from his prolific writings in periodicals as well as from books such as *The New Geography: How the Digital Revolution Is Reshaping the American Landscape* (New York: Random House, 2000).

10. *Caller-Times*, Mar. 7, 2010.

11. Harland Bartholomew and Associates, *Report upon Economic and Area Resources, Coastal Bend Region of Texas* (St. Louis: Harland Bartholomew and Associates, 1967), 2.

12. "Outlook: Energy to Expand" supplement, *Caller-Times*, July 29, 2001.

13. *Caller-Times*, Sept. 3, 2012.

14. Corpus Christi Regional Economic Development Corporation, *Economic Development Plan, Corpus Christi Metropolitan Area* (Corpus Christi, 2006), draft in author's possession, 1; James Connolly, ed., *After the Factory: Reinventing America's Industrial Small Cities* (Lanham, Md.: Lexington, 2010); Sean Safford, *Why the Garden Club Couldn't Save Youngstown: The Transformation of the Rust Belt* (Cambridge, Mass.: Harvard University Press, 2009).

15. Martin Associates, *The Local and Regional Economic Impacts of the Port of Corpus Christi* (Lancaster, Pa.: Martin Associates, 2004), 4–5; *Caller-Times*, "Horizon '99: Industry" supplement," Jan. 31, 1999, 10–11; *Texas Regional Outlook: The Coastal Bend Region* (Austin: Texas Comptroller of Public Accounts, 2002), 10–11.

16. Richard Florida, *The Great Reset: How the Post-Crash Economy Will Change the Way We Live and Work* (New York: Harper, 2011), esp. ch. 18.

17. Elizabeth Tandy Shermer, "Sunbelt Boosterism: Industrial Recruitment, Economic Development, and Growth Politics in the Developing Sunbelt," in *Sunbelt Rising: The Politics of Place, Space, and Region*, ed. Michelle Nickerson and Darren Dochuk (Philadelphia: University of Pennsylvania Press, 2011), 31–57.

18. Quotation: CCREDC, *Economic Development Plan*, 2006, 31; *Caller-Times*, Mar. 7, 2010; see also Fantus Company, *An Analysis of the Development Potential of the City of Corpus Christi* (Millburn, N.J.: Fantus, 1982), 38; Corpus Christi Industrial Commission, *It's a Good Move to the Sparkling City by the Sea, Corpus Christi, Texas*, booklet, c. 1976, in author's possession.

19. See, for example, David Schuyler, *A City Transformed: Redevelopment, Race, and Suburbanization in Lancaster, Pennsylvania, 1940–1980* (University Park: Pennsylvania State University Press, 2002); Howard Gillette Jr., *Camden after the Fall: Decline and Renewal in a Post-Industrial City* (Philadelphia: University of Pennsylvania Press, 2005). In *Boardwalk of Dreams: Atlantic City and the Fate of Urban America* (New York: Oxford University Press, 2004), Bryant Simon deals with a decrepit, conflict-ridden resort city. For references for the Rustbelt Midwest, see Connolly, *After the Factory*.

20. Richard Florida, "How the Crash Will Reshape America," *Atlantic*, Mar. 2009, 44–56; see also Florida, *Great Reset*.

21. Char Miller and David R. Johnson, "The Rise of Urban Texas," in *Urban Texas: Politics and Development*, ed. Char Miller and Heywood T. Sanders (College Station: Texas A&M University Press, 1990), 12 (see also chs. 2, 9); Abbott, *New Urban America*, 44–49.

22. Quotation: David R. Johnson, "San Antonio: The Vicissitudes of Boosterism," in *Sunbelt Cities: Politics and Growth since World War II*, ed. Richard M. Bernard and Bradley R. Rice (Austin: University of Texas Press, 1983), 235; see

also David R. Johnson, John A. Booth, and Richard J. Harris, eds., *The Politics of San Antonio: Community, Progress, and Power* (Lincoln: University of Nebraska Press, 1983).

23. "Leaving Their Mark: Powerful Leaders of the Past Worked behind the Scenes for Good of Area," *Caller-Times*, Oct. 6, 1997.

24. City of Corpus Christi, *Community Renewal Program: Economic Study, 1973*, 25; Harland Bartholomew and Associates, *Preliminary Reports on Parks and Recreation and Colleges and Universities, Coastal Bend Region, Texas* (St. Louis: Harland Bartholomew and Associates, 1968), 32–33; Department of Development Services, City of Corpus Christi, *Citywide Growth Report*, 2007, Power-Point display in author's possession; *Brain Gain*, 3.

25. City of Corpus Christi, *Community Renewal Program: Economic Study, 1973*, 53 (quotation); *Choices Facing Corpus Christi* (Corpus Christi, Tex.: Goals for Corpus Christi, 1975), 26–28; Fantus, *Development Potential of Corpus Christi*, 38–40.

26. Fantus, *Development Potential of Corpus Christi*, 5; see also Industrial Economics Research Division, *Greater South Texas Cultural Basin: Strategies for Economic Growth* (College Station: Texas Engineering Experiment Station, Texas A&M Univ., 1976), 21–24.

27. Quotation: Bill Walraven, *Corpus Christi: The History of a Texas Seaport* (Sun Valley, Calif.: American Historical Press, 1997), 187; Bill Walraven and Marjorie Walraven, *Wooden Rigs, Iron Men: The Story of Oil and Gas in South Texas* (Corpus Christi, Tex.: Corpus Christi Geological Society, 2005); *Houston Chronicle*, Oct. 5, 2001; Center for Business Research (CBR), *Annual Report: The Corpus Christi Bay Area Economy* (Corpus Christi, Tex.: Corpus Christi State Univ., 1991), table 4.

28. CBR, *Annual Report: The Corpus Christi Bay Area Economy*, 1991, 13 and table 2.

29. Ibid., 12; "Outlook: Energy to Expand" supplement, *Caller-Times*, July 29, 2001.

30. These two paragraphs: *Houston Chronicle*, Jan. 2, 2011; *Caller-Times*, Feb.–Mar. 2011, Oct. 8, 2011, Feb. 14, 2012, May 9, 2012, Dec. 8, 2012.

31. "The Impact of the Corpus Christi's Port on the Community," *Business Monthly: The Magazine of Corpus Christi Business*, Mar. 1982, 36; Center for Business Research (CBR), *Annual Report: The Corpus Christi Bay Area Economy* (Corpus Christi, Tex.: Corpus Christi State Univ., 1990), 14; CBR, *Annual Report: The Corpus Christi Bay Area Economy*, 1991, 17; "Corpus Christi and Coastal Bend Economic Pulse," flyer produced by the College of Business, TAMU-CC, 1999; Martin Associates, *Economic Impacts of the Port of Corpus Christi*, 4–7.

32. Quotation: CBR, *Annual Report: The Corpus Christi Bay Area Economy*, 1990, 12; CBR, *Annual Report: The Corpus Christi Bay Area Economy*, 1991, 20; *The Texas Outlook: Corpus Christi Area Seminar* (Austin: Texas Comptroller of Public

Accounts, 1990), 5; *Caller-Times*, "Horizons—Military" supplement, Jan. 29, 1995; "Naval Air Station Corpus Christi; Corpus Christi Army Depot (CCAD)," GlobalSecurity.org, globalsecurity.org/military/facility/corpus-christi.htm (accessed Nov. 10, 2013).

33. Impact DataSource, "The Annual Economic Impact of Military Facilities in the Corpus Christi, Texas Region," July 2001, 13.

34. John Richards et al., *An Analysis of the Economic Impact and Effects of Reduced Military Activities in Corpus Christi* (Corpus Christi, Tex.: College of Business Administration, Corpus Christi State University, 1977), 10, 14; *The Navy in Corpus Christi, 1968: Unofficial Guide* (Lubbock, Tex.: Boone, 1968), 8, 30–31.

35. Corpus Christi Chamber of Commerce, *Building Corpus Christi: 1993 Annual Report, 1994 Program of Work*.

36. *Caller-Times*, Aug. 25, 2005; *San Antonio Express-News*, Aug. 25, 2005; see also Jim Lee, *Report on the Impact of the 2005 Base Realignment and Closure Committee Actions* (Corpus Christi, 2008), at www.ccredc.com/Reports_Re sources_Reports_Studies_Maps.cfm (accessed Nov. 10, 2013). On urban lobbying for military bases, see Roger Lotchin, ed., *The Martial Metropolis: U.S. Cities in War and Peace, 1900–1970* (New York: Praeger, 1984); Roger Lotchin, *Fortress California, 1910–1961: From Warfare to Welfare* (Berkeley: University of California Press, 1992); Ann Markusen et al., *The Rise of the Gunbelt: The Military Remapping of Industrial America* (New York: Oxford University Press, 1991).

37. *Caller-Times*, "Outlook" section, July 29, 2001.

38. Ibid., Mar. 11, 2000, Sept. 16, 2000, Dec. 6, 2000, Oct. 20, 2001.

39. Daniel D. Arreola, "The Mexican American Cultural Capital," *Geographic Review* 77 (Jan. 1987): 17–34; Arreola, *Tejano South Texas: A Mexican American Cultural Province* (Austin: University of Texas Press, 2002, ch. 7; see also Raúl A. Ramos, *Beyond the Alamo: Forging Mexican Ethnicity in San Antonio, 1821–1861* (Chapel Hill: University of North Carolina Press, 2008). Two standard accounts of how this initial flexibility yielded to Anglo exclusivity are Albert Camarillo, *Chicanos in a Changing Society: From Mexican Pueblos to American Barrios in Santa Barbara and Southern California, 1848–1930* (Cambridge, Mass.: Harvard University Press, 1979), and Thomas E. Sheridan, *Los Tucsonenses: The Mexican Community in Tucson, 1854–1941* (Tucson: University of Arizona Press, 1986).

40. Alan Lessoff, "Harland Bartholomew and Corpus Christi: The Faltering Pursuit of Pursuit of Comprehensive Planning in South Texas," *Planning Perspectives* 18 (Apr. 2003): 202–203.

41. *Corpus Christi Caller*, Jan. 16, 1973, Jan. 3, 1974; Dave Mann, "Políticos Conflictivos," *Texas Observer*, Jan. 30, 2004, 4–7, 18–19, 28.

42. On Truan, see *Caller-Times*, Apr. 10–11, 2012.

43. Fantus, *Development Potential of Corpus Christi*, 10; R. L. Cope to A. R. Ramos, Jan. 25, 1983, repr. in Corpus Christi Business Development Commission, "Community Response to the Fantus Study," Mar. 1983, binder in author's possession.

44. Newsletters consulted at the website of the Corpus Christi Hispanic Chamber of Commerce, www.cchispanicchamber.org (accessed Mar. 30, 2010; site later changed).

45. *A Proposed U.S.-Mexico Industrial and Tourist Development Partnership* (Corpus Christi, Tex.: Corpus Christi Chamber of Commerce, 1990); CBR, *Annual Report: The Corpus Christi Bay Area Economy*, 1990, 14.

46. Corpus Christi Chamber of Commerce, *Building Corpus Christi*; *Caller-Times*, Jan. 22, 1995 ("Horizons-Industry" supplement), Feb. 7, 1999 ("Horizons-Economy" supplement), Mar. 11, 2000, Dec. 6, 2000, Oct. 20, 2001, Nov. 17, 2001, Sept. 16, 2004, Dec. 2, 2007.

47. Texas Department of Transportation, "Port to Port Feasibility Study Report," executive summary, Dec. 2006, available at www.ccredc.com/Studies_Re sources_Reports_Studies_Maps.cfm (accessed Nov. 12, 2013); La Quinta Trade Gateway Terminal Project, www.portofcorpuschristi.com/related-links/la-quinta -trade-gateway.html (accessed Mar. 21, 2011, later moved); *Caller-Times*, Dec. 13, 2003, Sept. 2, 14, 2004.

48. *Caller-Times*, July 5, 1998, Sept. 18, 1998, Sept. 30, 1998, July 18, 2004, May 8, 2005.

49. Kaye Northcott, "Corpus Delicti," *Texas Monthly*, Jan. 1978, 110.

50. Port of Houston Authority, www.portofhouston.com; Port of South Louisiana, www.portsl.com; Port of Beaumont, www.portofbeaumont.com. For navigation statistics, see U.S. Army Corps of Engineers, Navigation Data Center, www.navigationdatacenter.us.

51. *Caller-Times*, Mar. 1, 2, 11, 14, 17, Apr. 6, 11, 20, 25, May 18, 22, June 8, Aug. 28, 2001, Nov. 24, 2004, Jan. 11, 12, 2005.

52. John Lewis, *The Economic Impact of a Deep Draft Inshore Port on Corpus Christi, Texas* (San Antonio: Clifford Cason and Assoc., 1973); Galveston District, U.S. Army Corps of Engineers, *Record of Public Meeting: Corpus Christi Ship Channel, Harbor Island, Nov. 2, 1977*; Port of Corpus Christi, *Fiftieth Anniversary Port Book, 1976*, (Corpus Christi, Tex.: Port of Corpus Christi, 1976), 44–45; Port of Corpus Christi, *Project 2001* (Corpus Christi, Tex.: Port Authority of Corpus Christi, 1987), 24–25.

53. Robert H. Ryan and Charles W. Adams, *Corpus Christi: The Economic Impact of the Port* (Austin: Bureau of Business Research, University of Texas, 1973), 55; Port of Corpus Christi, *Project 2001*, 15; Navigation Data Center, U.S. Army Corps of Engineers, "Port Series No. 25: Corpus Christi, TX," available at www. ndc.iwr.usace.army.mil/ports/pdf/ps/ps25.pdf.

54. Port of Corpus Christi Authority, *Comprehensive Annual Financial Report for the Year Ended December 31, 2008*, ix; *Corpus Christi Caller*, Jan. 13, 1989; *Caller-Times*, Aug. 13, 2000, Dec. 14, 2003, Sept. 2, 2004, Nov. 28, 2004, Dec. 11, 2004, Aug. 16, 2012; Richard Alan Laune, "The Battle for Prominence: The Port of Corpus Christi, 1840–2001" (MA thesis, Texas A&M University–Kingsville, 2002), 91–93.

55. *Corpus Christi Caller*, Sept. 10, 1986, June 16, 1987 (Storm quotation), June 18, 1987; *Corpus Christi Times*, Jan. 5, 1987; *Caller-Times*, July 6, 1987; Port of Corpus Christi, *Project 2001*, 38–43 (quotation on 40).

56. *Caller-Times*, Oct. 7, 1998, May 8, 1999, Nov. 17, 2001; Jim Lee, "The Economic Significance of Tourism and Nature Tourism in Corpus Christi," Corpus Christi Convention and Visitors Bureau, Apr. 2009. On tourism as an urban redevelopment expedient, see J. Mark Souther, *New Orleans on Parade: Tourism and the Transformation of the Crescent City* (Baton Rouge: Louisiana State University Press, 2006). On tourist promotion in the American West, see Hal Rothman, *Devil's Bargains: Tourism in the Twentieth-Century American West* (Lawrence: University Press of Kansas, 1998); David M. Wrobel and Patrick T. Long, eds., *Seeing and Being Seen: Tourism in the American West* (Lawrence: University Press of Kansas, 2001).

57. Quotations: Corpus Beach Hotel, undated pamphlet from 1910s, Kilgore 6234, Special Collections and Archives, Texas A&M University–Corpus Christi (this archive hereafter cited as TAMU-CC); see also *Corpus Christi, Texas: Sea—Sunshine—Soil*, Corpus Christi Commercial Club brochure, c. 1916, Kilgore 6258.

58. Urban Land Institute, "A Report to the Central City Committee of Corpus Christi: Findings and Recommendations," June 1965, 33.

59. *North Central Area Plan* (Corpus Christi, Tex.: City of Corpus Christi Planning Department, 1990), 3–5, 20–23, 33; Bill Walraven, *El Rincon: A History of Corpus Christi Beach* (Corpus Christi, Tex.: Texas State Aquarium, 1990).

60. *Corpus Christi Caller*, June 13, 22, 26, 1976.

61. Quotations: *Caller-Times*, Aug. 26 and Sept. 7, 2003; see also *Caller-Times*, Aug. 10, Aug. 24, Sept. 6, 2003; *San Antonio Express-News*, Aug. 30 and Sept. 9, 2003.

62. *San Antonio Express-News*, Mar. 4, 2004; see also *Caller-Times*, May 13, 2007.

63. *Caller-Times*, Nov. 9, 2013.

64. Lee, "Economic Significance of Tourism," 3–4, 9. Of the many guides to South Texas birds, see Jamie Ritter, *Birding Corpus Christi and the Texas Coastal Bend* (Guilford, Conn.: Falcon Guides, 2007). Among numerous websites, see www.ccbirding.com; Coastal Bend Audubon Society, www.coastalbendaudubon .org; and Corpus Christi Convention and Visitors Bureau, www.visitcorpuschris titx.org/Birding.

65. Harland Bartholomew and Associates, *The Comprehensive Plan: Corpus Christi* (St. Louis: Harland Bartholomew and Associates, 1967), 2:127; Harland Bartholomew and Associates, *Preliminary Report upon the Cayo del Oso and Corpus Christi Beach* (St. Louis: Harland Bartholomew and Associates, 1966).

66. R. Bruce Stephenson, *Visions of Eden: Environmentalism, Urban Planning, and City Building in St. Petersburg, Florida, 1900–1995* (Columbus: Ohio State University Press, 1997), chs. 6–9.

67. *Voice-Chronicle*, Feb. 9, 1950; Department of Development Services, City of Corpus Christi, *Mustang–Padre Island Area Development Plan* (Corpus Christi, Tex., 2004), 4.

68. *Corpus Christi Caller*, Dec. 8, 1973, Dec. 29, 1974, Oct. 9, 1982; Ben D. Marks, "Padre Island: Fitting Development to the Environment," *Urban Land*, July–Aug. 1972, 8–14.

69. *Caller-Times*, Sept. 22, 1991, Dec. 3, 1994.

70. Ibid., Apr. 10, 1994, June 6, 1999, Nov. 15, 18, 2004, Jan. 30, Feb. 15, 2005; Department of Development Services, *Mustang–Padre Island Area*, 4; "No End in Sight for Island Development," *Texas Coastal Enthusiast*, Summer 2007, 162–166.

71. *Flour Bluff Sun*, Sept. 25, 1987; *Caller-Times*, Sept. 3, 1972.

72. Henry Berryhill to Richard Borchard, Nov. 20, 1995, copy in box 4, Hans and Pat Suter Papers, TAMU-CC; *South Texas Informer and Business Journal*, Nov.–Dec. 1992, Jan. 1993; Mark Evans, "Marine Advisor," *Texas Shores*, Fall 1999, 24–28; *Caller-Times*, Apr. 18, 1999, Feb. 25, 2001, June 14, 2002, Feb. 16, 2005.

73. Berryhill to Borchard, Nov. 20, 1995.

74. *Vote No on Packery Channel*, flyer in Packery Channel clippings file, TAMUC-CC; *San Antonio Express-News*, May 21, 2000, Feb. 22, 2001 (quotation); *Caller-Times*, Nov. 11, 2000, Mar. 23, 2001 (quotation), Apr. 8, 2001, Aug. 23, 2003, Feb. 16, 2005; Department of Development Services, *Mustang–Padre Island Area*, 38–39.

75. Department of Development Services, *Mustang–Padre Island Area*, 39–40; *Caller-Times*, Feb. 16 and Nov. 15, 2005.

76. *Caller-Times*, June 14, 2002, Mar. 7, 2003, Mar. 16, 2003.

77. Ibid., Nov. 6, 2006, Nov. 8, 2006, Mar. 11, 2007; *Texas Observer*, Apr. 21, 2006.

78. *Caller-Times*, Jan. 30, 2005 (quotation), Feb. 5 and 8, 2011.

79. Ibid., Jan. 27, 2008, Mar. 25, 2011.

80. Florida, "How the Crash Will Reshape America," 53.

81. *San Antonio Express News*, Jan. 1, 2001.

82. *Caller-Times*, May 22, 2012, Feb. 15, 2013.

83. Quotations: ibid., June 24, 2007, May 22, 2009; see also June 26, 27, 2007.

84. Ibid., "Horizons '98: Medical Competition" supplement, Jan. 25, 1998; "Horizons-Economy" supplement, Feb. 7, 1999; *Texas Regional Outlook: Coastal Bend*, 11–15, 23–24.

85. Texas A&M University–Corpus Christi, *Engine of Community Change* (Corpus Christi, 2002), report 2: "Business and the Economy," 3.

86. Janet R. Daley-Bednarek, *The Changing Image of the City: Planning for Downtown Omaha, 1945–1973* (Lincoln: University of Nebraska Press, 1992), 227; Safford, *Garden Club Couldn't Save Youngstown*.

CONCLUSION

1. Spohn Hospital, *In the Footsteps of Christ, the Divine Healer*, booklet dated 1955, Kilgore 4628, Special Collections and Archives, Texas A&M University–Corpus Christi (this archive hereafter cited as TAMU-CC).

2. For Woods's writings and activities, see the Dee Woods Papers, TAMU-CC; Dee Woods scrapbook, Local History Room, Corpus Christi Public Library; Dee Woods, *Blaze of Gold: Treasure Tales of the Texas Coast, Mostly of Gold That Is Buried and Ghosts Which Are Not* (San Antonio: Naylor, 1942). New editions of this book appeared in 1946 and 1972.

3. Rachel Bluntzer Hebert, with illustrations by Antonio E. García, *Shadow on the Nueces: The Saga of Chepita Rodriguez* (Atlanta: Banner, 1942); *Chipita Rodriguez*, music by Lawrence Weiner, first performed by the Corpus Christi Symphony, 1982.

4. Quotation: back cover advertisement, Vernon Smylie, *The Secrets of Padre Island* (Corpus Christi: Texas News Syndicate Press, 1964); Smylie, *A Noose for Chipita* (Corpus Christi: Texas News Syndicate Press, 1970); see also the Vernon Smylie Papers, TAMU-CC; Keith Guthrie, *The Legend of Chipita: The Only Woman Hanged in Texas* (Austin: Eakin, 1990); Guthrie, *History of San Patricio County* (Austin: Nortex, 1986); Guthrie, *Raw Frontier: Armed Conflict along the Texas Coastal Bend* (Austin: Eakin, 1998); Guthrie, *Raw Frontier: Survival to Prosperity on the Texas Coastal Bend* (Austin: Eakin, 2000); Guthrie, *Texas Forgotten Ports*, 3 vols. (Austin: Eakin, 1988–1995).

5. There are many accounts of Ferber's association with Hector García, whose daughter, Wanda, retold the story in the *Caller-Times*, Aug. 6, 2011.

6. Edna Ferber, *Giant* (Garden City, N.Y.: Doubleday, 1952), 332–334.

7. Terrence McNally, *Corpus Christi* (New York: Grove, 1998).

8. Bret Anthony Johnston, *Corpus Christi: Stories* (repr., New York: Random House, 2005), 4, 263. On Johnston, see his website, www.bretanthonyjohnston.com.

9. Johnston, *Corpus Christi*, 141, 230, 251–252.

10. Ibid., 263.

11. "Celebrate 2000" supplements appeared in the *Caller-Times* on the last Sunday of each month, beginning on Jan. 29, 1999; 1st quotation: Jan. 29, N1; 2nd quotation, "Building Corpus Christi" supplement, May 30, 1999, L1; 3rd and 4th quotations, "The Light of Other Days" supplement, *Caller-Times*, July 18, 1999, L2, O2.

12. "The Light of Other Days" supplement, *Caller-Times*, July 18, 1999, L2.

INDEX

∽

48–52, 140; historic preservation in, 209–216; revitalization plans for, 51–52, 196–209, 241, 273–274

Celanese Corporation, 43, 104

Centennial House, 103, 214, 218

Centennial Museum, 167, 204

Center for Hispanic Arts, 121, 187

Chamber of Commerce, Corpus Christi, 76, 85, 102, 196, 259, 262–263, 282, 292: and boosterism, 11, 31–34, 68; building, 235. *See also* Hispanic Chamber of Commerce; Mexican Chamber of Commerce

Charles, Grace, 4

Chicano movement, 134

Choke Canyon, 38–39, 105, 289

Christaller, Walter, 24, 26

Cisneros, Henry, 134, 244

Cisneros, Jose, 131

Cisneros v. Corpus Christi Independent School District, 47, 131–135

Citgo, 44, 257, 260

cities: midsized, 13–14; secondary, 2, 283–284; southwestern, 40, 249–251, 284; systems of, 2, 24–26; Texas, 22–24, 79–81, 97

City Beautiful movement, 53, 101, 159, 161, 163–164, 167, 200, 326n9

Civil War, (American), South Texas and, 5, 62–64, 89, 92, 98

Coastal Bend, 5, 19, 67, 112, 136, 253, 275; and Corpus Christi identity, 34, 110; economy of, 197, 257, 259, 287; geography of, 27, 35

Coastal Bend Council of Governments, 105

Coastal Bend Regional Planning Commission, 38, 248

Cole, E. B., 213

Coleman, Lena, 106

Coleman, Sherman, 166, 180–184, 300n61

Coleman-Fulton Pasture Company, 64, 136

Cole Park (neighborhood), 213, 216

Coles, Solomon, 136–137

Colley, Richard, 51, 53, 184, 197, 200–201, 210, 217, 234–235, 241, 286

Columbus Fleet (*Niña, Pinta,* and *Santa Maria*), 143–151, 210, 232–233

Coppini, Pompeo, 161, 163–166, 169

Corn Products Co., 44

Corpus Christi: geography of, 35, 40–41; historical periods of, 61–72; incorporation of (1852), 62, 213; literature about, 93, 126, 291–293; maps of, 20, 21, 27, 43, 46; municipal politics of, 71–72, 104, 168, 179, 181–182, 205, 244–245, 263; satellite city in Texas, 24–28, 59, 288; South Texas ranching families and, 64, 93–95, 98, 101–102, 291

Corpus Christi, Lake, 37–38, 221

Corpus Christi Area Heritage Society, 214

Corpus Christi Army Depot, 56, 244, 258

Corpus Christi Arts Council, 167, 204, 220

Corpus Christi Bay, 28, 33, 52, 72, 97, 98–99, 285; origins of name, 84–86, 179–180; and public art, 165–166, 175

"Corpus Christi Bay" (song), 60

Corpus Christi Bayfront, 15, 28, 51, 84, 102, 139, 181, 184, 247; plans for, 193–198, 201–204, 206–207, 236–237, 273–274, 291; public art on, 154–159, 166, 168, 175–177, 180–184, 187–191

Corpus Christi Beach, 50, 51, 53, 144, 199, 206, 209, 212, 273, 286

Corpus Christi Byliners, 289

Corpus Christi Caller-Times, 48, 64, 93, 106–108, 175, 293–294; building, 48, 213; and Memorial Coliseum, 233, 235, 238; and Old Nueces County Courthouse, 226, 228–230

Corpus Christi Cathedral, 52–53, 214, 231

Sidbury House, 217–218
Sierra Club, 278
Sinclair (oil refinery), 43
Singer, Edwin, 168, 205–207
Singer, Patsy Dunn, 168, 170, 205–207
Six Points, Corpus Christi, 55, 213
Smylie, Vernon, 290
Solomon Coles School, 137, 216
South Bluff, Corpus Christi, 167, 199, 204, 215–217, 218
Southern Alkali Plant, 20, 37, 69, 102
Southern Minerals Corporation (SO-MICO), 103, 214
South Padre Island Drive (SPID), 55, 56, 57, 121, 154, 200
Southside, Corpus Christi, 20, 54–55, 121, 125, 133, 137–138, 140, 154, 199–201, 210, 213, 216, 235
South Texas: Anglo colonization of, 61–65, 67; Anglo lore in, 6–8, 76, 78, 80–92, 115, 291–293; Corpus Christi and, 25, 27, 31, 34, 72, 108, 288; Hispanic identity and lore in, 6–8, 66–67, 80–86, 109–120, 288–290; ranching in, 93–95
South Texas Drilling and Exploration, 255
South Texas Institute of the Arts, 187
Southwest, U.S.: cities and, 3–4, 8, 12–13, 39–40, 197, 203, 249–252, 284; and Corpus Christi, 30–31, 35–40, 60, 70, 285
Southwestern (oil refinery), 43
Southwest Writers' Conference, 289–290
Spanish American Genealogical Association (SAGA), 120, 144
Spanish heritage, 84–86, 114–120, 143–151, 180–185, 289
Spanish Revival style. See Mission Revival style
Splash Day, 82, 272
Spohn Hospital, 53, 93, 282, 286
Steamboat House, 220–221
Stern, Howard, 154
Stevens, George, 93, 292

St. John Baptist Church, 137, 138
St. Louis, Brownsville and Mexico Railway, 99, 101, 286
St. Matthew Baptist Church, 137, 138
Storm, James C., 270
St. Paul United Methodist Church, 138
Stryker, Rick, 145, 148–150
Sullivan, Ron, 164
Sunbelt: region, 3–4, 80, 198, 244, 249–250, 281, 287, 310n11; period, 9, 22, 24, 112, 197, 250, 284
Sunrise Mall, 55
Suntide (oil refinery), 43
Surls, James, 170–172, 174, 175, 189
Suter, Hans, 276
Suter, Pat, 276
Sutherland, Mary, 96, 100–102
Sween-McGloin, Brooke, 231

Tatum, Buddy, 154, 157, 178
tax increment financing (TIF), 279, 281
Taylor, Paul Schuster, 117, 136
Taylor, Zachary, 36, 62, 90, 98, 238
Tejanos. See Mexican Americans
Tejano South Texas, 8, 68, 110, 121, 139, 151, 288
Texana, Lake, 39, 69
Texas: cities and, 1, 9, 22–27, 79–81; Corpus Christi and, 13, 17–18, 24, 34–35, 58–60, 271–273; as Greater Texas, 23, 288; Hispanic population of, 111–112; history, lore, and myth in, 5–6, 74, 80–81, 87–88
Texas, Republic of, 23, 55, 61, 79, 90, 107, 260, 285
Texas A&I University. See Texas A&M University–Kingsville
Texas A&M University–Corpus Christi (TAMU-CC), 3, 56–57, 121, 126, 156, 167, 183, 186, 187, 206, 230, 247, 253, 272, 283
Texas A&M University–Kingsville, 56, 134, 167, 253
Texas Historical Commission, 214, 218, 225, 228, 230–232, 238